The Control of Late Ancient and Medieval Population

THE CONTROL OF LATE ANCIENT AND MEDIEVAL POPULATION

JOSIAH COX RUSSELL

The American Philosophical Society
Independence Square • Philadelphia
1985

To Ruth
In honor of our
Sixtieth Wedding Anniversary

Contents

Tables

Preface

Who controlled population in the Middle Ages ? One theory is that conditions of disease and subsistence regulated the numbers of people, and an obvious alternative is that people controlled their own numbers. Looking at extremes of population and their controls, however, one sees, for example, that those in Roman North Africa had the longest length of life and abundant food but population declined in the first three centuries of our era. In the second half of the fifteenth century amid some of the worst plague conditions during the Little Ice Age, many Italian cities and regions increased rather rapidly by medieval standards. In the face of these conditions, one can hardly accept a theory of automatic response of population to conditions of health and subsistence. Malthus, it seems, was wrong.

Did medieval people really think about the possibility of population control or did they act without thought in the matter? According to the rather fabulous account of the life of St. Gerald, Irish kings in the seventh century called a meeting of clergy, nobles, and people at Tara to consider the problem of overpopulation. Most of the assembly, including a famous saint, Fechin of Fore, wanted God to send a pestilence to Ireland "so that the rest might live better." Saint Gerald objected, saying that God would provide, as in the case of manna for the Hebrews in the wilderness and of the feeding of the 5,000 by Christ. According to the story, God was so angry that he sent a pestilence which killed off many of those who had petitioned for the plague, including St. Fechin. The story has its problems, as one can see, but two characteristic items stand out: the people were aware of overpopulation and the most saintly wanted to leave the matter to God.[1]

Unfortunately, the opinions of the illiterate seldom got into writing as did the story of St. Gerald. And, having placed the responsibility for population control upon God, the clergy said very little about it either. To understand medieval population control, most of the information must be gleaned from a study of many processes which actually helped to control it. This is the subject of this study. Although some outstanding historians have expressed deep interest in the study of population, among them Beloch, Lot, and Pirenne, little has been done to understand the problems of

---

1. *Vitae Sanctorum Hiberniae,* ed. Charles Plummer (2 v., Oxford, 1910) 2: 107-115, especially p. 113.
2. (Budapest, 1970). M.R. Reinhard, André Armengaud et Jacques Dupagnier, *Histoire Générale de la Population Mondiale* (Paris, 1962 and later). J. C. Russell, *"Late Ancient and Medieval Population," Trans. Amer. Philos. Soc.* 48, 3 (1958): 1-152. J.C. Russell, "Population in Europe 500-1500," *The Middle Ages. The Fontana Economic History of Europe* (6v., London, 1972-1975). 1 (1972): 27-70.

population control, since there has been a dearth of information bearing directly on the subject.[2] The vast amount of skeletal evidence prepared by physical anthropologists in the last generation, especially their improved skill in identifying age and sex in bones in a long series of excavations has aided greatly in the study of population.

There are at least four general demographic conditions affecting population in late ancient and medieval Europe: monogamy (except among certain Islamic groups); marriage for economic reasons; territoriality; breast-feeding by a large percentage of mothers, thus increasing the time between births; and finally a differential mortality to the disadvantage of women. These customs or habits produced little or no increase in population in the first thousand years of our era.

However, a population increase could occur when there was deviation from these customs. There were births outside of marriage, although this was frowned on. The extent of territory thought necessary for marriage was sometimes reduced, as happened after the year 1000. Control was apparently lost for example, in parts of Italy at the end of the Middle Ages. To speed up the birthrate wet nurses were often used thus reducing the interval between births. The differential sex mortality may have been reduced by a better diet and by less killing of female children. The possibility of increasing population was better than is often believed. Humanity *can* increase at will, as it unfortunately does today.

On the other hand, humanity can reduce its population or hold it even. Instead of marriage, celibacy was often practiced either voluntarily or by prescription by certain groups. Contraception was apparently not a common practice nor was abortion. The high sex ratio (number of men to a hundred women) suggests that female infanticide was quite general.

These are the key elements in the understanding of population control in late ancient and medieval society. They operated amid a variety of physical and microbial conditions which are not easy to understand. In their study of skeletal remains, physical anthropologists have set up age classifications, which are widely used by many: *infans* I (0-6 years); *infans* II (7-13 years); *juvenis* (14-19 years); *adultus* (20-39 years), *maturus* (40-59 years) and *senilis* (over 59 years). Their use of standard age divisions enables them to present relatively simple tables, easy to understand even if the language in which it is written is unfamiliar to anthropologists in other countries.

There are certain fairly common conditions which should be used to compare other data. The length of life or expectation at birth was about 30-35 years for men and 25-30 for women. At age 20 the expectation was a few years less. Usually slightly more than half of the population was above 20 years of age and a third belonged to infans I and infans II. Sex ratio at birth should have been about the usual 103-105, that is 103-105 males to 100 females. The average number of children born to one woman seems to have been about 4.2.—a small number,—but the death rate in the adultus period for women, was high compared to a smaller but considerable mortality of men.

An assumed generation was the time between the birth of a mother and the birth of her middle child—about twenty-seven years. The primogeniture generation, from father to first-born son was a little less. Women seem to have borne few children before nineteen or after forty. Given the age setup, about 3.5 children on the average were required to maintain the population level.

The measurements of density of population are also worth keeping in mind. The household, if nuclear (man, wife and children with grandparents, widows etc. living separately) would be about 3.5 persons. If this family shared the house with others, the average rose. In general the number of female householders in population should indicate the household average: if five to eight percent, the household should have been about five; if 15 percent, it should have been nearer 3.5. In cities the average density to the hectare should have been about 100-120, but greater in Islamic and larger places. For others, unless the city was tightly enclosed with walls, it should have been less. In agricultural areas the land would have been crowded at thirty or more to the square kilometer. A special problem is the density in garden areas outside of city walls in river valleys, especially around the Mediterranean.

The arrangement of the subject matter is somewhat of a problem. Much of the material is new and not well integrated yet into the fabric of history. The study of population may well begin by examining the size of the largest city and one that is typical; Rome and Pompeii. This should show whether people of the more complex communities were able to control their populations. It would be uncontrolled in the larger cities—Rome has been used as an example. Outside the city the cemetery and its importance for demography is studied, for European soil, with some exceptions, preserves bones and other artifacts well. From them much can be learned about age, sex, and even material conditions of the people. One chapter discusses the problems of converting cemetery evidence and tomb inscription data into that about living populations.

The next task is to try to estimate the conditions of age in the population and the availability of energy as well as of necessary dependence. An effort is then made to show how tuberculosis and bubonic plague spread in Europe, the latter in two medieval sieges and the former in a permanent and terrible destruction of life extending into modern times. Tuberculosis is primarily a disease of ages 15-40 and is usually responsible, until the present century, for a large part of the mortality in people of that age group. With care, the high mortality rates of those years may be used to illustrate the spread of tuberculosis. The plague has more definite characteristics; its mortality in its initial epidemics was ten to fourteen times the normal mortality and in later attacks much more than normal. It was more prevalent in summer than most others and, if the graves inspected are pointed to the rising sun, cemeteries with more plague deaths show a heavier proportion pointing north of east, that is, along the sun's path in the northern hemisphere.

The one chapter shows the processes by which medieval people controlled their population by methods already outlined in this preface. Three chapters trace the course of population through late ancient and medieval times. The first thousand years saw occasional changes, including the very severe plague of A.D. 540-750, but it was about the same at the end of the millennium as it was at the beginning. The feudal period (A.D. 1000-1348) saw a very rapid increase in many European areas as feudal lords encouraged population growth to increase their power during a period of relative royal and imperial weakness. Toward the end of the period the population was again brought into control, so that it did not gain much in the half century before the plague of 1348. In that year the plague began a course much like that of the sixth century and two types of reaction followed. In Italy and in a few other localities a tremendous effort was made to overcome losses and a rapid population increase even resulted. In other areas a very gradual increase occurred, bringing numbers up more slowly so that many were still less in 1500 than at the plague's beginning. The last chapter discusses the motivation of persons with respect to population change and certain other phases of population direction and influence.

Since this is the first extended treatment of the subject, it is a tentative endeavor in many respects and many would prefer, however the Malthusian methodology because it is widely known. But Malthus said little about the Middle Ages and obviously knew little about it.

Lack of evidence made research difficult. In the early stages Dr. J. Lawrence Angel of the Smithsonian Institution gave valuable leads and allowed me to use some of his unpublished material. Alden and Judith Redfield, just back from extensive participation in the excavations at Mistihalj, discussed problems with me. Sylvia Thrupp's critique of a paper in 1965 at Munich was helpful. Larry Claflin, of Texas A & I University, set up the program for the use of a computer in Kingsville, Texas and was most helpful in its operation. Early in my research I benefited from discussions in seminars of Professor John F. Benton at the California Institute of Technology and of Professor Phillip D. Thomas at Wichita State

University. John Hopper and L. Hatfield improved the text in many places.

Much of the research for this study was in the very conveniently arranged stacks of the Peabody Library at Harvard University. There, the librarian, Margaret Peabody Currier, gave me the benefit of her extensive knowledge of anthropological bibliography. The Widener Library and Library of Congress supplemented the sources offered by Peabody. I am indebted also to the Royal Anthropological Society for permission to use its stacks. My wife, Ruth, has been constantly helpful in discussion of many topics and in manuscript and proof correction, as she has done frequently in our sixty years together.

This volume is only the last of a long series of help from the American Philosophical Society. It supported with a generous grant in 1938-1939 research in England which led to my *British Medieval Population*. In 1956 it published my *Late Ancient and Medieval Population*, largely the result of research while I was a Fulbright Professor in 1952-1953. Again a summer grant in 1961 led to the publication of a long article in its *Proceedings* in 1962. I am deeply grateful for its help and encouragement, expressed by advice from its referees, Professors Sidney Painter and Joseph R. Strayer.

Professor Walter L. Wakefield very kindly allowed me to include (in appendix 1) the information which he had collected on burials of heretics in the Middle Ages.

Chapter VII appeared in an earlier form in *Viator* vol. 7, pp. 65-78 and is reprinted by permission (1976) of the Regents of the University of California. The first part of Chapter I is reprinted by permission of the editor, Dr. Anna Hohenwart-Gerlachstein of *Bulletin of the International Committee on Urgent Anthropological and Ethnological Research* (no. 19, 1977: 107.121.

I. The Population of Pompeii and Rome

For an understanding of population control, the study of cities is very important, larger areas being difficult to study in many phases of life. Rome is well known for its disorders in the first century B.C.; Pompeii had well documented troubles. Growth in numbers without a supporting economic base indicates lack of control. Rome, a vast metropolis of unemployed persons fed by distribution of grain and amused by public entertainment *(pan et circenses)* is a prime example. Fortunately, both Rome and Pompeii may be studied more carefully than ever before by using new and different approaches to their populations: environmental conditions as well as in the context of Classical civilization.

THE POPULATION OF POMPEII

In the vast literature about Pompeii and other sites covered by the great eruption of Vesuvius in A.D. 79, there are few studies that deal with the demographic aspects of the subject.[1] Two sets of guesses exist for the population of the city: one of about ten to fifteen thousand based on Fiorelli's estimate of 1873 and another of approximately twenty thousand derived from the apparent capacity of the amphitheater of the city.[2] Most authorities agree that about two thousand persons were killed in the urban area, based upon data from the two-thirds of the city already excavated.[3] However, there are good reasons for doubting that Pompeii was anywhere near ten to twenty thousands in size, while the two thousand dead would seem to be a minimum estimate. Little seems to have been done by physical anthropologists to determine the age or sex of skeletons, although Pompeii provides one of the largest collections of them. Since no ancient city, unlike its medieval counterparts, has left a census of its citizens, an analysis of the skeletons of Pompeii might be a good substitute. Much could be

---

[1]Giuseppe Fiorelli, *Gli scavi di Pompei del 1861 al 1872* (Napoli 1873), 13-14. The official record is called *Giornale degli scavi di Pompei.* It was first edited for the period before 1861 by Fiorelli with the title: *Pompeianorum Antiquitatum Historia ex Schedis Diurnique* (2 v., Napoli, 1860, 1862). Later *scavi* appeared in the *Atti della Accademia Nazionali dei Lincei. Notizie degli scavi di Antichità* (Rome, 1868-), listed by year. A. Maiuri, *Introduzione allo studio di Pompei* (Naples, 1948), 280. The section on Pompeii of this chapter appeared with the same title in *Bulletin of the International Committee on Urgent Anthropological and Ethnological Research* 19 (1977): 107-114.

[2]For instance, Augusto Mau, "Pompeii, a City Buried Alive," in Margaret Wheeler, ed. *History was Buried* (Rev. ed., New York, 1967), 319. M. Cary, *History of Rome* (London, 1964), 625, no. 6 suggests a population of 30,000.

[3]Mau, *Pompeii, Its Life and Art* (Naples, 1873), 23. His information apparently came from Fiorelli.

learned about the age and sex structure of the city from the skeletons, as studies of medieval cemeteries show today.[4]

The smaller estimates of the population of Pompeii derive from Fiorelli's study of the rooms of the excavated portion of the city. Fiorelli, an exceedingly able man, was responsible for the first very careful excavation of the ruins. He was not, however, a demographer. He estimated that there were so many houses with so many rooms, adding three rooms for each shop and nineteen rooms for public buildings.[5] Unfortunately he had no base for estimating the number of persons living in each room, nor did he actually count the number of rooms. His estimate of 3,347 rooms, adjusting for unexcavated portions of the city amounts to less than twelve thousand people. The importance of this estimate is that by its very limited number it raises a question about the very large estimates, not merely for Pompeii, but for Rome and other ancient cities.[6] Fiorelli's estimate fitted well into his belief that the amphitheater seated about 12,807 persons.[7]

Larger estimates for the capacity of the amphitheater have already been mentioned. Such a structure might also accommodate persons from the countryside, since Pompeii was a city-state as well as a city. In A.D. 59 a great riot occurred between Pompeians and citizens of Nuceria in which a number were killed in the amphitheater.[8] The Roman emperor, Nero, closed the amphitheater for a decade and only the influence of its leading families, relatives of his wife, opened it again.[9] One can hardly use the size of the structure as a reliable indication of its urban population.

The area of the city is more significant, hard to define with great accuracy because the wall was unfinished in one section and there were houses outside it.[10] The estimates are between sixty-four and sixty-seven hectares. No exact data remain from other Roman cities with which Pompeian data can be compared. The houses were basically single story. Upper stories were usually added to only parts of them.[11] These were comparable to houses of later medieval cities where the two-story—if not the three-story—

[4]Well illustrated by Gy Acsádi and Janos Nemeskéri, *History of Human Span and Mortality* (Budapest, 1970).

[5]Fiorelli, *Gli scavi*, 13-14.

[6]For instance, the accounts in R. Duncan-Jones, *The Economy of the Roman Empire* (Cambridge, 1974), 262-277. For Pompeii he accepts Beloch's estimate of 15,000. (276).

[7]Fiorelli, *Gli scavi*, 14.

[8]Maiuri, *Introduzione*, 280.

[9]Tacitus, *Annals*, xiv, 17. W. O. Moeller, "The Riot of A.D. 59 at Pompeii," *Historia* (Wiesbaden) 19 (1970), 84-95.

[10]Exactly 64,6826 hectares, according to H. Nissen, *Pompeianische Studien zur Städtekunde des Altertums* (Leipzig, 1877), 377-378.

[11]Pio Ciprotti, *Convocare Pompei* (Rome, 1859), 77-78: Mau, *Pompei*, 245, 247, 313, 373.

house was normal. There the average density to the hectare was about 100 to 120 persons.[12] The Pompeian house thus should not have had as many inhabitants to the hectare since the area of the Pompeian house was as great as the medieval one. The density of Pompeian population may be estimated at about a hundred persons to the hectare. This would indicate about 6,400 to 6,700 inhabitants for the city of Pompeii with a few hundred more in the suburbs, making a total population of about 7,000—several thousand less than even the lowest estimates yet given.

The only area within the ruins in which all seem to have died is the Villa of Diomedes where eighteen skeletons were found. The area of the villa is about 1,500 square meters, an average of eighty-three sq.m. to the person. If the villa's share of uninhabited areas, such as streets, fora, temples, and baths were included, the area per person would be near one hundred sq.m. to the person, suggested by the estimate of seven thousand persons for the whole city.[13] One may not press this sample very far, of course.

Another and probably better approach to Pompeii's population is in the information in Della Corte's *Case ed abitanti di Pompeii*.[14] The data come from inscriptions written on houses and other walls, largely during the hotly contested election for municipal officials which occurred some months before the eruption of Vesuvius on 24 August.[15] Most householders wrote on their walls their choices in the election and thus a remarkably full list of householders remains. In addition some non-householder names appear. Della Corte identified about 900 names within the city and about 114 outside. If we assume that this represents about two-thirds of the city, it would show about 1,350 names inside and 170 outside. Of these names about six percent are those of women.[16] This may give a clue to the index figure by which the number of householders should be multiplied for a total estimate. The smaller the percentage of women, the larger the index figure, according to medieval information. For about six percent of women, the index figure should be about five; at twenty percent, it should be reduced to 3.5. For Pompeii the total population may be estimated at about 7,600 for the city and its immediate environs.

---

[12]J. C. Russell, "Late Ancient and Medieval Population, *"Trans. Amer. Philos. Soc.* 48,3 (1958): 59-68. My original estimate of the population of Pompeii was 10,500.

[13]Michael Grant, *Cities of Vesuvius: Pompeii and Herculaneum* (London, 1971), 134; J. Overbeck, *Pompeii in seinem Gebauden, Alterthümern, und Kunstwerken* (Leipzig, 1884), 22.

[14]M. Della Corte, *Case ed abitanti di Pompei* (2nd ed., Rome, 1954). The recent reissue (1965) is a reprint as far as the data are concerned.

[15]J. C. Willing, *The Last Town Election in Pompeii* (1893); largely based on P. Willems, *Les élections municipales à Pompeii* (Paris, 1887).

[16]Della Corte, 3rd. ed., 408. The count of women is the author's.

Another clue is that of the *summa honoraria,* paid by elected officials, the *duoviri,* after the election. This was usually about a *denarius* to the inhabitant, presumably outside as well as inside of the city. The amount for Pompeii was ten thousand which fits well into other indications of the size of the city and its city-state.[17]

The evidence then would show that Pompeii on the day of the eruption had about 7,000-7,500 in the city and suburbs and several more thousands in the countryside. Why have higher estimates been so uniformly selected—because those doing the reconstructing tend to compare them with modern developments. The grandeur of the temples, the art and sculpture in private homes, and the large recreational buildings are what might be expected of cities of twenty or more thousand today. Pompeian life followed a different life style which is difficult for us to visualize. We tend to compare a minor part of our life (art, architecture, theater) with what was a major part of the Roman activity. This is the lesson of Pompeii and its ruins present it magnificently.

THE MORTALITY AT POMPEII

Fiorelli estimates that two thousand died during the eruption.[18] In his report of excavations in the years 1861-1873, he stated that he had uncovered eighty-seven persons and had filled in forms for seven more, a total of ninety-four. He does not seem to have estimated the number of deceased by units of area of excavation although he does give the size in hectares of each excavated area: their total for those twelve years seems to have been 4.884 hectares.[19] This would mean that Fiorelli had excavated about one-fifteenth of Pompeii. If that was a random sample, the total number of the deceased for the whole city should have been about fourteen hundred. This is a minimum estimate, as we shall see. Others state that in the period 1861-1878, he uncovered 116 skeletons.[20] His successors in charge of excavations, Sogliano and Maiuri, made reports on the progress of the excavations but did not give the number of human remains, except as found each day. The estimate that the total number of the deceased was about two thousand was accepted by Mau.[21] However, the present superin-

[17]Tenney Frank, *An Economic Survey of Ancient Rome* (5 v. Baltimore), (1933-1940), 5: 252-253: Russell, 1958: 67-68.

[18]Fiorelli, *Gli scavi,* p. 172. Maiuri, *Pompeii: Its Life and Art,* 23.

[19]Fiorelli, *Gli scavi.* At beginning of each section: 1, 10, 17, 24, 26, 38, 44, 50, 51, 54, 59, 65, 70, 76.

[20]Report by Overbeck, *Pompeii,* 21.

[21]For 1873-1900 Sogliano, in *Atti del Congresso Internazionale di scienze storici* (5 v., Rome, 1904) 5: 322; A. Maiuri, "Gli scavi de Pompei, dal 1879 al 1948," *Pompeiana: Raccolta di studi per il secondo centenaio degli scavi di Pompei* (Napoli, 1950), 1-21, map on p. 11.

tendent says that there are about two thousand stored in the Casa del Sarno and Terme Feminili del Foro besides the few in the museum.[22] These include some from the countryside, perhaps a couple of hundred. For the city itself, about twelve hundred would seem a reasonable estimate. If these come from two-thirds of the ruins and are a fair sample, the total number of those dying should have been about twenty-seven hundred.

Whether the estimate of twenty-seven hundred is based upon a fair sample depends upon at least two things: was the rate of mortality the same over the whole city in the days of eruption or did people drift in one direction in the city, causing more deaths in the area to which they drifted? Second, were corpses and skeletons taken away so that the present number is less than the original group?

Density of population probably varied from one part of the city to another and conditions during the eruption may have changed as people moved within the city. Vesuvius is northwest of Pompeii, its cone is about eight kilometers from the western edge of the city. Just below the cone lay the road to Herculaneum which would have been avoided by those trying to escape. That was where Pliny the Elder met his death.[23] The wind, according to the younger Pliny's account, prevented ships from leaving the Stabian shore and thus was from the north and west. Again, people thinking about the wind would normally not have fled that way. The sixty persons who died at an inn in Borgo Marunaro, two kilometers south of Pompeii, must have decided, perhaps hastily, to leave in that direction.[24] The main escape route then should have been ENE toward Nuceria twenty kilometers away. The unexcavated portions of Pompeii, except for the amphitheater, lie mostly in the northern and eastern sections of the city, precisely those to which persons should have drifted. Since Fiorelli's time, strips along the two larger streets leading east have been excavated. One might expect that the remaining portions will offer more than the average number of skeletons.

The initial explosion of Vesuvius must have produced something like an earthquake in Pompeii.[25] Of those Pompeians who remembered the quake of 5 February 63, the first reaction must have been fear that houses would crumble, as many had done earlier. Fleeing from under their roofs, they would soon see the approaching clouds of stones, gas, and ash. The more timid probably fled at

---

[22]For this information (as well as other items) I am indebted to Dr. Guiseppina Cerulli, Soperintendente at Pompeii of the Soperintendenza alle Antichità delle Province di Napoli é Caserta (in a letter of 26 June 1975).

[23]Pliny, *Epp.* vi, 16-20.

[24]*Notizie degli scavi,* 1901, pp. 423-440, especially 427.

[25]Pliny, *Epp.* vi, 16.

once and were saved in large numbers. Those who refused to be upset by the explosion and clouds, like Pliny the Elder at Stabia, were caught by the ash and gas and killed. Some eighty died in the Palaestra—gladiators and others who were chained or refused to be frightened by the volcanic activity.[26] Herculaneum, lying just under Vesuvius, seems to have had few dead: the first rumble probably sent them flying. Excavation of outlying villas has not recovered many bodies.[27] People may have been less fearful in the one story houses—more common in the unexcavated areas—thus those areas may have had a greater than average number of skeletons.

The second problem is more difficult. The first two waves of excavation were carried out so carelessly that uncovered bodies or skeletons either left no record or were not properly stored in the ossuaries provided for them.

Immediately after the eruption, many of those who escaped must have returned to see if they could recover some of their possessions. The northwest wind would have caused the ash to drift to the southeast of the larger buildings. If the average ash fall was twenty feet, the low spots would have been considerably less. Inscriptions discovered on buildings show some post-eruption excavation had taken place, one inscription suggesting that some fifty bodies were lying about at the time.[28] The corpses recovered in the digging should have been given proper ceremonies outside of the city. How much excavation took place is not clear; if several thousands of Pompeii's population returned, quite a lot could have been done. That much of value was recovered seems evident in the higher quality of surviving artifacts from Herculaneum compared to those of Pompeii.[29] The volcanic hardened surface over Herculaneum could hardly have been penetrated at the time. Among the areas which should have attracted attention would have been the larger houses along the Via dell'Abbondanza, precisely those which were excavated in the last century.[30] Their height would have caused them to be identified above their ash and their valuable contents attracted excavators, owners and perhaps others.

The excavation of Pompeii, beginning in 1748, was not designed to record properly the discovery of skeletons. These are seldom mentioned in the official reports unless several were uncovered together or were bedecked with valuables—rings, jewels or recep-

---

[26]*Notizie degli scavi*, 1939: 214-228.

[27]*Notizie degli scavi*, 1910: 396-397; 1921, 431; 1922, 459-485.

[28]M. Della Corte, "Esplorazioni di Pompei immediamente successive alla catastrofe dell' anno 79," *In Memoria lui Vasile Párvan*, (Bucharest, 1934), 96-109.

[29]Eugen Kursch, *Herculaneum* (Nürnberg, 1960), 11. Herculaneum was a small town of perhaps five hectares, of which two-fifths have been excavated.

[30]See map in *Pompeiana*, 11.

tacles of unusual quality.[31] Bones were sent to local ossuaries, mentioned above. One cannot be certain that all skeletons were stored properly or at all, although the latter is unlikely.

The aim of the excavators was to uncover the city of Pompeii and to find valuable artifacts for the National Museum at Naples[32] by digging down vertically at promising places, often at a rapid pace. It is not even certain that the dirt and ash was always carried outside of the town; thus more modern excavation may be of debris moved from an earlier excavated site.[33] An odd phase was the digging of areas, usually rooms, for the view of distinguished visitors. A guest usually got a room or two, but when Czar Nicholas I, of Russia, and the King of Naples arrived at the scene in 1846, they were given a six-room salute which took all day.[34] An official list of objects to be recorded remains: gold, silver, copper, iron, even ivory and bones. In one report as late as 1942, under 'bone' was included "un molare equino e un molare umano."[35] With more scientific archaeological exploration under Fiorelli, the work proceeded at a high level but as yet no research of an anthropological character has been done on the skeletal evidence.

The present skeletal evidence suggests that at least twenty-seven hundred died at Pompeii. Many were probably recovered in excavations following the eruption and have been cremated or buried outside of the city. Some may even have been lost in the haphazard digging of 1748-1861. Perhaps more than the average remain in the unexcavated third of Pompeii. The lowest estimate would then be that about a third of the city died; a higher estimate might even suggest a half.

If these estimates are accurate, Pompeian skeletal evidence offers an unprecedented opportunity for the physical anthropologist to reconstruct the age, sex, and other characteristics of a Roman population. The estimates, it must be remembered, rest heavily on the number of skeletons in Pompeian ossuaries and on the completeness of Della Corte's list of names, even though the less accurate evidence tends to corroborate them. The remaining skeletons differ from the total in including a few of those who could neither walk nor be carried away. The survivors should not have been much different from those who were caught in the catastrophe, since the reasons for either fleeing or remaining must have been many and perhaps a majority would have had the

---

[31]As of a doctor carrying his instruments. *Notizie degli scavi*, 1939, 221.

[32]"Si e lavorato senza rinvenire alcuno oggetto antico," Fiorelli, ed. *Pompeianorum* 2:443 (1845).

[33]Fiorelli, ed. *Pompeianorum* 2:443; Notizie degli scavi, 1939 215; M. Della Corte, *Pompei: I nuovi scavi e l'anfiteatro* (Pompei, 1930), 82.

[34]Fiorelli, ed. *Pompeianorum* 2 (1846) 450.

[35]*Notizie degli scavi*, 1942, 307.

decision forced on them. A thorough study of skeletal data of ancient history artifacts is perhaps the greatest need today. It is more important because the Roman custom of cremation has reduced the amount of skeletal evidence available for study.[36]

ROME AS THE IMPERIAL CAPITAL

In contrast to Pompeii, Rome's population has been the subject of much study over the past century. Estimates have ranged from less than two hundred thousand to more than a million inhabitants. The upper and lower estimates present two very different concepts of the city. The lower estimates would suggest a Rome with enough financial support from imperial revenues, such as salaries of civil servants, and farm income of the great families, to provide a satisfactory and even healthy civic life. Higher estimates indicate a vast urban complex of high-rise buildings housing a multitude of urban poor folk with insufficient economic support.[37] The differences in estimates might tempt one to retreat into complete skepticism.[38] However, the evidence is of considerable quantity and some has not been exploited as it deserves.

The hypothesis of a very large population is based upon two arguments: first, the *insula* meant an apartment house or at least a multiple group of apartments, and to estimate Roman population one would multiply the 44,000-46,000 *insulae* in the *Libellus de Regionibus* by an uncertain but large number.[39] Second, the distribution of grain and money made to 200,000-320,000 persons were given to adult, free males of the city of Rome which also presumes a very large population.[40] The argument here is that the *insulae* were just apartments which may be multiplied by a small number for a population estimate and that the grain and other distributions before A.D. 410 were for citizens of both Rome and other cities in Italy. In addition there are several other means of estimating the city's population, all of which are compatible with a

---

[36]While considerable progress has been made in deriving information from cremations, the results, especially if the cremations are very complete, are not very satisfactory.

[37]Low figures appear in R. S. Lopez, *Commercial Revolution of the Middle Ages* (Cambridge, 1976), 6; F. Lot, *La fin du monde antique et le début du moyen age* (Paris, 1951), 80; Russell "Late Ancient and Medieval Population," 65. For the very long list of others see Pierre Salmon, *Population et dépopulation dans l'Empire romain* (Brussels, 1974), 22: G. Hermansen, "The Population of Imperial Rome: the Regionares," *Historia* 27 (1978): 129-169, and literature cited in these studies. The most recent, G. Rickman, *The Corn Supply of Ancient Rome* (Oxford, 1980), 9-11 suggests more than a million.

[38]F. M. Maier, "Römische Bevölkerungsgeschichte und Inschriftensstatistik," *Historia* 2 (1953-1954): 322.

[39]Published and edited twice: by R. Valentini and C. Zuchetti, *Codice topografiche della città di Roma* (Rome, 1940) and by A. Nordh, *Libellus de Regionibus Romae* (Lund, 1949).

[40]That is, adult males, presumably seventeen years of age and older, who number less than one-third of the adult men. To them would be added women, children, slaves, and visitors. The total would have been about four times the number of grain recipients.

population estimate of 150,000-200,000 or less. The topic is complicated by the possibility of change in the size of the population during the period A.D. 1-542.

There are two clues that the population increased in the period. Writing before his death in A.D. 79, Pliny the Elder gave both the circumference of Rome and the number of local units (*compita,* cross roads) of the city.[41] The first was almost exactly the distance of the walls of Aurelian (A.D. 270-275). However, by Aurelian's time settlements had been made outside of the walls, so some increase may be assumed. The number of local units also increased from 265 to 310 by the early fourth century, about a 17 percent increase.[42] This is what might be expected of the imperial capital; the size of the empire had increased in the same period and the bureaucracy, so important a part of Rome's working class, did too. Both probably reached their greatest strength in the second century. The population of Rome should have decreased some with the declining population of the empire even before the sack of Rome by the Visigoths in A.D. 410. The establishment of a second capital at Constantinople might also have helped in a decline. Nevertheless, it is hard to reduce the size of a bureaucracy and the aristocratic holders of extensive lands in both Italy and outside of the peninsula probably remained much the same. Rome was probably not much different in size in the fifth century from what it had been in the first, although an increase of a fourth may have occurred in between. Temporary losses from the plagues of the second and third centuries may well have been restored by migration within a short time.

The city certainly deserved structures equal to its lofty position as capital. Dio Cassius, for example, wrote that the Emperor Trajan rebuilt and enlarged the Circus Maximus to a size suitable for the people of Rome.[43] The size of the circus was naturally conditioned by the needs of a racecourse rather than to the population, but such ancient structures usually accommodated most of the adult population of the city. The Circus Maximus seated perhaps a hundred thousand people which might indicate a civic population of perhaps 50 percent more. The seating capacity of the other large structures were given by the *Libellus de Regionibus* but were overestimated by about 50 percent. The theaters of Balbus, Pompey, and Marcellus actually held audiences of about seven to twenty thousand.[44]

Romans apparently left no estimates of their city's population, although many commented upon its size and beauty. Augustus and

---

[41]Pliny, *N. H.* iii, 5, 66.

[42]See table 3.

[43]Dio Cassius, lxviii, 7. R-E suggests a higher figure.

[44]Nordh, *Libellus,* 12-13, C. Huelson, *Bulletino Communale,* (1894): 318-324. Hermansen, 145, 164.

Claudius took the last censuses of Roman citizens and found between four and six million of them.[45] If a separate total for the city alone was made, it has not survived. Indeed, the concept of citizenship was not limited to the city walls and thus the *plebs urbana* might not be restricted to the city alone.

Literary evidence has suggested to Classical scholars that the city was very large. Juvenal, in his famous third satire, describes the street and housing conditions as wretched. He apparently lived on a third or fourth floor.[46] Martial occupied an attic, up three flights of stairs, with his wife and daughter and a servant. He suffered from the excessive noise and commotion, but mentioned that others living in the city enjoyed better conditions.[47] The orator, Aelius Aristides, in his panegyric on Rome, declared that, if the city were flattened, it would reach Otranto (in the heel of Italy).[48] Using these clues early modern opinion, believing that the capital of a great empire should equal the size of Paris or London assigned very large figures to the city, but these were thoroughly unwarranted by Roman writers' remarks. Yet the philosopher, David Hume, noted that Herodian had said that the Golden Palace (and grounds) of Nero was as large as Rome.[49] Presumably this meant that the mass of tall buildings in the center of Rome was about the extent of Nero's work, which occupied about eighty hectares.[50] Hume favored a small estimate.

Rome was capital of an empire equal in size to the United States of America. In 1880 it also had about the same population as the Roman Empire—some fifty million,[51] with Washington having about the same population as Rome, some 170,000 inhabitants. The two cities were alike in other ways: they had little commercial or industrial strength and no direct access to the sea; both had rather small bureaucracies; transportation was easier in the United States with its railroads than in the Roman Empire with its seaways, although the Empire had better roads. The population of both cities was supported by government and farming. There were vast differences in the geography of the two areas and the kinds of governments which they had. In some ways the Roman Empire was closer to the United States of 1880 than the latter is to our country today.

---

[45]Augustus, *Mon. Anc.* viii, conveniently translated by W. Sinigen, *Rome* (New York, 1965): 104-113.

[46]Juvenal, iii, 201.

[47]Martial, I, cxvii; VII, xcv; VIII, xxiii; XII, lvii.

[48]Orationes, XXVI, translated by D. R. Dudley *Urbs Romana* (Aberdeen, 1967), 222.

[49]David Hume, "On the Populousness of Ancient Nations," in *Essays, Moral, Political and Literary,* Essay 11, 1: 429. This edition edited by T. H. Green and T. H. Grose, (1776).

[50]A. Boethius, *The Golden House of Nero* (Ann Arbor, 1960). 108-109.

[51]Russell, 1958, 148.

Rome derived much of her economic support from the imperial court, the aristocratic landowners and officials, the bureaucracy, and the army. All of these brought money into the city from taxes and other income. Such income is a basic factor in the civic economy.[52] In general each basic income supports about six or seven persons, that is, if it is sufficient to support a family. It takes an equal number of nonbasic incomes to provide goods and services to a city. Thus if the number of basic sources of income can be ascertained, an estimate of population can be made. If a city is more than seven times its basic sources of income, it is obviously overpopulated.

This phase of Roman history has not been studied and, indeed, only an introduction can be made to suggest future research. The basic groups would include those paid from the fisc. Only a few estimates of numbers are available. The *vigiles* (police-firemen) numbered seven thousand. Of the *aquarii* (officials in charge of the aqueducts which supplied water to the city) 240 were paid by the Aerarium and 460 by the fisc of Caesar, according to Frontinus.[53] The former were paid for by charges for water and were thus nonbasic; the latter were basic. Apparently the Count of the Sacred Largesses at one time had 546 regular and 300 extra workers. Based on these facts a very uncertain guess of five thousand members of the bureaucracy might be made. The number of soldiers in the city is also uncertain. They varied in number and in income. A poorly paid single soldier would not be rated as providing for five or six others. An even more tentative guess of six thousand persons is made, assuming that the actual number was usually larger but not as important a factor individually.[54]

The 1780 *domus* of the *Libellus* were probably of senators, *equites* and other wealthy men. If one adds three for important assistants of each of these, there were about eight thousand basic persons of this class, although there may be duplications of assistants who lived in the *insulae*. As a guess, two thousand might be added as members of the imperial court, although here again many, even slaves, may have lived outside in the insulae. Perhaps another two thousand might be added with those who entertained visitors and residents, either in the inns or theaters or other public entertainment. Obviously these guesses need to be refined by whatever evidence remains.

---

[52]Russell, 1972, 34-38.

[53]Frontinus, *Les aqueducs de la ville de Rome*, ed. P. Grimal (Paris, 1961) 56. Joel Schmidt, *Vie et mortes des esclaves* (Paris, 1973), 199.

[54]L. Homo, *Roman Political Institutions from City to State* (New York, 1966), 356; P. R. C. Weaver, *Familia Caesaris* (Cambridge 1972), esp. 302. Brunt, 1971, 152 (note 82 below) suggests 20,000 after Tiberius.

The total of these estimates is about thirty thousand. However, there may well be duplications in assigning persons to special areas rather than to insulae at large. Multiplying this number by six and seven gives 180,000 and 210,000. If this is correct or nearly so, it suggests that Rome was not overpopulated and was living well within its means. This throws an interesting light upon the meaning of the distributions of grain and meat. They were merely additions to income, already sufficient, rather than an unemployment benefit.

Roman urban society was geared to administer the government of the empire, largely supported by salaries and fees from official sources and from farm income for the landowners. The distributions to the *plebs* may have been regarded as the equivalent in food for those who did not have farms. They were fringe benefits, like free public education and various other compensations which citizens feel are quite proper for government to give today.

ROME AS AN INLAND CITY

The cities of the ancient and medieval world fall easily into two categories: inland and seaport. The difference between them was primarily the result of the much less expensive transportation by sea than by land, even with the aid of the splendid Roman roads. A second difference was the ready access of seaports to seafood, especially where the on and offshore breezes made for inexpensive fishing. A third was the actual distance between the city and the sea, since even a few kilometers allowed citizens to prepare to withstand armed attacks by pirates and enemies. These advantages affected the size and shape of cities and even the variation of population density within their walls. Rome was definitely an inland city, akin to others like it such as Antioch and Athens in the ancient world, Florence and Paris in the medieval.

Antioch was a caravanserai, a caravan city, of great extent, with a population estimated between 150,000 and 300,000, perhaps closer to the former figure. With its extensive commerce and some industry, it had perhaps 150 to 200 persons to the hectare in its densest sections.[55] If Athens had about fifty thousand at its height, it would have had a density of more than two hundred to the hectare. Before the Black Death of 1348 both Florence and Paris approached one hundred thousand. With its 630 hectares the density of Florence's population would have been about 158 to the hectare, while Paris with 430 hectares would have been about 233 to the hectare.[56] With these in mind, one might well question any

---

[55]Russell, 1958, 82 for a figure of 90,000.

[56]Russell, 1958, 77, for Athens; 1972, 44-45 and 150-151 for Florence and Paris respectively. For the last two also, L. Genicot, "Les grandes villes d'occident en 1300," *Économics et Sociétés au Moyen Age. Mélanges offerts à Edouard Perroy*, ed. J. Schneider (Paris, 1973), 211, 215. Some believe that Paris had a half million.

estimate of Roman population of over two hundred and fifty persons to the hectare. Even allowing Rome an extent of 1620 hectares (240 in the thinly settled areas outside of the walls), a population of a half million would have demanded three hundred to the hectare while a million would have required an unbelievable six hundred. The inland city tended to have its business districts in its center, as in the forums of Rome. And since the people preferred to live near their place of work because there was no public transportation, the density of population was greater there. Other business centers might be near the periphery, as in the hog market near the northern limits of Rome and the granaries, piers and warehouses on the Tiber to the south. Secondary centers were apt to lie along the main highways into the city. In Rome some were in the regions of the Via Lata to the north, Templum Pacis and Esquiline to the east, Porta Capena to the south and probably in Trastevere in the west.[57]

Cities tended to be square or round, but their shapes were often distorted by rivers or other geographical features. The seaports, by contrast, had available resources of seafood and easier access to the great grain markets of Sicily, North Africa, and Egypt. They were, of course, also supplied by the neighboring countryside. The shape of most seaports was more like a capital D with the seafront as the straight side. Most business and commercial activity tended to concentrate along the wharfside where a high degree of population density developed. As well illustrated by fourteenth-century Barcelona, most people tended to live near the sea front.[58]

This concentration along the dockside resulted in a greater density of population in the entire city. Ostia, restricted by river and swamp, averaged nearly four stories in height of houses compared to a mere two stories in Rome, as we shall see. Her population density should have been double that of Rome and was probably near 300 persons to the hectare for a total of eighteen to 27,000 persons. If one compares the number of tomb inscriptions giving ages of death in the third through the sixth centuries, Rome had about 6.75 times those of Ostia. Proportionately the Roman population then should have been about 121,000 to 182,000.[59] Ancient Alexandria had perhaps 216,000 in its 920 hectares or about 235 to the hectare. Medieval Venice had its 100,000 within 324 hectares or about 309 to each hectare.[60] Both of these cities drew support from the Mediterranean. In addition Alexandria was supplied from the Nile Valley while Venice drew from the Po Valley and the more distant Apulia.

---

[57]Nordh, 1949.

[58]Russell, 1958, 114. The more populous quarters, De la Mer and Pi were on the sea.

[59]Russell Meiggs, *Roman Ostia* (Oxford, 1960), 240; J. E. Packer, "Housing and Population in Imperial Ostia and Rome," *Journal of Roman Studies* 57 (1967): 90-95.

[60]Russell, 1958, 79; Russell, 1972, 64-66.

Other examples of seaports and inland cities might be given, but these are sufficient to illustrate the advantages of the seaports and the disadvantages of Rome and other inland cities. Rome had little in the way of commerce and industry as a base for population. One would expect then a density of no more than two hundred persons to the hectare.

The logistics of the Roman food supply implied an intimate connection of highways and food. Mommsen and Marquardt showed this a century ago in a famous work, discussing such titles as *curator viae et praefectus alimentorum* employed in the *cura alimentorum*.[61] About twenty roads entered Rome, but they were narrow, and the better roads with their stone surface were hard on feet and hooves. Hogs, more like razorbacks, driven from southern Italy to Rome, were alleged to have lost a fifth of their weight en route. Probably cattle, sheep and goats also lost badly although some doubtless came down the Tiber in boats.[62] Carts carried loads of about twenty-five *modii* (less than two hundred kilograms), a form of carriage so expensive that it doubled the cost of grain in thirty miles or so. The movement of heavy industrial products was also expensive.

Much had to come to Rome by water, but here also there were problems. Rome was twenty-five kilometers from sea by land and thirty-five kilometers by river. Some small ships were rowed or hauled upstream if conditions were right. High water from spring floods or low water in summer often impeded river navigation. The Mediterranean saw little shipping from November until March. Not only was navigation seasonal, but North Africa was several days away by sea and Egypt several weeks farther. Cargoes of larger vessels had to be transshipped at Ostia or Portus and then hauled up the river or carried by road to the city. A day's supply of grain for even 200,000 persons was 25,000 modii and required 12.5 ships carrying 2000 modii apiece.[63] Transshipment probably required about 300 men working ten hours a day at the seaport and about the same number at Rome to get the grain to the warehouses. And what was done with wheat also had to be done with oil, wine, and other supplies.

FORMA URBIS AND LIBELLUS DE REGIONIBUS

Two important sources for demographic information about imperial Rome are the great marble map (*Forma Urbis*) of Rome

[61]T. Mommsen and J. Marquardt. *Römisches Staatsrecht* (Leipzig, 1872), 2, 2: 1029-1033.

[62]A. Chastagnol, *La Préfecture Urbaine à Rome sous la Bas-Empire* (Paris, 1960), 312.

[63]Chastagnol, 1960: 317; E. Tengström, *Bread for the People* (Stockholm, 1974), 27-63. M. C. Branch, "Rome and Richmond," *Journal of the American Institute of Planners* 28 (1962): 1-9. Rickman 1980, 14-21.

and the description (apparently for tourists) called the *Libellus de Regionibus*.

The great marble map of Rome was located on the north wall of the Templum Sacrae Urbis near the Forum of Trajan which was later converted into the Church of Saints Cosmos and Damian. The map was about eighteen meters in width and thirteen in height, composed of about one hundred and fifty slabs, many about one by two meters in size.[64] It was on a scale of about 250 to 1, varying to as little as 300 to 1, a very detailed map. The horizontal axis is NE-SW and the vertical SE-NW. The former runs roughly through the Viminal Hill and the stretch of the Tiber River below the island; the other (going clockwise) along the Via Appia, Circus Maximus and the stretch of the Tiber north of the island. In general the most important area (Forum, Palatine) is on the lower right. This differs from the normal *decumanus-cardo* arrangement which often lines up in a NS-EW direction.[65] The map is a cartographic achievement of the first order, and deservedly belongs among the architectural triumphs of the Severi emperors. Such a building and map were appropriate as part of a municipal rather than an imperial *setup*.

The map is obviously designed to facilitate communications with the inhabitants of the housing units. Thus there is normally only one doorway for each unit although there was probably more than one door for some, especially those which had streets on either side of them. The stairwells indicate the number of stories and flights of stairs.[66] The stairways are normally at the end of blocks of units. It seems that the stairways lead to long halls, opening all units on that floor to outside communication. This assumption gives a maximum estimate of height in any calculation of average height of structures. Since some six hundred fragments of the map survive, a sampling process must be used to estimate the average number of stories in the buildings of the city. For the number of buildings of two or more stories in height, the total number of instances is used in table 1. The comparative number of single-story buildings is secured by counting all buildings in which two units appear in a fragment. From the table, it seems that the average height of structures in Rome was a trifle less than two stories in height, actually 1.84. When compared with Ostia which had an average building height of about four stories, the popula-

---

[64]G. Carettone and others, eds., *La Pianta Marmorea di Roma Antica* (Roma, 1960) for both text and tables. For the scale and accuracy, also O. Richter, *Topographie der Stadt Rom* (Munich, 1901). 5. An earlier edition was by O. Richter, *Forma Urbis Romae* (Berlin, 1874).

[65]G. Carettone, *La Painta Marmorea*. Richter 1901, 2-4.

[66]Pavil Zicans, "Über die Haustypen der Forma Urbis," *Opuscula Archaeologica* 2 (1941): 183-194.

Table 1

The Height of Roman Structures
in the *Forma Urbis.*

Number of stories	Number of flights of stairs	Number of structures	Number of stories
One	None	(300)	300
Two	One	157	314
Three	Two	62	186
Four	Three	5	20
Five	Four	13	65
Six	Five	20	120
Seven or more	Six or more	3	21
	Total	560	1026

Source: Carettone, *La Pianta Marmorea.* (Note 64)
There seem to be about seven units or insulae for each structure and that the 560 represent about 4,000 insulae or about a twelfth of the total city building units.

tion of Rome should have been about half as dense as stated earlier.[67]

The question naturally arises whether the fragments of the map are a fair sample of the total. Perhaps a tenth remains. Only forty-one of the areas have been located on the map of the city, but they are scattered fairly evenly over a considerable area. They fall naturally in certain sections of the city where identifiable monuments appear, either because they are named on the map or because of their distinguishable shape.[68] The Circus Maximus, for instance, fixes the location of several. Only five regions have no identifiable fragments: I, II, V, VI and VII. The first two were thinly settled, the others lightly. Two other regions. IX and XIV, the two most thinly settled, are not well represented. The unidentified fragments are probably scattered widely over the city and show a variety of building and street types. There seems no reason to doubt that the fragments represent well the whole map. The *Forma Urbis,* then, does not enable one to locate accurately all of the areas where population was dense but it does show that if restricted to structures of only two stories in height on the average, it could hardly have exceeded one hundred and fifty to the hectare. This would give a total population of about two hundred thousand at most.[69]

---

[67]See n. 59. and table 1.

[68]For instances: R. A. Staccioli, "Terme minore e balnea nelle documentazione della Forma Urbia," *Archaeologia Classica* 13 (1961): 92-103.

[69]Like those of medieval Europe, Russell, 1958, 59-63.

The second important source, the *Libellus de Regionibus*, covers somewhat the same subject matter as the *Forma* and may have been partially derived from it. Like the *Forma*, the *Libellus* lists monuments, forums, and facilities of the city. Beyond these, it lists officers, camps of the *vigiles*, and the numbers of *domus* and *insulae* in each region. The *Libellus* also gives the lengths of the boundaries of regions. With this information Von Gerkan has outlined the limits of the regions and estimated the size of the populated area by eliminating uninhabited areas, such as gardens, streets, forums, great monuments, and the Tiber.[70] This gives only 622 hectares of inhabited area. He apparently did not allow for vacant areas around structures, so that the land actually covered by buildings was considerably less. He paid little attention to the data represented by the *Forma Urbis*. He assumed that the insula was one floor of several storied buildings and that it was about 148 sq. meters in size with about twelve persons to the insula.

In a very recent article Hermansen makes a good case to show that *Libellus* was a tourist guide of the fourth century and subject to the inaccuracies and exaggerations that characterize such literature and make specific numbers (of which there are many) suspect. He tries to show that the insula means an independent building, normally an apartment house. He reasons that in law a word can have only one meaning, that laws show insula can mean an independent building and thus it must mean nothing else. However, he finds that the masters who carved the *Forma Urbis* were not interested in portraying independent buildings which is strange if insulae were so important, and that the insula was about 250 sq. meters in size.[71] This naturally eliminates any possibility that there were 44,000-46,000 of them in the city, so he arbitrarily reduces their number to about 25,000. He discusses von Gerkan's latest study and suggests corrections and changes.[72] He does not seem to prove that the insula cannot mean an apartment and the arbitrary reduction of the number of insulae is very questionable.

The *Forma Urbis* makes it certain that its authors were primarily interested in the apartment rather than in a collection of them. Since the apartments could easily number 44,000-46,000 within the walls of the city, "apartment" seems the correct definition of the insula in the *Forma* and in the *Libellus*. Historically, the insula was an isolated unit and probably remained that, usually for one

---

[70]A. von Gerkan, "Grenzen und Grössen der vierzehnten Regionen Roms," *Bonner Jahrbücher* 149 (1949): 34-63: estimate on 61; eliminated areas, 56.

[71]Hermansen, 1978, 129-169. (Note 37)

[72]Hermansen, 1978, on the insula see also: G. Hermansen, "The Medianum in the Roman Apartment," *Phoenix* 24 (1970): 41-47; J. E. Packer, "The insulae of Imperial Ostia," *Memoirs of the American Academy in Rome* 31 (1971): 70; B. W. Frier, "The Rental Market in Early Imperial Rome," *Journal of Roman Studies* 67 (1977): 27-37.

family even after houses were joined together as apartment houses. In writing of the destruction of the great fire under Nero, Tacitus spoke of the loss of "domuum et insularum et templorum."[73] The fire razed three regions, damaged seven others, and left four intact. Yet the city was alleged to have been rebuilt in stone with lower buildings and wider streets in a relatively short time.[74] Suetonius wrote of the porticoes which Nero ordered built in front of the "domos et insulas."[75] Unfortunately the remains of ancient buildings in Rome are not helpful in solving the problem of the insula.

How many lived in the insula? The inscriptions showing the ages of the Roman deceased give some interesting clues. Sixty percent of both freedmen and slaves were male. Only the freedmen had a normal sex ratio (52.5). The proportion of slaves of the great families was even more masculine: two-thirds or more.[76] This would indicate that at least a tenth of the population were adult, unmarried males, many of whom would be living in the insulae. Furthermore, the average age of death was low: only 4.6 percent of the men and 2.4 percent of the women died after the age of sixty, with a combined total of 3.7.[77] By contrast lowland Italy showed a 4.1 percent of both sexes dying after sixty, while the healthier highlands had 5.5.[78] Fewer older people usually meant fewer living with the nuclear family (man, wife, children). Such a simple family in times when the population was not increasing rapidly usually numbered 3.5 persons. Even slaves at Rome often had their own households.[79] One seems justified in multiplying the number of insulae by 3.5 (or at most, four) to estimate Roman population.

A test of the reasonableness of these numbers to insulae (and ten to the domus) is whether the regional totals based on them seem proper. These totals are in table 2. The densest population would be in the three central regions: Circus Maximus with 322 to the hectare, Forum with 281 and Palatine with 274. Few medieval cities averaged so large. Many high-rise buildings would have been

---

[73]Tacitus, *Ann.* 15, 41.

[74]Tacitus, *Ann.* 38, 40, 43.

[75]Suetonius, *Nero.* They also appear together in *Caesar,* 41. The ancient houses are discussed in G. Lugli, *Itinerario in Roma Antica,* (Rome, 1870), 84, 124, 324, 325, 361, 395, 531 and 435, where pictures of them are given.

[76]J. Szilágy, 1962, 358. For the great families, Susan Treggiari, "Domestic Staff at Rome in the Julio-Claudian Period, 27 B.C. to A.D. 68," *Historie Sociale* 6 (1973): 248. Treggiari, "Jobs in the Household of Livia," *Papers of the British School at Rome* 43 (1975): 58.

[77]Russell, 1958, 26 from tables 21 and 22.

[78]Russell, 1958, 27 from tables 25 and 26.

[79]Slaves were apparently encouraged to gain their freedom. For one estimate of the number of slaves in Rome, the totally impossible 138,500, see Lugli, "Quanti erano gli schiavi in Roma," *Nuova Antologia* fasc.1715 (October, 1943).

Table 2
Area and Density of Roman Regions

Number and Name of Region	Area (hectares)	Number of Insulae Domus in region		Population	Number persons to hect.	Area of Insula (hect)	Size of Insula (m²)
I Porta Capena	57.5	3,250	120	12,575	219	36.2	111.4
II Caelimontium	68.0	3,600	127	13,870	204	43.4	120.6
III Isis et Serapis	166.5	2,757*	160	11,250	68	60.3	218.7
IV Templum Pacis	53.5	2,757*	88	10,530	197	36.2	131.3
V Esquilinae	103.0	3,850	180	15,275	148	48.8	126.8
VI Alta Semita	203.6	3,403	146	13,370	66	72.4	212.8
VII Via Lata	63.5	3,805	120	14,517	229	38.0	99.9
VIII Forum Romanum	47.9	3,480	130	13,480	281	24.5	70.4
IX Circus Flaminius	296.5	2,777	140	11,120	38	77.3	106.8
X Palatium	37.0	2,642	88*	10,127	274	18.2	68.9
XI Circus Maximus	31.0	2,600	88*	9,980	322	17.5	67.3
XII Piscina Publica	86.5	2,487*	113	9,834	114	42.2	169.7
XIII Aventinus	124.0	2,487*	130	10,004	81	64.5	259.3
XIV Trans Tiberim	280.0	4,406	150	16,918	58	43.0	97.6
Total	1,628.5	44,301	1,780	172,850		622.5	

Sources: Titles as in Nordh (note 37), pp. 2-19. Area, from von Gerkan, *Grenzen* (note 70): p. 55. It includes extramural areas of 5 hectares in Region III, 5 in VI; 75 in IX; 7 in XII and 188 in XIV. The number of insulae are from Nordh, 2-19. Von Gerkan (p. 63) gives 1,790 with several regional differences. Population: each represents adding 3.5 times the number of insulae to ten times the number of domus. Density: population divided by area (number of hectares). Area of insulae is von Gerkan's calculation in *Grenzen*, p. 64. Size of insula; area of insulae divided by number of insulae.
*Pairs of identical figures are naturally suspect. Templum Pacis would seem to have too few insulae. Nothing seems obviously wrong with the other sets of numbers.

needed to house that dense a population. A city with half a million the size of Rome would have required a fantastic density in the center. These three regions covered about 117 hectares which was not much larger than Nero's palace and grounds which Herodian compared to Rome. The Capitoline and Palatine hills with the high-rise mass about them dominated the eastern half of the city.

To the numbers living in the insulae must be added the people in the domus and in the barracks. While slaves in some numbers lived with the great families in their domus, many also probably lived in the insulae. The families of senatorial and equestrian rank numbered only a few hundred and many of them lived outside of the capital. It seems, then, that ten might be a reasonable number by which to multiply the 1780 domus, a total of 17,800. The problem of the barracks is that one cannot be certain how many soldiers actually lived there; the barracks do not occupy much space. Many, particularly after marriage was permitted, would probably have occupied some of the insulae. The total population may be estimated by using 3.5 or four to the insula. Thus the larger and smaller estimates are as follows: the larger of about 200,000 (172,880 in the insulae; 17,800 in the domus and 10,000 in the barracks) and a smaller of 183,350 (155,500 in the insulae, and the same for the smaller in the domus and barracks). A rough estimate of 180,000-200,000 for imperial Rome is not large by modern urban populations, but it was very large for the ancient and medieval world. The number does not suggest crowding, except in the central regions of the city. As the Roman satirists witness, the Romans disliked the idea of crowding in densely settled areas.

THE GRAIN AND MEAT DISTRIBUTIONS

An early argument for a very large Roman population was the large number of recipients of grain and money from Augustus and later emperors. This argument assumes that the numbers were correct and that the recipients were adult, male Roman citizens living at Rome. Any large round number in ancient and medieval statements is open to question.[80] The matter of the distributions must be considered not merely as one of phraseology but also in actual practice.

The primary statements are in the biography of Augustus, his *Res Gestae*.[81] For his position as emperor he was deeply indebted to his army, many of them from cities and towns all over Italy, most of whom were Roman plebs.[82] He tells of his censuses which enrolled

[80]For a good statement of the difficulty of believing medieval and ancient numbers, K. Lamprecht, *Deutsche Wirtschaftsleben im Mittelalter* (2 vols. Leipzig, 1885), 2: 9-16.

[81]*Mon. Anc.* viii, 9-12, 15.

[82]The soldiers still came from Italy, for the most part. P. A. Brunt, *Social Conflicts in the Roman Republic* (London, 1971).

more than four million Roman citizens. He said that he gave a number of gifts, none less than 250,000. Then: "in the eighteenth year of my tribunician power, I gave sixty denarii to each of 320,000 of the urban plebs." He also said that more than 200,000 of the plebs were receiving public grain. If these were residents of Rome alone, the total population of that city was at least 200,000 and in the case of 320,000, at least a million and a quarter, since adult male citizens would be only about one-fourth of a population, including women, children, slaves and free noncitizens.

Neither plebs nor *plebs urbana* need refer to the inhabitants of Rome alone. Most of the four or more million Roman citizens were plebeians living outside of Rome, many of them in Italian cities. "Urban" might have been used to distinguish urban from rural citizens. The latter would presumably have been fed by their own grain and meat. Other Italian cities than Rome might also have needed grain and other distributions, particularly in supplying Rome as seaports or markets. The test would be to find if other Italian cities were receiving grain from the Roman supply.

Large estimates for the city's population have also been made from data in the biographies of later emperors.[83] The estimates were very large, obviously sufficient for the 200,000 regular recipients mentioned above. Recently, an authority on the housing of Rome has written, "Without question Ostia and Portus were fed from the grain shipped to Rome and, indeed an often quoted passage from the Vita of Severus (xxiii), suggests that Rome served as supply depot not only for Latium but also for all of Italy."[84]

In the fourth century, grain allotments were being shifted from one Italian city to another, even from the Roman *canon* or supply.[85] A.H.M. Jones presents cases of this kind. Puteoli, which had received a grant of 150,000 modii a year, had its grant halved by Constantine who then brought it back up to 100,000. Professor Jones also wrote:

A number of these Campaian cities, including Capua, also received corn grants, no doubt to assist them in delivering hogs to Rome.[86] Under Gratian, Capua complained that Cerealis, the perfect of the city in 353-355, had cut the corn grants from the Roman *canon* by 38,000 modii, and Gratian ordered a restitution of the old allotment.

---

[83]W. J. Oates, "The Population of Rome," *Classical Philology* 29 (1934): 101-106; Tengström 1974, 27 ff.; Chastagnol 1960, 313.

[84]Packer, 1967, 89.

[85]All from Q. Aurelius Symmachus, *Relationes*, ed. G. Meyer (Leipzig, 1872), 40.

[86]A. M. H. Jones, *The Later Roman Empire*, 702-703 and 709. Chastagnol 1960, 301. The data are in F. W. Barrow, *Prefect and Emperor: The Relations of Symmachus* (Oxford, 1973), 6. J. Beloch, *Bevölkerungsegeschichte der griechischeromischen Welt*, (Rome, 1886), 399, 402.

One can understand why a *tessera* for grain would name the home city of the holder.[87] Thus the grain given to these and probably other Italian cities went to the plebs urbana, even as early as Augustus.

If allotments of grain were being shifted from one city to another with no reference to population, they are not very helpful as a demographic source. Perhaps a better clue is the apparent capacity of the city's mills. The *Libellus* gives the number of mills in the middle of the fourth century as 254.

Somewhat earlier Trajan had enacted a law that a Latin Rights owner of a mill, grinding not less than a hundred modii of corn daily for three years, should be entitled to citizenship.[88] If a hundred modii was the average daily output of the mills, the total should have been about 25,400 modii a day. Since a modius was supposed to feed eight persons a day, the number should have been about 203,200.[89] This clue has the advantage of dealing with a distribution which should have included the whole population of the city itself. In the year 419 there were apparently fed in the city itself 120,000 persons, when the city was probably somewhat reduced by the Visigoths' sack in A.D. 410.

This is the same as the number of persons alleged to have been given pork rations in that same year.[90] The pork distribution apparently began in the reign of Aurelian (270-275) about the time that he began building the city wall. The size of the pork distribution is also known for two other years: to 317,333 persons in 367 and 141,120 in 452. The size of the 452 distribution is believable, as evidence of the recovery of the city from the sack of 410. The problem then is the very large figure for A.D. 367. One possibility is that it is a mistake. Another is that the figure refers to a distribution including other cities in Italy, as did the grain distribution. If the last alternative is the explanation, the list of those outside of the city should have outnumbered those in the city. Probably both the grain and pork distributions to other cities ceased with the capture of Rome in 410.[91]

All of this creates a different picture of the grain and pork distributions. Of the 320,000 of Augustus's allotment, perhaps only 140,000 went to Rome itself, leaving about 180,000 for the other cities. The rather casual information about those cities show

[87]A. van Berchem *Les distributions de blé et de l'argent à la plèbe romaine*, (Geneva, 1939), 33-57, especially 42.

[88]F. de Zulueta, *The Institutes of Gaius* (Oxford, 1946), 1, 34: Jones, *Later Roman Empire*, 699.

[89]Jones, 699; Packer, 1967, 88; Tengström, 1974, 80; Van Berchem, 1939, 85.

[90]Chastagnol, 1960: 326-329; Jones, *Later Roman Empire*, 702, 703; Tengström 1907, 85.

[91]Although the Visigoths moved on, they thoroughly destroyed the government of the countryside.

traces of three groups. The first were nearby ports, like Ostia and Portus; the second, farther ports, Tarracina, and Puteoli. A third would be farther cities, like Capua, an important city of Campania, important in the hog trade. It is unlikely, however, that distributions were limited to these cities; they do not have the population to have created a sufficient demand for the amounts of grain in question. Perhaps other nearby ports were included, such as Antium and Caere, and further ports, such as Misenum and Naples and more inland centers, such as Praeneste, Tusculum and Tibur. These cities were part of the system that fed Rome.[92]

If the evidence about size and distribution of population has been interpreted properly, the quantitative aspects of public order and local government may be examined more carefully. The *Libellus* tells something about the forces of the region and its division, the *vicus*.

Each region had two *curatores* and 48 *vicimagistri*. In addition the city had 7,000 *vigiles* (police-firemen) and an indefinite but large number of soldiers. Some of these existed as a part of the dignity and clientage of the emperor, but they were available for control of the city, if needed. If there were even five thousand soldiers available, the total force ready for action was nearly thirteen thousand—a figure large enough to maintain order easily. The region, however, seems to have been purely an administrative district. It had no shrine and little history, apparently dating back only to Augustus.[93]

The smaller local division was the vicus or *compitum*, the former a street or street with the buildings alongside it and the latter, a crossroads, presumably crossing of streets.[94] The vicus ranged in size from nearly fourteen hectares in Region III, Isis and Serapis, down to less than two hectares in three central regions. In number of persons they varied from nearly two thousand in Region II, Caelimontium, to 169 in Region XIV, Trastevere. The last two were quite exceptional; the next in size was 1316, with the average about 410-470 inhabitants. In the central regions a vicus could have been merely two sides of a block while in the least densely populated areas there were 11-13 buildings to the hectare, probably single storied detached dwellings.

The *Libellus* also gives information about facilities available to the inhabitants of Rome. It states that there were 254 bakeries and 393 markets, but they were not scattered evenly over the regions. On the average there was about one of each for the vicus. There

---

[92]The possibilities stem from the data in R. MacMullen, "Market Days in the Roman Empire," *Phoenix* 24 (1970): 333-341, esp. 340.

[93]Suetonius, Augustus, 30.

[94]"In oppido vici a via quod ex utraque parte viae sunt aedificia," Varro, *De lingua latine*, V, 14, 5. See also RE under "*Compitum*."

were also 856 baths (*balneae*) and 1,352 water outlets (*laci*), or about two of the former and three of the latter for each vicus. Lack of refrigeration and of water outlets within the insulae made it necessary for people to visit the facilities quite frequently, producing wide acquaintance among the members of the vicus.

These small communities had a variety of names which indicate something of their individuality.[95] Many were named after temples: Bellona, Diana, Fides, Festis Fortunae (several), Hercules, Honor et Virtus, Isis, Minerva, Venus et Vesta, and Victoria. Some were named after statues and *simulacra*; others after local sites, gates of the city, hills, baths, markets or water outlets. Many were named after callings: *fabricius, frumentarius, sandalarius, unguentarius*: enough to suggest that many vici were primarily groups engaged in a particular trade. A type of name that rarely turns up is ethnic or geographical—*Africus* is an exception. Of course, the names of only about one-fourth have survived. Sufficient evidence remains to show that, like small districts in cities everywhere, the vici tended to be homogeneous and shared something of a common life.

The *Libellus* mentions the number of aediculae after the number of the vici for each region and it is always the same, so we presume that each vicus had one. Pliny said that each compitum had a shrine, probably in the *aediculum*. At one time each vicus had apparently had four vicomagistri.[96] It was there that the bride was expected to pay a small sum before marriage. The authorities apparently made announcements through the vicus.[97] It seems to have resembled and possibly succeeded the early curia and it could have continued in the parish of the Catholic Church. It was probably through the vicus that the imperial government directed its efforts to keep out those who had no valid reason to be in Rome.[98] The vicus was evidently a fairly intimate, sturdy group which did not really need much disciplining in the empire, however much it may have participated in the struggles of the republic.

Imperial Rome stands out more clearly from this study, if it has interpreted the evidence properly. It was a modest city by modern standards of about 180,000-200,000. The insulae were apartments and the distribution of grain and pork went to other Italian cities as well as to Rome. Although there were many high buildings, as shown by the *Forma Urbis*, the average was only about two

---

[95]O. Richter, *Topographie der Stadt Rom*, index under vicus.

[96]"In singulis vicis quatuor magistri inveniuntur": Castagnoli, *Fontes in Urbem in Universam Pertinentes* (Rome, 1952): 170, 90, and 130.

[97]P. Grimal, *Love in Ancient Rome*, tr. A. Train, Jr. (New York, 1952), 57; Suetonius, Augustus, xliii, 1.

[98]R. H. Barrow, *Prefect and Emperor: The Relations of Symmachus, A.D. 384* (Oxford, 1973), 6.

stories, and the area covered by the domus and insulae was small because of extensive open spaces and public places. The city had a population of the density expected of a capital with little commercial or industrial base and of an inland city. The city had a basic financial support from the court and fisc together with incomes of the great families, quite adequate for its size. Its residents were members of small sturdy communities of about 400-500 in average size with a long tradition of local responsibility. All in all Rome was a well knit, well governed city, which deserved the high compliments which were rained on it by contemporaries.

This picture of a lean and effective metropolis is spoiled by the data about age and mortality in the city of Rome. Table 3 shows that it was about the unhealthiest place in the Roman Empire. A mortality rate of 65 percent for men and 75 percent for women in the age period 20-40 (adults) is extremely high. It is not much less for the first and second centuries than for the third and later centuries, thus the pestilences of the second and third centuries can hardly be the cause. Perhaps lead poisoning was a factor in the mortality, particularly among the ruling class of the city who could afford the wine, sweetened by lead products and contaminated by lead dishes and containers, even by lead pipes.[99] The very heavy mortality must have tended to destroy the ruling families gradually and force the government more and more into the hands of migrants from healthier areas of the empire.

Table 3				
The Mortality of Men and Women in Rome: I-II and III-IV Centuries. (Percent)				
Time Group	I-II Centuries		III-IV Centuries	
	Men	Women	Men	Women
Inf I	22.8	17.8	24.9	26.2
Inf II	17.6	16.1	17.4	29.4
Juvenis	19.5	25.5	17.0	27.2
Adultus	62.5	75.2	59.3	78.5
Maturus	57.9	65.3	66.4	60.2
Senilis	100.0	100.0	100.0	100.0

Source: Szilagyi, 1963: 131-132.

[99]S. C. Gilfillan, "Roman Culture and Dysgenic Lead Poisoning," *The Mankind Quarterly* 5 (1965): 3-20.

II. The Villages of the Dead

The cemetery and the burial rites performed there serve several needs of a society. The first and obvious one is disposing of the deceased, a need readily satisfied by burial under a foot or so of earth or cremating the remains and burying them in an urn. The second is by responding to the feeling that something follows death, in spirit at least—a belief encouraged by the alleged occasional appearance of apparitions which resemble the deceased. Cemeteries also provide a place to produce conditions surrounding the corpse like those of life. The position of the grave in the cemetery, the bones of the dead, and the grave furniture and artifacts buried with the deceased often survive the centuries and preserve much information about the deceased and the life of the community of which the burial was a part. This study is limited to the elements which are essentially demographic: length of life, sex ratio, and other vital information that may be derived from the evidence. The data throw much light upon the vital conditions of the late ancient and medieval society and unexpectedly upon the diseases of the period. From the data also comes evidence about population control. While the core of the information is cemetery data, other evidence, particularly of later Middle Ages, is helpful.[1]

Cemeteries and their remains have been studied by generations of anthropologists and archaeologists with increasing skill and understanding, especially in the last few decades. Working in museums and universities, they have produced models of the societies whose cemeteries they have excavated and fitted the data into earlier archaeological and literary studies of the period. The research is interesting in itself as well as for the picture of the past that it has helped to reveal.

DEATH AND BURIAL CUSTOMS

The custom was to inter the deceased in the earth. People knew, of course, that eventually the body was reduced to bones, which, in most soils, endured for great periods of time. Cemeteries survived even longer, and sometimes with more than bones, in the bogs of northern Europe and in the sands of Egypt. Evidence of reported appearances of apparitions and spirits made it seem clear that something survived separate and free of the body. The result of freeing the body could be accomplished much faster by fire, particularly by the use of oak and other very hot burning wood. The remains could then be placed in an urn and be preserved even more satisfactorily than in the earth alone. Cremation was com-

---

[1]A. C. Rush, *Death and Burial in Christian Antiquity* (Washington, 1941). For customs and ideas on death, Aries 1977: 16-67.

mon, not merely in the Classical world but even for a time in the barbarian north, until Christianity took hold and forbade it. As usual, there was a tendency for the very rich and powerful to be buried outside of the earth in ossuaries and raised tombs—even in the churches. Christians believed in the resurrection of the body, but the state of the body in resurrection was not very clear.

Ancient burial customs were more sophisticated around the Mediterranean than those of northern peoples in the period. An extensive Greek mythology related to the deceased which suggested that the soul crossed the River Styx and had to pay a coin to Charon for the passage. These coins, usually placed on the forehead, normally bore a date which has enabled archaeologists to determine the time of burial.[2] Unfortunately such a custom never developed in regard to St. Peter. The Romans, moreover, liked to prolong the memory of the careers of their deceased by placing short accounts of them on tombs together with the deceased's ages, and the pleasant parting "S.t.t.l. (Let the earth lie gently over thee.)". Usually Roman bodies were cremated and the ashes placed in special *mausolea* or *columbaria* if not in individual tombs. The mausolea often resembled contemporary habitations while the niches were like apartments (insulae) in the cities. They were usually placed outside the gates along the highways and thus illustrate the common tendency to make conditions around the dead as much as possible like those of the living. The evidence about ages in the inscriptions has been subjected to extensive if inconclusive study and will form an important part of the cemetery evidence.[3]

To the north of the Roman Empire life was more primitive. The tendency to treat the dead as nearly like the living as possible meant an adjustment to the forces of nature: earth, sun, winds, rain, and snow. Each community had its burial traditions, often brought in by tribes from other areas. Near the village the cemetery was usually on a hillside, probably in imitation of the village site, although it may have had a ritual significance. It was obviously easier to see the rising sun from the hillside and the road provided access to the cemetery.[4]

The early cottage or house was often begun by excavating a foot or two of earth. This permitted the inhabitants to share the warmth of the earth and reduced the necessary superstructure of

[2]Donna C. Kurtz and J. Boardman, *Greek Burial Customs* (Ithaca, 1971). For later periods Eva Kolnikova, "Totenobulus in frühmittelalterlichen Gräbern in der Slowakei" (summary of Slavic original), *Slovenská archeologia* 15 (1967): 189-254 with map on 193. Other instances are in Burger, 1968 and Lethridge, 1933.
[3]J. N. C. Toynbee, *Death and Burial in the Roman World* (Ithaca, 1971); Friedlander, *Roman Life and Manners under the Early Empire*, tr. from German (London, 1963) 3, 282-302. A. D. Nock, "Cremation and Burial in the Roman Empire," *Harvard Theological Review* 25 (1932): 321-359.
[4]Salin, 1949, 1: 422-429;; 2: 3-51; Meaney, 1943: 303-304.

adobe, stone and later bricks. The grave likewise began with a trench to hold the body, sometimes enclosed by boards or stones for further protection.[5] Tombs of the leaders were often mounds of earth or sand above the burials, sometimes under ships, with valuable artifacts, presumably for the assistance of the deceased in a future world. Sometimes even horses were interred.[6] In general little effort to preserve the identity of the deceased was made, except among the Romans. Adjustment to the earth was as to a kind mother who in most cases preserved the bones and other remains effectively.

ALIGNMENT AND POSITION OF GRAVES

The sun, source of light and warmth, was also a strong, perhaps even dominant influence. Again with some exceptions, graves were lined up toward the east as the sun rose over the horizon. The early morning burial apparently followed a night of mourning with wailing and singing.[7] Houses also seem to have been lined up, usually east and west. Probably the house absorbed more heat lying east and west in the winter and provided more shade on the north side in the summer. The direction of the graves, pointing to the rising sun, gives clues of the time of year of the burial since the sun moves along the horizon with the seasons, north of it in summer and south in the winter. The burials in the late spring and summer point north of east and those in the late autumn and winter point south of east. Since some diseases are seasonal, notably the plague, which occurred in warmer weather, the direction of graves can be significant for estimating the prevalence of the disease. In the graves the heads were generally placed toward the west, although this custom varied. Sometimes the heads of

---

[5]A scattering of samples of village house construction: England, B. Cunliffe, "Saxon and Medieval Settlement Patterns in the Region of Charlton, Hampshire," *Medieval Archaeology* 16 (1972): 1-12; J. G. Hurst, *Medieval Village Excavation in England* (London, 1970): 258-270. France, H. D. Cloret, *Themes on the Historical Geography of France* (London, 1977): 372-375. Germany, H. Dannheimer, "Die mittelalterliche Siedlung bei Kirkheim," *Germania* 51 (1973): 152-166; D. Eckstein & W. Liese, "Jahrringchronologische Untersuchungen zur Altersbestimmung von Holzbauten Haithabu," *Germania* 49 (1971): 155-168; L. Ohlentoth, "Zum Hausbau des frühen Mittelalters in Suddeutschlands, "*Mannus*" 29 (1957): 535-544. Slovakei, H. Haborstigis, "Die mittelalterlichen Bauerndörfer des 10-13 Jahrhunderts in der Slovakei," *Archeologicke Rozhledy* 27 (1975): 297-304.

[6]With horses: Cilinska, 1953: 308; Jaskanis 1977; Laszlo 1955: 110; Paulsen 1967; Schmidt 1953: 107-110; Schmidt 1961: 82-89; Schulz 1933.

[7]*Archaeologia* 73 (1922): 193; *Archaeologia* 74 (1923): 211-288; Burger 1966; Dastugue 1964: 15; K. Horedt, "Der östliche Reihengräberkreis in Siebenburgen," *Dacia* 21 (1977): 251; Lethridge 1936: 2; Salin 1949: 2: 190; Skerlj 1958: 119; B. Somerville, "Instances of Orientation in Prehistoric Monuments of the British Isles," *Archaeologia* 73 (1922): 193; 74 (1923): 211-288. "If, by calling on Almighty God to witness, he forbids the diabolical songs which the lower elements of the common folk are accustomed to sing at night over the dead and loud laughter which they affect then," J. de Q. Adams, *Patterns of Medieval Society* (Engelwood Cliffs, 1969), 108. At Prüm A.D. 906.

males were in one direction and females in the other. When this occurred it made sex determination easy. Occasionally males and females were separated in the cemeteries.[8]

Nevertheless, the configuration of graves varied frequently. Although most lay east to west, they sometimes were scattered about, while many of the early medieval ones pointed north. In Hungary, under the Avars, some families were buried in groups around the grave of the matriarch of the family.[9] At the other extreme in pattern are the cemeteries of carefully marshalled graves often more in line than the village houses themselves, although even these varied if pointing toward the rising sun. These are called *Reihengräber* and may possibly have been associated with German warrior clubs.[10] Graves seem usually to have been dug next to each other without attempts to keep families together. Soldiers were occasionally buried near their leaders and criminals may have been buried separately.

Children were occasionally buried by themselves but usually were scattered among the adults.[11] The length of their graves indicate their approximate age even after the disappearance of their bones, which naturally disintegrated faster than those of the adults. They also were often buried with toys or other distinguishing artifacts. However, the number of buried children is seldom as large as it should have been. This is probably because, not merely in Germanic, but also in Roman and Christian societies, the child was not regarded as part of the family, nuclear or extended, until he has been formally accepted. As a result less effort was made to preserve the bodies in burial, especially of the very young and females. The acceptance into the society of the clan or family was a very formal ceremony among Greeks and Romans. As will be seen, the amount of infanticide even among Christians was large— baptism a formal acceptance by family and church at birth coming into practice only very gradually. Indifference to children some-times led to careless burial in houses. Perhaps in time of plague

---

[8]Salin 1949, 2: 189-191.

[9]G. Laszlo, "Etudes archéologique sur l'histoire de la Société des Avars," *Archaeologia Hungarica* 34 (1955): 110; K. Mesterhazy 1949: 131-178.

[10]A. H. Price, "Differentiated Germanic Social Structures," *Vierteljahrschrift fur Sozial- ind Wirschaftsgeschichte* 55 (1969): 433-446; burial of soldiers about their leader: Dambski, 1950 and 1955; S. C. Hawkes, "Crime and Punishment in an Anglo-Saxon Cemetery," *Antiquity* 49 (1975): 118-122.

[11]Budinsky-Kricka, 1956; Dollfus, 1968 and 1968-1969; Voinot, 1904: 73-74. Also A. B. Aldridge, "Notes on the Children's Burial Ground in Mayo," *Journal of the Royal Society of Antiquaries of Ireland* 49, 1 (1969): 83-87. M-A Dollfus & M. Guyot, "Sépultures de nouveaux-nès dans les fouilles de Fleurheim à Lyons-la-Forêt (Eure)," *Annales de Norman- die* 18 (1968): 283-399 (2-4 centuries).

Table 4

Preplague and Plague Mortality by Months,
Late Medieval England.

Month	Percentages of Mortality				
	Preplague 1340-1348	Plague, Epidemic Years	1348-1375 Endemic Years	1376-1400	1476-1500
January	9.8	0.9	6.9	6.4	6.6
February	12.2	5.8	7.4	7.8	7.4
March	5.5	5.1	10.6	5.6	8.4
April	9.5	5.5	6.6	7.4	7.9
May	7.3	6.7	8.3	6.3	9.1
June	4.7	8.3	8.6	6.8	7.3
July	3.7	10.6	6.1	6.7	6.3
August	9.2	17.3	11.4	13.3	10.5
September	8.3	14.1	13.9	16.2	10.4
October	11.7	14.3	6.9	7.1	12.8
November	11.4	7.2	6.9	8.5	7.7
December	6.7	4.2	6.4	7.9	5.6

Source: Russell, 1948: 197. Cf. Skerjl 1952 for north Balkan area and Dols, 1977, 179 for conditions elsewhere.

people were buried in multiple interments in large graves but none of any great size has been discovered.[12]

Christianity gave more importance to cemeteries since they were associated with prospects of the Christian heaven. The cemetery was moved more and more into the village and located near the church itself. The graves tended, like the church building itself, to lie east and west. It was supposed to point in the direction of Jerusalem, approximately in an eastward direction. The alignment with the rising sun declined, although such customs occasionally persisted. Since it is sacrilegious to disturb a Christian cemetery, few have been excavated, except in communist countries. Exceptions are, of course, necessitated by the building of modern highways, removal for artificial lakes, and new buildings in cities, the so-called "rescue" operations.[13]

If Christians protected their own cemeteries, they did not respect those of pagans. Since these often had valuable artifacts,

[12]Acsàdi & Nemeskéri, 1970: 224; Gejvall, 1960:38; Schaeffer 1963: 222. Buried in house: E. Bendann, *Death Customs* (New York, 1930), ch. 3. Possible instances of multiple burial: Salin, 1949: 309, 369; Aries, 1977: 45. Lepers were sometimes buried separately: C. Wells, "A Leper Cemetery at South Acre: Norfolk," *Medieval Archaeology* 11 (1967): 243-248; V. Moller-Christensen, *The Lepers from Norestver, Denmark* (Copenhagen, 1953).

[13]For change from pagan practices, Aries, 1977: 37-49. J. T. Noonan, "Intellectual and Social History," in D. V. Glass and R. Revelle, *Population and Social Change* (New York, 1972): 115-135, esp. 122.

they were often plundered, even in the Middle Ages. The plundering of the Lombard cemeteries after they left the Balkans for Italy has been well documented.[14]

Burial in Christian cemeteries was not only limited to members of the faith but also to those in good standing at the time of death. There were cemeteries for some heretics, but their bodies were not generally entitled to burial.[15] Sinners of certain types were excluded and Jews were allowed to have their own cemeteries. A famous one at Montjuich in Barcelona has been carefully excavated.[16]

VALUE OF SKELETAL DATA

If a cemetery is largely intact, whether Roman, barbarian, or Christian, its skeletal evidence may be used to determine its population over a period of time. Certain conditions should exist, however. One should be able to assign dates to graves or groups of graves so that the number of generations involved may be known. As an example, take a cemetery of six hundred graves with an existence of one hundred and fifty years and apparent continuity of size over the period. If the length of the generation was thirty years, the cemetery and village should have existed for five generations with about thirty in each generation. Adjustments must be made, however, if the village varies in size over the period.[17] There may have to be a correction for the missing children.[18] This type of information will not be used much in this study since it concerns other phases of demography.

For the pre-Christian period the study of tribal wanderings has focused on skeletal evidence, (since this is one of our chief sources of information, although transient settlement leaves a less satisfactory body of evidence). Sometimes a massacre of a whole community is shown in an excavation, or the decimation produced by plague.[19] Cemetery evidence presents much human information about former residents of the village and how the ordinary folk lived—short and simple annals of the poor.

Other than the total population of the village, skeletal data make it possible to reconstruct the sex-age setup of the inhabitants. The usual method is to construct a life table, of which a sample is given

[14]H. Adler, "Zur Ausplunderung langobardischen Gräberfelder," *Mitteilungen des anthropologischen Gesellschaft zu Wien* 100 (1970): 138-147; for other cases S. Rappoport & H. Kelright, *Archaeology* 106 (1963).

[15]See appendix 1.

[16]Fusté, 1949; Prevosti, 1951; Bay, 1941-1942.

[17]Acsádi & Nemeskéri, 1970: 67-72; for Halimba, Acsádi & Nemeskéri in *Homo* 8 (1957): 141-145.

[18]Chapter IX below.

[19]Lagore Crannock, Ireland, Hencken 1950; Marrina Drive, England, Brothwick, 1962.

Table 5

Life Table, Mikulcice

	q_v	l_c	d_x	L_x	T_x	e_x^o
Total: Males, Females, Uncertain						
I	28.4	71.6	2018	575	11251	55114	27.3
II	12.3	87.7	1443	177	9393	44453	30.8
J	9.6	90.4	1266	122	7230	35060	27.7
A	27.8	72.2	1144	413	14880	27830	24.3
M	91.9	8.1	731	672	7900	9080	12.4
S	100.0	0.0	59	59	590	590	10.0
Males						
I	19.1	80.9	848	162			
II	7.6	92.4	686	52			
J	8.5	91.5	634	54			
A	25.7	74.3	580	149	10110	15140	26.1
M	91.6	8.4	431	395	4670	5030	11.7
S	100.0	0.0	36	36	360	360	10.0
Females						
I	21.2	88.8	807	171			
II	8.2	91.8	636	52			
J	8.2	91.8	584	48			
A	45.3	54.7	536	243	8290	11640	21.7
M	91.6	8.4	293	272	3140	3350	11.4
S	100.0	0.0	21	21	210	210	10.0

Sources: Poulik, 1957; Poulik, 1963; Stloukal, 1962;
Stloukal, 1963a; Stoukal, 1964; Stloukal, 1967.

in table 5. It is from Mikulcice, an important city in Moravia at the height of the Great Moravian Kingdom in the ninth century. It provides a very typical pattern of the Middle Ages.[20] If the village has a relatively stable population, the problem is fairly simple. One assumption is that each age group is properly represented in the bones that have survived. At Mikulcice the number of infant remains is close to the estimate. The problems of reconstructing the life table are discussed in the next chapter.

Even the bone content and conditions yield information. There are the so-called Harris lines which indicate that the person has suffered nutritional deficiency some time in his life.[21] The bone content is being studied biochemically by outstanding Hungarian physical anthropologists with remarkable results, what they call

---

[20]See table 5.

[21]Calvin Wells, *Bones, Bodies and Disease* (London, 1964), 55.

"the total biological reconstruction." From this comes information about blood type[22] and data about conditions of health and disease in various periods of life.[23] One anomaly that appears, for example, is that the skeletons of men show a much higher number of pathological cases (102 of 226 men) than women (38 of 203) and yet the men lived longer.[24] Not much total research along these lines has been finished so it will not figure much in this study. It is perhaps the best illustration of the magnificent research that is being done in this field.

Conditions operate very differently upon cemeteries. Peat land in northern Europe has preserved bodies and even clothing better than the sands of Egypt.[25] In other cemeteries poor soil composition has destroyed most of the skeletal information, although bone is a very durable substance, as the survival of prehistoric bones attests. Much evidence has been lost. In some places corpses have been removed from graves to mortuaries, to make room for other corpses. This process has destroyed valuable associations of the graves themselves, and the less sturdy bones of women and children suffered more and were less numerous than the remains of men.[26] At Hythe, a well known ossuary of England, where the size of the place might lead one to anticipate a low sex ratio, that is, a more equal number of the sexes, the identified are 326 men and 230 women, a very high sex ratio of 142.[27] This suggests that the disparity was the result of greater loss of more fragile bones.

A similar process of removing skeletons from graves to museums has resulted also in greater losses of female bones. In one large collection in a museum 84 percent of the male skeletons were complete while only 35 percent of the female were.[28] Early Europe saw the custom of cremation of bones spread widely and disas-

---

[22]I. A. Langyel, *Palaeoerology: Blood Typing with the Fluorescent Antibody Method* (Budapest, 1975): esp. 204.

[23]J. Nemeskéri, "Problémes de la reconstruction biologique en anthropologie historique," VI Congrès International des Sciences Anthropologiques et Ethnologiques, Paris 1960: 1 (1962): 669-775; I. Lengyel & J. Nemeskéri, "Application of Biochemical Methods to Biological Reconstruction," *Zeitschrift für Morphologie und Anthropologie* 54 (1963): 1-56, with detailed bibliography at end. J. Nemeskéri & L. Harsanyi, "Die Bedeutung paläopathologischer Untersuchung für die historischen Anthropologie," *Homo* 10 (1959): 203-225.

[24]Nemeskéri & Harsanyi, 1959: 222-223.

[25]H. Jankuhn, "Moorfunde, Neue Ausgrabungen in Deutschland," *Römisch-Germanische Komission des deutsches Archaeologischen Instituts* (Berlin, 1958), 243-257.

[26]Acsádi-Nemeskéri, 1970, 58.

[27]Parsons, 1908, 423. For Rothwell, F. G. Parsons, "Report on the Rothwell Crania," *Journal of the Royal Anthropological Institute* 40 (1910): 483-504.

[28]From Ostrow Lednicki, Wokroj 1955, 52. On methods: J. Nemeskéri, L. Harsanyi & G. Acsádi, "Methoden zur Diagnose des Lebensalter in Skelettfunden," *Anthropologischer Anzeiger* 24 (1960): 70-95. Schwidetsky, 1957, 1958.

trously, although modern anthropologists have devised ingenious methods of determining age and sex of cremation remains.[29]

Modern excavation by properly trained anthropologists and archaeologists is very different from earlier work. Enthusiastic amateurs ripped up hundreds of sites, trying to find valuable artifacts and destroyed volumes of important data. In writing of one dig, the excavator remarked that there was "nothing but bones" there.[30] Even today weekend dilettantes dig up ancient mounds, hoping to find pottery or other artifacts to grace their homes. The amount of irrecoverable information lost in such unfortunate activities is appalling. Well into this century excavators displayed great ignorance. They identified males from females with difficulty and classified skeletons as those of young, mature, and elderly persons. In most cases the evidence about age is not very helpful; few tried even to identify the sex of teenagers. When interest centered more on the skeletons themselves, emphasis was on racial phases, producing long tables of measurements of bones—particularly of the skull. Various series of *Crania*[31] appeared, defining persons by the shape of their heads. Grave furniture offered opportunities for cultural study paralleling the racial study. Some is very good.

As in other scientific fields, the advance in physical anthropology in this century has been rapid. Much of this has been the result of change of status of museums. Earlier, they tended to exhibit only permanent cases of material from excavations which too often had been poorly managed, without pictures or descriptions of the actual processes of excavation. Now much museum effort is essentially laboratory operations where the exhibits are only one part of the museum's activities. The larger part is the careful research that leads to the publication of valuable monographs. Parallel to this has gone the laboratory activity of university departments of anthropology and archaeology that frequently have their own

---

[29]Dzierzykray-Rogalsky, 1966; K. K. Jazdzewski, "Report on Excavation 1950 of an Early Medieval Cemetery at Lutomiersk." Summary of Polish report. *Materialy Wczesnosrednioieczyn* 2 (1950): 257-264; A. Malinovski, "Synthèse des recherches polonaises effectuées jusqu'à present sur les os des tombes incineration," *Przeglad Anthropologiczny* 35 (1969): 127-. C. Müller, "Methodisch-kritische Betrachtungen zur anthropologischen Untersuchungen von Leichenbränden," *Praehistorische Zeitung* 42 (1964): 1-29. U. Schaefer, "Grenzen und Moglichkeiten des anthropologischen Untersuchung von Leichenbränden," *Bericht V. International Kongress Vor- und Fruhgeschichte, Hamburg,* 1950, 717-724. U. Schaefer, "Beiträge zum Problem der Leichenbranuntersuchung," *Zeitshrift für Morphologie und Anthropologie* 55 (1964): 277-282. Judita Gladykowska-Rzeczycka, "Anthropological investigations on the bone remains from crematory cemeteries in Poland," *Homme* 25 (1976): 96-116.

[30]A. F. Griffith and L. F. Salzman, "An Anglo-Saxon Cemetery at Alfristan, Sussex," *Sussex Archaeological Collections* 56 (1914-1915): 16-57; 56: 197-210.

[31]The various *Crania* studies. A good illustration is F. S. Kollman, "Altergermanische Gräber in der Umgebung des Starnburger Sees," *Sitzungsberichte der math.-phys. Kl. der K. Akademie der Wissenschaften zu München* 1 (1873): 295-344.

museums. The motion picture shorts of the excavations at Sutton Hoo and Stonehenge have shown what can be done to explain and even to popularize meticulous research in archaeological fields.

Research in this field, indeed, is moving so fast that it is hard to keep abreast of it. Some general articles that cover even the less advanced countries indicate the extent and nature of the work there.[32] Today the computer is used; however, the research is still very uneven and the knowledge of its results not known as widely as it should be.[33] Even today our interdisciplinary enthusiasm often fails to cross departmental lines.

GRAVES AND POPULATION

The roughly fifteen centuries covered by this study might be expected to show several different types of vital experiences. Two great plague periods occurred, the first often called the Plague of Justinian from about 542 and lasting well into the eighth century. It has been defined as the bubonic plague. The second was the Black Death beginning in 1347-48 and continuing well into the modern period. The drastic effects of these plagues in producing a peculiar age-specific setup in the population make it easy to consider these two divisions of the period. This leaves about 500 years before the first plague which has a political as well as demographic pattern of some consistency. The long period between about 750, the end of the first plague, and the outbreak of the second should obviously constitute at least two periods. Demographically two may be selected with a dividing line about 950-1000, when population in much of western Europe as well as Egypt and possibly Syria began to increase.[34]

The periods differ considerably in amount of data available. The first period (0-542) has most of the inscriptions which the Roman world enjoyed writing as well as a considerable amount of grave data, some of which fortunately comes from outside the Roman Empire. The Germanic and other invasions are interesting to French, Germans, and Hungarians (among others). This has led to much excavation in central Europe for first plague data. Indeed, without it the limits of the disease could hardly be defined. The extreme west now lost interest in graves but the east and south of Europe maintain an interest well past the year 1000. The second plague period shows little grave data but much of other types; yet

---

[32]Fon Avars: Laszko, 1955; for Great Moravia, Poulik, 1959; for Rumania, E. Condurachi, *Rumanian Archaeology in the Twentieth Century* (Bucharest, 1964). For Hungary, J. Nemeskéri, "Fifteen years of the Anthropological Department of the Hungarian National History Museum (1945-1960)," *Annales Historico-Naturales Musei Nationalis Hungarici* 53 (1961): 615-639. (With maps of sites of excavations).

[33]*Archaeologiai Ertesito* 93 (1966): 284-290.

[34]Russell, 1958: 71-112.

Table 6

Population Estimates (in millions) at Specific Times,
0-1500 A.D.

Area	0	500	650	1000	1340	1500
Greece and Balkans	5	5	3	5	6	4.5
Italy	7.4	4	2.5	7	10	9
Iberia	6	4	3.5	7	9	8.3
Mediterranean	18.4	13	9	17	25	21.8
France—Low Countries	6	5	3.5	6	19	16
British Isles	0.4	0.5	0.5	2	5	3
Germany-Scandinavia	3.5	3.5	2	4	11.5	7.5
West and Central Europe	9.9	9	5.5	12	35.5	26.5
Slavic	4	5	3			2
Russia				6	8	6
Poland				2	3	2
Hungary	0.5	0.5	0.5	1.5	2	1.5
East Europe	4.5	5.5	3.5	9.5	13	11.5
Total	32.8	27.5	18.0	38.5	73.5	59.8

Sources: Russell, *Late Ancient and Medieval Population*, 148; somewhat revised by articles later: for Balkans in *Journal of Economic and Social History of the Orient* 2 (1960): 269-270; for Italy, J. Beloch, *Bevölkerungsgeschichte Italiens* III (1961): 344-352.

the outlines of its age-specific mortality are not as well known as those of the first period.

The population of the area changed quite a bit in the course of the centuries. The greatest change was in the loss of population in the first half century of both plagues. This is estimated at about forty percent with a subsequent decline of another ten percent by the end of the first century of each plague. This was followed by a gradually accelerating increase which caused the population in the first plague to regain pre-plague figures in two centuries and in the second plague in a century or so. The period A.D. 1000-1348 saw another great increase in population in most of the area. The beginning of the first period was one of decline for much of the Roman Empire, more in the west than in the east. The balance of population also altered much between northern and southern Europe. Only after the year 1000 did a rapid increase of central and western Europe cause it to surpass the Balkans and Mediterranean states in numbers.

The figures which are given in table 6 are only approximate even when they seem more specific. The data upon which they are

based are rather rough and serve only to give some idea of the
order of figures with which one deals in that period. It is better to
have a general idea of the population than to be entirely without
estimates. With total figures come also some idea about the density
of population, and even the size of cities and villages.[35]

The table shows, of course, the great increase from the year
1000 to 1348, which is well known. However, what is not so well
known is that the population also increased heavily between the
low point after the first plague, about 650, and the year 1000. The
very fact of such a long and large increase must be considered in
any history of length of life and related studies. Up to 650 the
population had been relatively sparse in the north and thus to
some extent protected from disease. Diseases might come in from
the great centers of animal and bacterial life in Africa or Asia, but
they would not have survived without sufficient population to
preserve them. The first plague died out in the west, for instance.
Now with denser population the chances were greater that more
diseases would appear and remain permanently, as we shall see in a
later chapter in the case of tuberculosis. The second plague,
appearing in 1348, was to survive until well into modern times.
Some diseases, notably those of children, cannot as yet be traced
and there are few references to them except in medical manuals of
the period.

In terms of total population two eras can be seen; the first—
from the beginning of time to about A.D. 950-1000. Population at
the end was, except for Russia, about the same as it was at the
beginning. The second era lasted until the end of the Middle Ages,
when both before 1348 and in the last two generations the increase
was very marked. These will be the basis for the discussions in
chapters IX-XI, where the developments that led to both the first
great increase (950-1348) and the recovery at the end of the
period in some countries (1440-1500) are considered in terms of
length of life, area of habitation, and especially sex ratio and
replacement rates.

MOTIVATION AND RESULTS OF MODERN STUDY

The motivation for anthropological work on graves varies from
country to country, although now there is a general appreciation
of its value for the history of peoples. Most countries show some
interest in the subject. Table 7 shows the number of graves and
skeletons which have been examined and used in this study, and
how greatly the number varies from area to area. The study was
originally the archaeologist's responsibility but has gradually
shifted to the anthropologist. For countries such as England,

---

[35]Russell, 1972: 15-30.

Table 7
Number of Skeletons by Time and Areas

Time	Total	1 Mediterranean	2 France	3 Britain	4 Germany	5 Hungary-Balkans	6 Bohemia-Alps	7 Scandinavia	8 Poland
1	5804	440	288	1652	690	1101	592	315	726
2	7959	47	772	595	2893	2005	1447	56	144
3	13324	1190	29	380	578	4796	5551	551	249
4	10274	765	—	143	544	3798	780	1491	2753
5	4585	113	83	594	340	970	420	1532	533
	41946	2555	1172	3364	5045	12670	8790	3945	4405

France, Italy, Portugal and Spain, Roman remains attracted attention early, especially from Classical scholars. This tended to slow up the study of medieval anthropology. However, increasing interest in the German tribes and their history has encouraged anthropological research, particularly in England, France, and Germany. Even in Spain the Visigoths have received attention. The Roman habit of cremation, although it declined in the empire, still tended to discourage the physical anthropologists, yet the most magnificent collection of skeletons, that of Pompeii, has never attracted attention. This is unfortunate, since it is the most significant collection of skeletons produced at one time in history. It provides the opportunity to examine anthropologically much of the population of a sizable city. This is especially important since it seems that perhaps forty percent of the Pompeians were caught at that holocaust.[36]

Table 7 shows that by far the most extensive work has been done in Hungary and Bohemia. Hungarian anthropologists are in the forefront of this field, both for quantity and quality of their achievements, relating in long series of articles in a number of periodicals the uncovering of the cemeteries of the Avars, Hungarians and others of that country. These anthropological studies carried out under the auspices of the universities and especially of their museums are doubly important because there is a shortage of documentary evidence about Hungarian history. Bohemian scholars have concentrated upon a brilliant epoch which is best illustrated by these studies, the Great Moravian Kingdom of the ninth century. Magnificent volumes have been devoted to the cities of that epoch: Mikulcice, Staró Mesté and others.[37] Work in Rumania is interesting because of the Roman influence there. Fortunately scholars in these countries usually give summaries of their articles in western languages and Russian as well as in their own. The development of standard tables for recording data also helps. Hungarians produce most of their articles in western languages since they have little hope that western scholars will learn Hungarian.

The Scandinavian countries have shown a great interest in their early forebears, the Vikings, producing excellent volumes, monumental in scope, on Birka and Westerhus. German efforts though more scattered are of excellent quality and often transcend national boundaries, for example, their interest in the Canary Islands and Visigothic Spain.

Anthropologists have produced a very large amount of information that should be integrated in the historical writings of their

[36]See above, ch. 1.
[37]See note 32 above.

countries. As we shall see, data about life and health are of great value in understanding underlying conditions. The study includes the Roman Empire because it had a profound effect upon the countries of Western Europe even from a physical, anthropological standpoint. The empire's system of roads allowed not only men but bacteria to travel easily from one end of the empire to the other, to the detriment of the health of the citizens. The roads also made migration easier for the various tribes which entered the empire.

The data from the cemeteries have their limitations. No evidence of marital conditions survives, except among the Avars. This applies also to household size. The number of infants and perhaps of others is too small but an estimate can be made. Apparently no plague pit has been disovered although they are mentioned in literary sources. There is also unevenness of information about cemeteries. In Italy and Spain the greater interest in the prehistoric and Classical periods has usurped interest in the late ancient and medieval. The only medieval cemetery in Italy, at Cannae, was excavated in the mistaken hope that it was where the slain in the great battle with Hannibal and the Carthaginians were buried. Each country has its own field of interest; unfortunately certain periods of the Middle Ages have not interested some countries.

Nevertheless, cemetery data do present much new information about length of life and sex ratio. Upon this information much may be added to indicate phases of the social and economic life of the people. If, as Professors Pirenne and Lot once wrote, "Demography is perhaps the most important of all the social sciences,"[38] its study should be of value to historians.

---

[38]Ferdinand Lot, *Recherches sur la population et le superficie des cités remontant à la période Gallo-Romaine* (3v. Paris, 1945-1950) 1: vii.

III. To Quicken the Dead

Much of the study of control of population consists of data gleaned from skeletons; other evidence deals with information about age of death. However, for the purposes of demography information about a population when it was alive is also needed. This chapter analyzes the problems of converting information about the dead to reconstructing a living population. The sources of skeletal information are given in the bibliography appended to this work. Bibliographical and skeletal evidence are then discussed.

BIBLIOGRAPHY AND CLASSIFICATION

Any study of cemetery evidence may well begin with the *History of Human Life Span and Mortality* by Acsádi and Nemeskéri, two of the outstanding authorities in the field.[1] It considers the principles of physical anthropological study of the evidence from the beginning of human history well into the twelfth century. Geographically, the emphasis is upon central Europe, especially Hungary, a center for some of the better studies of cemetery evidence. Fortunately, the subject is such that politics is not likely to prevent scholars on either side of the Iron Curtain from exchanging views, but further research is needed on both sides. The results of the study have unfortunately not been standardized. What little information there is has appeared in one periodical devoted to the study of the history of population.[2]

For older articles and recent research there is a section in the bibliography of the *Anthropologischer Anzeiger* entitled "Vor- und frühgeschichtliche Skelette." *The Yearbook of Physical Anthropology* contains information easily available.[3] Since references to studies in archaeology such as those provided by the Council for Old World Archaeology (COWA) since 1955 and the Royal Anthropological Society of London since 1962 seldom state whether the articles have sections devoted to physical anthropology, these are not so helpful.[4] The Peabody Library (of anthropology) at Harvard University keeps an up-to-date file on authors and their works.

---

[1] Budapest, Akadémiai Kiadó.

[2] *Annales de démographie historique* (Paris, 1971-).

[3] Published by the Instituto Nacional de Antropologia Historica, Universidad Nacional Autonoma de Mexico (Corduba 45, Mexico 7, D.F.) for the American Association of Physical Anthropology, 1962).

[4] I acknowledge my gratitude to the Society for access to its stacks in the autumn of 1974.

Physical anthropology has benefited from a reasonable classification for age groups set up by Rudolf Martin in his comprehen-
sive *Lehrbuch der Anthropologie in systematischer Darstellung*, first
published in 1914.[5] This was based upon certain rather obvious
developments of the human skeleton in the following age groups:

A	Infans I	1st six months	B	0-6 years
	Infans II	Years 0-6		7-13
	Infans III	7-13		
	Juvenis	14-19		14-19
	Adultus	20-29		20-39
	Maturus	30-49		40-59
	Senilis	50-		60-

His idea has been generally accepted, but the ages were changed
to the B grouping above.[6]

Martin's original classification has been continued in Poland and
some other places but the revised groupings are more common
elsewhere. Martin's work is often the basis for a table such as
follows:

	I	II	Juvenis	Adultus	Maturus	Senilis	Total
Male							
Female							
Uncertain							
Total							

Such a table is international and may be used easily, much like
mathematical or algebraic signs. One must be certain, however,
that the revised table is used, for sometimes inf. III is not included,
even when the original Martin table appears. It is, of course,
troublesome to convert one into the other. Even more confusing
are the tables drawn up by some scholars (mostly English) which do
not conform to the standard ones.

The use of skeletons to discern the actual age of persons
developed slowly. Table 8 gives the classification used by authors
over the decades of this century. For many years they tried only to
differentiate the old from the young or the young from adult men
and women. In fact earlier studies were often limited to skulls to

---

[5] Jena, 1914. The third edition is under the names of R. Martin and K. Saller, Munich,
1959-1964: age division and sex ratio, 2841 and length of life, 2852.

[6] There seems no account of the adoption of the modified age divisions. The older division
(dropping infans III but including infans I the years from birth to seven) is still used in
Poland and elsewhere occasionally.

determine race of individuals or groups rather than their other measurements of age or sex. Gradually the more skilled scientists extended their range of discrimination of age and sex until today many determine age within a few years for adults and within months for children. They can even determine the sex of the very young. In fact growing numbers of scientists tend to list results by five-year periods. For most purposes, however, the six anthropological age groups are sufficient for our use.

Table 8 also shows the tremendous advance in the number of recent articles published on the subject, the peak being reached in the 1960s. Interest has shifted in part to the sociological study of cultures which involves looking closely at extinct villages to plot the extent and area of huts, granaries, and other buildings, as well as examining dumps for evidence of artifacts and even of animal bones for their use as food. These findings are valuable in determining population by estimating size of household. It is doubtful if the small huts would have held more than the nuclear family. Of course housing conditions and diet had a very important influence upon human health.

Table 8

Types of Data provided by Anthropologists: by date of publication with respect to age and sex.

By Age Groups	By Sex	To 1920	1920-1929	1930-1939	1940-1949	1950-1959	1960-1969	1970-1978	All
1 Adults and Children	None	3	0	2	1	4	8	0	18
2 AMS and I II J	AMS	12	4	15	6	26	37	0	100
3 All six groups	AMS	2	1	4	8	32	44	24	115
4 All six groups	JAMS	2	0	3	5	33	62	32	137
5 All six groups	None	0	1	2	2	8	12	3	28
6 All six groups	All	1	1	3	2	7	32	18	64
Total		20	7	29	24	110	195	77	462

The date is the date of publication.
Many skeletons were not sexed because of limitations of the remains or of the author.

PROBLEMS OF THE DATA

Data used in determining age or sex present some problems, especially with the older evidence. Only a few of these are considered here.

The study of sex ratio (number of men to each one hundred women) is complicated by the relative inability of earlier scholars to determine sex in skeletal remains, even before the discovery that childbirth produced notches in the pubic bones, thus clearly indicating the sex of the person. Earlier studies, therefore, often had a larger number of undetermined sex. One would wish to know the nature of the bias. Five earlier studies of English scholars (all before 1950) show 107 men and 87 women, a sex ratio of 129. Ten studies since 1950 suggest 159 males and 141 females, a ratio of 113. If the unusual cemetery of Marina Drive is excepted, the ratio drops to a normal 105.[7] All of these studies occurred during the plague conditions of A.D. 540-750 in England when the sex ratio would have been normal since the losses of life during the plague should have made infanticide inappropriate.

Another problem was whether the earlier estimates of age had a bias. Age has been determined by comparing a skeleton whose age is known with one that is conjectured. Most of the testing was on modern persons since so few skeletons of ancient or medieval persons can be identified by age in written evidence. The question, of course, remains whether the skeletons of persons aged more rapidly in earlier times. Acsádi and Nemeskéri studied a series at Kerpuszta, using the older "classical" methods and found a "sharply protruding mode" at ages 30-34. Using more recent methods, that mode shifted to "middle adult age" (that is 40-59). It would seem, if this is a typical case of what happened in the older calculations, that former estimates of age were too low rather than too high. The figures for deaths at Kerpuszta are:

	Old	New
20-29	32	
30-39	43	38
40-49	40	45
50-59	59	
60-69		

Presumably the change would result in the alteration of the "new" age above, increasing life expectation at age thirty by a third of a year and at forty by less than that.[8]

---

[7]Russell, 1976, 70; see also Chapter VII, note 20.

[8]Acsádi & Nemeskéri, 1970: 190.

The introduction of data from inscriptions and other written sources raises two other questions affecting the number of persons in each age group. The first is the obvious exaggeration of the higher ages in some lists, most obvious in the inscriptions from Roman North Africa. The second is the more general prevalence of rounding numbers, the use of tens and fives rather than more exact figures even on inscriptions and other documents. Numbers tend to be concentrated first in tens, then in fives, and less often in even numbers. The problem is often "corrected" by using running numbers, that is, by averaging each five or other numbers in a row. This assumes that persons will use the nearest rounded number. However, it is possible to check this against accurate documents in medieval England—inquisitions and proofs of age.[9] The latter give almost exact dates, even actual days of month and year for many persons thus showing the numbers were rounded when used in other documents. Furthermore, early years of heirs (say, one to five years of age) are also very accurate when compared to proofs of age (usually at twenty-one for men). And, after all, if an heir inherits at one or two years, his age cannot be much mistaken by contemporaries. Now, this comparison of documents shows that rounding is usually downward to the nearest round number. Thus those listed as "thirty" in documents actually average thirty-four in more accurate documents. Similarly those called forty actually average forty-five years; those said to be fifty, average fifty-four, while those at sixty average sixty-two. Thus the rounding would be equivalent to saying that a man was in his thirties, forties, and so on. Those rounded to fives usually average a couple of years older. Many figures seem to represent actual numbers: thirty-six, for instance, seems to mean thirty-six. Actually a very simple and reasonably accurate method would be to take a person said to be in a bracket, say the twenties, and multiply by twenty-five to get the total number of years lived by the group.

It must be remembered that sometimes forty or even thirty years may just mean that a man is grown up. And for the higher ages the greater of several estimates probably is the more accurate. Single numbers for the very high ages tend to be exaggerated.

How much would the correcting change the expectation? If we assume that the overestimating of age over seventy equals the loss by rounding, the results for Pisa in 1427 can be surmised. It is assumed that two years will be added for the rounding at the fives and the additions will be as above; four for twenty and thirty-five for forty, four for fifty and one for sixty. This would result in the following changes:[10]

---

[9]Russell, 1948: 110-114.

[10]Herlihy, 1958: 282-285. For the entire catasto of Florence; Herlihy & Klapisch-Zuber, 1978: 360-370.

	Simple	Corrected	
Expectation at age			
Twenty	25.4	26.9	+1.5
Thirty	21.8	23.5	+1.7
Forty	17.5	19.5	+2.0
Fifty	15.0	13.5	+1.5
Sixty	9.5	10.6	+1.1
Seventy	6.1	6.8	+0.7

The result, then, is that rounding lowers the estimates for life expectancy a year or two.

It is harder to estimate the effects of exaggeration of age beyond seventy. The number of persons at that age is not high and correction for exaggeration would greatly affect only the expectation at the elderly. The possibility that persons would have ages recorded merely because they were very old is more important. This may explain why the numbers of persons over age seventy is high in Roman Empire figures. This also prolongs the expectation of persons over seventy.

Another factor is the size of cemeteries. Larger cemeteries usually present more satisfactory information about age and sex divisions than smaller ones because they are less subject to chance conditions. The cemeteries of the tribes during the great migrations were often small, produced by skirmishes with settled communities or by sudden epidemics. After stays of often short duration the tribe moved on, leaving traces of their experience in the cemetery. Or modern construction may uncover a few graves of a large cemetery, mostly concealed under large buildings. The use of these data are naturally limited by knowledge of their extent in time and place. Archaeologists are helpful in determining the approximate area and dates of the burials. The data about cemeteries are given in very succinct form in the bibliography which should be consulted when they are pertinent. And, of course, for more detailed information the articles themselves should be consulted.

THE ROMAN INSCRIPTIONS

From the Roman World, chiefly of the period A.D. 1-600, come thousands of inscriptions on tombs, many of which give the alleged age of the deceased. Actually the amount of evidence is second only in volume to the cemetery evidence from earthen tombs. The value and usefulness of these data have been variously assessed by a succession of writers—some presenting valid objections.[11]

---

[11]Chronologically the studies upon Roman data are: H. Seidal, *Über römische Grabinschriften* (Sagan, 1891); A.F. Harkness, "Age at Marriage and at Death in the Roman

In general they question: 1) the patterns of deaths which do not conform to the patterns of modern backward countries; 2) too high a death rate, especially for women from fourteen years of age to forty; 3) too many quite elderly people; 4) too high a sex ratio (too many men with respect to women); 5) failure to show enough infants and small children; and 6) lack of sufficient evidence for various professional and other groups. One reason for entering a field which has been well worked is that the inscriptions have never been compared to skeletal data. Of course, the amount of such data has been limited by the custom of cremation. Relatively few skeletons remain, making them all the more valuable. It is, indeed, the scarcity of such evidence that makes the possibility of studying Pompeian data so promising.

The first objection must be dealt with because it is pivotal to the whole question.

The only conclusion possible is that, even on the assumption of a stationary population, which is in itself fragile, ages of death derived from Roman inscriptions cannot be used to estimate expectation of life at birth or subsequent ages.[12]

But why should Roman expectation conform to modern, even if primitive, patterns of longevity? Diseases, which greatly influence length of life are different, as are climatic conditions, and even density of population has changed—all making comparisons difficult.

The second objection, too high death rates, especially for women aged 14-40, illustrates the effects of disease.[13] A later chapter will discuss the spread of tuberculosis—the cause of the very high death rate among young women. The generally high death rate of children after infancy probably came from the prevalence of children's diseases: diphtheria, measles, polio and others which have become much less threatening. The roads of the Roman Empire made it easy for diseases to move from the great disease centers of the ancient world, India and central Africa, into the west.

Empire," *Transactions of the American Philological Association* 27 (1891): 35-72; K. Pearson, "On the Change in the Expectation of Life during Period 2000 B.C. to the Present," *Biometrika* 1 (1901): 261-264; A. De Marchi," Cifre de mortalitá delle iscrizioni romane," *Rendiconti R. Istituto Lombardo de Scienze e Lettere*, ser. 2.333 (1903): 1025-1034; W. R. Macdonnell, "On the Expectation of Life in Ancient Rome," *Biometrika* 9 (1913): 36-80; B. Hombert & C. Prèaux, "Note sur la durée de la vie dans l'Egypte greco-romaine," *Chronique de Egypte* 20 (1945): 129-146. J. C. Russell, 1958: 24-30; J. D. Durand, "Mortality Estimates from Roman Tombstone Inscriptions," *American Journal of Sociology* 65 (1960): 364-373; K. Hopkins, "On the Probable Age Structure of the Roman Population," *Population Studies* 20 (1967): 245-263.

[12]Hopkins, 1967: 246.
[13]Hopkins, 1967: 247-249, 260-263.

Table 9

Comparison of Roman Inscription Numbers
With Cemetery and Archival Data, over age 60.
(Percent of population over 20 years of age of those over 60)

Area	Sex	l_{60}/l_{20}	T_{60}/T_{20}	e_{60}^0
Cemetery	all MF	18.9	(7.6)	(9.4)
Calabria	MF	21.7	10.1	13.0
Bruttii, etc.	MF	16.6	9.2	12.0
Latium	MF	14.2	13.8	18.5
Aemilia	MF	18.8	10.1	12.2
Gaul	MF	15.9	12.5	15.0
Britain	MF	16.0		13.0
Asia, Balkans	MF	20.8	10.9	11.9
Egypt	MF	18.7	11.1	13.7
Average 1427		17.9	11.1	13.7
Cemetery	all M	22.9	(8.5)	
England	M	22.5	9.2	10.4
Iberia	M	17.5	9.9	13.7
Rome		17.1	12.0	
Cemetery	all F	15.2	(6.8)	
Iberia	F	29.9	15.0	12.3
Rome		8.3	7.5	
N. Africa	M	46.0	14.8	18.8
	F	39.4	22.2	18.4

Source: Russell 1958: pp. 25-29.

The third criticism is well taken: there seem to be too many elderly in comparison with those under sixty.[14] This is especially true of North Africa. Yet the chances are that the longevity there was due to the absence of tuberculosis and its slow advance in the ancient world. Very good age-length statistics are given by the English inquisitions post mortem and do not show (table 13) too much difference. The percentage of very elderly is not high and thus does not affect life expectancy data especially for those under the age of fifty.

The high male to female ratio is verified by skeletal data for the non-plague periods of the Roman and medieval eras. Refusal to accept it comes from a noble inability to comprehend widespread infanticide as a population control, particularly for females. In earlier periods of history infanticide was a logical choice over over-

[14]Hopkins, 1967: 249-253; Herlihy & Klapisch-Zuber, 1978: 353-354. For bibliography of modern times see I. Rosenwaike, "A Note on the New Estimates of Mortality of the Extreme Aged," *Demography* 18 (1981): 257-266.

population. Its practice as one of the methods of control will be considered in a later chapter.

The fifth objection, failure to show enough infants, is characteristic also of the other cemeteries. The indifference to infanticide morally is paralleled by an indifference to burying children, especially infants, carefully. However, it is possible to estimate the number of children, as we should, from pubic bones which seem to show an average of about 4.2 children per woman.[15] The number can also be judged by estimating the number of potential children possible for women in their child-bearing years. Using this information, one may vary one's estimate of the possibilities. The high sex ratio of North Africa, for instance, is a natural corollary to the low death rates of women there between 20 and 40.

The sixth objection has some point, particularly with respect to ages of specific classes.[16] Generals obviously died at a greater than average age, simply because they did not become generals as a rule until they were mature men. Their expectation was comparable to that of men of forty than to children. The same would be true for any group that had an age qualification for entrance. Freedmen, at least of the first generation, would be older than slaves at death, since they usually were not freed until they were adults. However, the differences among persons in a simple age, such as the Roman, can easily be overemphasized. Slaves who lived within a family, shared its diseases and its environment. Doctors were not very effective and it was hard to prevent slaves from sharing the food of the family. The ancient world, even more than the medieval, enjoyed a sense of spaciousness, inherited from their close connections with the countryside. Most country people actually lived in villages with the isolated homestead as a rarity. As we have seen, even in the city of Rome, people lived in what functioned as villages.

Another approach to the question of the value of the Roman inscriptions is a comparison with other inscriptions of the same area and character. Take the cemetery of the army camps of Lorch (Lauriacum) and Trentholm and the inscriptions of their provinces of England and Noricum.[17] The percentage of infans I and II is higher in Lorch (13.3) and Noricum (11.7) than in Trentholm (5.0) and England (9.6). Similarly the percentage of the elderly (over 60) is higher in Lorch (13.6) and Noricum (23.9) than in Trentholm (0. 0) and England (7.9). However, at army camps the sex ratio is much higher; 462 for Lorch and 390 for Trentholm against 127 for Noricum and 200 for England. While these figures

---

[15]See pp. 147-148.

[16]Szilágyi, 1962: 322-336 for data. Lorch, Kloiber 1957, 1960, 1962; Trentholm, Wenham 1968; Noricum, Szilágyi, 1962: 238; Britain, Szilágyi, 1961: 132.

[17]Acsádi & Nemeskéri, 1970: 60-72.

do not prove the authenticity of the inscriptions, they do fall in line with what would be expected of the places and their provinces.

THE LIFE TABLE

For a study of the demographic structure of any population the life table has value. Its parts, well known and well defined, can be understood at once by demographers and should be easy for medievalists and others to learn. It is a kind of basic device like the alphabet or multiplication table, and can be understood even in foreign-language articles. Though it has its limitations even other methodologies use parts of the life table. Several will be used in this study. It must be kept in mind, however, that the life table assumes a stationary population.

The age divisions used in a life table are arbitrary. It is more convenient for medieval and late ancient use to employ the five-year system since the tables about Roman inscriptions and those from the Inquisitions post mortem of England come in this form. Even here the problem does not affect those over 20 years of age. Actually the divisions of the anthropological systems, Martin or revised, are sensitive enough to give an accurate impression of vital relationships. The division by age—x to x^{tn}—(column 1) is the core of the life table and its composition is fundamental.

In the second column of the life table (q) is the mortality rate of those alive at the beginning of the interval during the interval. The third column is the reciprocal of the second. The fourth column (1) is the number alive at the beginning of each interval. The fifth column (d) is the number dying during the interval. The sixth column (L) is the number of years lived during the interval. The seventh is the number of years lived in the interval and all later years. The eighth is the average number of years of life remaining at the beginning of the interval. All of this provides a very convenient body of useful information about the hypothetical structure of a stationary population based on the data from cemeteries.

The life table may include all persons or divide them into tables for males and females. The tendency to include all was encouraged earlier because of the difficulty of distinguishing sex, particularly those under the age of twenty. Acsádi and Nemeskéri believe that with the most modern methods a very high degree of sex determination is possible, providing that sufficient bones are available.[18] The problem in using earlier studies is that there may have been a bias in selecting sex in questionable cases. It seems that the degree of sexualization (characteristics of sex in bone structure) slightly

---

[18]Ibid., 73-100.

Table 10

Life Table, Nonplague Periods

Age		q_x		l_x	d_x	L_x	T_x	e_x^o
0-6	I	15.2	84.8	25441	3874	158717	835652	33.1*
7-13	II	9.3	90.7	21567	2013	142917	683115	31.7
14-19	J	8.5	91.5	19554	1670	113314	540194	27.6
20-39	A	42.9	57.1	17884	7672	280960	426880	23.9
40-59	M	79.0	21.0	10212	8072	123520	145920	13.6
60-	S	100.0	0.0	2140	2140	21400	21400	10.0

Source: data in personal files and in bibliography.
*Probably too large since deaths of the very young were often not properly buried. The expectation at birth should be about that of age seven.

favors the identification of females (that is, their characteristics are easier to identify) and thus scholars have left more males in the undetermined states than females. Given this situation, the apparent shortage of females in most cemeteries is not due to bias against their identification. It is true that in cemeteries where many graves have too few bones for identification, the great disintegration of female bones must be considered. The development of certain chemical tests have reduced chances of mistaking or failing to identify sex.[19]

Besides comparing living and dead populations the life table has other uses. The mortality rate for each interval is secured by dividing the number of dead at the end of the interval from that at the beginning (l_x). Its reciprocal (subtracting from 100) gives the chance of surviving the interval. At the right of the life table is the expectation of life at the beginning of each interval. It is secured by dividing T_x by the number in column 1 in the same line. It must be remembered that for the late ancient and Middle Ages there is nearly always a relatively uncertain quality of the figures used. The use of figures should not lead one to believe in the absolute accuracy of figures, so that the difference of a year or so in calculations has little meaning. Lest one compare the data unfavorably with modern, let us remember that modern censuses have disturbing errors and uncertainties. If the United States Census of 1980 were within two or three million of the exact number, it would be happy. There are always too many centenarians in the census, perhaps a third too many. Others list age twenty-one far in excess of probability while considerable numbers

---

[19]Ibid., 100-137.

of parents forget to record their newborn babies. In dealing with population and censuses one does not deal with exact sciences.[20]

The total life table using most of the available and usable evidence needs explanation. The table has certain probems which are partially avoided by using all the data for only the older four classes (juvenis, adultus, maturus, and senilis). Until recently few scholars attempted to give the sex for persons under fourteen or even twenty, as is stated above. In the next chapter an effort will be made to show the more probable ages for the uncertain periods in the total life table. Even the complete table as given here, has too few persons in the youngest ages and thus the life table overestimates the true average. However, a distinction must be made for the two plague periods which definitely lowered the average for the entire Middle Ages. There were two distinctly different standards for the period.

LIVING AND DEAD POPULATIONS

From the life table, which is based upon a dead population, it is possible to reconstruct a living population, assuming that it is stationary, and not changed much by migration or other factors. Of course, the process could be reversed by starting with the T_x column of a living society and working backward from it. However, desirable information comes primarily from a live population. The differences between the two are caused by differing lengths of lives. In the life table those who died young count for much less than in the dead list where the years lived do not count. For study of modern data there is little use for the dead table since it is the conditions of living today which are usually studied. The percentages of death at each age group are important.

For the late ancient and medieval period not much data from live populations are available. There are lists of citizens by ages only for several cities in the fifteenth century. The most detailed, and that which covers the largest area, is the great survey of the year 1427 which included Florence and several cities under its rule. Pozzuoli has such a list for 1489. Some data have survived from a list made at Reims, France, in 1422 and a partial list from Treviso in 1384. From the lands of St. Victor, Marseilles, there are partial age data which show some distribution by age in the seventh century. A massacre at Lagore Crannock in Ireland (seventh to tenth century) gives the population at that particular time. A relatively short list by age remains for an area in fourth-century Asia Minor. If Pompeian skeletons were studied carefully by anthropologists, the results would be the best introduction to Roman population by age and sex that is available.[21]

[20]Table 11.
[21]Ibid.

Table 11

Comparison of Living Population with Hypothetical Living Population, Skeletal Data
Percentage of Deaths by Age Groups.

Place and Period	Infans I (Years)			Total	Infans II		Juvenis		Total Persons
	0	1-3	4-6		Percent	Total to Age 14	Percent	Total to Age 20	
Asia Minor 4 century				19.4	19.4	38.8	6.5	43.3	31
Skeletal Data, I				19.9		32.6		51.4	
Lagore Crannock 7-10 cent.				5.5	16.7	22.2	11.1	33.3	36
St. Victor, Marseilles 7 century	4.0	5.8	8.1	17.9	12.2	30.1			719
Skeletal Data, III				19.2	16.2	35.4	14.3	49.7	
Treviso 1384						21.6	14.9	36.4	2151
Reims (part) 1422	2.2	4.8	3.4	10.4	12.7	23.1	14.7	37.8	1272
Florence 1427	2.9	9.2	8.1	20.2	16.3	36.5	9.4	45.9	36932
Tuscany, contado 1727	2.6	10.7	7.9	21.2	13.1	34.3	9.0	43.3	264210
Pisa 1427				25.0		34.5	8.4	43.9	747
Pistoia 1427	4.1	13.7	7.2	19.4	10.8	35.8	8.1	47.2	15775
Pozzuoli 1489	1.9	9.2	9.3	19.4	12.4	31.8	14.7	36.4	2528
Skeletal Data					18.0	37.4	16.4	53.8	

Sources: Asia Minor, A. H. M. Jones, *The Later Roman Empire* (Norman, 1964): 2: 1044. Lagore Crannock, Hencken, 1950: 199-203. S. Victor, Marseilles, Russell, 1958: 31 assuming 29.42.58 and 88 to infans I; filii, filie and baccalarii to infans II. Treviso, Beloch, 1937: 24. Reims, Desportes 1966: 497. Florence, Tuscany, Herlihy & Klapisch-Zuber, 1978: 656-664. Pisa, Cassini, 1965: 88-89. Pistoia, Herlihy, 1967: 283-285. Puzzuoli, Beloch, 1937: 29-30.

At least these living data offer opportunities to compare with the dead data. From table 12 comparisons may be made of these living data with the results of skeletal information. The fourth-century Roman data from Asia Minor have been criticized as suggesting "that few children survived and also that the general mortality was high and that men married late in life."[22] All three are open to question. By medieval standards the expectation of life derived from these data show a length of 21. 8 years at age twenty, not very low, as is also the total life estimate of 26. 3. The number to a dwelling was the normal 3.5 and the number under the age of twenty is actually a little high. The population was certainly not declining if this small sample of thirty-one persons is representative of the total population. The men are alleged to have married late because evidence showed a 65-year-old man with a fifteen year-old-child. But this was not necessarily his first marriage. And the children from a first marriage would probably appear as separate householders with children of their own. In other words the remarks are illustrative of a lack of knowledge of these demographic realities.

The data from the lands of St. Victor of Marseilles are quite difficult to interpret. If the *baccalarii* (both men and women), were only transient workers, not a real part of the communities, the percentages for the age classes would be more nearly similar to the skeletal evidence. The shortage of very small children may reflect a certain mercy toward the very young in the massacre at Lagore Crannock. These data are included among the live data since the victims all were alive at one time and show a live situation.

Table 12

Percentage of Persons aged below Twenty Years of Age in Plague Times, City and Britain

Britain, Landed Class	Percent	City and Date	Percent
Born before 1276	56.4	Europe, 1000-1348	50.1
Born 1276-1300	52.3		
Born 1348-1375	44.2	Reims, 1422	37.8
Born 1376-1400	43.9	Pisa, 1427	43.4
Born 1401-1425	49.9	Pistoia, 1427	47.2
Born 1426-1450	54.4	Pozzuoli, 1489	56.1

Sources: See Table 11.

[22]Ibid.

The fifteenth-century data show rather marked coincidences of development between the experience of the cities and of the cemeteries. Since this was the period of the plague, the divergence of the numbers between plague and nonplague periods are clearer. It seems that in the second half of the fifteenth century the plague lost its influence and the conditions resembled the nonplague era.

Skeletal data seem to present a fairly coherent picture of the changing conditions of demography during the Middle Ages. There were general conditions over much of Europe as the plague and other conditions shifted about over the continent. The picture also is quite reassuring with respect to the available evidence. It is certain that with more data and better approaches to the evidence the picture of the demographic conditions will become clearer. It is also probably true that the perfected picture will look very much like that presented in this study.

IV. How long did they live?

In his well known *Etymologies,* the seventh century Spanish bishop of Seville outlined a system of six ages of man.[1] Infancy (*infantia*) went from birth to seven years: childhood (*pueritia*) to fourteen years; adolescence (*adolescentia*) to twenty-eight years; youth (*juventus*) to fifty years; gravity (*senior, id est gravitas*) to seventy years; and old age (*senectus*). Those six ages commence like the anthropological series with two ages of infancy and childhood (like Infans I and II) and follow with a normal adolescence. Here the unexpected begins. Adolescence continues well into manhood and then youth goes on to fifty years. There seems to be no middle age in the Middle Ages. A sixth age is allotted to those over seventy. From this one gathers that Isidore and presumably the medieval readers of the thousand manuscripts of his work were not as impressed with the shortness of medieval life as we are. Do we not read of the brevity of life in the Middle Ages or in the Classical world for that matter? And yet a standard medieval author allows a sixth age from seventy years to the end of life.

Of course Isidore lived in Iberia which had one of the longer expectations of life at that time—the longest belonging to North Africa, with a close second in the Canary Islands. Another long-lived group was that of the pillar (stylites) saints.[2] The problem is that while some, even in less favored places than these, lived long lives, many died young and thus pulled down the average, which is what is usually meant by the length of life. It is not a very satisfactory measure since it depends so much on the unsatisfactory data for infancy. It is better to calculate the expectation some years after birth, perhaps even as late as the twentieth year.

OLD AGE EXPECTATION

Sixty years is a convenient if arbitrary time to select as the beginning of the period of old age (senilitas), more important as a point in a decimal system than for any significance biologically. The bodily changes at this time seem slow and regular. Consideration of a biological rather than chronological age is interesting but hard to document. Obviously some age in appearance faster than others; but whether there is a corresponding change in bone and other conditions which indicate biological aging is another and undecided matter.[3] The approach here is strictly chronological, but even the matter of chronology is complicated by the lack of

---

[1]*Isidori Hispalensis Episcopi Etymologorum sive Originum Libri XX,* ed. W. M. Lindsey (Oxford, 1911): XI, 11, 1 (47). Herlihy & Klapisch-Zuber 1978: 202.

[2]H. Delehay, *Les Stylites* (Louvain 1895).

[3]Acsádi & Nemeskéri, 1970: 102-104.

exact data: no birth certificates and limited certificates of death. What one deals with are alleged ages at death and of data of anthropologists estimating ages at death from skeletal evidence. About much of both types of evidence there is some uncertainty in the late ancient and medieval world.

The results are reported in two forms as indicators of the standards of senescence. One is the expectation of life at age sixty, the number of years that, on the average, persons lived after that age. The second is the proportion of persons over a given age who live past sixty or are living at one time after that age, the living and dead age group mentioned in the last chapter. In the life tables the information is supplied by the e_x^o column for expectation of life and the l_x and the T_x columns for the other two indexes.

The most accurate information about the elderly comes from the inquisitions post mortem of England in the period after the middle of the thirteenth century. The length of life is based on two figures: the year when the man entered his holding and the interval until his death, given in a second writ. Now the dates given for entrance are rather accurate since a large part of them came into their holdings in their twenties when ages are given very accurately.[4] This avoids the tendency to exaggerate which is apparent when persons or their relatives give ages. Furthermore, the expectation of life of those over sixty was not much affected by the plague after 1348: actually the expectation increased! The data are set up by generations. Here are given (1) the percentage of persons at age 20 who reached 60 (lo_x) and the percentage of the population over age 20 held by those over age 60 (T_x). The percentage of total population would be roughly double that over 20 but is not given since it involves the less reliable figures of infancy. The expectation is given also (e_x^o).

	$^l60/^l20$	$^T60/^T20$	$^e60^o$
Born before 1276	25.7	8.4	9.4
Born 1276 - 1300	22.2	7.3	8.3
1301 - 1325	17.6	6.9	9.3
1326 - 1348	18.1	8.8	10.8
1348 - 1375	22.4	10.2	10.9
1376 - 1400	19.3	9.0	10.0
1401 - 1425	29.7	10.6	10.5
1426 - 1450	25.0	12.4	13.7
Average	22.5	9.2	10.4

---

[4]Russell, 1948: 181-185, 199-214.

Table 13

Percentage of *seniles* of Total Population over Age 20
and Expectation of Life at 60 in Fifteenth-Century Cities.

City, date		$l_{60/120}$	$T_{60/T20}$	e_{x60}^0
Florence-total	male, 1427	26.3		
	female, 1427	25.7		
Pistoia,	male, 1427	26.0		9.6
	female, 1427	23.0		9.5
Reims (part),	male, 1422	17.7	12.2	10.3
	female, 1422	16.6	10.4	11.8
Pozzuoli,	1489, female	8.5	16.0	9.8
	1489, male	14.2	16.3	12.0

Sources: Florence; Herlihy-Klapisch-Zuber, 1978, 317.
    Pistoia: Herlihy, 1967, 282-285
    Reims: Desportes, 1966: 97
    Pozzuoli: Beloch, 1937: 29-31.

The English documents show a number of very long lived persons. One alleged centenarian did his witnessing in bed.[5] Alina de Marechale was said to have been ninety when she inherited some lands but she lived another seven years. In one inquest a Reginald de Colewick was said to have lived a century. His son probably lived a very long life, while his grandson passed eighty, indicating that their longevity as well as their land was inherited. Of about 2,950 persons whose ages at death are known, some sixteen lived past ninety. Oddly ten of these were in the generation born from 1426 to 1450. In fact that whole generation had an expectation three years longer than the average for the landholders. The data are so well documented that the long life of that generation seems believable.[6] They do not rest upon opinions of neighbors.

The contemporary data from Pozzuoli (1489) gives one man said to have been ninety-six, two women centenarians and three female nonagenarians. Reims of 1422 claimed one man of ninety. The Florentine documents of 1427 show ninety-seven alleged centenarians![7]

For earlier periods data are less abundant. Jusuf ben Tashfin, emir of Africa and enemy of El Cid, apparently lived more than a century. The famous warrior and author, Usamah ibn Munqidh,

---

[5]R. H. Helmholz, *Marriage Litigation in Medieval England* (Cambridge, 1974): 83.
[6]Russell, 1948: 192-193, 202-207.
[7]Beloch, 1937: 29-31; Desportes 1966, 97; Herlihy & Klapisch-Zuber 1978: 659 and 663.

died at ninety-three while his nurse reached a hundred. A complication here is that the Islamic century was shorter than the Christian, if only by a few years. The early centuries of the Middle Ages were marked by the long lives of the Stylites, several living to or near the century mark. Theodore of Tarsus at nearly seventy was sent to England as archbishop of Canterbury and governed there for twenty-one years.

It would seem then that the span of life, the age which a person might possibly reach under the best of conditions, was about one hundred years. It seems also that the percentage of people alive at one time over sixty years of age might well be a fifth of the adult (over twenty years) population. There was then no lack of mature men and women in the population There were exceptions. Only one member of the English royal family, either male or female, lived to be over sixty-eight. The exception was Robert Curthose who spent the last twenty years of life confined to a prison.

The Canary Islands had a very long lived population in the eleventh century, but only in the northern areas. The difference can be seen in this comparison.[8]

	North	South
Adultus	28	91
Maturus	37	98
Senilis	38	25
Percent over 60	36.9	11.7

As indicated above in table 13, the average for Italian cities was about 25 percent of those over twenty lived to be sixty. Those in the south of the Canary Islands saw only about 12 percent above sixty while nearly 37 percent of those in the north lived to great age. It is a striking illustration of the influence of environment. The northern part was rainy, fruitful, and heavily settled while the southern part was very dry, poor, and thinly settled. Roman North Africans also lived to a great age and were proud of it.

The percentage over age twenty who survive to sixty is probably a better test for longevity than the average length of life or the percentage over sixty in a living population. The latter, in part, must depend upon an estimate of the length of life of the very old, who are most subject to exaggeration of age. The estimate of ten years of expectation over age sixty should be reasonably accurate but it does not distinguish much among percentages of those over sixty in the skeletal evidence.

The percentage of those in the United States over twenty who reached sixty in 1935 was just about 70 percent but is, of course,

---

[8]Fustè, 1961; Schwidetsky, 1960, 1963.

Table 14

Percentage of Those Twenty and Above who Survived to Sixty Years of Age: Male and female.

Region	Period 1 1-540	Period 2 540-750	Period 3 750-1000	Period 4 1000-1348	Period 5 1348-1500
1 Mediter-ranean	30.2-30.8		15.6-19.1	14.8-19.1	33.3-25.6
2 France	25.0-40.7*	22.4-21.0			
3 Britain	7.2-11.8	4.9-9.9	25.0-28.0*	27.6-50.0*	5.9-0.0*
4 Germany	6.2-6.2	8.8-5.9	0.0-0.0*	7.5-0.0	2.6-0.0
5 Hungary-Balkans	15.0-22.7	0.0-2.4	21.1-19.2	10.8-10.1	2.9-0.0
6 Alps-Czechoslovakia	14.3-9.4	0.0-0.0	15.2-12.2	16.3-7.4	20.0-23.1*
7 Scandinavia	15.2-10.2		5.4-3.8	9.8-11.4	3.3-0.0
8 Poland	20.8-28.6	0.0-0.0	0.0-0.0*	9.3-8.0	9.0-8,6*
Period Total	15.9-17.4	6.0-5.1	16.9-16.4	6.3-10.5	7.1-4.6
Grand total	13.5-12.9				

*Less than 20 in group.

somewhat greater today. The general average for available medieval data is 13.5 percent for men and 12.9 percent for women. There is a great difference between plague and nonplague periods. For nonplague periods the average is about one percent higher: 14.8 for men and 14.3 for women. The plague periods show only 7.1 for men and 4.6 for women. The percentage of persons over sixty ought then to be a test for the presence of plague.

The grand averages for the five periods are as follows:

	Male	Female
To 540	15.9	17.4
540 - 750	6.0	5.1
750 - 1000	16.9	16.4
1000 - 1346	9.3	10.5
1346 - 1500	7.9	10.8

The surprising figures are the low ones for the fourth period and the high numbers for the first. It raises doubts, for instance, whether it was a natural failure of fertility which caused the decline of population in the Roman Empire.

If one turns to geographical areas for evidence of old age percentages, there are other surprises. First, there is the high level of old age in northern Europe in the first period. This should have meant a warmer climate at the time, when there was great expansion of tribes. Throughout the time the Mediterranean saw larger numbers of older people. North Africa, if we may use the Roman evidence, had a very high proportion of older persons. The percentages according to inscriptions of the Roman Empire were:[9]

	Male	Female	Both
North Africa	46.0	41.3	
Iberia	29.9	17.5	
Asia Minor, etc.			22.1
Rome	9.4	8.5	
Latium			14.2
Egypt			18.7
Cisalpine Gaul			15.9
Calabria, etc.			21.7
Sicily, etc.			16..6
Aemilia, etc.			18.8
Gaul, Narbonensis			16.3

When one compares these figures which are for l_x one sees an apparent difference between the Mediterranean countries and those to the north. The l_x figures are clearly larger in the Mediterranean than in the areas to the north, although there are exceptions. Only North Africa seems clearly out of the range of the possible.

THE MATURUS AND ADULTUS DATA.

For purpose of computing life tables the number 10 is apparently accurate enough for the expectation of the senilis class. The problem then is to find numbers to use for the next two classes, maturus and adultus, respectively set at forty to sixty and twenty to forty. There are sufficient numbers of cases where the age estimates are given in terms of five years or even ten years to see the proportion who died in the shorter periods and thus to get a figure for the entire classification (usually for a life table) if only the larger classifications of adultus and maturus are available. The available evidence shows the following:

adultus male average	30.8	or 10.8 for it.
adultus female	30.1	10.1
maturus male	49.7	9.7
maturus female	49.5	9.5

In all cases ten seems close enough to the averages to use it satisfactorily in the calculations. Since the figures are above ten for

---

[9]Szilágyi, 1961, 1966.

adultus and below for maturus, any calculations which involve both will tend to offset the bias of the two. The smaller figures show how long these lived in each period and who died.

The information about age is most reliable for the adultus and maturus groups. The data are not skewed by exaggeration for the most advanced groups nor hindered by lack of information about the youngest ages. The expectation of life at twenty and forty are much more reliable than for younger ages and are given in tables 15 or 16. There the shortness of life during the two plague periods can be seen as well as the greater expectation of the period A.D. 750-1000. There are exceptions which. in some cases, are probably due to lack of available data. It is especially unfortunate that there is so little data available for Gaul and France since it had one of the largest area populations in the Middle Ages. It can be seen also that the mature age group did not have the same amount of difference in the plague periods as did the others. The plague apparently did not strike so heavily in the upper ages.

The mortality within the two periods is probably the most accurate age data for the periods. As we shall see, the mortality of tuberculosis was most heavily concentrated in the period from twenty (or fifteen) to forty and thus is a good clue to the presence and spread of that disease. For women it might be an indication of losses in childbirth but this seems to have been a minor factor. The two ages, adultus and maturus, constitute the years of greatest physical activity and will be of value in estimating the amount of dependence and active life in the population. The chief difference in the lesser length of life among women seems to have been a factor of diet which will be considered in the next chapter.

JUVENIS AND INFANS II AGE GROUPS

The years from seven to twenty are more difficult to handle in a study of age and sex. Until recently most anthropologists refused to estimate either within those years. To do so requires a much more exact knowledge of bone structure. One must fall back on other evidence to supplement the little that is known. Less interest in physical anthropology now makes it unlikely much more data will be available about the infans II and juvenis groups within the next decade. It must be admitted that these, while important, are not easy to distinguish on a year to year basis. Physical growth seems to vary from person to person. Especially between the ages of ten and fifteen individuals vary considerably in growth. In schoolrooms of children seated by height, some move forward or backward quite suddenly in those years of age.

The chief problem in constructing the life table for those ages is to ascertain a proper number by which to multiply the number dying within the limits of the two age groups. For the juvenis group Roman inscriptions offer considerable evidence.[10] Of the ages

Table 15

Expectation of Life at Age of Forty by Time and Area.

Area	1-542		542-750		Time 750-1000		1000-1348		1348-1500	
	M	F	M	F	M	F	M	F	M	F
All-Average										
1-Mediterranean	26.8	23.8			14.2	15.9	15.0	15.8	20.0	20.0
2-France	17.0	17.6	15.7	15.3	15.5	20.0				
3-Britain	16.5	17.4	12.7	18.7	14.1	14.7				
4-Germany	12.8	13.0	12.0	12.1	14.3	13.1	14.1	14.7	10.9	10.0
5-Hungary-Balkans	13.6	14.9	11.2	11.3	15.0	15.9	14.4	14.8	13.8	12.7
6-Alps-Bohemia	13.9	13.2	11.0	12.0	13.4	13.9	15.3	13.4	12.0	12.1
7-Scandinavia	19.3	18.2			12.7	12.9	10.2	13.2	11.6	10.9
8-Poland	16.7	21.1	10.0	10.0	14.2	14.7	11.9	13.7	10.3	10.5

---

[10]Szilágyi, 1961, 1966.

Table 16

Expectation of Life at Age Twenty by Time and Area

Area	1-542		542-750		Time 750-1000		1000-1348		1348-1500	
	M	F	M	F	M	F	M	F	M	F
1-Mediterranean	29.4	27.7			27.9	26.8	24.6	26.3		
2-France	27.9	23.5	28.7	28.1	20.0	20.0				
3-Britain	19.6	19.8	17.7	16.2	26.8	23.5				
4-Germany	21.4	19.9	17.1	20.1	23.5	19.2	23.9	20.1	17.1	14.1
5-Hungary-Balkans	22.5	25.4	20.0	17.9	25.7	23.7	27.1	22.2	22.6	19.1
6-Alps-Bohemia	26.0	19.6	20.7	18.1	27.6	23.3	27.7	20.4	23.2	19.0
7-Scandinavia	22.4	26.5			21.8	16.0	23.6	20.0	18.2	16.9
8-Poland	26.7	26.0	15.9	12.4	23.9	20.3	22.2	20.3	21.1	20.2

Table 17

Percentage of *Juvenes* dying of Total Deaths,
by Area and Time. Both sexes.

| Area | Times | | | | |
	1-540	540-750	750-1000	1000-1346	1346-1500	All
1 Mediter-ranean	0.5	.0	0.4	3.2	12.2	
2 France	23.1	13.2			30.0	
3 Britain	9.3	13.7	26.7		(2.3)	
4 Germany	14.2	13.0	9.1	16.8	9.8	
5 Hungary, Balkans	13.6	7.8	11.4	8.7	11.1	
6 Czecho-slovakia, Swiss, etc.	7.8	6.4	10.1	8.6		
7 Scandinavia	1.9		5.1	8.7	14.0	
8 Poland	27.2	26.1	16.7	5.7	(3.3)	
All	9.2	11.0	8.2	6.7	9.1	

Source: private collections of author
(too few)

fourteen through nineteen, fifteen was the most common year—a
result of rounding. The even numbers were more used than the
uneven, although seventeen appears frequently—an age when the
Roman boy attained his manhood. Nineteen was used least,
probably because it was next to twenty, although apparently the
tendency was to round to lower numbers. However, the pairs of
even-uneven numbers between thirteen and twenty do not differ
much in size. In the cities the number of boys aged twelve or
fourteen may be higher because apprentices migrated from the
countryside to the city at those ages. Three seems a satisfactory
number for the length of time that boys who died in the juvenis
period (14-19) lived in that period and is used in the life tables.

Table 17 is based upon a relatively small amount of evidence for
the juvenis period. This explains the considerable variation in the
percentage for the several countries. There is more evidence (table
19) for the infans II group—a seven-year period. Heavier mortality occurred during the first three years of the seven, so that
three seems a better number than four by which to multiply the
number dying as infans II to estimate the experience of the group.
The mortality was about 50 percent higher than for the juvenis
group, but less, of course, than for infans I. The data came mostly
from central Europe.

	Table 18				
Percentage of Infans II dying of Total Deaths by Area and Time.					
Areas			*Times*		
	1-540	*540-750*	*750-1000*	*1000-1348*	*1348-1500*
1 Mediter- ranean	ˋ1.8			6.8	7.5
2 France	25.8	41.9			19.0
3 Britain	9.2	19.1	6.4		(2.8)
4 Germany	30.2	13.0	11.4	15.8	18.4
5 Hungary, Balkans	10.3	23.3	23.8	18.4	21.7
6 Alps Cze- choslovakia, Swiss	7.8	18.6		30.0	
7 Scandinavia	5.7		5.1	7.1	16.4
8 Poland	4.7	(52.2)	29.5	4.0	(4.3)
All	14.2	25.2	15.0	10.5	8.8

INFANS I

Tables (20 and 21), give information about the mortality during period of infans I, the first seven years of life, the most difficult and elusive period of life to judge. In the first place there is the question of definition of years. One can speak of the first year of life or year zero, which is baffling. The years show more diversity of mortality than later life which makes them individually important. Then occasionally scholars give the total by pairs or even three or more years. In table 20 these are distributed: that is, if there are seven assigned to years three and four, each is given 3.5. The total for the first year of life is thus 454.5. Table 21 compares the mortality by the data without correction. Then it gives the mortality in percent for the total assuming that the total is 4.2 times the number of females over the age of 20. Eight of the cemeteries show an average of mortality in the first year of life as 13.4 while six others give a average of 12.3 with more for the assumed correction. Thus they are not far apart.

One purpose of this chapter is to set up coefficients of the periods for use in the life tables. That is, if a person died during infans I how long is he supposed to have lived? This can be estimated by the proportions lived by each and the length of the year or years lived. We assume that those who lived only a part of the first year lived .3 years, and that those who died in 1-3 years averaged 2.5 and those 4-6 years averaged 5.5 years—we are dealing with completed years in each case. Those dying in 1-3 had completed either one or two or three years and thus the average

Table 19

Specific Years of death assigned to Infans II Skeletons.

Place-Date	7	8	9	10	11	12	13	Total	Author-Year
Gabara 5-1	4	4		1	1			10	Necrasov 1969
Sabaoni 5-1	1	1	1	2	1			6	Necrasov 1969
Trentholm 3-1	2		3		2	4	3	14	Wenham 1968
Nové Zámké 4-2	3	3	4	4	3	2	1	20	Stloukal 1966
Sontheim 4-2	2	1	1	1		1		6	Creel 1966
Zelovich 6-2	10	9	10	10	9	5	5	58	Stloukal 1974
Zwölfoxen 6-2	2	1	1			1		5	Lippert 1969
Brandisek 6-3					2			2	Chochal 1961
Pilismarot 5-3	6	2	3	2	2	2	2	19	Fettich 1965
Bilina 6-4	3	3	2	2	1	2	2	15	Hanáková 1971
Fonyod 5-4	3		4	4	3	1	1	16	Nemeskéri 1963
Kerpuszta 5-4	10	5	4	3	2	2	3	29	Nemeskéri 1952
Pawlow 8-5	1		1				1	3	Miszkiewicz 1968
Total	47	29	34	29	26	20	18		

Numbers assigned to series of years (e.g., 9-11) have been distributed among those years.

Table 20
Specific Years of death Assigned to Infans I Skeletons

Place-Date	0	1	2	Years of Life 3	4	5	6	Total	Author-Year
Odry 5-1	2	1	2	1				4	Kmiecinshiego 1968
Gabara 5-1		3	3	3	3	3	5	22	Necrasov 1969
Sabaone 5-1	20	10	9	4	1			44	Necrasov 1969
Trentholm 3-1		1			3	1	4	9	Wenham 1968
Bankälla 7-1	28	3	2	2	1	1	1	38	Sähkstrom 1954
Sontheim 4-2		2	3	2	2	2	1	12	Creel 1966
Alattyan IV 5-2	20	2	2	10	10	7	7	58	Kourig 1963
Zwölfoxen 6-2	45	11	6	6	3	2	6	79	Lippert 1969
Pilismarot 5-3	4	3	2	3	2	2	2	18	Fettich 1965
Dessau 4-2	1		1	1	1	1	1	6	Krüger 1967
Nóvy Zamké 4-2	7	9	11	9	9	5	4	54	Stloukal 1966
Moravicanech 6-3		1	1	1	1		1	5	Stloukal 1964
Zelovich 6-2	27	19	21	20	34	20	21	162	Stloukal 1974
Alsónémedi 5-3	8	2	1	1				12	Nemeskéri 1952
Brandysek 6-3	3	3	2	2	1	1	1	13	Kytlikov au Csav 1968
Libice 5-3	66	29	34	24	18	18	11	200	Hanáková 1969
Zalavar 5-3	3	6	5	4	2	2	6	45*	Tetramondi 1971
Bilina 6-4	6	7	5	4	3	2		27**	Hanáková 1971
Kerpuszta 5-4	64	10	11	10	12	8	10	125	Nemeskéri 1952
Opolo 8-4	1	1	4	1		1	1	9	Miszkiewisc 1968
Fonyod 5-4	6		6	7	8	5	3	36	Nemeskéri 1963
Westerhus 7-4	120	6	11	15	6	12	8	178	Gejvall 1960

Table 20
(Continued)
Specific Years Assigned to Infans I Skeletons

Place-Date	0	1	2	3	4	5	6	Total	Author-Year
					Years of Life				
Cara Insula 7-5	6	2	3	3	5	5	5	29	Isager 1936
Mistihalj 5-5	44	14	3	3	4	3	4	75	Redfield 1968
Pawlow 8-5	1	1	2	3	2	2	1	12	Miszkiewicz 1968

*Another 17 with no age.   **Another 18 with no age.

Table 21

Deaths During the First Year of Life

Place and Date	Birth	Weeks				Months												Average
		1	2	3	4	1	2	3	4	5	6	7	8	9	10	11	12	
Bankälla 7-1	24																	.04
Pilismarot 7-3		1						1	1		2	1		1	1	1	2	.9
Mikulčice 6-3	12	50	7	16	14	3	49	50	52	16	15	10	8	9	2	2	2	.263
Alsónémedi 5-3						1	1	1	1	1		1	1		1	1		.76
Libice 6-3	22					6	6	6	6	5	6		4	4				.067
Westerhus 7-4	7					8	8	8	15	15	14	12	11	11	4	4	3	.43
Mistihalj 5-5	11	3	3	3	2	4	4	3	3		1	1	1	1	1	1	1	.245

Numbers are distributed over the range of the figure: i.e., 15 for five years is listed as three each year.

Sources: Bänkalla Sählstrom, 1954; Pilismarot Fettich, 1965: Mikulice table 5; Alsónémedi Nemeskéri, 1952; Libice Hanáková, 1969; Westerhus Gevall, 1960; Mistihalj Redfield, 1968.

would be 2.5. It can be seen that the average would be a little more than 2.5 for the lower three and a little less than 5.5 for the second:

0 year	.44 x .3	.132
1-3	.34 x 2.5	.800
4-6	.22 x 5.5	1.320
	1.00	1.892

The average then is close enough to suggest two as the number to be used for those who died in infans I.

The table about the mortality of the first year of life is not very extensive, limited to eight places in only three areas: Czechoslovakia, Hungary and Scandinavia. One may expect that rapid advances in this very backward area will occur in the future. Much more data from female pubic bones should give credence or provide variations in the 4.2 index used in this study. In the second place the recently developed methods of distinguishing age in the very young are being used more and more.[11] So the data here are naturally to be regarded as very tentative. Furthermore, the data show, what appears elsewhere, that very young children were not always buried. Westerhus might seem to have included even the youngest. Mikulcice provided a fair number.[12] The number by which the year one should be represented in the life table experience appears here as about .4 years. However, the number at Mistihalj seems closer to the correct figure[13] and the number of the missing is so great that it seems best to use .33 as the index for average length of life lived by those who died in the first year of life.

The number of cemeteries about which some estimate of the percentage of children may be made is about eighty-seven. The problem is the age included in childhood. Presumably it should be about twenty but it may have been earlier. The estimate had to be made upon bone development as defined by Martin which should have been close to twenty. The list shows about the following:

[11]Acsádi & Nemeskéri, 1970: 104-113; Redfield, 1968.

[12]Gejvall: for Mikulcice Poulik, 1963, 1967; Stloukal, 1962, 1963c, 1964, 1967.

[13]Redfield, 1968.

Percentage children	Number of Cemeteries
15-19	2
20-24	9
25-29	17
30-34	20
35-39	13
40-44	11
45-49	5
50-54	4
55-59	4
60-	2
	87

The median is about 33.3; the modal group is that of 30-34, but the average is about 36.4 for all of the data. This is, as one would expect, somewhat lower than the approximation based on deaths of the three lower ages, which is about 43 percent. It tends to show that about a third of the children were not buried in the cemeteries. A considerable proportion would have died or been allowed to die at birth. At Westerhus, where even the foetuses were buried, 120 of 364 had not reached the second year of life.[14]

The cemetery evidence also reveals something about the health of children in the late ancient and medieval world. If a woman had on the average only 4.2 children even in ten years, the children had the benefit of proper age spacing. This in itself should have made for relatively healthy children. The mother usually nursed her children which also benefited them. The primitive housing had the advantage of keeping the children out of doors and in the sun. As a result rickets seems to have been infrequent, even in such a northern place as Westerhus, Scandinavia.[15] There seem to be relatively few cases where mother and child were buried together at time of childbirth. There is little evidence of broken bones in children. Probably the greatest harm was done by children's diseases but very little is known about them. Once accepted by the family, the child seems to have done reasonably well.[16]

What was the total mortality of childhood? Some try to answer this by adding together the mortality for the periods of childhood as they have been secured. Two approaches have been made: the data approach, using the figures that have been secured and an assumed mortality, allowing for infanticide.

---

[14]Gejvall, 1960: table 1.
[15]Gejvall, 1960: 93-94.
[16]Ibid.

	Data	Assumed
Infans I (first year)	15	20
Infans 2-7th years	0	10
Infans II	11	11
Juvenis	8	8
	44	49

This would show then that approximately 50 percent of persons died by the age of twenty.

These figures may be compared to the recently published data derived from parish registers of churches from about 1559-1750. These were secured by "family reconstitution," a very careful use of data covering long periods of years and requiring very long periods of time for the studies. Naturally relatively few have been accomplished, mostly by the French, who developed the method. Flinn has summarized the data produced by Fleury, Henry, Goubert and others following their methods. Converting the data into the form used here, the results appear to be the following percentages of mortality:[17]

	English	French	Swiss	German	Danish	Spanish
0-1	18.7	27.1	28.3	15.4	20.6	25.1
1-7	14.6	18.6	15.0			
7-14		5.1	6.1			

Here, as elsewhere the failure to follow the standard system of Martin, used generally elsewhere, makes comparisons more difficult. Futhermore, the possibility of infanticide, especially in England and Germany, makes the figures somewhat suspect, since the victims of infanticide would probably not figure in the registers. The results, however, are about as might be expected. People in the Middle Ages were obviously healthier than in the early modern period.

TOTAL LENGTH OF LIFE

If one divides the areas into above average, average, and below average length of life divisions, the results are:

[17]Flinn, 1981: 92, 93, 131-132, 133-137. He has a good discussion of methods on 1-12.

Period	Above Average	Average	Below Average
I	Mediterranean		
	France	Bohemia, etc.	Britain
	Hungary	Scandinavia	Germany
	Poland		
II	France	Hungary	Britain
	Germany		Bohemia
			Poland
III	Bohemia		Hungary
	Mediterranean		Scandinavia
IV	Britain	Bohemia	Germany
		Poland	Hungary
	Britain	Scandinavia	
V	Mediterranean	Hungary	Germany
	Poland		Scandinavia

This is based upon allotting three points for above average, two for average and one for below average and dividing by the periods in which the area appeared.

If the cemeteries are divided according to area groups, instead of by chronological divisions, a fairly common pattern persists across Europe. The French and Czech-Swiss groups seem to include more of the below twenty persons although it means little in the case of France because the total is low. The Scandinavian and Polish cemeteries present fewer children than the others. The Hungarian-Balkan, German and English are about the same, the median is near the 40 percent mark which is about the same as the death rate for the children in their first year of life. However, the mystery remains and is not further clarified by the evidence arranged by country. Whatever the reason, the custom of not including more children was apparently universal in Europe and changed little in the period concerned.

Some evidence remains about the length of life of medieval regular clergy (monks, nuns, friars, etc.) but it shows little difference from that of the laity. In the Gallen Priory cemetery, Ireland, about 1100-1300 the monks seem to show a better expectation at age twenty and a less at forty: 23 percent survived to sixty among the laity and 20.5 percent among the monks. The plague period cemetery at Leipzig shows a very poor expectation even for that period: 18.1 years at age twenty and 11.5 at forty.[18] In contrast the evidence for great length of life (if we interpret it correctly) for Canterbury Cathedral monks (Christchurch) was very good, if we assume that they entered religion at about twenty—an age when most people decided upon their careers.[19]

---

[18]Gallen, Ireland; Howells, 1941; Leipzig; Schott, 1961.

[19]Russell, 1948: 189-192.

Before the plague the average *monachatus,* years of being a monk, was about 30.6. During the plague period this dropped to about 27 years while those dying between 1456 and 1471 had experienced 33.2 years on the average. This record was almost three years better than that of contemporary English landholders. The plague mortality in the other English monasteries does not seem much different from that of the clergy at large.[20] The latter was high in the first plague (perhaps 35 percent) but probably because, besides being often more exposed, they lived in small households where the chance of being bitten by the limited number of fleas was greater than in larger households. In Florence the Dominicans at Santa Maria Novella lived as friars about 32 years before the plague and about 26 during the time after 1348, an experience very similar to that of Christchurch, Canterbury.[21]

As might have been expected, the worst experience was in Greenland.[22] Its records are limited but show the following mortality:

	Inf. I	*Inf.* II	*Juv.*	*Adultus*	*Maturus*	*Senilis*	Total
Male			1	4	8		12
Female	1	7	4	23	8		32
							12

From these raw data the expectation of life was only about 23.5 and, of course, it would be even less if we add the large number of children whom we might assume that the women had and who disappeared without a trace. The awful difference in the numbers of men and women must have been as the result of accidents by land and sea in Greenland's climate. An even lower length of life appears at Westerhus in Scandinavia due to the careful burial of so many infants in its cemetery.[23] The length of life in those unfavorable climates was much like that of prehistoric man. The highly unfavorable conditions in imperial Rome and surrounding Latium allowed an expectation of only fifteen years at birth.[24]

Perhaps the most startling result of the study of this chapter is the difference of length of life of men and women at age twenty—largely the result of heavy mortality of women between twenty and forty. More female deaths occur in that period than between forty and sixty. For all three periods ten proves to be a reasonable guess for length of time lived within the period by those who die in it—

[20]Russell, 1948: 222-223.

[21]Herlihy, 1974: 254.

[22]Fischer-Møller, 1942.

[23]Gejvall, 1960.

[24]Szilágyi, 1963: 131-132; Russell, 1958: 26.

primarily a problem for the life table. There are notable variations in length of life by country and period, factors which need dicussion. The length of life, so long and so questioned for Roman North Africa, probably should be reduced for years after seventy, but length of life there was still much longer than elsewhere. Exceptions also exist for the Canary Islands and the pillar-dwellers (although they were seldom in Europe). The reason was lack of contact with contagion rather than, with the exception of Greenland, climate and geography. The plague periods, 570-700 and 1348-1500, show a much shorter length of life than the other periods. It seems then that at 20 male expectation was about 25 years and female 23 but at 40 and 60 they were not much different. Some, as today, lived to great ages. Thus if life was short in the Middle Ages, it must be remembered that this life is a statistical concept, an average. Some few lived even as today past the century mark. The length of total life expectation at birth is a much more difficult problem.

Perhaps the most satisfactory life table is that of the period A.D. 750-1000 in table 47. The nearest to the proper totals for infans I and infans II seem to remain for that period, so the estimate for total length of life is not inflated by too few children. The table also shows the longest length of life for a period of the Middle Ages.

V. Potential Energy and Dependency

Potential energy, one of the factors in the dynamics and control of population, is conditioned by several factors, among them: human age and health, climate and supplements of animal and machine power. Considerable numbers of early deaths meant a heavy loss of potential energy. If the percentage of children was high, the requirements of energy for their care was large. If, however, there was more use of animals and machines, there was more energy available to replace human hand labor. If foods which improved human efficiency were produced, further sources of energy were tapped.[1] More energy would be clearly shown in increased percentage of persons living in the cities, since cities rest upon the surplus of human energy available beyond immediate needs of subsistence.[2] For a more immediate index of human energy the life table offers convenient and direct information. One may start with a discussion of age of employment as a factor in potential energy. Employment is used here in the very general sense of useful work.

AGE OF EMPLOYMENT

The poll taxes of the fourteenth century, which presumably were levied primarily upon wage earners, were usually set at fourteen for both men and women.[3] If one entered an apprenticeship of seven years at twelve or thirteen years, he would end it at nineteen or twenty. Guild masters found it to their advantage to postpone the finish of apprenticeship in order to get as much of the young men's labor as possible before they began paying them.[4] Both in shops and for servants in homes, work was doubtless more exacting than the simple duties on the farm for the less skilled.

Many English manors, however, set twelve as the age at which the penny was exacted once a year for boys when they entered the tithings and their responsibilities.[5] Feudal pages apparently started earlier—to judge from Scarborough death rates in the five-nine year group.[6] At the International Economic History Congress ten was preferred as a proper age for an estimate of the beginning of

---

[1]Few new foods appeared, so a book on ancient foods is relevant: Don and Patricia Brothwell, *Food in Antiquity* (New York, 1969); Bullough and Cameron, 1980: 317-320.

[2]For size of cities and demographic relations: Russell, 1972, esp. 275.

[3]Russell, 1948: 118-146; Russell, 1958: 47-52.

[4]Thrupp 1948: 192-194. (See note 24 below)

[5]W. A. Morris, *The Frankpledge System* (Cambridge, Mass., 1910), 14, 70. There were exceptions.

[6]Todd 1927: 497 The number of deaths jumped so markedly at the early age, presumably because pages were hired at an early age.

labor for farm children—it is accepted here.[7] It means allowing the infans II period (7-13 years) to be divided between dependency and employability. Isidore, it will be remembered, set fourteen as the beginning of youth,[8] a period which would continue to age twenty-eight. Feudal lords had even more reason for postponing the coming of age of male heirs which took them out of wardship and cost the lords a highly profitable right. It is rather odd that until recently democracies retained this high age just because greedy feudal lords had established it for their own profit. The Romans set seventeen as the age that boys entered the army and modern societies in spite of their preference for twenty-one as voting age have usually set eighteen as the age for conscription into the army.

Isidore is not so helpful in setting limits to an active life. He set it at seventy but apparently had in mind intellectual activity.[9] Sixty is a more common age for letting men out of responsibilities on the manor and elsewhere.[10] The problem is that the health of men varied so widely. Many suffered from arthritis and other afflictions reduced their efficiency or caused them to retire. Sixty would seem

---

Table 22

Employability: Percentage Alive 10 or 20 to 60.

Period	All (10-60)	All (20-60)	All (20-60)	Females (20-60)
I (1-540)	59.2	55.8	58.1	56.0
II (540-750)	56.2	49.6	52.1	48.7
III (750-1000)	55.0	58.4	63.6	62.0
IV (1000-1348)	57.5	61.0	61.0	57.9
V (1348-1500)	51.1	49.5	51.0	48.8

Sources: for period 1 table 44; for period 2 table 34; for period 3 table 47; for period 4 table 49; for period 5 table 35.

---

[7]At Munich August, 1965 I suggested fourteen as the limit of dependency. The suggestion was subjected to severe and informed criticism. The paper, somewhat revised, reappeared as the "Effects of Pestilence and Plague," *Comparative Studies in Society and History* 8 (1966): 464-473. It is followed by a discussion of the paper by S. Thrupp, 474-483. Article by D. Herlihy in *The Medieval City* (New Haven, 1977), 17-20. Also P. Riche, "L'enfant dans le haut moyen age," *Annales de demographie historique* 1973: 95-98. Among the Visigoths the majority was at age fourteen, among the Anglo-Saxons and Burgundians, fifteen. Cf. also Herlihy & Klapisch-Zuber, 1978: 375, 571-578.

[8]Isidore, *Etym.* XI, ii, 4.

[9]Isidore, *Etym.* XI, ii, 6-8.

[10]Russell, 1948: 293. Probably sixty.

to be a good average. The age for women is not so clear. Sixty is also set for them although a case could be made for a lesser number of years.

We assume that the ages of dependence were from birth to about ten and from sixty to death, leaving about fifty years as the age of potential energy. Actually, during the years from ten to sixty many were ill and others unable to work because of various disabilities. What we wish to know is how much of the time between ten and sixty years of age persons were actually able to work, assuming that they could only work then. The actual number of years lived is given in the T_x column of the life table. By dividing the actual number by the potential a percentage can be secured. This is done in table 23 for the five periods of time covered by this study. Since data are scarce for the years from ten to fourteen and the sex not carefully determined, a separate test for the persons by sex is given for each period from age twenty to sixty.

The period of longest employability was between A.D. 750 and 1000. The data represent best the conditions in Hungary and central Europe and may not be accurate for western Europe. The decline in years of work may have been due to shifting from a pastoral economy to one based on the plow in central Europe in that period. Even in the west there was a shift to a heavier plow which may have forced more hard work from the plowmen. One interesting feature is the closeness of the figures for the two plague periods and their sharp differences from the nonplague areas and times. The position of women seems to have been best in the third period (750-1000). From the standpoint of health in the areas outlined, the third period must have been a kind of golden age, even if historians have described it as a dark age.

The figure for "all" include some who were identified only by age and not by sex. Furthermore,, it must be remembered that the numbers for age groups are not strictly comparable since the geographical areas differ from period to period, as a result of the availability of data. The ancient-medieval figures of from 51 to 67 percent is very different from the figure of more than 94 percent for the United States of 1949-1950. The figure for U.S. employability is about the same for other European and some other nations today. Perhaps the improvement in living conditions is shown better in these figures than in others.

In general the heavy loss of employability during the plague periods stands out. Not only was there the well-known high mortality but also those who were left suffered heavier losses than the population in normal times, thus creating severe placement problems. Furthermore, the ratios of employment varied for men and women. Women were hit harder in the first plague (A.D. 542-750) but also recovered faster in the succeeding period. After

A. D. 750, however, women did much worse than men. The period of best health from ten to sixty seems to have been the postplague period for women and from A.D. 1000 to the second plague for men. The record of the two plague periods would also tend to show that men suffered more in the late medieval plague than did women, as people of that time alleged.

The problems of determining the amount of dependency is complicated by the failure of anthropologists to distinguish males from females in children and also because a large number of them disappeared from the cemeteries. The best evidence of the type needed comes from Mikulcice of the ninth century. It places the dependency rate at about 30 percent. There are some curious deviations from the 30 percent figure, for example, the Italian cities of Pozzuoli and Pistoia, which show an unbelievable number of persons over sixty. The records were as inaccurate as the North African Roman cities except they seldom list a person as a centenarian. And at Reims the number of the dependents is very low. The second plague period shows also a very high number of older persons, but that also occurred among the English landholders where the data is about as good as can be secured. Apparently the plague did lead to an increase in the percentage of older persons, perhaps because it killed so many of the young ones.

It cannot then be said that the burden of raising children was heavy in the Middle Ages. The greatest loss was obviously the high death rates among the adult persons. Enough older persons lived so that there was no loss of experienced persons. In the Italian cities it would seem that it was a privilege to be an older person. There is a possibility that some of the advances of the Renaissance were the result of the large number of experienced persons in the population.

Data about favorable health conditions of the Mediterranean rests partly upon the exceptional length of life recorded in the Canary Islands. The total evidence for the first region is not extensive and is important only for certain times (tables 15, 16). There is little evidence from Mediterranean cemeteries after A.D. 1000. The last period, marked by the Black Death, found conditions very bad (table 23). For the first period the Roman inscriptions show North Africa with the best health and energy. After the first period, unfortunately, there is no data for North Africa.

It is surprising that the next healthiest areas were the extreme northern countries: Scandinavia, Britain, and Poland. The first two were aided by the Gulf Stream and probably did not suffer from extremes of weather as did Central Europe. Poland may have benefited by its isolation during most of the Middle Ages. The better climate of Scandinavia would tend to explain why it provided so many of the tribes which spread out and conquered much of Europe in the early Middle Ages. The area profited from

Table 23

Dependency: Percentage of Persons 0-10 and 60 on of Total.

Area	Date	0-10	60+	All Dependents	Total Population	Percentage Dependency
Europe	1-542	30208	2610	32818	118717	27.6
Europe	542-740	43887	2080	45967	148067	31.0
Europe	750-1000	94527	8460	102987	323872	31.8
Europe	1000-1348	87428	7100	94528	294528	32.1
Europe	1348-1500	23103	1420	24103	70957	33.9
Mikulcice	9c.	15947	390	16337	55114	29.6
Reims, male	1421	95	25	120	630	19.0
Reims, female	1421	108	21	129	638	20.2
Pistoia male	1427	2517	1150	3667	8306	44.1
Pistoia female	1427	2110	1040	3155	7469	42.2
Florence male	1427	5460	1893	7853	19953	39.4
Florence female	1427	4903	2080	6983	16956	41.2
Tuscany, contado, male	1427	39544	19954	59298	137993	43.0
Tuscany, contado, female	1427	32356	18209	50565	125645	40.2
Pozzuoli, male	1487	428	53	481	1395	34.5
Puzzuoli, female	1487	352	74	426	1133	37.6

Sources: Europe 1-542, table 43; Europe 542-750, table 34; Europe 750-1000, table 35. Mikulcice, table 5; Reims, Desportes 1966; Pistoia, Herlihy, 1967, appendix 2; Florence and Tuscany, Herlihy & Klapisch-Zuber, 656-663. Pozzuoli, Beloch, 1937, 29-31.

the quite warm climate which Europe enjoyed for much of that period. The combination of a people ready to expand and a favorable set of political conditions may have been responsible for the outpouring of Germanic tribes from that area.

HUMAN SIZE AND INVENTIONS

Man's physical makeup is a factor in human control of population. The largest concentration of population in the late ancient and medieval world was near the Mediterranean. Circa A.D. 350 there were about twelve million people near that sea: roughly four in North Africa, four in Italy and Iberia and two in southern Gaul. North of these countries there were three million in northern Gaul, three and a half in Germany and Scandinavia, three hundred thousand in Britain, and uncertain numbers to the east. The population of the Mediterranean area was well organized in the Roman Empire and should have been able to keep the northerners out.

However, the Germans and Slavs had an advantage in height and weight. Mediterranean men, on the average, were about 1.57 meters in height (five feet, two inches) and weighed about 54.4 kilos (120 pounds). Germans were nearly six inches taller (1.73 meters in height) and weighed eighteen kilos more. The Slavs, (to judge from samples) were somewhat shorter (1.67-1.68 meters) and probably heavier, since they tended to be broad of shoulders. The advantage in weight is obvious; the advantage in height, though only a few inches placed the eyes well above those of opponents of the south.[11]

Of course, the original technical advantages of the Romans offset the superior height and weight of the northern men, but as Germans joined the Roman armies in ever greater numbers, they too acquired technical knowledge. As Germans migrated, armies of Germans moved south but they numbered in the low hundred thousands and only slightly raised the overall stature of the south. The factor of size thus has to be considered.

An interesting anthropological study has suggested that a shortening of the skull (brachycephalization) occurred to a considerable extent in the late ancient-medieval period.[12] One might assume

---

[11]Wiedrcinska, 1973, 373-377.

[12]F. Weidenreich, "The Brachycephalization of Recent Mankind," *Southwestern Journal of Anthropology* 1 (1945), esp. p. 27 for great change at the end of the ancient and beginning of the medieval period. He suggests that two factors (expansion of the brain and adjustment to erect posture) probably determined the change. "It may well be that the conditions of life and nutrition—dearth or abundance of iodine or calcium or other substances—influence the skull form of individuals." (p. 47). N. Lahovary, "Les brachycéphales et la question de la brachycéphales progressives," *Bulletin der schweitzerische Gesellschaft für Anthropologie und Enthnologie* 23 (1946—1947): 23-63; Schwidetsky, *Annales Historico-Naturalis Musei Nationalis Hungarici* 71 (1960): 357-359; 72

that this was part of a general reshaping of the human figure to produce a sturdier body with relatively less accentuation of arms and legs. The change from dependence on animals (herding, hunting) to a plow culture was partly responsible for the change. Technically, it might even have been the reason for a shortening of life, since the plow would entail heavier physical labor for men and women.

The change in the shape of the head to a broader, shorter form might have resulted from an alteration in function of nose and jaw. The notable warming of the climate, particularly if accompanied by dampness, might shorten and widen the nose. The presence of long sustained diseases, bringing with them high temperatures, might have aided in the change. Similarly the substitution of more grain for meat may have lessened the need for powerful jaws. Apparently few new foods came to Europe then, although the use of legumes seems to have increased, notably in the tenth century.[13] A lack of iron was a distinct problem, especially for women.[14]

The implications of such inventions as better harnesses, horse collars and horse shoes need further study, particularly as they affect human health. These, however, were to be offset by the smaller farms for large populations, necessitating heavier labor, developed under pressure by feudal lords in the tenth to fourteenth centuries.[15] The lords were largely responsible, along with monastic institutions, for the development of mills and their fish ponds, which contributed to a better diet. Animal husbandry apparently declined with the fall of the Roman Empire.[16] The emphasis of feudal society upon the horse should have produced some results in the breeding of the war horse. Horses seem to have been used more for plowing as the agriculture became more intensive in the later Middle Ages.

The Romans had developed a good heating system for houses but it was lost in succeeding centuries. The earlier cottages were often very small, dug well into the earth with a fire in the center of the room. They must have been quite as comfortably warm as the windy, large open halls of the nobles and gentry.[17] In the colder parts of the continent conditions favored a sort of semi-hibernation during the winter. To meet the increasing chill of the later

---

(1970): 369; I Kiszely, "Representation of the Longobard Man in the Light of Anthropological Funds," *Acta Facultatis Rerum Naturaïum U. Comanianae Anthropologia* 20 (1976): 123—125.

[13]Brothwell 1969. Not many additions to the ancient diet.

[14]Bullough & Cameron, 1980: 317-323.

[15]See below pp. 177-179

[16]S. Bokinyi, " The Development and History of Domestic Animals in Hungary," *Annales Historico-Naturales Musei Nationaiis Hungarici* 73 (1971): 640-754; R. Trow-Smith, *A History of the British Livestock Industry to 1700* (London, 1957); lists of *bubulci* (ox-drivers) with number of oxen each owned: M. C. Ragut, *Cartulaire de S. Vincent de Macon* (Macon, 1864), 20. Early 12c. 2 oxen, 1; 3 oxen, 3; 4 oxen, 6; 5 oxen, 8; 8 oxen, 1.

[17]See ch. III, note 6 above.

Middle Ages people wore clothing as a kind of second skin. The problem of the summer heat was not so serious: shade and night were the most helpful. The Little Ice Age produced a serious decline in temperature from the end of the thirteenth century.[18]

The question of the amount of energy needed to meet the requirements of church and state are important. The church eventually received a tenth of the income of adherents and varying amounts of other bequests and gifts. A. H. M. Jones thought that the very heavy imperial taxes were a factor in Rome's decline. The cities also have been thought to have been parasitic, but that idea is in part the result of overestimating urban population.[19] These are topics treated here quite cursorally but which need further study.

DEPENDENCY

Dependency is the burden carried by society for those who are too young, too old or too feeble to contribute their share of society's work. It is assumed that the "too old" are over sixty and the "too young" under ten years of age. Estimates of dependency can be secured from the life tables. Unfortunately, the numbers of the dependents are among the least trustworthy because of the tendency to overestimate the ages of the very elderly and lack of interest in the very young. The index of dependency is secured by adding the L_x the number of infans I age, one-half of the L_x number for infans II and the L_x number for senilis and dividing that total by the T_o number, the number at the top of that column. The tendency will be to underestimate the number. The estimates are:

Entire period, all areas	30.1
I (A.D. 1-542)	31.2
II (542—750)	30.8
III (750-1000)	31.8
IV (1000-1348)	27.1
V (1348-1500)	34.6

About the best information, certainly the most complete, is from the study of the Great Moravian city of Mikulcice, from the late eight and ninth centuries.[20] Its index is 31.6 and thus very close to the other estimates. The estimates do not vary greatly between the plague and nonplague figures and thus seem to be a medieval standard of about 30 percent.

Other evidence for the fifteenth century plague period shows a higher dependency rate. Pistoia had a rate of 43.2 percent for men

---

[18]See ch. XIII, figure 1.

[19]A. M. H. Jones, *The Later Roman Empire*, 284-602 (Norman, 1964): 465-468. See table 5.

and 45.4 for women. The countryside had a rate of 42.5 and 47.5 for the city itself.[21] The landholders of England had a very low 28.0 preplague rate but the generation born in 1348-1375 had the high rate of 49.9.[22] However, in both the plague periods the population was declining for several generations. This should have been as a result of fewer children and a lowering of the index. In the preplague period of the later Middle Ages, the population was increasing, producing more children and raising the index. The result should have been to bend the rates toward the middle, at about a third in nonplague periods and two-fifths in plague times. This is roughly the same today. In 1949-1950, the United States had a ratio of 31.2 for the same age limits.[23] However, dependency today lasts much longer and is more burdensome to parents, since children require a longer period of education and care.

At the other end of active lives there was a more gradual transition to retirement than there is today, where sudden ending of a life work is often a traumatic experience. London merchants seem to have felt old age coming on in their fifties and they retired gradually as their sons or other heirs took their places in the guilds.[24] About an eighth of the men on the Winchester manors retired early, which would place their retirement at about the age of sixty.[25] Often the retiree left the house to his son or son-in-law or other heirs and moved into a cottage on the edge of the village. His successor in the holding then was able to marry and assume full status as a member of the farming community. The cottages were simple to construct and probably not very substantial, but the older folk were masters of their own homes and had the dignity of ownership. In the later Middle Ages, and in some places earlier, older persons lived in the same houses with their children, partly because of colder weather which seemed to call for more durable dwellings. It may be because inhabitants of cottages seemed to die in greater numbers than those in larger houses and larger families.[26] The results of living under the same roof were often bad. Tensions which developed may have been a factor in the rise of the witchcraft mania then. The move to a cottage usually carried with it the right to a small garden and perhaps a few acres, or even a portion of the returns from the old holding. As retired parents passed away, the newly born children succeeded to the portions of their grandparents.

---

[21]Herlihy, 1967. See table 24.

[22] Russell, 1948: pp. 180—186.

[23]William Petersen, *Population* (New York, 2nd ed.) 211.

[24]S. Thrupp, *The Merchant Class of Medieval London 1300-1500* (Chicago, 1948), 192-194.

[25]M. Postan and J. Titow, "Heriots and Prices on Winchester Manors," *Economic History Review,* second ser. 11 (1959): 398-409.

[26]This agrees with other evidence, see pp. 228-229.

Normally a widow with a dependent child or two would be willing to move into a cottage while her son or son-in-law took over the working of her estate. Often when a woman of forty or so inherited a farm holding, the bailiff of the manor would offer her in marriage to someone who would till the farm—there being no scruples about a young man marrying a much older woman. There were advantages in that there would be few children to raise. In general the wishes of women, especially widows were respected.

Dependency includes also those mentally retarded and the insane. Places were usually found for the retarded as herders, for instance. Indeed, herder might connote mental slowness. At their best in simple repetitive jobs, the retarded were often ideal for this important task, since they did not mind the monotony of the work and found comfort in association with the animals and in the importance of their duties. The conditions of the insane are not so certain since they exhibited a wide variety of conditions and were not so docile. The cities were obviously not suitable for them nor for the retarded who were subject to ridicule when they did not adjust easily to circumstances. There was less scope for their activities and more occasions for the rise of tension. During a plague, a highly emotional time at best, unusual persons aroused feelings of distrust or fear, leading to accusations and persecutions for witchcraft.

The effects of medical care in the late ancient and medieval world are hard to assess. Before the nineteenth century development of sanitation, surgery, and bacteriology, it must have been modest at best. Many doctors prescribed a variety of remedies and most people got well naturally, attributing their recovery to the doctors, then as now. These doctors doubtless thought that they were responsible. However, the doctors had one relatively simple problem in handling tuberculosis, probably the most common illness, for rest and good food (the rest cure) was needed—so simple that anyone could have ascertained it, but apparently none did. Probably the medical profession was most successful on the psychosomatic side, giving confidence to the ill when they needed it. They could diagnose many illnesses but seldom had a remedy which would be regarded as effective today. One story has come down to us from the fourteenth century. In France the graduates of the medical schools refused to permit a woman to practice medicine although she charged nothing, and many testified that she was an effective practitioner, curing many cases in which the regular doctors had failed. In another instance a woman who tried to practice medicine was apparently buried alive.[27]

---

[27]P. Kibre, "The Faculty of Medicine at Paris, Charlatanism and Unlicensed Practices in the Later Middle Ages," *Bulletin of the History of Medicine*, 27 (1953): 9-12.

Only in the Greek east did institutions develop which resembled hospitals for the ill. Hospices for travelers, both pagan and Christian, were fairly common, needed by the traveling public of the ancient and medieval world. The hospitals of the West were apparently derived from Byzantine models, of which the most successful and effective were those of the Order of the Hospital St. John. [28] The hospitals were at best only moderately effective. When the need was for food and careful attention, they succeeded. The problem was that, until the nineteenth century, medicine itself could really offer little. Furthermore, the concentration of disease within the walls of hospices and hospitals was a very effective way of spreading disease, in view of the lack of careful sanitation. For the unattended and the poor they were satisfying refuges. The medieval hospitals must be classed as social institutions rather than medical.

LESSER DISEASES

The great destroyers of the period, tuberculosis and the bubonic plague, will be taken up later. For other diseases the problem of identification and effects are not easy: there were so many of them with symptoms often similar to each other: rising temperatures, sore throats, aches, and pains. Most diagnoses must be based upon statements, written in documents or literary works. Since with very rare exceptions, only skeletons survive, the conditions of only the bones remain. At Westerhus in very poor climatic conditions in Scandinavia, rickets were not evident although the infantile mortality was very high. Gjevall suggests that breast feeding kept the incidence of rickets low. Many cases of disc degeneration occur in skeletal evidence which show that backache must have been a most common complaint. At least a third of adults had pathological conditions of the skeleton. Teeth, however, were in surprisingly good condition at many places but not so satisfactory at others. This study includes only a few of the many comments upon bone appearances, a topic upon which very much more might be written. In general, the conditions of teeth seem to have been better than at present, perhaps even a little better in the medieval than in the ancient world.[29]

[28]T. S. Miller, Knights of St. John and the Hospitals of the Latin West," *Speculum* 53 (1978): 708-733.

[29]Gejvall 1960; W. F. Loomis, "Rickets," *Scientific American* 223, no. 6: pp. 72-71. In general see Calvin Wells, *Bones, Bodies and Diseases* (New York, 1964). For teeth, pp. 122-125, especially figure 19, about incidence of dental caries. I. Tattersall, "Dental Paleopathology for Medieval Britain," *Journal of the History of Medicine and Allied Sciences* 23 (1938): 380-385; Malinowski 1966: Malinowski & Wybych, 1966 (bad teeth); Stenberger, 1953 (good teeth): Stloukal, 1963.

Disease and accidents were important causes of temporary and permanent dependence, yet direct information about them in the ancient and medieval world is scanty. Medical writers often described them accurately but give few indications of mortality rates. Chroniclers and others are notoriously generous in their attribution of numbers in epidemics. "So many died that the living could hardly bury the dead," occasionally was remarked. The plague is the easiest to follow because it treated severe alterations in the age and sex setup of the population as well as of time of death. Tuberculosis was probably the most common deadly disease and can be detected by its very heavy mortality in the fifteen to forty-year age group. Other epidemics occurred but are hard to identify. Smallpox (variola) should have been easy to identify and occasionally occurred.

Increased accuracy in the study of skeletal remains has advanced knowledge of pathological conditions beyond the obvious incidence of broken bones, arthritis, and similar conditions. Upon two well known epidemics more may be said tentatively: the first concerns the second and third century epidemics which spread over the Roman Empire; the other is the edipemic which accompanied the famine of 1315-1317, probably the most serious epidemic between the two great plagues. Something also may be said about the incidence of appendicitis.

The epidemics of the second and third century have been the subject of a fine study by J.G. Gilliam, who stresses that information about them comes from later and less reliable chroniclers who probably exaggerated.[30] No description is available and these epidemics probably had no outstanding characteristics such as those of small pox which was apparently picked up in Seleucia, the valley of Mesopotamia, and brought back first to Rome and then to Gaul and Germany. Galen saw it in Rome and later among the troops at Aquileia. One possibility is that it was the more severe form of malaria, the one associated with warmer climates. Now, if the epidemic was carried to Gaul and the Rhineland by soldiers, it should have been there in the late second and third centuries, when inscriptions show very poor expectation of life in those areas. Again in the damp and hot sixth century, malignant malaria was rampant in those areas. The weather seems to have been exceptionally warm then. And evidence about malignant malaria seems to die out in the seventh century, particularly in Gaul. The terrible conditions of health in Rome and Latium must have been in part the result of this malignant malaria. While it is devastating

[30]J. G. Gilliam, "The plague under Marcus Aurelius," *American Journal of Philology* 82 (1961): 225-251.

[31]"Malaria," *Encyclopaedia Britannica*, 14th ed. 1930, p. 707; S. F. Kitchen, "Falciparum Malaria" in *Malariology*, ed. (Philadelphia, 1949): 995-1026.

to the young, it affects all and is a seriously debilitating disease, weakening people so that they fall victim to other sickness. That it moved with the army from Seleucia to Italy suggests that it was carried in the human system, like malaria.

Certain areas seem to have had a higher rate of mortality between twenty and forty than even the 60 percent tuberculosis could account for. This was true at Rome, Ostia, Aquileia, and Milan as well as at Salona in Dalmatia. The cities of Gaul, Arles, Bordeaux, Lyon and Vienne all had a mortality of over 70 percent, but this dropped later in the north. The mortality however, in Italy, remained high.

This might be attributed to P. falciparum, the most malignant form of malaria which spreads best in areas of high temperature, such as in Italy but is rare north of the Alps. Of course, one might expect that as a form of malaria, it would be recognized and described as such by writers of the time because of its occurrence at regular two, three or four day intervals. However, P. falciparum "does not tend to the chronicity in the absence of reinfection as do other forms."[31] So its clinical relationship with other forms of malaria may not have been recognized. The disease could have been carried easily by soldiers since it presumably remained with a carrier a long time. The high mortality at the Roman army camps at Carnuntum, (near Vienna) (between twenty and forty of 55.6 for males and 77.8 for females) and at Trentholm near York, England (66.0 for males and 84.0 for females) seem to indicate malignant malaria as well as tuberculosis.[32] At both places the mortality should have been low, given the favorable climatic conditions. Conditions outside of the cities and camps were much better then.

The later history of malignant malaria seems to have been what might have been expected. It remained endemic in the Po Valley, at Rome and elsewhere in Italy where the high temperature kept it alive. It was a terrible menace to pilgrims going to Rome from the north and to northern armies coming to help crown Holy Roman Emperors at Rome.[33] Perhaps with the rise in temperature in the fifth and sixth centuries, it reentered southern Gaul: many miracles involving malaria occurred then. Like tuberculosis it was not as prevalent in the mountainous areas as it was on the plains.

One result of malignant malaria may have been the movement of villages to higher levels, creating those picturesque Italian hill towns. This would have been largely from A.D. 180 to about 300—the period of the civil wars, which would have been a contributing factor, especially along the great Roman highways

---

[32]Kloiber, 1957, 1962. Warwick and Wenham, 1968.

[33]A. Celli, *The History of Malaria in the Roman Campagna* (London, 1933): chs. 2-6.

subjected to pillage by passing soldiers as well as by invaders from outside of the Empire. The solution was to live in new villages above the level of the mosquitoes and to be protected by town walls.

The pestilence and famine of 1315-1317 were probably the causes of the worst catastrophe which the Middle Ages experienced between the two great medieval plague periods of 542-750 and 1348-1500. A good account of this has been written based largely upon the reports of the chroniclers who tended to accept rumors as facts and featured the more lurid stories of the time.[34] According to them, in 1316 even in England the living could scarcely bury the dead and parents ate their children. Official accounts of that year show that from May to October some two thousand died in Bruges and three thousand in Ypres. There is a problem here of the proportion of the population from which the dead were counted: was the mortality merely from the cities or did the dead also include the starving who came in from the countryside, often from considerable distances? Other sources from England seem to give reasonably accurate accounts of the mortality. The data about peasants on the manors of the bishopric of Winchester show about a 25 percent mortality for the decade 1310-1319 and this tallies with the expectation of fiefholders in England in the same period.[35] This mortality was enough to halt the increase of population and perhaps to even reduce it slightly.

The pestilence in England is described by the chronicler, Trokelawe, as a "dysentery" which brought acute fever and suffering of the throat (gutturosa). However, dysentery suggests that 'gutturosa' should read "guttosa," that is, of the intestines.[36] The attribution to bad food as the cause suggests a short time for incubation, indicating bacillary dysentery rather than amoebic. Indeed, the symptoms of bacillary dysentery are much like those of food poisoning. Of course a diagnosis of a disease from medieval statements is always hazardous, but in this case the attribution of the age of victims seems appropriate to dysentery. The particular type of dysentery was probably the sonne, which is said to appear in epidemic form in temperate climate and to be prevalent particularly in England. It has a high rate of carriers (20 percent).[37]

---

[34]H. S. Lucas, "The Great European Famine of 1315, 1316 and 1317," *Speculum* 5 (1931): 343-77, esp. pp. 355-357. For the Ypres and Bruges data, H. van Werveke, "La famine de l' an 1316 en Flandre et des les regions voisins," *Revue du Nord* 41 (1959): 5-14.

[35]Postan & Titow, 1958 and note following by P. Longden, 417. For fiefholders, computation cards on the data of their lives, Russell, 1966, 468-469.

[36]*Chronica Monasterii S. Albani* (Rolls Series) 3: 94. For use of "guttosa" see NED under "gut". It would be natural to correct from a less common word (guttosa) to a more common one (gutturosa) by a copyist, assuming that a dash for "ur" had been omitted carelessly in the original.

[37]R. J. Dubos, ed. *Bacterial and Mycotic Infections of Man* (3rd ed. Baltimore, 1957), 350-3B7; Manson-Baur, *Synopsis of Tropical Diseases* (Baltimore, 1943), 79-83.

However, the pestilence, presumably of the same type, touched all of Europe from Tuscany northward. The waterlogged condition of the soil in that continent after the long rains of 1315 and 1316 and consequent poor conditions of food, particularly among those crowded into the cities, offered ideal conditions for the spread of the disease. The course of the Bruges and Ypres epidemics shows that it was largely a spring and summer epidemic in 1316, as it was in the high mortality years of 1322, 1323 and 1324 in Britain.[38] The age and mortality seem appropriate to dysentery but the slight evidence does not show such child mortality.

Today dysentery is described as a "frequently terminal infection in other debilitating diseases, such as malaria and tuberculosis."[39] The sample from the fiefholder mortality seems to confirm this. The average number of deaths for the years in the group for 1313 and 1314 was about 51 with 1315 showing only 42. However, 1316 and 1317 show 68 and 62 deaths respectively, while the average for the four years following was only about 43. Thus the pestilence (since the famine could hardly have affected the fiefholders) merely eliminated a little earlier those who would normally have died in 1318—1321. Even the very high mortality at Bruges and Ypres may probably be regarded as a proportion of the half-million or so persons living in Flanders rather than just the thousands of the two cities. The starving of the countryside seem to have drifted into the cities seeking both urban and monastic charity, according to contemporary accounts.[40]

The effects of the pestilence and famine do not seem to have been permanent. In England the percentage of the survival of children in 1320-1335 was as good as for any earlier period of the years 1255-1346: the death rate among children in 1315-1317 can hardly have been very high, though dysentery usually brings severe child mortality.[41] It is possible that for children as for adults the disease struck them a little earlier than other normal serious diseases. The economy of Europe recovered in the harvest of 1318 and was apparently quite stable until 1348. The life table for 1340-1342 shows a lesser mortality than for either 1280-1282 or for 1310-1312.[42] Since many people suffered from either malaria or tuberculosis, the pestilence of 1315—1317 merely hurried them to their deaths.

---

[38]Using dates of death in *Calendars of Inquisitions post Mortem* vols. V Rd VI (English Public Record Office.)

[39]Manson-Baur, 79.

[40]As in note 21.

[41]Lucas, 369, 363 and 375 respectively.

[42]Russell, 1948, 190-191. "The use of cow's milk was ideal to spread both dysentery and enteritis but nursing by women probably prevented the wide spread of other diseases." C. Wells, *Bones, Bodies and Diseases,* 107-108.

Like food poisoning, acute appendicitis probably caused more deaths in the late ancient and medieval world than is usually recognized. Today careful diagnosis and early surgery have reduced this to a relatively minor place among the causes of illness and death, but in the earlier period most cases would probably have been fatal. Since its cause was not known, the food or other poisoning were usually blamed. King Stephen apparently died of appendicitis, while his son, Eustace, had the proper symptoms for it. Appendicitis does run in families. The diet of nobility and royalty ran heavily to meat and avoided the more bulky vegetable foods which seem effective in preventing appendicitis. It frequently struck persons in the best of health and often when asleep, leading to the belief that a person was poisoned by his enemies. If one can assume that as large a proportion of persons who are now hospitalized for appendicitis would have died of it before modern times, the mortality might run as high as four or five percent, which would make it a rather deadly disease.[43]

The study of the potential years of labor and the periods of dependency show that the healthier periods in the north of Europe were between the great plague of Justinian and the Black Death of 1348. The healthiest of all areas was North Africa in the later Roman Empire with the Canary Islands nearly as free from sickness. The vitality of the people was strongest, not in the times usually considered the "greatest," the thirteenth century, the early Roman Empire and the Renaissance, but in earlier more uncomplicated societies. Perhaps that is the price of "progress," as the term is usually understood. And the idea of a "golden age" in the past has some basis in fact.[44]

---

[43]Russell, 1978, 87, 89-90.
[44]There seem few studies of the health of the Middle Ages. Examples are: M. Stloukal, "Die Gesundheitsausstand des Gebisses bei der Population von Grössmahrischen Mikulcice," *Anthropologie* 1 (1963: Prague): 3541. Acsádi-Nemeskéri, 1970; 254-262; Bullough & Cameron, 1980.

VI. The Spread of Tuberculosis in the West

Until about A.D. 1912 tuberculosis was the greatest killer in the West with the exception of the plague, yet its history is not too clear. One of its less common forms, Pott's Deformity, (spinal collapse) can be detected in skeletal evidence but does not appear in the West until A.D. 400-1000.[1] Perhaps it had appeared even earlier among the Chinese and Indians.[2] The description of the disease by Hippocrates (about 300 B.C.) suggests a widespread epidemic form, the old "galloping consumption" and thus was probably a new disease in the west, since diseases are usually more lethal when they first appear.[3] He noted that the most afflicted age was between eighteen and thirty-five years, and that a combination of it with malaria was unusually dangerous.[4] In the first century A.D. Celsus wrote more about it, as did Galen in the second century. Their descriptions are so accurate that there is no doubt about identification of the disease. The very widely distributed *Etymologies* of Isidore of Seville (sixth century) repeated this information and added that it was called 'phthysis' in Greek because it consumed the body. Following it he said that 'tussis' was so called in Greek because of the depth of the cough. The deep coughing at daybreak of "lungers" is an awful sound of the tuberculosis communities.[5]

The tendency of tuberculosis to peak in the juvenis and adultus periods (14-40 years of age) offers an opportunity to use data of deaths in those periods as indications of its predominance. Even deaths from typhoid fever and child birth in these periods cannot compare with the incidence of tuberculosis.[6] This study assumes that variations in the deaths in those two age periods result primarily from the presence or absence of tuberculosis in the population. After its arrival the doubling or worse of the death rate would show that it was responsible for half or more of the deaths.

EARLY TUBERCULOSIS IN THE WEST

Tuberculosis has a peculiar course. Infants pick it up early and carry it in their system for years, often "breaking down" from it in

---

[1]D. R. Brothwell, "Palaeodemography," in *Biological Aspects of Demography*, ed. W. Brass, pp. 111-130. S. A. Wakeman, *The Conquest of Tuberculosis* (Berkeley, 1966): 16-19, 49-50.

[2]G. Wolff, "Tuberculosis and Civilization," *Human Biology* 10 (1938): 106-120.

[3]*Aphorisms*, ed. W. H. S. Jones (London): at end.

[4]Hippocrates, *Air, Waters, Places* X. *Epidemics*, I, xxiv. Celsus, De Medicina, ed. W. G. Spencer (Cambridge, 1935) 1: 125, 135, 143, 325-353.

[5]Isidore, *Etymologies*, IV, xii, 17.

[6]L. I. Dublin and A. J. Lotka, *Twenty-Five Years of Health Progress* (New York, 1937): 16, 82, 103-104, 359-361, 364-368.

their early twenties. It is not certain what precipitates it, but workers in carefully run sanitoria seldom get it. Conditions of life in childhood and adulthood often determine whether one becomes tubercular, and even then its course varies. With some, the disease runs a rapid course to death. Many struggle with it over several decades, finally dying of other ailments, often pneumonia. A large group overcome it after months or even years.

Tuberculosis seemed to be worse in warm and damp weather and so many went to higher altitudes or drier climates. The rest cure was discovered only at the end of the nineteenth century, and often depended upon the skill of doctors in prescribing the amount of proper rest. The success of doctors was as much a factor in successful cures as that of climate.

City environment was apparently also a negative influence. Presumably families living in cities might develop a resistance to the disease over generations—a slow process because of the time lag in exhibiting the disease and the fact that many had children before they died in their twenties and thirties. Jews are sometimes thought to have built up a resistance to it. A Jewish cemetery at Barcelona does show a relatively low mortality (36 percent) for the period from twenty to forty years, which is in line with the idea.[7] The people in large, arid areas of Roman North Africa show as low or even lower deaths in the period, a fact that can be used only with care, since aridity may also have reduced the incidence of malaria and other diseases.

Several instances of Pre-Roman death rates of the adultus period are given in table 25. These show, in general, that there was a higher mortality, especially for women in places around the Mediterranean than north of the Alps. The mortality of men shows that of those alive at about twenty, 20 to 40 percent were dead by the age of forty. For women, although there seems to have been only a 30 percent mortality at Mezocsat, at least a 50 percent mortality was normal elsewhere. Mezocsat, Hungary, apparently had no tuberculosis yet and, as a nomadic area, the populace was not burdened with heavy field labor.

Athens apparently suffered from tuberculosis during the Classical period but probably did not have it earlier. The later high death rate for women, about two thirds from twenty to forty, after a 20 percent loss in the teens, would seem to indicate this. The problem is that only a third of the men seem to have died in the adultus period. Many young must have lost their lives fighting away from the city and have been buried abroad.

In the centuries following the fourth and fifth centuries at Athens few cemeteries remain. In the West cremation was the

[7]Fusté, 1951.

Table 24
Percent of deaths, ages 20-39 (*adultus*).
Some Pre-Roman Cemeteries.

Place, period	Percent dying, 20-39 years.			Percent dying, 10-19 years.			Acsádi and Nemeskéri, pp.
	Male	*Female*	*Both*	*Male*	*Female*	*Both*	
Tiszapolgar- Basa-tanya, copper age	37.3	38.5	38.			15.6	276-283
Alsonemedi, copper, 1400-1200 B.C.	22.1	54.4	35.2			10.8	282-284
Mezocsat, middle bronze	46.5	64.53	49.7			20.1	285-286
Larna, middle bronze	64.8	80.0	71.3	10	20		212
Lower Austria, bronze age.	42.3	71.0	52.6				
Sarata-Monteoru, bronze (1800-1400)			67.8				214
Athens, late bronze eight cent. B.C.	40.5	56.2	47.3	8.7	20.0		
Mezocsat, early iron	13.54	29.03	19.3			11.0	210
Athens, Classical	34.9	67.7	48.6			20.7	

Data not by Acsádi, and Nemeskéri, 1970 by courtesy of J. Lawrence Angel, Smithsonian Institute.

usual form of caring for the deceased leaving little skeletal data. For this reason it would be particularly valuable if the remains at Pompeii should be examined carefully by physical anthropologists. Perhaps a third of the city died in that awful night when Vesuvius erupted. A survey of the evidence would give a very accurate picture of the age and sex composition as well as other skeletal evidence for the city.[8]

GENERAL OVERVIEW OF MORTALITY, AGES 20-40

Despite the criticism of Roman epigraphic data, they still are the best basis for understanding mortality in the empire.[9] Table 25 gives the figures for the Roman provinces from the inscriptions. Here they appear without regard for time and usually for the entire population. Later they will be discussed in more detail for time and location as well as for sex. The provinces that show the highest mortality were in the areas which were apt to be marshy and wet: Latium, Cisalpine Gaul and Gaul around Narbonne (table 25). There nearly two-thirds of the people between twenty and

Table 25		
Death Rate, Ten-Forty in Roman Provinces.		
Area	*Loss, ages 10-20*	*Loss, ages 20-40*
Low rate		
Africa, both sexes	11.1	32.3
Africa, male, 24	9.9	30.0
Africa, female, 23	12.7	35.6
Medium		
Iberia, both	15.0	51.0
Iberia, male, 18	14.0	44.1
Iberia, female, 17	16.4	55.3
Egypt, 30	18.3	52.0
Aemilia, 27	18.0	52.1
Brutium, 26	22.9	55.1
Asia Minor, 19	19.9	55.4
Calabria, 25	29.3	56.1
High rate		
Narbonne, Gaul, 28	26.1	63.1
Latium, 29	35.8	65.5
Cisalpine Gaul, 20	25.6	66.0

Source: Russell, 1958, pp. 25-29. Numbers are to tables.

---

[8]Chapter I above.
[9]pp. 46-50 above.

forty died in those years. Obviously malaria as well as tuberculosis was rampant as noted by the ancient physicians. The best record was made by the North African provinces with a 35 percent mortality. This is probably a little low since many persons were recorded primarily because they lived to a great age and thus skewed the mortality record downward for those dying before sixty. In between were the rest of the provinces, with a loss of just more than half of the population. The provinces of Iberia did better than others north of the Mediterranean largely because of the high dry Meseta: Egypt, probably because of its dampness in times of irrigation, did not get full benefit of its aridity.

While inscription data tends to come from cities, the cemetery evidence is mostly from the countryside (table 26). It shows a lower mortality for all except the British Isles and Alps. These two areas were dominated, at least for some time, by the Roman armies garrisoned in them—precisely the groups which would be responsible for the spread of tuberculosis. In the period before A.D. 540, tuberculosis was coming into most of Western Europe only slowly and primarily in the cities. Indeed it may be doubted if it got into the Balkan Peninsula or much of the Alpine territory. Similarly both Poland and Scandinavia were largely spared, although the data are rather meager for the first and third periods of time. In general it seems that the small villages of Europe of the north had little tuberculosis, in the cities, however, during most of the Middle Ages there was more. An unfortunate feature of the data is that there are so few for the Mediterranean and France. In both, of course, the primary reason is that few Christian cemeteries have been excavated.

The city of Rome, the largest in the West, at least in the early Middle Ages, also had a very high mortality of the young adults. The Rome of the Empire showed a male mortality from ages twenty to forty of about 61.0 percent while that of the females was 77.0. The loss from ten to twenty years of age was apparently about the same: 32.0 and 31.2.[10] Migration creates problems for the data, of course; few other cities had as high an influx of foreigners as did Rome, although efforts were made to keep them out. Some, like Juvenal, returned to their native villages and cities to die. However, the mortality rates of Latium, lying all around Rome, are as high as those of the city. Only an extensive immigration could have kept up the population of the city and Latium, since they did not adopt the pronatalist policies of the Renaissance areas.

North Africa was in sharp contrast to Rome and Latium. Not much evidence is available for the time immediately preceding the

---

[10]Szilágyi, 1963: 131-132.

Table 26

Mortality Rates between Twenty to Forty Years of Age.

Areas	Period 1 M-F	Period 2 M-F	Period 3 M-F	Period 4 M-F	Period 5 M-F
1 Mediterranean	33.2-58.9		26.4-45.7	41.6-36.8	33.3-50.0*
2 France	33.7-51.1	33.7-53.1	35.3-40.0		
3 Britain	58.1-64.9	66.0-78.3		59.0#	62.6#
4 Germany	48.3-57.0	55.9-54.4	44.3-60.2	46.3-59.3	66.2-59.1*
5 Hungary-Balkan	47.0-38.1	53.0-62.0	34.8-47.0	29.8-51.0	46.9-55.1
6 Alps-Bohemia	33.2-58.9	64.8-63.3	24.6-57.4	35.3-55.4	37.3-59.2
7 Scandinavia	43.9-41.7		47.9-62.2	34.8-37.6	32.8-67.2
8 Poland	42.1-76.5	75.0-71.4*	42.4-58.4	44.4-58.7	44.8-50.2+
	35.9-55.9	56.0-60.1	36.5-41.7	39.1-44.6	45.5-55.2

* Less than one hundred skeletons considered.
# Russell, 1948: pp. 181-185.
+ Simple averages of all but less than one hundred cases;

Roman Empire, but some evidence remains from paleolithic times which indicates that men in some areas of Morocco lived a surprisingly long time.[11] In the caves near Oudja and Taforalt people seemed to have had only a 50 percent loss from twenty to forty years of age and an even more remarkable record of less than 10 percent (8.6) from the age of ten to twenty. It was a healthy area from an early date.

The slow movement of tuberculosis from man to child often with a wait of decades before it appeared tends to make it a local disease with wide variations in incidence and mortality. Whereas some diseases swept over a country in weeks or months, tuberculosis moved more by decades. Fortunately, the data available for North Africa is so extensive that an effort to show the movement of the disease there is worthwhile.

The chance of a child getting the disease from an infected adult, and the probability that something would reduce the resistance of the young person so infected, set up a wide variety of conditions favorable or unfavorable to contracting the disease. Conditions varied greatly. Obviously the spread of the disease would occur primarily in the cities, especially in the larger ones. Conditions of life for the young people would also affect the chance of contracting the disease. Such occupations as mining and factory work in the cities increased susceptibility. The Roman army's travels provided a particularly effective means of spreading it. Youths at seventeen were eligible for the army, just at an age when they might be likely to break down with the disease. At that age they went on exhausting marches and had strenuous physical exercises as part of their military duties, often in areas to which they were not acclimated, thus making them vulnerable to various diseases. They were often housed in barracks in distant army camps and placed in contact with nearby civilian populations. These were ideal conditions for the spread of tuberculosis. The Roman army fought and lived over much of the Mediterranean area, even before the end of the Republic in the first century B.C. There is little evidence about the spread of the disease before the period of the Empire.

The literary men of the first century, especially Cicero, do not mention it. The situation changes in the second century. Pliny mentions it several times, noting especially the discovery of a plant which seemed a specific against tuberculosis. It appears in the writings of Martial, Juvenal, and Vitruvius also. It would seem to have been widespread in Italy in that century. Ammianus Marcellinus commented upon the healthiness of the countryside,

---

[11] Ascádi & Nemeskéri, 1970: 153-154 and 158.

particularly in the mountainous areas.[12] In the period of the empire tuberculosis spread widely.

Breaking down the mortality rate for the adultus period by the two spans of time (1-2 centuries and 3-5 centuries), the city of Rome was particularly hard hit: for men 62.5 and 59.3 and for women 75.2 and 78.5.[13] The tall apartment houses of central Rome must have been perfect breeding places for tuberculosis infection. The situation was even worse in Ostia: 71.2 for men and 85.2 for women.[14] Unlike Rome which had extensive areas of low density housing, Ostia was a mass of apartments. It was probably more frequented by eastern Mediterranean immigrants also. Puteoli also had a high mortality, but Miseunum and Brindisi did much better[15] with a lower mortality than the mass of smaller places in Italy which had a record of 60.7 and 47.4 for men and 68.9 and 64.8 for women.[16] It should be noted that both men and women did better in the second period. A very large percentage of Roman troops came from Italy in the first century A.D. but less from later centuries. Rome was thus a center for the spread of the disease. Merida in Spain was set up in the second century B.C. by Rome as a colony for veterans. It probably reflects the health of Roman soldiers from Italy at that time. If so, their condition must have been rather good since Merida's record for the two imperial periods was 43.2 and 11.1 for men and 52.0 and 52.6 for women: the number of tombs was small, however.[17] Spain was fortunate to have been invaded by Carthaginians among whom the mortality rate was apparently low and by Romans before they were severely infected by tuberculosis. And they had a climate which helped fend off the disease.

NORTH AFRICA, ITALY AND THE BALKANS

The mortality rates for the adultus period of the Roman provinces of North Africa are very low. If one divides the rates into five-year groups, the mode of high mortality (highest point) lies in the 20-29 age groups. The longer tuberculosis exists in a population the later the mode seems to be, presumably because a population tends to build up a resistance against it over time. Tables of black and white mortality from tuberculosis in the United States show that the mode for blacks' mortality lay in the 20-24 year group, while it was highest after thirty years of age for

---

[12]Pliny XX, 46 XXIV, 28; XXVI, 38; XXVIII, 230, XXXI, 62. Martial XI, xxi, 7. Juvenal XIII, 95. Vitruvius II, 9. Ammianus Marcellinus XXVII, 44.
[13]Szilágyi, 1973: 131-132.
[14]Szilágyi, 1963: 133-134.
[15]Szilágyi, 1963: 135-136 and 134-135.
[16]Szilágyi, 1962: 301-303.
[17]Szilágyi, 1973: 144.

both white men and women.[18] Blacks seem to have been exposed to tuberculosis only after they came to America, giving them exposure of only two or three hundred years, while the Whites have been exposed for centuries. If American conditions are comparable to African, the lands of North Africa should have been exposed to tuberculosis for five or more centuries, perhaps even longer. The trade of Carthage with the eastern Mediterranean must have gone back to Phoenician associations of several centuries before Christ. However, transmission of the disease to the interior must have been slowed both by limitations of trade and by climatic conditions unfavorable to the spread of tuberculosis.

The data about North African mortality show that the places of highest mortality were primarily along the great highway from Carthage to Lambaesis and Timgad by way of Sicca Veneria and Theveste, while a second highway from Rusicade to Sitifis by way of Cirta had other centers of high mortality.[19] One problem of ascertaining mortality is that the figures of the Four Colonies (Cirta, Milev, Chullu and Rusicade) are returned as one unit, possibly obscuring a higher mortality for the two larger cities. Other cities of high mortality: Sigus, Caesarea and Carthage were naturally exposed as coastal cities to influences from the east. Two unusual characteristics of the North African data are that the differences between male and female mortality rates are not large and that these rates do not differ much with respect to the two periods of time. However, the difference in mortality grew in the age period ten through fourteen years during the third-fifth centuries, probably the result of other than tuberculosis. Some of the higher mortality may have resulted from the presence of Roman army camps, such as that of Lambaesis near Timgad.

The experience of North Africa would suggest that it did not get tuberculosis from central Africa. The disease only went to the interior of Africa in the last century or so. The tubercular bacillus does not stand up well under direct sunlight, which, of course, the Berber settlements and villages were subjected to.

In the north of Italy the mortality of three cities, Aquileia. Milan and Ravenna, can be compared with that of the sum of the data from the smaller places.[20] The average of the 20-40 mortality as a whole was 58.8, very high and indicative of tuberculosis, probably with malaria as an aggravating factor. For males the average for the first two centuries was a high 60.5 which dropped to 47.8 for the succeeding three centuries. For women the rate arose from 65.2 to

---

[18]Dublin and Lotka (note 6): 16 and 82.

[19]See table 27.

[20]For the smaller Italian cities: Szilágyi, 1962: 301-302. Aquileia 297-298; Milan 299-300; Ravenna 300-301.

Table 27

Percentage of Mortality of Adultus Period (20-39 years) of Roman North Africa I-II and III-V Centuries.

City	Centuries I-II		Centuries III-V		Pages*
	Male	Female	Male	Female	
Altava	50.0	33.3	25.0	36.7	261
Ammaedara	34.5	41.2	26.7	43.2	241
Arsacal	20.0	20.0	20.3	23.9	249
Auzia	21.7	35.3	17.6	44.4	248
Caesarea	46.7	73.3	44.8	45.2	247
Calama	47.8	42.9	30.9	31.9	250
Castellum Celitanum	16.6	21.0	18.3	18.1	313
Castellum Tidditanorum	30.5	35.4	25.6	30.7	237
Carthage	44.1	58.3	41.8	50.3	315
Four Colonies	31.8	39.3	30.2	33.8	309
Lambaesis	30.3	46.0	30.9	44.4	311
Mactaris	20.0	30.2	20.3	26.1	244
Madaurus	25.5	20.3	22.8	22.1	318
Masculula	23.8	20.0	27.0	25.9	258
Mastar	26.2	24.6	30.2	30.7	240
Maxula	20.0	23.1	24.4	30.2	355
Mustis	18.9	21.7	31.3	29.4	257
Sicca Veneria	35.5	34.7	38.4	37.8	317
Sigus	29.6	29.0	22.9	42.5	243
Simitthus	20.0	32.1	16.7	52.4	260
Sitifis	41.4	38.1	36.4	44.0	251
Thagaste	16.7	16.3	15.4	26.7	259

Table 27 (Continued)

Percentage of Mortality of Adultus Period (20-39 years)
of Roman North African I-II and III-V Centuries.

(Continued)

City	Centuries I-II		Centuries III-V		Pages*
	Male Female	Male	Female		
Thala	34.5	34.8	26.8	36.0	254
Theveste	36.0	42.3	35.6	37.3	238
Thibilis	27.8	27.7	27.9	27.0	245
Thurbursicum Bure	22.7	20.0	20.5	21.4	252
Thurbursicum	35.8	37.5	28.7	38.4	320
Numidarum	21.8	34.4	30.4	33.3	235
Thugga	33.3	33.3	17.1	11.3	262
Timgad	18.8	21.1	13.3	26.1	256
Uchi Major			26.6	33.4	
Average	29.4	32.9			

*Sources: Szilágyi, 1965; 309-321; 1966; 235-263.

68.3. The cities also showed a better condition for men from the first to the second period: Aquileia from 86.7 to 44.4; Milan from 80.0 to 35.9 and Ravenna from 38.2 to 35.9. Even the women did better in the cities as time went on: Aquileia from 93.8 to 73.3, Milan from 93.8 to 71.0, and Ravenna from 100.0 to 72.7. However, the data were very limited in number, especially for the cities. Small as they are, they seem to show that conditions were getting better, except for women in the country villages and small cities. The situation would seem to suggest that tuberculosis had not been introduced long before the first two centuries; first through the cities and still making no large inroads in the countryside. Ravenna likewise stands out as having a quite healthy populace although it is not far from the Adriatic; no wonder that the Adriatic fleet was located near it at Classis, rather than at Aquileia whose terrible mortality suggests it as a plague-ridden spot. Even though Aquileia seems to have improved in health, it was still less attractive to the Roman emperors when they moved from Rome to north Italy in the later Empire and chose Ravenna for their residence.

Table 28 gives the percentages of mortality of the Illyrian provinces or Balkan provinces beginning from the eastern end. A great through road ran from Byzantium, (later Constantinople), to Italy along which a fair amount of traffic and passengers must have passed. Nevertheless the main way to the West was on the Mediterranean and the area was to some extent not in the main current of action. Dalmatia with its port, Salona, had the highest mortality (51.6, 69.3) in the group, although Dalmatia's mortality rated among the lowest of the Roman provinces. Dacia, across the Danube, was in the empire only a century or so and had a very low mortality (38.9) while Raetia, in the Swiss mountains with its 35.6 percent was nearly as healthy as North Africa. The other three in the 40 percent group were also quite low in mortality. These might be regarded as among the less civilized portions of the empire. As they became more civilized, they might be expected to have a less healthy condition and that is what happened. With the exception of Dalmatia (and women in Pannonia) both sexes experienced a higher mortality in the third and fourth centuries than in the earlier period.

Data for the provinces do not include data from the cities. Of the twelve cities, seven had higher mortality rates than the provinces in which they were located; four were lower and one was about the same. Four on important cross roads were all higher: Aquincum, Carnuntum, Virunum and Viminiacum. Emona on a main highway was lower. The two Dacian cities may have been mining centers. It seems then that tuberculosis came in slowly along the highway and Adriatic and spread out over the countryside from the first to the fourth century. Evidence from cemeteries is sparse

Table 28

Percentage of Mortality ages 20-39: Balkan provinces
and cities, I-II and III-IV centuries

Provinces	Total	I-II	Male III-IV	I-II	Female III-IV	Page
Dacia	38.9	31.1	33.3	50.0	51.1	309
Moesia	45.9	25.8	36.0	50.0	45.9	307
Dalmatia	51.6	62.9	38.4	62.4	52.9	303
Pannonia	45.9	27.3	46.7	75.0	37.5	315
Noricum	49.1	43.8	58.0	45.3	57.6	319
Raetia	35.6	14.3	39.1	33.3	53.8	320
Cities						
Apulum, Dacia	50.0	45.0	50.0*	50.0*	75.0*	309
Sarmizegetusa,						
Dacia	42.9	35.7*	31.6*	40.0*	61.1*	308
Viminacum, Moesia	31.7	29.2	27.3*	50.0*	50.0*	306
Salona, Dalmatia	69.3	70.0	60.6	80.7	72.2	303
Aquincum, Pannonia	50.5	34.1	55.3	57.1*	75.0*	312
Brigetio, Pan.	53.2	44.0	50.0	50.0*	72.2	313
Carnuntum Pan.	57.4	55.6	77.8*	41.7*	66.7*	310
Emona, Pan.	35.5	25.0	33.3*	45.8*	42.1*	313
Intercisa, Pan.	45.5	28.0	47.1*	75.0*	37.5*	314
Celia, Noricum	45.4	36.2	40.5	52.6	60.5	317
Ft. Solva, Nor.	48.1	31.8	71.4*	42.9*	72.7*	318
Virunum, Nor.	82.1					318

The pages are Szilágyi, 1962.   *Small samples.

for this period and area but what does remain shows about the same picture as the inscriptions.[21]

The west European provinces are more in line with the conditions in Italy than with the northeastern areas. Their mortality rates (50-65) for the adultus age are higher than either of the others. There are some interesting problems involved in their data.

Britain was conquered only in the middle of the first century A.D. and hardly subdued before the end of that century. However, three legions were sent there which normally marched through London along the highways to the three camps at the three corners of England. The Roman soldiers made up a considerable part of the population of England which was very sparsely inhabited.

[21]Zurich: Schreiter, 1929 (.47; .90); Lorsch: Kloiber, 1957 (39.7; 59.1); Schwechat bei Wien: Seracfsin 1936 (-, 33.); Szentendre (Lombard cemetery, mid sixty century) Keszthely, 1966 (.38; .30); Kaiseraugst, Switzerland: Bay, 1968 (.31; .50); Warna, Bulgaria: Hajnis, 1965 (.67; .88); Tisice, Hungary: Chochol, 1973 (.11; .06) Czakrak, Hungary: Nemeskéri, 1956 (.14; .50); Gabara and Sabaro, Rumania: Necrasov, 1969 (both.57).

4. Western Europe

Provinces	Total	Male		Female			
		I-II	III-V	I-II	III-V	10-20	Page*
Britain	51.5	50.0	48.2	50.0	68.4	13.6	136
Gaul	63.6	69.2	52.3	80.0	72.6	21.5	141
Germany	54.3	52.1	61.0	46.2	53.8	10.2	131
Cities							
Arles	52.5	83.3+	23.2	90.0+	60.0	25.0	140
Bordeaux	59.0	75.5	29.3	81.0	46.9	5.5	136
Lyon	56.5	78.6	37.1	73.5	72.5	25.4	134
Vienne	46.7	75.0+	39.5	—	48.4	7.4	138
Cologne	47.4	46.2	—	62.5+	75.0+	9.5	130
Mainz	53.8	45.2	75.0+	84.6+	70.0+	7.1	130
Trier	54.4	—	51.4	—	59.1	27.2	137

Table 29

**Percentage of Mortality ages 20-39;
Western European Provinces and Cities:
I-II and III-V Centuries.**

* Source: Szilágyi, 1961 and pages in table.
+ Numbers small.

However, the information about mortality there before the plague of 542 is scarce. The inscriptions suggest a reasonable mortality of about 50 percent during the adultus period in the first-second centuries. The data from four cemeteries would suggest a much higher mortality. The very extensive cemetery at York, heavily male and therefore probably containing Roman soldiers, has a 66 percent male mortality of the adultus age. The smaller cemetery at Verulamium (St. Albans) also shows a high mortality rate, as do two others.[22] The inscriptions show female mortality in the 68 percent area, while two of three fifth-century cemeteries agree in this.[23] It seems that the Roman troops brought tuberculosis to the island where it spread, causing, as usual, a higher rate of mortality among the women. The Romans tended to move soldiers to opposite ends of the empire which would bring soldiers from the eastern part where there was presumably more tuberculosis.

In Gaul the mortality rates of both men and women declined from the first two centuries into the next two. Tuberculosis seems

---

[22]York: Wenham, 1968 (.74; -) Verulamium (St. Albans: Keith, 1936; Maiden Castle: Wheeler, 1943 (high); Abingdon: Leeds, 1919 (high).
[23]Bedford: Humphrey, 1922 (.60; 68); East Shelford; Peake, 1915 (57, 45); Orpington: Tester, 1963 (60, 65).

to have arrived there earlier than in Britain, since Gaul put up a better resistance to the disease. The four cities of Gaul all enjoyed a lower mortality rate than did the rest of the country—a rather unusual situation. One possible explanation is that malaria was so widespread in a period of great warmth that it fostered the more malignant form. The death rate for ages ten to twenty years also suggests that disease. Very little information comes from three small cemeteries of the period.[24] It was not a favorite period for archaeologists. Gaul had a very high mortality rate for the adultus age then.

German mortality rates were, in general, somewhat less than those of Gaul, about 50 percent from ages twenty to forty, except for some higher rates in the third-fifth centuries. A number of smaller cemeteries show conditions then.[25] For the first part (2-3 centuries) both males and females seem to suffer about a 50 percent mortality. In the following two centuries the rate continues among women but the average for the males (contrary to the inscriptions) declines. The large cemetery of Mungedorf near Cologne shows lesser mortality than that of the inscriptions for the city. Most of the cemeteries of Germany were outside of the boundaries of the Roman Empire and illustrate rates of mortality there.

The mortality between twenty and forty years of age was less in the third period (A.D. 750-1000) than it had been in either of the two preceding periods (tables 29 and 30). Indeed it seems to have been the healthiest period of the late ancient-medieval period. Part of this may be an illusion reflecting simply the greater number of data coming from central Europe where conditions were more pastoral than in the western parts. It is surprising that both France and Germany show a lower mortality in the plague period than in the late Roman period, even though the anthropological data make it clear that the plague was there in the second period. The sharp increase of mortality in Hungary and the Balkans fits in with the theory that the plague also appeared there.

The relationship of tuberculosis to the plague is also perplexing. The plague struck hard at the people aged seven to twenty and thus overlapped somewhat the age of heavy mortality of the other

[24]Mt. Augé: Lautier, 1948 (1.0; .50); Cortrat; Picard, 1963 (.0; 1.00); St. Aubin-sur-Mar, Dastugue, 1971 (.33; .0).

[25]Leuna-Merseburg, Grimm, 1953 (.25; .50) Hassleben: Schultz, 1933 (.25; .50); Mecklenburg: Asmus, 1939 (.88; .67); Prositz: Fricke, 1960 (Both .50): Rügen Grimm, 1959 (.33; .67). These are the best for the first and second centuries. For the third and fourth centuries: Alt-Weddington; Nowak, 1966 (.67; .50); Ammarn: Sellman, 1905 (.0; .33); Grone: Hampe, 1959 (.38; .60); Gross Surding: Gläser, 1935 (.71; .71): Köln Mungedorf: Fremersdorf, 1955 (.33; .67); Niemburg: Schmidt, 1964 (-; .50); Oggau: Ehgarten, 1947 (.50; .50); Poysdorf: Jungwirth, 1968 (.25; .50); Weissling, Keller, 1971(.23; .50); Zauswitz: Grimm, 1969 (.30; .67).

		Period 2				
Area	Men—Number alive at	Died in interval	Mortality percent in interval	Women at 20	Died	Mortality
all	615	317	51.5	512	352	68.8
Mediterranean	—					
France	98	33	33.7	39	21	53.8
Britain	102	73	71.6	81	60	74.1
Germany	113	44	38.9	102	44	43.1
Hungary-Balkans	168	88	52.4	165	121	73.3
Czechoslavakia, Swiss	117	67	57.3	108	91	84.3
Scandinavia	17	12	70.6	17	15	88.2
Poland						
		Period 5				
all	354	199	56.2	133	83	62.4
Mediterranean	63	21	33.3	20	10	50.0
France	—					
Britain	17	10	58.8	10	7	70.0
Germany	38	24	63.2	9	5	55.6
Hungary-Balkans	34	16	47.1	20	12	60.0
Czechoslavakia, Swiss	10	1	10.0	13	3	23.1
Scandinavia	83	124	67.8	49	38	75.6
Poland	14	5	35.7	12	8	66.7

Table 30

Mortality, ages 20-39, periods 2 & 5, areas in Europe

disease. It seems probable then that the two struck at the same types of persons and thus the survivors were also of similar types.

For areas outside of the Empire some evidence exists, though it is not abundant. One fair-sized cemetery of Bohemia, at Luzec, shows a very low mortality.[26] Several cemeteries in Poland show a very high mortality, averages in the high sixties and seventies.[27] Most are for the first two centuries, since only one, Milowov, is of the second half of the period. A complication is that one cannot always be certain that the older scale of Martin which has adultus ranging from twenty to thirty, is being used, as it normally is in

[26]Luzek, Chochol, 1970 (.20; .57). For diagnosis of tuberculosis in an Avar community: A. Marcsik, "Diagnose einer generalisierten TBC-Erkrankung und einem Awarzeitlichen Skeletten," *Anthropologiai Kozlemenyek* 16 (1972): 99-103.

[27]Poland first and second centuries. Gostkowo: Florkowski, 1970 (.41; .67); Korzen: Wiercinski, 1968 (.50; .7 or .62; .48); Odry: Kmiecinskiego, 1968 (.78; .67); Pommerania: Malinowski, 1973 (.61; .43 or .89; .84); Jadwing at Szwajcaria: Dzierzykray-Rogalsky, 1962; Zakrzow: Gralla 1964 (4 adults only). Later Wołownia: Dzierzykray-Rogalsky, 1966 (.19; .43 or .55; .76).

Poland. The poor climatic conditions of Poland were probably responsible for the high mortality. Scandinavia is represented by only four cemeteries, three in the first and second centuries. The first three: Bankälla, Mellby, and Vallhagen, show mortality ranging from 35 to 55 percent. The other cemetery (A.D. 250-500) shows a much higher mortality of 50-56 percent. It suggests that tuberculosis may have reached Scandinavia by the third century, but the evidence is too weak to make this more than a suggestion. In this Skedemoss evidence the mortality of the males is much higher than for the females.[28]

After the first plague (542-750) the skeletal data show the mortality so low in the Switzerland-Austrian-Czechoslovakian area that one wonders if tuberculosis had entered the area to any extent. The same is true of Scandinavia and Poland for the same period. However, the mortality of the adultus group increased markedly just before the second plague, that is, in A.D. 1000-1348. This should indicate that tuberculosis had arrived not long before and was just getting a stronghold then. The mortality increased even more in Germany which suggests that the gradual urbanization of Germany, even more than of other central European areas, was encouraging the spread of tuberculosis. Hungary and the Balkans, which had a modest mortality in the Roman period saw increased rates in both the third period (A.D. 750-1000) and the fourth (A.D. 750-1348) and thus tuberculosis had spread and become more of a problem.

Data before the plague about mortality by age are rather scarce. The landholders of England, mostly male, who were born before 1276 and thus lived mostly in the thirteenth century, had a mortality between the ages of twenty and forty of only 34 percent, an excellent record, nearly as good as that of North Africa in Roman times.[29] This average fell rapidly: those born 1276-1300 had a record of 41.4; and those of the next generation 46.9, a typical plague record. It would be very difficult to separate the plague deaths from those of tuberculosis in Britain. The same would be true of three other places: Reims in France and Pistoia and Pozzuoli in Italy in the fifteenth century. These cities present a distinct problem in migration which must have tended to fill the places of those who died of the plague. Reims in 1422 (if one may assume a stationary population) had a mortality between ages of twenty and forty of 50.5 for men and 40.5 for women.[30] For Pistoia in the foothills of the Apennines and thus presumably less

[28]Bankälla: Sahlstrom, 1954 (.50; .56); Mellby: Gejvall, 1951 (.38; .39); Vallhagar: Gejvall, 1955 (.32; .46); Skedmosse: Gejvall, 1968 (.61; .38).

[29]Russell, 1948: 182-188.

[30]Desportes, 1966: 97.

ravaged by malaria had a 43.6 loss for men and 42.7 for women, assuming again a stationary population.[31] The countryside showed a 43.9 percent loss for ages 20-40 while the city had only 40.7. It must show a heavy migration into the city, although a case can be made that the scattered population suffered more from plague. In Pozzuoli in 1489 the loss was about 66.6 for men and 59.7 for women.[32] It might seem that plague struck harder at men than at women. If the English low mortality in the adultus age group was typical of northern Europe, some resistance to tuberculosis must have developed by that time.

Ancient and medieval physicians suggested various cures for tuberculosis but none offered the rest cure, the simplest remedy, although prescriptions like sea travel might have inadvertently suggested it. Actually many prescribed various forms of exercise, perhaps one of the reasons for the high death rate from the disease. The failure to discover the rest cure must rank among the greatest of human failures. In a lingering disease such as tuberculosis many died of complications from other diseases such as pneumonia and malaria. Furthermore, breakdowns were brought on by crises or overwork, so that the energetic and hardworking were frequent victims.

Many died during early marriage and thus the birthrate was cut down by the disease. Then if particular types of persons were particularly susceptible, their numbers in the population should decline. Data from modern Lisbon showed that the long-headed suffered more than the round-headed.[33] It seems that taller persons were affected more than shorter.[34] As mentioned earlier there was a distinct brachycephalization of European population in the Middle Ages; a change in which tuberculosis played a part. Not much evidence remains for tuberculosis of the bones.[35] Some study has been made of the influence of the disease upon the thinking of its victims but hardly enough to justify conclusions.[36] In any case tuberculosis has been a heavy burden on humanity, but its influence came primarily on the Roman Empire before the first plague and must be considered one of the factors in its decline.

---

[31]Herlihy, 1958: 282-288.

[32]Beloch, 1937: 29-31.

[33]G. Olivier et M. E. de Castro e Almeida, "Forme de Crane et Mortalité differentielle per Tuberculose," *L'Anthropologie* 76 (1972): 471-499. Data from twentieth-century Lisbon.

[34]K. Hess, "Körperhöhe und Laṅger-Breiter Index bei Tuberkulosenkranken," *Bulletin der schweitzerlichen Gesselschaft für Antropologie und Ethnologie* 23 (1946-1947): 64-68.

[35]V. Møller-Christensen, *Middelalderenes Laegekunst i Denmark* (Copenhagen, 1944). English summary 219-222.

[36]G. F. Dorner, *Aspects of the Psychology of the Tuberculous* (New York, 1953). This is based upon only thirty-two cases.

VII. The Earlier Medieval Plague in the British Isles.

Gildas acknowledged the devastation of the plague of A.D. 542-546, a key to his lamentations upon the sins of the British.[1]

> How doth the city sit solitary, that was full of people!
> She is become a widow, that was great among the nations!

Though the effects of the plague in those islands were apparent to him, they have not been to recent historians. Two articles have concentrated upon the course of plague epidemic, mostly around the Mediterranean. They agree that it was a factor in the success of Muhammad, but the more recent asserted that it did not disturb northern Europe.[2] Two new books on Britain from 350 to 650 touch lightly upon the plague. One even asserted that, although it affected Wales and Ireland, it hardly touched England.[3] Much other written data has been overlooked or misunderstood, while archaeological evidence—the direction of graves in cemeteries and skeletal information indicating conditions typical of plague periods—has not been presented. In comparison with the extensive literature upon the later plague of the fourteenth and fifteenth centuries little indeed has been published.[4] Yet if the earlier plague had anywhere near the influence in northern Europe that the other had, it should be well worth studying.

THE ALIGNMENT OF GRAVES

Some facts about the plague are well known: it prefers a moderately high temperature and a similar degree of moisture.

[1] Lamentations 1.1; Gildas, pref.; ed. J. Stevenson, *Gildas de excidio Britanniae* (London, 1838), 2: "Videbamque etiam nostro tempore, ut ille defleverat. 'Solam sedisse urbem viduam, antea populis plenam.'" In the present study, the term "Britain" includes Ireland. This chapter appeared as an article by the same title in *Viator* 7 (1976): 65-78.

[2] Russell, 1968, 174-184: Biraben and Le Goff, 1969, 1484-1510. "Pour l'Occident, enfin, une hypothèse est tentante. Il est sur que les îles Britanniques, le Nord de la Gaule, la Germanie, dans sa majeure, ont été épagnées par la peste. Si l'on pousser loin, trop loin, sans doute, cette hypothèse, on avancerait que la peste justinienne . . a pu aussi expliquer Charlemagne" (1508).

[3] John Morris, *The Age of Arthur* (New York, 1973), 223. "There is no reason to suppose that the disease ever took hold of the main body of the English," but this may be limited to the first epidemic. Leslie Alcock, *Arthur's Britain, History and Archaeology. A.D. 367-634* (New York, 1971), 23, 54. For other guesses: W. P. MacArthur, "The Identification of Some Pestilences Recorded in the Irish Annals," *Irish Historical Studies* 6 (1949) 169-181: J. D. F. Shrewsbury suggests that the plague was smallpox, *Journal of the History of Medicine and Allied Sciences* 1 (1949): 5-47.

[4] For a recent introduction, W. M. Bowsky, *The Black Death, a Turning Point in History?* (New York, 1971).

For Europe this means that it is generally more prevalent in summer, less so in the spring and fall. The pneumonic form, moving from person to person, was nearly 100 percent fatal, but fortunately it was not common. The bubonic form ran about 60-80 percent fatal, but for some reason individuals rather than families usually contracted it. Thus such groups as elderly persons or clergy living in smaller units tended to have a higher mortality. Its prevalence was conditioned by the rat which often experienced cycles of expansion. Another factor was the sensitivity of the flea to the smell of certain common animals and plants: horse, camel, cattle, and he goats, as well as to olive oil, walnuts and ground nuts.[5] Such sensitivity would suggest that the flea was also sensitive to certain persons. This seems evident in areas where there are fleas. Perhaps half of the people in Europe survived because the flea did not like them. Those who died of the plague left evidence in their age groupings and eventually their sex ratio as well as in the direction in which their graves pointed.

Early medieval burials apparently took place at sunrise. The graves were usually lined up with their longer axis pointing toward the sun.[6] The point of sunrise moves with the seasons, being farthest north about 21 June and farthest south about 21 December. The direction of graves then gives good evidence about the season of burial: summer burials pointing north of east and winter south of east. Since people die in all months of the year, the graves point in an arc, northeast to southeast. Archaeologists usually mention, sometimes in great detail, how the graves point. If they give a general direction, it means that the midpoint of the directions lies there. Fortunately, this information is one of the easiest to secure and is generally given.[7]

A summary of information about the direction of graves is given in table 31—data from about 460 cemeteries in four periods from A.D. 1 to A.D. 1348. In the nonplague periods more cemeteries have a median direction south of east than north of east, while more are pointed north of east in the period A.D. 542-700, the period of the plague. It is well-known, of course, that more cases of plague occur in warm weather than in cold. The ideal conditions of plague occur when both percent of humidity and degrees (Fahrenheit) of temperature are between 68 and 80. The evidence of direction of graves then suggests that the plague occurred in sufficient quantity to alter the seasons of burial for much of northern Europe. However, more careful attention should be given to Britain.

---

[5]Biraben and Le Goff, 1488.
[6]Perhaps the best illustration: B. Skerlj, 1958, 119.
[7]See above chapter II.

England has been much interested in archaeology for a long time; long enough for a series of earnest but ignorant amateurs to tear up hundreds of graves, looking for Anglo-Saxon jewelry and other artifacts. In our century better work has been done and at present highly trained and professional scholars are at work. The same is true of most European countries. Even the poorer of the amateurs sometimes recorded the direction of graves. The period of the plague corresponded to much of the early barbarian era of Anglo-Saxon occupation which has attracted the most attention, leaving relatively little interest for later medieval centuries. The information about England is sufficient to draw conclusions based upon the evidence.

That the plague did occur more frequently in the summer in England is indicated by data from the inquisitions post mortem of the second plague period (after A.D. 1348). The data between 1340, some years before the outbreak of the plague and 1375 shows these percentages of mortality for those years.[8]

	Preplague (1340-1347)	Plague (1348-1375)
May-August	24.9	44.6
November-February	40.1	22.8

The climate was probably warmer in the period A.D. 550-750 than in the later Middle Ages, assuming that the British climate moved like that of Greenland.[9] This should have meant that the contrast in death rate would have been even sharper between winter and summer in the earlier period, since warmer weather came sooner and lasted longer.

The direction of graves in a cemetery is that of the midpoint in the arc of directions of the several graves. However, in some cases the excavator merely says that the graves point in a given direction. Actually for our purpose if more graves point north of east the presence of plague is suspected. In England one site, Melbourn, shows a north-northeast alignment.[10] Three are northeast: Finglesham, Kent; Holdenby, Northamptonshire; and Marina Drive, Bedfordshire.[11] Twelve point east-northeast: Abington, Berkshire; Ardwall Isle, Kirkudbrightshire; Camerton, Somerset; Chadlington, Oxfordshire; Holborough, Kent; Leighton Buzzard, Bedfordshire; Mitcham, Surrey; Parkburn near Lasswade and

---

[8]Russell, 1948, 180-183.
[9]W. Dansgaard, S. J. Johnsen, J. Moller, "One thousand Centuries of Climatic Record from Camp Century on the Greenland Ice Sheet," *Science* 166 (1969): 377-381.
[10]D. M. Wilson, 1956, 29-41.
[11]Sonia Chadwick, 1958, 2; E. T. Leeds, 1909, 91; D. R. Brothwell in John Morris, 1962, 43.

Camp Hill near Troughton, Midlothian; Sutton Courtenary, Oxfordshire; Chapel High near Balladoone, and Church Island, near Valencia, County Kerry, Ireland.[12] Eight are described as pointing east: Addiston near Lauder, Berwickshire; Alfristan. Sussex; Lymynge, Kent; Petersfinger, Wiltshire; Wallingford, Berkshire; and Winterbourne Gunner, Wiltshire.[13] Only Little Eriswell, Suffolk shows an east-southeast direction.[14]

Four of those described as east lie near the south coast, but this is just the area Bede described as the original location of the plague of 664. Cemeteries of other late ancient and medieval times in Britain as well as those on the continent, seem to point largely in a south of east direction.[15] The acceptance of Christianity did not seem to affect direction of graves at first, since Christian graves were supposed to point in the direction of Jerusalem, known in general as east. Comparisons with Christian burial grounds are difficult because few Christian cemeteries are disturbed today, except for rescue operations necessitated by removal of burials to make way for modern roads or other construction.

AGE AND SEX COMPOSITION

A second characteristic of any plague visitation was that a higher proportion of men aged between twenty and forty died than was the case for those forty to sixty.[16] Those born before 1276 (and thus seventy-two years of age before the plague struck) show 236 dying between twenty and forty and 279 between forty and sixty. On the other hand, of those who were born after 1325, 111 died between forty and sixty while only 695 passed away between forty and sixty. The relatively few data of the British cemeteries in the sixth-seventh centuries show 103 dying in the age group 20-40 and only twenty-six in the older period. The proportion was actually 59-4 at Abingdon, 7-1 at Little Eriswell, 1606 at Holborough, 11-1

[12]E. T. Leeds and J. B. Darden, 1936; A. C. Thomas, 1967, 132; E. Horne, 1928, 62; A. C. Thomas, 1971, 57, 69; V. I. Evison, 1956, 86; M. Hyslop, 1963, 161-200; H. F. Bidder, 1906, 47-68; A. S. Henshall, 1958, 252-285; Leeds, 1940 52; Leeds in R. H. Hodgin, *History of the Anglo-Saxons* 1 (Oxford, 1936): 222, respectively.

[13]A. C. Thomas, 1971, 55; A. F. Griffith and L. F. Salzman, 1914-1915, 16-57; T. C. Lethridge, 1948 45-70; R. F. Taylor, 1966-1967, 67-69; Alan Warhurst, 1955, 69; E. T. Leeds and H. de Shortt, 1953, 62; E. T. Leeds, 1938, 93-101; J. Musty and J. E. D. Stratton, 1959, p. 88.

[14]Calvin Wells in P. Hutchinson, 1966, 21-28.

[15]In the *Victoria County History* the sections on "Anglo-Saxon Remains" are not as informative as the title suggests. They were done mostly in the first decade of this century by Reginald Smith who occasionally mentioned direction of graves. In general they vary much but give little chronology. See, for instance, Derbyshire 1: 272; 1: 349, 367, 368; Northamptonshire 1: 229, 233, 237; Oxfordshire 1: 351, 358, 361; Staffordshire 1: 200; Sussex i: 345. The section of Kent is a good description of the awful damage that amateurs have done, with the best intentions, to English cemeteries.

[16]Russell, 1948, 180-185.

Table 31

Direction of Graves by Period and Area

Period	NE	ENE	E	ESE	SE	Other	Ratio NE,ENE / ESE,SE
A.D. 1-541	1	8	22	12	3	5	0.66
A.D. 541-750	69	70	103	26	21		2.78
A.D. 750-1000	3	10	23	20	13	2	0.39
A.D. 1000-1348	4	8	18	18	3	2	0.40
Period A.D. 541-750 (by Area)							
France	19	4	13	5	5		2.30
Britain	4	12	8	1			16.00
Germany	28	45	72	18	6		3.04
Hungary-Balkans	10	7	5	1	9		1.70
Bohemia- Switzerland- Austria	8	2	5	1	1		5.00

Sources: chapters 7 and 8.

at Marina Drive and 4-0 at Winterbourne Gunner, but at Chadlington more survived (3-2) into the later years as also at Lymynge (11-4).[17]

According to some chroniclers, the plague epidemic of 682 caused high mortality among children *(puerorum)*. The original epidemic of 542-546 struck at all ages, probably pretty much alike. However, later attacks found a much higher percentage of children than adults vulnerable to the disease. The plague was carried, as is well known, by fleas on rats. The variation in number of rats, a 3.8-year cycle, seems the reason for epidemics of that interval or its multiples. Apparently some persons, as mentioned earlier, were saved from the disease because fleas did not like them. Usually by age thirty most people had either been killed by the disease or spared permanently, since expectation of life at thirty was about the same in plague or nonplague eras.[18] The heaviest mortality seems to have been of children after the earliest years (when they were kept close within the family). Thus the years called by anthropologists infans II (7-13 years) were among the most fatal.

---

[17]For references see notes 10-14 above.

[18]See life tables at age thirty Russell, 1948, 180-185.

They were scarcely less fatal than infans I (0-6 years usually). In Britain the results were:[19]

	Infans I	Infans II
Abingdon	21	18
Holborough	6	2
Little Eriswell	4	1
Lymynge	3	3
Marina Drive	6	8
Melbourn	1	3
Petersfinger	6	5
Winterbourne Gunner	1	1
	48	41

These figures must be read with the realization that the number of infant remains is so small that obviously many of the babies were not buried in the cemeteries. On the continent more infans II than infans I turn up in the cemeteries of the period.

The study of the sex ratio (number of men to 100 women in this case) is complicated by the relative inability of earlier anthropologists to determine sex in skeletal remains, even though the discovery that certain notches in the pelvic bones may indicate the number of children that a woman has borne.[20] The uncertainty about determining sex seems to be the reason why the sex ratio is higher in the estimates of the earlier studies. The five earlier studies (all before 1950) show 107 men and 83 women, a sex ratio of 129. The ten studies published since 1950 suggest 159 males to 143 females for a sex ratio of 113.[21] If the very unusual cemetery of Marina Drive is excepted, the ratio drops to the normal 104. Earlier anthropologists tend to assume that big bones indicated males, disregarding the quite common occurrence of big women among the German tribes.[22] In other periods before 1348 in the Middle Ages the sex ratio appeared to be about 120 or higher. This seems to have resulted from heavy female migration from villages to the cities (quite questionable) and infanticide of female

---

[19]For references to places see notes 10-14 above.

[20]J. L. Angel, "The Bases of Palaeodemography," *American Journal of Physical Anthropology* 30 (1969): 432.

[21]Abingdon 51-44; Camerton 24-17; Chadlington 5-5; Holdenby 4-3; Mitcham 23-14. For the ten: Little Eriswell 10-12; Holborough 16-12; Lymynge 18-18; Melbourn 13-9; Marina Drive 18-6; Parkburn 10-14; Petersfinger 21-18; Sewerby 20-20; Stratford-Alveston 29-28; Winterbourne Gunner 4-4. Sewerby data P. Rahtz 1960, 137 and for Stratford-Alveston, A. Meaney 1964, 253.

[22]An interesting case is the "fisherman from Barum," Gejvall, *Fornvännen* (1970): 281-289.

babies.[23] The low sex ratio in England in the period A.D. 540-750 is another indication of plague conditions in Britain.

The data for the plague show many characteristics of the later plague. From 1348 for three centuries, at least, the plague struck periodically in great epidemics but was endemic at other times.[24] It is probable that the same was true for the earlier period. Three great epidemics occurred about A.D. 544, 664 and 682, as we shall see. If a great epidemic killed eight to ten times more than the usual yearly mortality, it had a great effect on other aspects of human thinking. For instance, since nearly equal numbers of male and female deaths appear in plague periods, the depleted number of females caused less frequent resort to infanticide. Furthermore, even the two great epidemics of 664 and 682 seem to have no connections with epidemics of Mediterranean areas.[25] One has to assume, then, that reservoirs of the disease developed during the period in the British Isles. The archaeological sources thus tell us much about the plague.[26]

Written sources are better than might be expected. The Welsh chronicle known as *Annales Cambriae*, apparently contemporary though limited, seems accurate.[27] Good chronicle data about the plague remain from Ireland from an early eighth-century compilation.[28] This was the basis for several Irish chronicles of a later date which occasionally added items of their own.[29] Nennius and the Anglo-Saxon Chronicle seldom mention the plague. Gildas was obsessed by it and Bede gives a variety of precious data. Irish saints' lives mention it. Adamnan's life of Columcille is a most valuable source.[30] Nevertheless, serious questions remain, particularly about the Irish Annals.

---

[23]Suggested by low sex ratios in cities and high sex ratios in village cemetery evidence.

[24]Russell, 1948, 216.

[25]Biraben and Le Goff, 1969, 1497.

[26]Discussed in Russell, 1973, 525-530.

[27]*Annales Cambriae*, ed. J. Williams ab Ithel, Rolls Series (London 1860). On its sixth-seventh century data reliability see J. C. Russell, "Arthur and the Romano-Celtic Frontier," *Modern Philology* 48 (1951): 145-152, esp. 147-148; on origin and validity, T. Jones, *Brut y Tywysogion: Red Book of Hergest Version* (Cardiff, 1955).

[28]L. Bieler, "Sidelights on the Chronology of St. Patrick," *Irish Historical Studies* 6 (1948-1949): 246; E. MacNeill, "The Authorship and Structure of the Annals of Tigernach," *Erin* 7 (1914): 30-113, esp. 89-108, T. F. O'Rahilly, *Early Irish History and Mythology* (Dublin, 1946), 252-255.

[29]The Clanmacnoise chronicle is edited by Dennis Murphy, S. J., for the Royal Society of Antiquaries of Ireland (Dublin, 1896). The Innisfallen Annals were edited by S. Mac Airt (Dublin, 1950); "Tigernach" by Whitley Stokes in the *Revue Celtique* 16-18 (1895-1897); and the Ulster Chronicle by W. M. Hennessy (Dublin, 1887). A facsimile edition of the Annals of Innisfallen has an excellent introduction by Eoin MacNeill, Royal Irish Academy (Dublin, 1933).

[30]Charles Plummer, *Vitae sanctorum Hiberniae* (Oxford, 1910) 2, cx-cxi; clxxi; II, 113. A. O. Anderson and M. Anderson, *Adomnan's Life of Columba* (London, 1961) 459-460. The name seems to be spelled either Adamnan or Adomnan.

THE FIRST AND SECOND EPIDEMICS

The first epidemic began in the eastern Mediterranean late in 541. It had reached Arles by 543[31] and thus it is not surprising that it struck Ireland in 544. The Annals of Ulster tell of the great mortality, called *blefed,* in which Mo-Bi Chlarainech died.[32] Apparently this is the year referred to in the *Lorica,* ascribed, probably correctly, to Gildas.[33]

> Ut non secum trahat me mortalitas (5)
> Hujus anni neque mundi vanitas.

This rather frenzied poem asks aid from all the supernatural host and names in minute detail all parts of the body which are to be protected.

> Ne de meo possit vitam trudere (87)
> Pestis, febris, langor, dolor corpore.

These lines define the order of symptoms of the plague: a very high fever, languor, and terrible pain as the buboes develop. Other diseases have the same symptoms, but these, at least fall in line. The second prologue begins:

> Deus, inpenetrabilis tutela,
> Undique me defende potentia. (30)
> Mei gibre pernas omnes libera,
> Tuta pelta protegente singula,
> Ut non tetri demones in latera
> Mea vibrent ut soleant iacula.

The *pernas,* so prominent in these lines, seem to mean haunch with meat on it or ham, referring to the glandular situation which was the seat of the most prominent symptom of the disease.[34]

The *Lorica* is one of the few pieces of plague literature and it indicates the depth of Gildas's feeling with regard to it. It was probably written in the same year (*huius anni*) that the plague was raging. Gildas's second writing, his famous *De excidio,* came later and may have been his reaction to a second visitation of the plague. Maelgwn, king of Gwynedd, the outstanding ruler of Britain, died in an attack of the disease in the year 547 (or 549) according to the *Annales Cambriae,*[35] but he is mentioned as alive by Gildas. His

---

[31]Biraben and Le Goff, 1969, 1494.

[32]Hennessy (note 29 above), 49-50; Mac Airt (note 29 above), 70-71.

[33]Edited by Whitley Stokes along with *A Medieval Tract of Latin Declensions* (Dublin, 1860), 133-151. For the authorship of Gildas, 133-134. The numbers within parentheses are the numbers of the lines of the poem. The Latin has local words, like *gibre* for *vir.* Other obscure lines may connect the disease with the plague (73-74):

> Tege trifidum jacor et ilia
> Marcem, reniculos, fitrim cum ogligia.

[34]The poem needs to be studied further by specialists in the Latin of the period.

[35]*Annales Cambriae* (note 27 above), 4; Alcock (note 3 above) suggests 549 as the proper date.

terrible lamentations are evidently the result of the plague, since the Britons had experienced a generation of prosperity and success against the Anglo-Saxons before the plague. Gildas is the outstanding contemporary authority for sixth-century Britain and his reaction to the plague is important.

Perhaps in the same year, 549 (or 552) Saint Finian of Clonard, the great teacher of the saints of Ireland, perished in the plague. According to his life, he may have done so as a voluntary sacrifice for the Gaels.[36] His death adds to the possibility that the first plague actually came in two epidemics or waves.

The cemetery at Marina Drive has already been mentioned as one with unusual age and sex counts.[37] The community cannot have been large, however, as its burial ground argues for a small colony of Kentishmen established in a hostile territory in Bedfordshire in the last years of the sixth century. There they fought for survival for a decade or two before they moved on to other fields, returned whence they came, or were overwhelmed by their enemies. Their chief enemy then would have been the plague. The heavy proportion of young men suggests a military outpost; the number of children in infans II (7-13) is typical of the plague. The number of ornaments in the children's graves and the lack of artifacts in the adults would suggest that the children had received attention because they died first and because many died at the same time, they had been buried hastily. The dates suggested are from 570/600 to 600/620.

The account of Saint Gerald recorded in the Preface and the meeting of kings and others at Tara to decide what should be done about overpopulation following the recovery of population after the first plagues must have occurred a little later. The story, it will be remembered, was that God did send a plague but that it killed off great numbers of the very people, the rich and the mighty, who had wished for a pestilence.[38] It is interesting folklore about the plague and why so many important persons died of it.

Bede mentioned the second great plague, that of 664, several times. The most detailed description is:

In the year of the Lord 664 there was an eclipse of the sun on May 3 (actually May 1) at four o'clock in the afternoon and the same year a sudden pestilence (*lues pestilentiae*) first devastated the southern parts of Britain and afterward attacked the kingdom of Northumbria, raging far and wide with cruel devastation and laying low a vast number of people.

---

[36]C. Plummer, "Cain Ermine Bain," *Eriu* 4 (1910): 39, citing *Lismore Lives*, 82. The data: 552 from Annals of Innisfallen, ed. Mac Airt (note 28 above) 71; 549 from Plummer (note 30 above) 1: lvii.

[37]John Morris, 1962, 44. (note 3 above)

[38]Plummer (note 30 above) 2: 113-114. On its value 1; lxxi-lxxii.

Bede mentioned only Northumbria in the north and thus seems to confirm Adamnan, as we shall see, in his statement that parts of the north were spared. In another place Bede stated that the pestilence "quickly followed" the eclipse and thus suggests that it started in May or June.[39] He also wrote of the survival of Cuthbert although the saint had a tumor in his thigh (*tumor in femore*), which is excellent identification clinically that he suffered from bubonic plague.[40] King Egbert also survived, while Bishop Cedd of the East Saxons died at Lastingham.[41] As sites of the plague, Bede designated Barking near London (4.7, 8); Ely near the Wash (4.19); Lichfield in the center of England (4.3); Lastingham (23.3); Wearmouth (Hist. Abb. 8); Lindisfarne (*Vita Cuthberti* 27) and Carlisle (*Vita Cuthberti* 27), all in the north of England.[42] The list illustrates a typical distribution of places, in that chroniclers nearly always write more about the area in which they live.

According to Bede, the plague was very deadly in Ireland.[43] The early source for the Irish chronicles said that the plague arrived in August by way of Leinster at a place called Moyith or Camp Itho in the area of Fothart.[44] This seems to have been in the Kilkenny-New Ross area in the southeast of Ireland, nearest the south of Britain. A great number of important persons: kings, bishops and other religious are listed as victims.[45] The next year (665) four abbots of Bangor died, emphasizing a distinctive feature of the mortality.[46] The plague made a profound impression in the islands, perhaps more than the first one, but a more literate populace may account for the difference.

THE THIRD AND LATER PLAGUES

In 679, according to the Anglo-Saxon Chronicle, the abbess Aethelfryth of Ely died, after prophesying her death and that of

---

[39]Bede, *Historia Ecclesiastica* 3: 27; 4, l. B. Colgrave and R. A. B. Mynors, *Bede's Ecclesiastical History of the English People* (Oxford, 1969), 310-313; *Vita Cuthberti* 33. The *Anglo-Saxon Chronicle* (ed. G. N. Garmonsway [London, 1953] 34-35) quotes from Bede, since it also had May 3 instead of the correct May 1.

[40]*Vita Cuthberti* 8; used by MacArthur (note 3 above).

[41]Bede, *H. E.* 3. 27; 3. 23.

[42]The list is given in William Bright, *Chapters in Early English Church History* (Oxford, 1907): 348.

[43]Bede *H. E.* 3. 27; Colgrave and Mynors (note 37 above), 312-313.

[44]664: "The mortality raged at first in Ireland in Magh itho of Fothart," Annals of Ulster, ed. Hennessy, 118-119; "The great mortality began at Moyith the first of August," Annals of Clonmacnois, p. 106; "Mortalia magna in Hibernia pervenit in ipsis kal. Augusti i.e. in Campo Ithad in Lagenia," Annals of "Tigernach," ed. Stokes 17, 198. Given under 666 in Annals of Innisfallen, ed. Mac Airt, 96-97. See note 27 above.

[45]Virtually the same list in all, from the archetype.

[46]Annals of Clonmacnoise, 108; Annals of "Tigernach," 200; the dates vary but it evidently was the second year of the plague.

many of her nuns.[47] This was three years before the "third great plague" or the "mortality of the children." (It was called by both names.)[48] It appeared in Wales apparently before it reached Ireland in October 682.[49] Presumably it was in England in that year also. Bede tells of a double monastery in which the nuns' part had just been added and in which a light from heaven directed where the deceased nuns should be buried. The monks' area had already suffered as "daily one or two men were carried off to the Lord." Saint Cuthbert, who had been stricken in the 664 plague, carried on through the third one.[50]

In Ireland where the mortality had been heavy in 682, it continued as the "mortality of the children" in 683.[51] Perhaps it was during this plague that there arose the story of the vicarious deaths of Eimine Bain and forty-nine of his monks to save the lives of Bran ua Faelain, king of Leinster and forty-nine of his chiefs. Bran died in 692.[52]

Toward the end of the seventh century, Adamnan, a monk of Iona, wrote about the life and miracles of Saint Columba or Columcille and included the following:

This also I consider should not be reckoned among the lesser miracles of power, in connection with the plague which twice in our times ravaged the greater part of the surface of the earth. Not to speak of the other wider regions of Europe (that is to say, of Italy and the city of Rome itself, and the provinces of Gaul this side of the Alps and the Spanish provinces, separated by the barrier of the Pyrenean mountains), the islands of the Ocean, namely Ireland and Britain were twice ravaged by a terrible pestilence, excepting two peoples only, that is the population of the Picts and of the Irish in Britain, between which peoples the mountains of the spine of Britain are the boundary. Although neither people is without great sins, by which the Eternal Judge is often provoked to anger, yet until now he has spared both of them enduring patiently. To whom else can this favour conferred by God be attributed, but to Saint Columba, whose monasteries, placed within the boundaries of both peoples, are down to the present time held in great honour by both.[53]

Adamnan was writing about A.D. 688-704, thereby corroborating the chroniclers' statement that two great epidemics had

[47]Bede, *H. E.* IV, 19: death reported in the Anglo-Saxon Chronicle, ed. Garmonsway (note 39 above), 38.

[48]Annals of Ulster, ed. Hennessy, 134-135; Annals of "Tigernach," 218; called the third plague in the Annals of Innisfallen, ed. Mac Airt, 98-99.

[49]*Annales Cambriae* (note 27 above), 8. Annals of Ulster, 134-135 and "Tigernach," 208, give the month of October.

[50]Bede, *H. E.* 4: 7; *Vita Cuthberti* 33.

[51]Annals of Ulster, ed. Hennessy, 134-135.

[52]Plummer (note 36 above) 39. King Bran died in 693; Annals of Ulster, 143.

[53]Anderson and Anderson (note 30 above), 458-463.

occurred. Biraben and Le Goff record no plagues of 664 and 682 unless the second was part of the one that touched Syria and Egypt in 684-686.[54]

Adamnan had gone to England in the reign of King Egfirth "while the pestilence continued and devastated many villages on all sides" (p. 461). Egfrith ruled from the death of his father Oswiu in 670, until his own death, fighting the Picts in 685.[55] The area thus protected by Saint Columba would have been about the Solway Firth and across the hills into the Midland Plain of Scotland. The evidence would show that the Pictish kingdom and the Irish of Dalriada somehow escaped the ravages of the plague. This occurred occasionally, even in the fourteenth century. Van Werveke showed that the Netherlands largely escaped the attacks of the plague in 1348-1351, although they were devastated by later epidemics and seem to have had no inherent protection against it.[56]

There is some evidence that epidemics occurred after 682. Abbot Easterwine and many monks of Jarrow died in 686; the time that young Bede and the abbot succeeding Easterwine kept up the services together.[57] In Ireland another plague occurred in 699-701, just fifteen years after the end of the 682-684 one; and seven years later, in 708, a plague with dysentery occurred.[58] It is possible that these were not the bubonic plague even though the intervals between them and earlier ones suggest it. In any case the cemetery evidence reviewed earlier indicates that the bubonic plague had been endemic in the British Isles most of the period 544-700 and perhaps later.

THE EFFECTS OF THE PLAGUE

The islands before 540 had become well populated by the standards of the time so that there was even emigration from them. Not much pressure from the continent was likely. In January 516 Arthur had defeated the Saxon army at Mount Badon, producing a generation of peace, while there was general stability among the Celts. Elsewhere, the very great similarity between the epidemics of 542-700 and those of 1348-1500 have been noted.[59] Probably in

[54]Biraben and Le Goff, 1969, 1497.

[55]At Nechtenesmere near Dundee. F. T. Wainwright, *Antiquity* 22 (1948): 82-97. Wainwright, *The Problem of the Picts* (London, 1955), 8.

[56]"Plague in the Netherlands during the Middle Ages," a paper read at the Economic History Association meeting at Cambridge. England, 1953, a copy of which he gave me. Probably the same as his "Nogmalls de Zwarrer Dood in de Nederlanden," *Bijdragen de Geschiednis der Nederlanden* 8 (1954): 251-258.

[57]*Vita abbatum* 10; Bright (note 42 above), 389; Colgrave and Mynors (note 38 above), xx.

[58]Annals of Ulster, ed. Hennessy (note 29 above) 148-149, 156-157.

[59]For migration see F. M. Stenton, *Anglo-Saxon England* (Oxford, 1943), 5; for the date of the battle, Russell (note 26 above), 149-150. For similarity of the two plagues in time, Russell, 1958, 41.

the sixth and seventh centuries, the British Isles declined as did England in the later period: a drop of 20-30 percent in the first years followed by a further decline to at least 50 percent by the end of the century and a low level well toward the seventies of the next century. However, the epidemics of A.D. 682-683 may have reduced British population proportionately below the fifteenth-century level.

Three possible effects seem worth considering. First, the plague tended to decimate the less densely settled areas because of the rat's territoriality, that is, one rat and his limited number of fleas had a definite area, so that the more people in that area, the less chance of infection. Thus the Celtic hamlets suffered more than the larger Anglo-Saxon villages. The advance of the Anglo-Saxons just after A.D. 550 may be explained by this hypothesis.[60]

Second, the plague with its terrible mortality tended to create a crisis situation. And in a crisis a few usually take advantage of opportunities offered to advance their own interests and increase their power. Now the Tribal Hidage shows England divided into perhaps four greater states (Kent, East Anglia, Wessex, Northumbria) and a number of medium-sized tribes of perhaps 7,000 hides (land areas) each (East Saxons, Hwicce, Gagas, Westerna, Wreconseitna and Lindisfarona).[61] The last group, in large part, quickly amalgamated with neighbors to form Mercia, perhaps even before the marked effects of the plague. However, in the time of the plague, a very large number of the remaining tribes, perhaps two dozen in number, were absorbed into the larger units. Somehow the leaders of the larger states broke down the status quo which had respected the identity of the smaller tribes and forced them into union with the larger powers: rulers like Ceawlin, Centwine, Edwin, Penda, and Oswiu. It is somewhat parallel to the failure of regions to continue development after the outbreak of the Black Death of 1348, although there was a promising outlook for them earlier.[62]

Third, a further factor was the apparent failure of the plague to damage much of the Scottish areas of the islands. Well past the second plague of 664 Northumbria seems to have pressured the north in the time of King Oswiu and as late as 670 by King Egfrith. The latter even led an invasion of Ireland in 684. However, 685 saw the terrible defeat of Egfrith at Nechtanesford near Dundee in Scotland, a battle in which the Picts brought death to the king and

---

[60]Morris (note 3 above) suggests that the English profited by not suffering from the plague, 223-224.

[61]J. C. Russell, "The Tribal Hidage," *Traditio* 5 (1957): 200-201. Compare G. Sheldon, *The Transition from Roman Britain to Christian England* (London, 1932), 98.

[62]Russell, 1972, 214-247.

a considerable part of his army. Their king, Bruide mac Beli, "ruled for twenty-one years and made himself the strongest power of the north" from 672 to 693. "The Picts regained the land which the English had held and the Irish who were in Britain and part of the Britons regained their liberty," Bede said.[63] Here one may see clearly the effect of the plague mortality, especially of 682-684. Once the momentum of the English advance had been lost by that battle, the weaker potential of the English became apparent: seldom again did the English attempt a conquest which would be followed by colonization. Adamnan gave as a miracle of Saint Columba that he saved "his territories," that is, the area of modern Scotland (except the most southern parts) from the plague. One wonders how far that idea spread: it could have been a help, in addition to the feeling that Columba had Christianized the area, in furthering the sentiment for unity in the north.

During the plague the Irish and Welsh converted the Scots and helped with the conversion of the English—the beginning of a remarkable missionary movement which spread to the continent. These were natural results of the religious zeal stirred by the mortality of the plague. Society was simple then and it took the next step in religious development: conversion and missionary activity in Britain—as in the contemporary Islamic world. This was in marked contrast to the fourteenth century when neither conversion nor missionary effort was appropriate. The next step then appeared in hysterical manifestations such as those of the Flagellants, the religious and witchcraft persecutors and the devotees of the dance of death. Others simply disbelieved in religion. Gildas, reacting like those of the later preplague visitation, was too early to be appreciated. Adamnan believed that sin brought on plague but was not willing to say that it was lack of sin which saved Scotland from the plague. He belonged to an age which did not try to explain everything.

The fact that the second and third great epidemics did not reach into central and northern Scotland suggests that it had a tenuous grip in the north. The mystery of the disappearance of the plague also remains: perhaps the lesser number of people did not provide sufficient human reservoirs for the disease, or the cooling of the climate rendered the environment less propitious, or it was just a matter of chance. Population was greatly reduced and society simplified. The slight demographic advantage of the English in the first epidemic was offset by the exemption of much of Scotland. The balance was preserved: the English kings grew stronger but fought among themselves, and the Celts felt less pressure for another four hundred years.

---

[63]Stenton (note 59 above), 57.

VIII. The Earlier Medieval Plague on the Continent

The plague's course and effects seemed to have received more attention for the eastern half of the Mediterranean basin than for the western part.[1] This may have been because the East's greater political unity and more intellectual activity in the early Middle Ages provided more and better information about the plague. An extensive study would show that in the West there were relatively few items (about thirty) about the plague. Two-thirds of these came from Gregory of Tours (who died about A.D. 594) and Paul the Deacon (died about 800), with Gregory providing more than Paul. The maps illustrate the location of fifteen epidemics from 542 to 767. The plague appeared in the West in only four of nine epidemics after A.D. 600 mostly in Italy and only one as far west as Marseilles. In fact, after the death of Gregory there was very little plague in the west.

There is useful information for Italy and Spain where there is little non-literary evidence to determine occurrence of plague. The sites are quite naturally on the main highways and consist mostly of large cities. Anthropological information is therefore of very great value for continental Europe as well as for the British Isles.

THE MEDITERRANEAN COUNTRIES AND FRANCE

More literary information about the plague should have come from Italy than from other areas, being the western center of literacy and education and home of the Papacy and the traditions of the Roman Empire. Actually most of the information about plague there comes from Paul the Deacon (ca. A.D. 720-800), the historian of the Lombards, who was associated with the Abbey of Monte Cassino and the court of Charlemagne in the course of his life.[2] He supplies about one half of the information about the plague in Italy. He says that it touched all of Italy in 580 and mentions specifically its appearance at Ravenna, Grado, and Pavia. Other authors mention its occurrence in Italy in 543, one, Gregory the Great, tells of its effects on Rome in 580. Gregory of Tours comments upon its occurrence at Rome, with later casual items about plague visits to Sicily and Naples and South Italy in 746-747

---

[1]Biraben and le Goff, 1979. For the course of the plague in the later plague and general conditions of the epidemic: M. W. Dols, *The Black Death in the Middle East* (Princeton, 1977), esp. 39-67.

[2]Coveniently translated by William Dudley Foulke, *History of the Lombards by Paul the Deacon* (New York, 1907). A good description of the plague and its effects occurs on 56-58. Other references: 160, 200 (A.D. 617-618), 238. For Paul's life, xv-xxxv, and his historical work, xxv-xlii. For the manuscript and editions, xxxii-xxxv.

and 767.[3] There is no archaeological evidence in Italy from this period since few Christian cemeteries are excavated. It is odd that Procopius said so little about the plague in Italy. He wrote at length about the Byzantine armies there and his account of the plague in Constantinople is the best account from the early medieval world.

Iberian graves thus far have not yielded much information about the plague period. Like other Mediterranean countries Spain has been more interested in prehistoric and Roman archaeology than in medieval. However, some German archaeologists have excavated in Visigothic cemeteries of the plague period: Daganzo near Madrid, Duraton near Segovia and Silveirona in Portugal. At the last named, though data are scarce, twenty were male and six female; only one each of infans I and II appear. In general the graves point northeast, the sex ratio is typical of migrating groups.[4] Written evidence is sufficient to show that the plague was present in 542-543 and 588. Isidore defines plague as *pestilentia, contagium, inguina,* and *lues* and he comments upon the rapid course to death of the disease and its frequency. The information about *contagion* rather suggests that he knew of the pneumonic form. The high, dry meseta with its hot summer temperature and large animals should have held the disease in check. In the late medieval plague, Spain seems to have suffered less than France or other western European countries.[5]

The chief source of information about the plague in western Europe was, of course, the works of Gregory, Archbishop of Tours who wrote about A.D. 574-594. He lived near the center of Gaul and as archbishop traveled widely over the country thus being in a position to get news. Gregory had deep interest in weather and disease including much about both in his writings, especially about the Black Death which appeared in the west when he was about five years old. According to him, the first attack came in by way of Marseilles and reached as far north as Trier. The second was in 571 (and is mentioned) as being at Chalons-sur-Saône as well as at Lyon, Bourges, Clermont, and Dijon. It occurred in the south in 580-582 as well as in 588-590. Other sources indicate its ap-

[3]Gregory of Tours, *Hist. Franc.*

[4]Daganzo: Fernandez Godin, *Junta Superior de Excavasiones Antiq.* (1930); Duraton: A. Moliero Perez, "La necropolis visigoda de Duraton (Segovia)," *Acta Archaeologica Hispanica* 4 1948: 88; Silveirona (Estremoz, Portugal): Xavier de Cunha 1955. Graves at Deza (Soria) Hinojar de Pey, Suellacatras and Pamplona all aligned E-W may be preplague. Zeiss, *Die Grabfunde aus den spanischen Westgotenreich* (Berlin, 1934), 161, 163, 166, 178, 190.

[5]Isidore, *Etym.* IV, vi, 17-19. Pestilentia. Idem et contagium a contingendo, quia quemquem tetigerit, polluit. Ipse et inguina ab inguinum percussione. Eadem lues a labe et luctu vocata, quae tanto acuta est ut non habeat spatium temporis quo aut vita speretur aut mors, sed repentinus languor simul cum morte venit. This was a very popular book, surviving in a thousand medieval manuscripts.

pearance in 599-600 and 630-635.[6] Gregory mentioned the
plague rather casually as an item of interest rather than with
careful explanations of the spread of the disease.

Two other references may be added which may refer to the
plague.[7] St. Maur died in the epidemic of 588 along with 115 of the
140 monks of his monastery. The second concerns a case at Noyon
at the time of the death of St. Eloi in 659. Noyon is a bit farther
north than Trier, the farthest north of the items vouched for by
literary evidence.

A summary of the French evidence follows.

Direction of graves in cemeteries (number of cemeteries)[8]

North east	19		
East northeast	4	North of east	23
East	13		
East southeast	5		
Southeast	5	South of east	10

---

[6]According to Gregory the first attack of the plague came by way of Marseilles and
reached as far north as Trier (HF IV, 5; Liber Mir. xvii, 4). The second, of 571, touched as
far north as Chalons-sur-Saône as well as Lyons, Bourges, Clermont and Dijon. (HF VI, 14,
33; VII, l) as well as 588-590 (HF IX, 21-22; X, 23-25). Other sources indicate its
reappearance in 599-600 and between 630 and 635. Biraben-Le Goff.

[7]W. W. Skeat, ed. *Aelfric's Lives of the Saints*, Early English Text Soc. 68, 82 (Oxford, 1881):
169. "Denique eo tempore vastabit morbus acerrime nunnullas civitates Francie. Case of
a woman with a pustula on her neck. Migne, *Patrologia Latina* 81: 581. In one grave several
burials: at Herpes, C. Barriere-Flavy, *Étude sur les sépultures barbares du midi et l'ouest de
France. Industrie Wisigotique* (Paris, 1892), 190.

[8]Northeast-southwest: Abainville (Meuse); *Gallia* 32 (1974): 342; Andresy (Seine-Oise);
Salin 2 (1948): 195. Billy (Moselle) *Gallia* 32 (1974): 343; Bousserancourt (c. Jussey),
Thevenin, *Les cimetières merovingiennes due Haute Saône* (Paris, 1968), 29; Champigny-sur-
Yonne, la Pannetière, *Revue d'Est* 3 (1952): 37; Clamanges (Marne), P. Coudray et P.
Parrazot, "Le cimetière merovingien de "La Pannetiere à Campigny-sur-Yonne," *Revue
archéologique de l'Est et de Centre-Est* 3 (1952): 35-49. Plan, 37. Conlie (Sarthe): Cochet
1851: 134; Dampierre-sur-le Doubs (Doubs); *Revue archéologique d'Est* 20 (1969): 291;
Envermeu (Seine Inferiour), Cochet 1851, 187; Fère-Champenoise (Marne): Coutier, etc.
"Fouilles d'cimetière merovingienne a Fère-Champenoise," *Bulletin de la Société Prehistori-
que franque* 26 (1929): 523-524, Plan 524. Grathe-Loup (Yonne). *Revue archéologique de
l'Est* 4 (1953): 308-319. Plan 310. Lezeville (Meuthe-Moselle) Salin, 1922. Mont-Joly
(Normandy): Dastugue, 1959; Ouville-le-Rivière Cochet, 1951, 134. Roanne (Loire): R.
Perrot, *Revue archéologique de l'Est et de Centre-Est* 25 (1974): 17-26. Plan on 18. S.
Marguerite-sur-Mar (Normandy): Cochet, 1951, 134; S. Pierre d'Èpinay: Cochet, 1951,
134; Sauville (Loire): *Bulletin de l'Association Lorraine d'Ètudes anthropologiques* 1
(1928-1929): 49-74. S. Aubin-sur-Scie, Cochet, 1951, 134.

East-northeast. Blondefontaine (Haute-Saône): A. Thevinin, *Revue archéologique de l'Est
et de Centre-Est* 20 (1969): 291-303. Plan 292. Eply (Lorraine): *Gallia* 32 (1974): 339.
Estagel (pyrenees orientales): Lantier, 1949, S. Sulpice (Vaud): Reymond, 1911.

East-southeast. Bislee (Meuse): *Gallia* 32 (1974): 343. Haine-St.Paul: G. Faider-Feytmans, *Les nécropoles merovingiennes - - - de Musée de Mariemont* (1970): 21. Holgerlungen: Salin,
1949; 2: 184. Piñedes (Herault): Arnal 1979 Sublanies: Cordier 1974. Varangeville: Salin,
1946. Plan 202.

Southeast. Blossangeaux (Doubs): Mery, 1968. Bourgogne (Loire): Scheuer, 1909. Ciply:
Feider-Feytman, 1970, 148. Félines S. Peyre (Herault): Méroc, 1961.

This is impressive evidence, because it has so few problems in it. In other periods there are always more facing southeast (excepting the second plague period).

Of eighteen cemeteries where the set of skeletons has been determined, five show a female majority, seven male and in two there are an equal number.[9] A problem here is that in early cemetery excavations, there is doubt about the accuracy of sex selection. In other periods the sex ratio is high. The total number of skeletons in these cemeteries is: men 375, women 368 for a sex ratio of 102.

The data for the other two tests are not so decisive: seven cemeteries have more infans I skeletons than infans II, with 80 infans I skeletons and 37 infans II. Six cemeteries have more male skeletons over forty years of age with only one having less: the total skeletons are 111 over age forty and 69 under that age.[10]

The evidence from the cemeteries comes for the most part from areas in France not touched by the written sources. In the northwest the Norman provinces and in the northeast the departments of Haute Saône, Loire, Marne, and Aube have each more than one cemetery while Yonne in the center has several. Even some of the cemeteries which have a preponderance of graves pointing south of east show characteristics of plague influence. Blossangeaux has 13 men to 18 women while the number of infans II and of men dying under forty is large. Bourogne has 101 males to 132 females. Few cemeteries of the plague period have been subjected to excavation and examination. However, there seems little reason to believe that the plague did not touch the area.

THE GERMAN DATA

Archaeological information about German areas is conspicuously greater than for France, largely because the plague occurred during the second half of the Völkerwanderung, a period

---

[9]More men: Grathe-Loup (see note 8), 13-9; Lezévile: Salin, 1922; Lyons, St. Lawrence, Choulans: Wuilleumier, 1949; Sublaines: Cordier, 1974. Billy (see note 8) 75 men, 2 women. Chaouilly (Merthe-et-Moselle): Vornet, 1904. Equal number, men-women-Varangeville: Salin, 1946. Fleury-sur-Orne (Calvados): Dastugue, 1964. More women than men. Blossangeaux (Doubs): (see note 6) SE; Bourogne (Loire): Scheuer, 1909; Estagel: Lantier, 1949; Mont July: Dastugue, 1959; Piñedes: Arnal, 1959.

[10]The Infans I numbered more than Infans II in: Blossangeaux: Mery, 1968; Chaouilly: Vornet, 1904; Ennery: Heuertz, 1957; Estagel Lantier, 1949; Lyons: Wuilleumier, 1949; Piñedes: Arnal, 1959;
   Infans II had more than Infans I in Fleury-sur-Orne: Dastugue, 1974.
   More male skeletons over 40 than under: Blossangeaux: Mery, 1968; Chaouilly: Vornet, 1904; Fleury-sur-Orne: Dastugue, 1964; Lyons: Wuilleumier, 1949; Piñedes: Arnal, 1959. Sublaines: Cordier, 1974; Ennery.
   More males under 40 than over: Mont-Joly: Dastugue, 1959.

Table 32

Direction of Graves in Collections of German Data,
during Plague Period, A.D. 542-750.

Place	NE	ENE	E	ESE	SE
Bindung		9	3	2	1
Dannheimer	4	1	14	1	1
Garsha		6	5	1	
Koch		3	5	2	
Reim		2	4		
Schmidt 1970	3	3	8	3	2
Schmidt 1976		2	7		
Other places	21	19	26	9	2
	28	45	72	18	6

Sources: C. Bindung, "Bericht über Ausgrabungen in Niederrheinischen Kirchen," *Rheinische Ausgrabungen* 10 (1971): 219-241.

H. Dannheimer, *Die germanische Funde der Späten Kaizerzeit* (Berlin, 1960).

Friedrich Garsha, *Die Alamannen in Sudbaden* (Berlin, 1970).

Ursula Koch, *Die Grabfunde des Merowingerzeit aus dem Donautal zum Regensburg* (Berlin, 1968), *Germanische Denkmaler der Völkerwanderungszeit*, A, 10.

Hartmann Reim, "Fundstellen des Merovingerzeit aus Baden-Würtemberg und kr. Tuttlingen," *Fundberichte aus Baden-Würtemburg* 1 (1975): 628-641.

Berthold Schmidt, *Die späte Volkerwanderungszeit in Mitteldeutschland*, southern part (Berlin, 1970).

Berthold Schmidt, *Die späte Volkerwanderungszeit in Mitteldeutschland*, north and east parts (Berlin, 1976).

of great interest to the Germans. The information comes in two forms: data from individual sites and collections from specific districts. Both are given in table 32. Few had thought of cataloging data with respect to the plague period and thus one must sort it out from material organized upon other bases, usually geographical but not chronologically correlated to the plagues. The importance of direction of graves was not recognized then and with few exceptions the direction has not been given very exactly. Most tend to be quite general: east often includes variation from exact east. Similarly there is variation for NE and SE. For our purposes mere statements that the graves lie north or south of east is valuable.

In the mass, about seventy-three cemeteries show their graves lying more to the north than the south of east; only twenty-four lying south of east. Outside of this plague period the mass of cemeteries show a heavy majority of graves pointing south of east. The exception is the evidence from the south and east in central Germany in Schmidt's data. Even here the north and south

Table 33

Comparison of German Data of 542-750
with those of 750-1000

	542-750	750-1000
Cemeteries—with more males than females	20	9
—with more females than males	13	3
Males in same cemeteries	1445	209
Females in same cemeteries	1240	146
Sex Ratios of the skeletons	117	149
	— — — —	
Cemeteries—more Infans I than II	11	7
Cemeteries with less Infans I than II	5	1
Skeletons—number of those with more Inf. I	228	60
—number of those with less Inf. I	176	21
Ratio of I to II — — — —	.77	.35
Cemeteries with more Adultus males than older	9	2
with less Adultus males than older	6	7
Males over 20 in cemeteries with more Adultus than older males	486	51
Older males in cemeteries with less Adultus than older	520	80
Percent of total Adultus	48.3	38.9

The number of skeletons is not the same because information about all types is not available for the cemeteries.

pointing graves seem about equal which should indicate some spread of the disease.[11]

The other indications of plague, from skeletal information, are decisive only when compared to conditions earlier and later than the plague period. A comparison with the succeeding period shows less females, infans II and deaths before forty in the postplague population than earlier. The same is also true for the preplague period. Germans seem to lose interest in the archaeology of the postplague period, in part because with more Christian churches and churchyards, there have been fewer excavations.

In any case there is little reason to doubt that plague extended over much of Germany. Probably with further study, especially in more carefully defining the chronological limits of cemeteries, a more accurate picture of plague in the German area can be

---

[11]The mass of the data is so great that it seems necessary to give details of location only for the data other than that to direction of graves. It can be seen that the data in the collections roughly parallel in number those of the other areas. There is some small overlapping, of course. Other areas. B. Schmidt, "Opferplatz und Gräberfeld bei Oberwerschen, kr. Hohenmö lsen," *Jahrbuch für mitteldeutsche Vorgeschichte* 50 (1966): 275-286. Map 276; direction of graves slightly ENE.

outlined. There are few chronicles or other literary evidence for Germany in this period. The people were just beginning to become Christian and thus, throwing off the old forest taboos, to extend the farming areas on a large scale.[12] Except for such cities as Cologne, Mainz, and Trier in the west there were probably few cities of any size. The archaeological data then is very valuable in showing that Germany suffered severely from the plague.

THE AUSTRIAN-BOHEMIAN-SWISS DATA

Austria, Bohemia, and Switzerland lie south and east of Germany and share many of its geographical characteristics. The direction of Swiss cemeteries runs NE 8, ENE 2, E 5, ESE 1 and SE 1. Like the German evidence the Swiss shows more infans I than II and all cemeteries have a majority of males over age 40. The one large Bohemian cemetery of Zelovich has 258 women to 153 men, but the other figures are 162 infans I to 58 of infans II and 112 males under to 41 males over 40. The other three Bohemian cemeteries show a direction of graves either E or ENE.[13] Again the evidence that the plague existed in the area becomes stronger by comparison with the evidence for the next period. In this period Switzerland had a majority of women in six of eleven cemeteries.[14] For the next period also Bohemia had men in the majority in fourteen of eighteen cemeteries and the antiplague setup (more infans I than II and more men over 40 than under) in all of its cemeteries for which there are indications of direction.

THE OTHER EASTERN AREAS

Fortunately Hungarian archaeologists and anthropologists have a deep interest in both the plague period (A.D. 542-750) and

---

[12]A. H. Price, "The Germanic Forest Taboo and Economic Growth," *Vierteljaheschrift für Sozial- und Wirtschaftsgeschichte* 52 (1965): 368-378.

[13]Austria: graves NE: Aargebiet: Hug, 1940; Basel: Laur-Belort, 1957; Breitenschutzing: Kloiber, 1966; Katzendorf: Geiblinger, 1953; Lauriacum: Kloiber, 1957, 1960, 1962; Premploz: Viollet, 1908 (?): Pieterlen: Tschumi, 1943; Pitten: Hampl, 1971; Rudelsdorf; Kloiber, 1964a; Wartmannstette: Hampl, 1961. ENE: Deersheim: Schneider, *Nordharzer Jahrbuch* 3 (1967): 7-19. Kaiser Augst: Viollier, 1909; Petinesin Tschumi, 1940. East: Beggingen-Lobern: Guyan, 1958; Beringen (Schaffhausen): Viollet, 1911; Hafeld: Kloiber, 1964a; Mannersdorf am Leithegebirge: H. Mitscha-Marhein, *Archaeologia Austriaca* 22 (1957): 45. Rohrendorf-Expersdorf: Hampl 1965. ESE., Traunmündung: Hertha Ladenbauer-Orel, *Das baierische Gräberfeld an der Träunmündung* (Vienna, 1960) plan 80. Zelovich: Stloukal, 1974. NE: Mikulcice, *Prehled Vyzkumo* 65 (1967): 58; Uberske Hradiste: *Prehled Vyzkumo* 65 (1967): 40. East: Brazno: Pleinerova; *Archeologicke Rozhledy* 23 (1971): 713. Staré Zemke: *Prehled Vyzkumo* 65 (1967): 69.

[14]More women: Beggingen Lobern: Guyan, 1958; Beringen: Viollier, 1911; Buochs: Hug, 1962; Elgg: Trudel, 1938. Traunmündung: Ladenbauer-Orel, 1960. Rudelsdorf: Kloiber, 64a. Less women than men: Bernerring (Basel): Laur-Belart, 1948. Breitenschutzing: Kloiber, 1964a. Kaiser Aust: Viollier, 1909. Lauriacum: Kloiber, 1957, 1960, 1962. Rohrendorf-Expersdorf: Hampl, 1965.

the following period (750-1000). The first coincided with the Avar invasion and conquest and the second with the Hungarian. Thus there is available data for both the plague period and the following centuries, so that their characteristics may be compared for indications of plague. The direction of the graves for the plague period is: NNE-NE 10; ENE 7; E 1; ESE 1; SE 9. While these cemeteries have only a slight tendency toward the north, the direction during the postplague period is heavily toward the ESE and SE.[15] The differences with respect to the other tests are as follows:

	542-750	750-1000	
Male-female majority	11-15	12-8	3 even
Inf I-Inf II majority	5-12	10-8	1 even
Males-20-39 vs 40 and over	13-7	13.5	2 even

In all three categories of skeletal evidence the Hungarian cemeteries tend to show existence of the plague, over much of the country. The Danube Valley, one of the principal trade routes to Constantinople from western Europe, ran directly through the country. It would be surprising if the plague which seems to have come from the east had missed Hungary. As might be expected the larger places, on the trade routes, seem to show stronger evidence of the plague: the four cemeteries of Alattyan show proper proportions of the data if added together. Eloszalles and Tiszavasvars have fewer in infans II than in I while the two Üllo cemeteries show more deaths in those over 40.[16] The late Avar period which fell after the plague shows distinct tendencies for graves to lie toward the southeast.[17]

---

[15]Graves pointing NE: Avar: Kourig, 1963, 93-97; Cimpie: Salamon, 1969; Ciko: Kourig, 1963; 93. Csepel: Sos, 1961. Dunaszekesö: Kourig, 1963, 94. Kiszomber: Torok, 1962 (actually NNE). Kornye: Salamon, 1969. Martonkasar NE of Szekesfeher: G. Rosner, *Alba Regia* 1 (1960): 171-174. Szigeszentimiklós-Haros: *Archaeologiai Ertesito* 80 (1953): 51. Ujhalasto: Garan, 1972. Varpalata-Szucs (Malan, 1952).
    Pointing ENE: Andoc: Garan 1972. Batida: Balint, 1937. Budapest: Liptak, 1963. Szentes-Kajan: Wenger, 1955. Szentes-Kukenyzug: Csallany, 1961, 25. Szentes-Nagyhegy, Csallany, 1961, 44. Szeged-makkoserdo: Kourig, 1963, 93. Ujhalasto (two cemeteries): Garan, 1972. Zamardi: *Somogvi Muzeumok Kozlemenyei* 1 (1973): 7.
    East: Vors: Sagi, 1961.
    ESE. Szentendre: Kiszely, 1966.
    SE. Alattyam Kourig, 1963 (2 cemeteries). Dunaszecso: Burger, 1966. Kerepes: G. Torok, *Folia Archeologica* 24 (1973): 118. Kiskoros: *Somogyi Muz. Kozlemenyei* 1 (1978): 70. Tiszavasvar: Wenger, 1972. Unbropuszta: see under Kiskoros above, 70. Varpalata: ibid. 72.

[16]Alattyan: Kourig, 1963; Alattyán-Tulát: Wenger, 1952, 1957; Avars: Laszlo, 1955, 1957; Batida: Balint, 1937; Budapest: Liptak, 1973; Csakbereny: Toth, 1972; Csapel-Insel: Sos, 1961a; Dunaszekcsö: Burger, 1966; Elöszellás: Wenger, 1966 (Bajcsihegy); Hegykö: Toth, 1964, 1967; Janoshida-Tótkerpuszti: Wenger, 1953; Mélykút-Tsanedülö: Farkas, 1971; Szebeny: Toth, 1961; Szentes-Kazan: Wenger, 1955; Tiszavasvar: Wenger, 1973; Üllo: Sos, 1955. Kornye: Salamon, 1969; Kunszállás Liptak, 1971, Parducz, 1963, Sagi, 1961.

[17]Especially Alattyan: Kourig, 1963: 93-97, esp. 97.

There is really little information about the early plague period in Yugoslavia and Rumania. What little there is shows a consistent NE or ENE direction of graves sugesting that the plague was prevalent in both of those countries. This is as might be expected since they lay between the north of Europe and the plague ridden south.[18]

The information about Scandinavia and Poland is scarce indeed for this period. In the former only data about Ihre remain: orientation was primarily SE but the sex ratio was low with 34 men and 32 women.[19] For Poland data remain for only three cemeteries and one of these may be from an earlier period. Osowa, a fifth-sixth century cemetery, has a plague cast with 5 men and 13 women and more men over forty than under, but a 5-4 advantage is not very impressive. Karmazyny has barrows and thus no easy orientation while its 15-13 male-female division again is not typical. At Cialopynch males outnumbered females twelve to eight and infans I over infans II three to one, but more men died as adultus than as maturus, a ratio of eight to two. The information is thus very tenuous. Poland, however, is not too far from the Asiatic steppes, recently supposed to be the seat of the plague.[20] Presumably Poland had its share. One may doubt, however, that it reached Scandinavia—unless the Norsemen had the longboats for which they were later famous. In which case they would probably have carried the plague home.

A COMPARISON OF THE EARLIER AND LATER PLAGUES

Little doubt exists that the plaque spread over Italy, Iberia, and southern France. Apparently it ranged much farther north. The preceding chapter shows that it touched most of the British Isles except Scotland and some of northern England. It seems also to have covered all of France and southern and middle Germany. Some areas even in northern Germany were also affected, but the lack of evidence may be the result of lack of research upon northern and eastern sections. There is little evidence for or against the presence of the plague in either Scandinavia or Poland. In Germany the Rhine and Danube valleys show much evidence of plague, so it is not surprising that Austria, Czechoslovakia, and

---

[18]Jugoslavia: Bled Ptuj Skerlj 1952, 1958; for Romania: Bratei (Sibis): *Materiale si cercetari archeologice* 10 (1973): 191-201. Mormintul: E. Condurachi, *Histria* (Bucarest, 1966): 326; Veresmort (Univea); *Studii si cercetari de istorie veche* 4 (1973): 645. ENE. Piatra Frecatei, *Materiale si cercetari archeologice* 8 (1962): 580-581. Obirsia (Ott): *Dacia* 10 (1965): 164 (plan) Prueni (Buzau); *Dacia* 13 (1969): 526.

Ihre: Stenberg, 1961.

[19]Osowa: Dzierzykray-Rogalsky, 1962: Karmazyny: Cebak, 1955: Cialopynch: Dzierzykray-Rogalsky,1961.

[20]Russell, 1958: 40-45.

Hungary also saw much of the disease. Since the disease moved along the great seaways and roads, one might have expected that it would have reached most of Europe. As we have seen, however, it did not always spread everywhere, thus one cannot be certain about its extent. The cause of its disappearance also remains unclear. Perhaps the great loss of population also depleted the reservoirs of infection which were needed to keep the disease circulating; or there may have been a depletion of men whom fleas would attack or of the disease itself.

How much was the mortality of the plagues of the sixth-seventh centuries and how did it affect the course of population change in the period? The quite considerable data available cannot produce an estimate directly, as one can for the late medieval plague. That series of epidemics apparently reduced the population perhaps a quarter in the first epidemic and by much lesser numbers in the succeeding epidemics. By 1377 the population was down probably 40 percent from the preplague figures and continued downward until 1440. For much of the fifteenth century the population remained the same, but began increasing with various rates of growth into the next century.[21] Did the earlier plague have a similar course?

One big difference between the milieu of the two plagues was the much greater number of people in Europe in 1348 than in 542: about seventy million as against perhaps thirty, more than double the population. However, this difference would be of much importance only to pneumonic plague, carried from mouth to mouth. The bubonic form moving by flea and rat was carried more precariously and limited by the territoriality of the rat. Even in densely populated modern India usually only one or two members of even large families contracted the disease. A second difference was the climate which from 1350 to 1500 was probably cooler than from 542-600 and thus not as propitious for the spread of the plague.

The course of the epidemics in the two periods had elements in common. Both entered areas which had not experienced the plague in the recent past and thus had little immunity against it. One terrible epidemic, lasting for perhaps three years, was followed by endemic periods of eight and twelve years (542-4 to 552 and 1347-50 to 1369). The epidemics then recurred at cycles of about 3.8 years, a rat cycle. In Britain there had been a marked decline in plague mortality before its recurrence in 664 and in the fourteenth century there was a similar period of not so high mortality beginning about 1440. If the evidence about other

---

[21]Russell, 1948: 206-207. Compare mortality rates of ages five to twenty-five in tables 9.9 and 9.10.

effects of the plague is similar one might tend then to assume that the courses of population change were about the same.

In both periods the sex ratio generally declined since the mortality made the saving of both male and female lives valuable. After the first epidemics of the two periods, the children, principally of infans II, suffered so heavily that the epidemics were called plagues of the children, but it is difficult to estimate the quantitative losses. In fact this is one of the least known facets of the late medieval epidemics. The shifting of deaths to the summer is evident, both in the figures of monthly deaths in Britain and in the direction of graves. Actually this shift seems greater in the earlier than in the later period. All in all it seems that the mortality of the first plague was as heavy as that of the second.

Biraben and Le Goff suggest cautiously that the plague was responsible for the power of Charlemagne by differential reduction of population, setting up a preponderance of population in the European areas over which Charlemagne was to rule.[22] Obviously if northern France and much of Germany was affected by the plague, there is little to commend this thesis. However, the plague by reducing population in general would have weakened the human resources necessary to expand political boundaries of the period. Frankish interference in both Italy and Iberia declined in the period 542-700, perhaps as a result of the plague. The population decline in Italy has been thought to have enabled the Lombards to come into Italy and take it over even early in the plague period. The military impotence induced by the plague may have aided in the limiting of military operations in northern Europe. The Germanic migrations from Scandinavia seem to have ceased for a time then also. This might suggest that Scandinavia had actually suffered from the plague also; otherwise, northern Europe, like Italy should have attracted migrants from farther north. More excavation then in the era of plague may give an answer to the question of its exsistence in the north.

The plague had two types of results: an immediate one upon a region where it occurred and an indirect one upon the world at large through differential mortality of differing regions. Within regions it simplified life merely by declining numbers. Cities were smaller and thus the industrial and commercial life was reduced and less diverse. The number of surplus men also declined and reduced the base for military expansion. In the west the English ceased to try to conquer Scotland and even Ireland. The Franks ended their adventures in Iberia and Italy. The differential mortality was naturally to the advantage of the drier and hotter land, principally of the great semi-desert and desert areas. Islamic areas

---

[22]Biraben and Le Goff, 1969: 1508.

Table 34

Life Tables, Plague Period, A.D. 542-750.

	q_x		l_x	d_x	L_x	T_x	e_x^o
			Total: Males, Females, Uncertain				
I	12.8	87.2	5029	644	31983	149067	29.6
II	11.5	88.5	4385	503	23807	117084	26.7
J	9.1	91.9	3882	355	22227	92277	23.8
A	56.6	43.4	3527	1996	50580	70050	19.9
M	86.4	13.6	1531	1323	17390	19470	12.7
S	100.0	0.0	208	2080	2080	2080	10.0
			Males				
I	0.5	99.5	1882	10			
II	0.5	99.5	1872	9			
J	3.5	96.5	1863	66	10980	48430	26.0
A	49.5	50.5	1797	890	27040	37450	20.8
M	92.6	7.4	907	840	9740	10410	11.5
S	100.0	0.0	67	67	670	670	10.0
			Females				
I	0.9	99.1	1858	17			
II	1.8	98.2	1841	34			
J	6.3	93.7	1807	114	10500	43610	24.1
A	56.8	43.2	1693	961	24250	33010	19.5
M	90.2	7.8	732	660	8040	8760	12.0
S	100.0	0.0	72	72	720	720	10.0

for example, developed at this time, about 610-732, at the expense of their neighbors. In the west it meant expansion first into North Africa and then into Iberia in 711. If it had any share in the power of Charlemagne, it was probably because of the impetus created by the rise of population after the plague. More likely Charlemagne was the beneficiary of one of the most amazing series of one man - one son (or successor) developments in history.[23] The statistical chances of that series is almost too great to believe.

The skeletal data for the second plague period are helpful only for those over the age of twenty. In most cemeteries there are few skeletons of younger people up to the age of twenty. Some of the data come from museums and ossuaries where movement of the bones has been destructive to the smaller bones of women and children, particularly of children. This results, for one thing, in a higher sex ratio when the sexes were nearly equal in numbers. Nevertheless, this raises some questions. In the time of the later plague was there less careful handling of corpses? There seems to

[23]J. C. Russell, "Aspects démographiques des débuts de la Feodalité," *Annales Économies, Sociétés, Civilizations* 20 (1965): 1120-1122.

Table 35
Life Tables, Plague Period, A.D. 1348-1500

	q_x		l_x	d_x	L_x	T_x	e_x0
			All (Males, Females, Uncertain)				
I	6.4	93.6	2543	264	16481	70957	31.8
II	6.3	93.7	2279	143	13245	64478	28.3
J	8.0	92.0	2136	171	12303	51233	24.0
A	50.9	49.1	1965	1001	26450	38930	19.8
M	85.3	14.7	964	822	11060	12480	12.9
S	100.0	0.0	142	142	1420	1420	10.0
			Males				
I				1			
II	5.0	95.0		1			
J			1206	60	7062	30472	25.3
A	48.7	51.3	1147	580	15820	23410	20.4
M	87.1	12.9	587	511	6630	7590	12.9
S	100.0	0.0	76	76	760	760	10.0
			Females				
I				1			
II				2			
J	7.0	93.0	718	50	4130	17158	23.9
A	55.7	44.3	668	372	8820	13030	19.5
M	85.9	14.1	296	255	3370	4210	12.0
S	100.0	0.0	41	41	410	410	10.0

be little evidence remaining of actual plague pits, that is, where numbers of corpses were dumped indiscriminately in time of epidemics.

A comparison of the two life tables for the plague periods shows a very remarkable similarity of the two and, of course, differences from life tables of nonplague periods. The shortage of data for early years of life makes comparison of expectation for the first twenty years of life of little value. The expectations at twenty and forty years of age for men and women are quite alike, except for the expectation of forty-year-old men. In the first plague their expectation was only 11.5 years, even less for the women at that age. In the second plague it had jumped to 12.9 years. The female expectation at age forty was twelve years exactly for both plagues.

Skeletal data do not give the same accuracy for chronological analyses that the inquisitions post mortem of late medieval England do.[24] The first generation subjected to the plague (those born 1326-1348) had an expectation at forty of 15.72 years and this increased for each generation until those born 1426-1450 had

---

[24]Russell, 1948: 180-185.

20.44 much longer than suggested by the skeletal data. The increase indicates that the plague tended to destroy not only those who had little resistance to the plague but to any other diseases. In general a population which had undergone a long period of plague should have been healthier than preplague populations.

Even at the end of the discussion of the plague there are at least two questions which still require answers. The first is the question of whether the house rat was the only important carrier in the early medieval plague.[25] The second is whether the medieval plague, like the modern, was suffered by only about one person in each household.[26] It remains a mysterious topic.

[25]J. Rackham, "Rattus rattus: The Introduction of the Black Rat into Britain," *Antiquity* 52 (1979): 112-120.
[26]R. Pollitzer, "Plague" in J. M. May, *Studies in Disease Ecology* (New York, 1961): 473.

IX. The Threat of Too Many Mouths.

Late ancient and medieval people lived close to their means of subsistence. Often their animals spent the night in the next room or at least just outside the house, unless they were in the flocks within the lord's folds. Their gardens were nearby, the grain supply was in jars within the house or in barns. They knew what the nearby ponds and streams held and how much would come from orchards or scattered nut trees. They could see what they might expect to eat during the long winter and anticipate what would be coming during the following spring and summer. From all of these they could estimate how many persons would live off of the available food. The chances that it would increase over the years were not good and if it just satisfied the number of persons who were living and growing, the prospect of additions to the population was not a happy one. Yet it was one which had faced other rather primitive peoples for centuries back. Folk tradition and custom had evolved to meet the problems. What they were is not very clear. At least the textbooks do not discuss the question of how they met the problem of population and the danger of overpopulation. Many today believe that they did not need to, that the birthrate was about that of the death rate and that variations in numbers were caused by disease and famine alternating with good crops and healthy years.[1]

This chapter will discuss the factors involved in population change and stability: the length of a generation and the difference in years of parent's age to their children. The relation in number is the replacement ratio. The potential of childbearing may be considered in terms of years of possible marriage as well of some uncertain evidence from female bones. It is assumed that breast-feeding was normal and that the spacing of children largely depended upon it. The number of children could be increased by wet nursing. The possibility of marriage hinged upon the availability of means of subsistence; that is, no job, no marriage, a considerable restraint upon the number of children. High death rate among girls was a factor, particularly the apparent prevalence of infanticide. And plague might increase the availability of land holding and speed up the rate of marriage. There was thus considerable opportunity to increase or decrease the number of children voluntarily, without the aid of illness and famine.

---

[1]Coming primarily from Malthus and his contemporaries. For their views see J. J. Spengler, "Malthus's Total Population Theory," *Canadian Journal of Economics and Political Science* 11 (1945): 83-110; 12 (1946): 234-264. Recent biographies are: Patricia James, *Malthus* (London, 1979) and William Petersen, *Malthus* (Cambridge, Mass. 1979).

THE GENERATION AND REPLACEMENT RATES

What constitutes a generation has been discussed recently and is obviously a key factor in demographic history.[2] The relation of the age of children to that of their parents determines in part the rise and fall of population. The generation is thus a moving calculation, the result of continuous deaths and births year by year. And this makes it difficult to define a generation in terms of so many years, assuming that people born within certain years will have certain characteristics or types of thought or action. Traumatic events or general conditions prevailing within a number of years might leave lasting impressions upon contemporaries which would not be shared by those not yet living or even not old enough to understand and feel what was going on. So also will waves of public opinion, styles and fashions which seem to develop suddenly and sweep over vast areas. Do they have a permanent effect upon people of a particular age group and thus stamp perrnently that generation in a particular mold?[3] Important as the questions are, our interest here is primarily demographic.

One form of generation is that of primogeniture, from a landholder to his oldest son or other heir. Good evidence for this form of succession is available for the landholders of late medieval England and Wales from about 1250 to 1500.[4] Along with age of succession and death the average expectation of life at time of succession is given. In every case the expectation is shorter than the length of the generation. The reason is that in some cases a grandson succeeded and thus a generation was actually skipped and in others the successor was a nephew or even more distant heir. In some cases an heiress married and it is the age of the husband which is given. However, son succeeded father in a very large percentage of cases. It is not surprising that the age of heirs declined sharply during the plague period, from 24-26 years before the plague to 18-21 during the plague until the last plague generation. Since the age of marriage of girls was not low before the plague, their age probably declined also during the plague and is certainly lower in the fifteenth century.[5] The length of the generation, however, only declined from about twenty-eight to twenty-four years. It suggests that the death rate was much less for the years after succession—that the plague was largely a disease of the children of young adults.[6]

[2]Herlihy, 1974: 347-364. Bibliography on p. 348, note 1.
[3]Herlihy, 1974: 347, 350 on definitions of generation.
[4]Table 36.
[5]Russell, 1948: 156-158.
[6]See p. 115.

Table 36

Data about the Generation among English Landholders,
about A.D. 1250-1500.

Date of Birth	Age at succession	Age at death	Length of generation	Expectation at age of succession
Before 1276	28	54	26	25.0
1276-1300	24	50	26	23.8
1301-1325	23	47	24	22.3
1326-1348	19	47	28	22.7
1348-1375	18	42	24	22.3
1376-1400	21	47	26	21.6
1401-1425	19	52	33	29.4
1426-1450	26	54	26	25.6
Average	22.3	49.1	26.6	24.1
Plague average (1348-1425)	18.7	46.7	27.7	

Sources: Age at succession: Russell, 1948, 202-207: midpoint of "number exposed". Age at death: midpoint of "number dying." Expectation at age of succession: calculated from tables 8.2-8.9, Russell, 1948, 180-185.

Another form of generation should stretch from the marriage of father or mother to a midpoint in the number of their children. Since, as we shall see, marriage was apt to come a few years after age twenty, the midpoint of family size may well have been about thirty years of age[7] in normal times and perhaps five years younger in times of the plague. The latter would be produced both by the shortening of the lives of parents and the earlier marriages.

A striking point about the figures in table 36 is the differences in lengths of generations. The group born in A.D. 1401-1425 lived an average of thirty-three years, six years more than the average, twenty-seven. That generation began to be influenced in its thinking at about seven years of age or about 1408 and continued for another thirty years or to about 1438. The events of 1408-1438 may have had a profound effect upon its generation and a more enduring effect upon history. It was the time of England's second attempt to take over France and its subsequent defeat. It was also the age of the Great Councils and their failure.

The table also enables one to secure replacement ratios of generations.[8] A common error is to believe that if fathers at death

---

[7]See below.

[8]Russell, 1948: 236-245. There called "succession of generations"; Herlihy, 1974: 348-350. Sylvia Thrupp, "The Problem of Replacement Rates in Late Medieval English Population," *Economic History Review* 2nd. ser. 14 (1961): 218-224.

are survived by an equal number of sons, the population remains the same. Obviously sons are not as old as their parents and many of the sons will die before they reach the age at which their parents died. An estimate of the replacement rates may be made by comparing groups in the life table (L or T) equally distant in age as the length of the generation, usually twenty-seven years (table 35). Using the life tables for the time periods 1-5, years 1-13 (infans I and II) may be compared to years 27-40 (two-thirds of adultus). The results are:

1	(1-542)	1.85	(21373/39583)
2	(542-750)	1.65	
3	(750-1000)	1.70	
4	(1000-1348)	1.85	
5	(1348-1500)	1.69	

The figures for Mikulcice (table 7) show 2.2, but there seems a relatively small number of older people in its population. The plague figures are probably too small because of failure to bury children in the cemeteries. The Mikulcice figures (table 5) are probably more typical of the plague period and compare to losses in England.[9]

We interpret this to mean that the numbers (1.75 etc.) are the number of sons needed to replace dead fathers or daughters to replace mothers, or that twice the number would be necessary for a family to replace itself. This assumes that the decline in numbers between birth and fourteen is about the same as the number dying between thirty and forty-four. Actually the life tables usually show more dying in the later than earlier period of life, but most life tables from skeletal evidence are lacking in persons of the earliest years of life.

There is a distinct difference in pattern of replacement of the plague from the nonplague periods, as one would expect. It is, in fact, so different that it should be an indication in itself of the presence of plague in a population.

POTENTIAL FECUNDITY AND ACTUAL FERTILITY

Fecundity denotes the number of children that women can have and fertility the number that they actually have. The outmost limits are set by age when procreation may take place. The evidence for the years when women did have children is rather sparse for the Middle Ages but tends to show that most mothers had their children between the ages of nineteen and forty. The number of children within these age limits was determined by a

---

[9]Russell, 1948: 203-208.

variety of factors: some natural and some set by mankind.[10] Of the number of children which they had, several types of evidence are available. Chronicles and other documents provide data for the upper classes. At the end of the period some data from parish registers are informative. The skeletal evidence gives length of life between twenty and forty years of age in various areas. Women usually nursed their own children and this custom, with other factors during pregnancy, would tend to reduce the appearance of children to one in each two and a half to three years. There is controversial evidence about the value of parturition scars in female pubic bones as indications of the number of children that women have borne.[11]

The usual assumption is that women may bear children soon after menstruation starts but this overlooks the rather common teenage infertility. A survey of ages at which medieval royalty and nobility had their first children shows that few mothers had children before the age of twenty,[12] although many were married at much younger ages. A few were married at age seven to nine, more at the ten to twelve years of age and a large number at fourteen. Blanche of Castile married Louis VIII when she was twelve, had her first child seven years later and a dozen more before she was forty. Isabel, wife of King John of England, also

---

[10]On the general problem of prenatal wastage, J. Bongaart, "Why High Birth Rates are so Low," *Population and Development Review* 1 (1975): 289-296.

[11]J. L. Angel, "Paleodemography and Evolution," *American Journal of Physical Anthropology* 31 (1969): 344; and articles cited there. For modern evidence: C. A. Holt, "A Reexamination of Parturition Scars on the Human Female Pelvis," *American Journal of Physical Anthropology* 49 (1978): 91-94. M. Nag, *Factors affecting Human Fertility in Nonindustrial Societies, a Cross Cultural Survey* (Yale, New Haven, 1962): 87, 107-113 and esp. 113-115. Although mostly modern it agrees with the 20-40 thesis. J. A. Post, "Ages at Monarchy Menopause: Some Medieval Authorities," *Population Studies* 12 (1971): 83-87.

[12]The dates are: birth, marriage, birth of first child, death (if under 22) and death of husband (if wife is under 22). Anne, dau. Edward I: 1475, 1495, -, -, -. Anne, dau Edward IV: 1475, 1495, -, -, -. Anne of Brittany: 1476, 1491, -, 1492-. Beatrice, d. Henry III: 1242, 1260, 2 daus.* Blanche of Castile: 1188, 1200, 1207, -, -. Blanche, dau. Henry IV: 1392, 1402, 1409, -. Catherine of Valois: 1401?, 1420, 1421, -, -, Christine de Pisan: 1364, 1378, 3 children.* Eleanor of Aquitaine: 1122, 1137, 2 daus.* Eleanor, dau. Henry II: 1161, 1176, 1180, -, -. Eleanor, dau. John: 1215, 1224, -, 1231, -. Eleanor, wife Henry III: -, 1235, 1239, -, -. Eleanor, wife Alphonso: 1161,*. Eleanor of Thuringia: 1207, 1221, 3 children, 1227, -.* Elizabeth, dau. Edward I, 1282, 1296, -, -, -. Elizabeth, dau. Edward IV: 1466, 1486, 1486, -, -. Isabel of Hainault: 1170, 1186, 1187, -, -. Isabelle of Angoulême: 1188, 1200, 1207, -, 1216. Isabel, dau. John: 1214, 1235, -, -, -. Isabel, wife Philip IV, 1247, 1262, 1271, -, -. Isabel, wife Richard II: 1389, 1396, -, -, 1399. Isabel of Bavaria: 1371 1385, 5 sons.* Isabel, dau. Edward III: 1332, 1365* Joan, William of Sicily: 1165, 1177, -, -, -. Jeane d'Acre 1271, 1289, -, -,?* Jeanne, dau. Edward II: 1321, 1328, -, -, -. Joan, dau. John: 1210, 1221, -, -, -. Margaret, dau. Henry VII: 1489, 1503, 1507, -, -. Margaret, dau. Edward III: 1346, 1359, -, 1361, -. Margaret, dau. James I: 1424, 1436, -, 1445, -. Margaret dau. Henry III: 1240, 1251, 1261, -, -. Margaret wife Louis IX: 1219, 1234, 11 children.* Mary, dau. Edward III: 1344, 1361, -, 1362, -. Mathilda, dau. Henry I-: 1102, 1114, -, -, 1125. Mathilda, dau. Henry II: 1156, 1168, 3 sons, 1182, -.* Philippa, dau. Henry IV: 1394, 1406,* Philippa of Hainault: -, 1328, 1330, -,-.*
*Not included in the calculations.

married at twelve, had her first child at twenty and only three more to the king before he died. However, she married at thirty-three and had nine more before her last was born when she was forty-seven. Just after the end of the Middle Ages Catherine de Medici (1519-1589) married at fourteen, had no children for ten years and then nine in a short time. The significance of this evidence is that so many did marry at an early age and thus had the chance of early childbirth. There were *few* advantages of early marriage for most farm women. In general not many children were born to women after the age of forty and, indeed, relatively few in the late thirties.

How many children could they have in those twenty years? Louis IX's queen seems to have had twelve children in twenty years. Eleanor of Aquitaine, following her second marriage to Henry II of England, had five children in five years but only three afterward. Edward I of England and his first wife, Eleanor of Castile, had ten children in fifteen years, after an initial decade without children. His grandson, Edward III, had ten in nineteen years with Philippa of Hainault. In spite of these outbursts of prolificy the average to the families of English royalty in the Middle Ages after the Conquest was only six. Furthermore they were shortlived: only one member, male or female, lived to be eighty, and no other lived past seventy. Many died in early life. The long-lived member was Robert Curthose who spent the last thirty years of his life in a comfortable prison. It seems clear that most of the children in the royal families were nursed by others than their mothers. Occasionally women who nurse their own children have babies every year but it is very unusual.

Data from the recently discovered Catasto of Florence of 1427 confirm the conclusion that women then bore children mostly after the age of nineteen.

It can be seen from the births of royal children that ten or twelve might easily be born in twenty years under favorable conditions, or an average of about one every two years. The nursing of one's children slowed the intervals between children, perhaps a year which would give about three years between children. A study of the effect of breastfeeding today shows the percentage of women who became pregnant while lactating at various months[13]

Three	.7	Fifteen	34.8	Thirty	76.4
Six	4.9	Eighteen	48.7	Thirty-six	88.9
Nine	13.1	Twenty-four	66.4	Forty-eight	96.1
Twelve	23.9				

---

[13]Louis Henry, "Intervals between confinements in the absence of birth control," *Eugenics Review* 5 (1959): 200-211. This deals with families of at least six children, very fertile families with long periods of fertility. Herlihy-Klapisch-Zuber, 1978: 555-562. Flinn, 1981, 30-39, 102, 117.

Table 37				
Age of Mothers at Birth of First Child				
Age of Mother at Marriage x	Number Married at age x	Number of births of firstborn at age x	Number of mother's death at age x	Number of mothers whose husbands died at age x
7	2			
9	1			
10	1			1
11	2			
12	7			
13	1			
14	6			
15	4		2	1
16	2		1	1
17	1	1	1	
18	1	1	1	
19	2	3		
20	3	4		1
21	1		2	
22		5	5	2

Source: footnote 11.
Explanation of first item in each column. The youngest girl was married at age 7. Two girls were married at age 7. 1 girl had a child at age 17. 2 girls died at age 15. The husband of one girl died when she was 10.

Normally the period before a woman could conceive (amenorrea), if not breastfeeding her child, would be only about four months. And the distance created by breastfeeding between childbirths increased with age and the number of children. It is obvious that breastfeeding is not a good form of birth control, although it usually postponed the next conception for about eleven months. And other complications tended to keep down the birthrate. Thus if both husband and wife lived through twenty years of marriage the normal number of children would be seven, although the tendency to slow down toward the end would limit the number to six. It must be remembered that these are averages.

Using the data above, it seems that a breastfeeding mother would be pregnant, on the average about twenty-three months after the birth of the last child. The time between births would then be about thirty-two months. However, the data are modern and, of course, do not concern children in the Middle Ages who were often affected by dietary deficiencies. Furthermore, certain times of year were obviously more suitable to having children (winter-early spring?) than others and folk wisdom may have tended to concentrate conceptions in definite periods to produce births at desirable times. These would tend to set up a three-year cycle of births—a cycle which should tend to prevent an unwanted combination of knee and lap baby at the same time.

Presumably the children of royal and noble families would have no problem of food deficiency, although one cannot tell just what might have been the attitude of people towards foods. The insufficiency of iron in medieval diet has recently been pointed out, and particularly its probable effect upon women during their childbearing period.[14] The deficiency was probably worse in the first part of the Middle Ages but is supposed to have declined with greater consumption of meats, beans, and vegetables after about the year 1000. That there was a difference in the death rate of men and women throughout the Middle Ages is clear and doubtless a deficiency of iron was partially responsible for it causing a loss of life expectation of a few years. There are problems yet in the pattern. Few women seem to have died in childbirth if the small numbers of newborn infants buried with mothers is indicative of the condition. If the information is accurate that more farm children were born in late spring, then there is a problem: this meant conceptions in July and August, just about the most strenuous season of the year for farm women. For the landholders of late medieval England the months of most births were March and August, which meant conceptions in June and November—this before the plague of 1348. After the plague (and probably due to its influence) most births occurred (by month) in November.[15] The monthly variation before the plague was not great. There were, as one might expect, few conceptions during Lent, showing a certain restraint then, as they heeded ecclesiastical advices. The yearly advantages of certain seasons might well have tended to draw births into a yearly pattern, tending toward a three-year interval for births.

However, women would have twenty years of potential childbearing only if they lived through the whole period from twenty to forty or more. Allowance must be made for deaths in those twenty years. Actually only about half of the women managed to live throughout the whole period. Some allowance might be made also for the deaths of husbands. However, their loss of life was not so high; furthermore many of the women remarried. As we shall see the high sex ratio with its fewer women suggests that they remarried after their husbands died. The calculation can be made easily by dividing the number of years lived in the period from twenty to forty (L_{20}) by the number of persons alive at twenty (l_{20}). For the total life table for the period for females is 62.470 (L_{20}) divided

[14] Bullough-Campbell, 1980, 317-325.
[15] Russell, 1948, 169-172.

by 41.68 (1_{20}) or 15.0. We assume then that the average number of children under the life table conditions was potentially five. The husbands lived an average of 16.3 years in the interval. If two average persons married and neither remarried their average would have been only 12.2 years for about four children. However, both women and men probably remarried which would increase the limit toward the woman's potential.

The women's potential for childbearing in the five time periods shows:

A.D. 1-540	15.0	at three	5.0	at 2.5	6.0
540-750	13.1		4.4		5.2
750-1000	15.6		5.2		6.2
1000-1348	15.1		5.0		6.0
1348-1500	13.8		4.6		5.5

The limitations of the data for the fifth period must be remembered, but they should not affect these data much since they deal only with skeletons of persons of age twenty and above. They would tend to show that the first plague must have had a serious effect upon population recovery as the later one.

If, as we have seen, the average births necessary to maintain the population was about 3.5 to the woman, there should have been, assuming all married, more than enough children to maintain the population, although not enough in times of plague. Nevertheless the difference between the plague average potential of 3.1 children and the 4.64 children necessary for maintaining the population during the first plague would mean a radical change in the normal conditions of marriage and life, unless the population was to continue declining indefinitely. The fact that the population did recover in the second period during the plague period and may have done so partially in the first plague would indicate a considerable change.

For the nonplague periods the average of about five-six children was ample even to increase population when only 3.5 children were necessary if every woman was married and had children throughout her natural life. Indeed five children under those circumstances would have meant a rapid increase of population such as appeared only in the period A.D. 1000-1380 or so in southern and western Europe with perhaps a long period in the eastern parts of Europe.

Outside of the skeletal information there are some uncertain data about the meaning of certain changes in female pubic bones. All agree that they are the result of childbirth stresses. Some authorities thought that these can be used to determine the number of births that the woman had experienced. From a series of studies on ancient and medieval cemeteries, the average to the woman seemed about 4.2. Recent studies upon the remains of women whose childbirth history is known has cast doubt upon the evidence, at least of modern women.[16] These later scientists have doubted that the method is satisfactory for modern cases and thus raise a serious question about the earlier evidence. There is, of course, the possibility that the childbirths of an earlier day were under conditions which would have left more obvious results in the bones of the mothers. That is to say, that a difference in position and of more stress under ancient and medieval practices would have produced more obvious and simpler results in the bones. It is unfortunate that such potentially valuable evidence cannot be substantiated.

Another source of evidence about total number of children in a family comes from parish registers, but unfortunately these come almost entirely after the Middle Ages. Some sixteenth-century registers give some clues to conditions in Europe at the time. Mols has compiled information on the subject: English: Banbury, 3.7; Cheltenham 4.8; Chesterfield 4.9; Leeds 3.3; Manchester 4.4; Romney 3.6; Sheffield 3.6; Tiverton 3.8; France: Metz 3.1; Strasbourg 2.9; Germany: Augsburg 3.3; Leipzig 2.8; Munster (Alsace) 3.7; Stuttgart 3.5; Weissenburg 4.0; Italy: Venice 3.4; Switzerland: Zurich 3.6.[17] The average of these is 3.7, quite a little lower than the 4.6 suggested by the skeletal evidence of women who had children in the second plague, or rather the potential if they all had children.

The number of children that a woman has is, of course, a lifetime total and not a very good indication of the size of her household at any one time. It is a part of the history of the household which is bound up with other phases of life and society.

TERRITORIALITY, MATRIMONY AND THE HOUSEHOLD.[18]

The household, despite its apparent simplicity, is a reasonably complex organism. Fundamentally, it begins with a union of male and female, a union which has its complications. Then there are added children and their problems; nurture, support, and education. The strength of the unit rests largely upon its economic base and assurance of future subsistence. This is the nuclear family. If to it are added grandparents or orphan relatives, it becomes more

---

[16]The data recently provided about birth intervals show a fairly consistent marriage at about 25 followed by the first child (Flinn 1981, p. 28, 33), in the period before 1750. The result is, on the average, the first child appeared at about 26, the second child 28-29, the third 32 and two or more later with the last child at about 38-40, on the average. (Flinn 1981, p. 84). This might have been much like the medieval.

[17]Mols 1955: 216-222.

[18]See, for instance, A. V. Stokes, ed. *Territory* (Stroudsburg, 1974); V. C. Wynne-Edwards, *Animal Dispersion in relation to Social Behaviour* (Edinburgh, 1962).

complicated. Furthermore, it is part of a community and region of individuals. In an age of great migrations this outside relationship may be of vital importance to communities and even regions. However, at present this study deals primarily with the simpler units and their relationships.

Among birds it is often noticed that when either of a nesting pair is killed, the survivor quickly recruits another of the same sex and carries on the nest. It assumes that the system produces more birds than the territorial system can support and that the unmated birds are a kind of reservoir on which to draw. The data about replace-ment ratios shows that there was a similar surplus of men thus creating problems of too many unmarried and unemployed to complicate governmental and social relationships. Yet the Middle Ages, up to 1348 at least, seem not to have suffered much from underemployment, unless it developed to some extent in the thirteenth century. Certainly for twelve centuries or so there seems to have been no serious problem, even though data tend to indicate more children than necessary to replace the population. In time of plague the problem was to provide enough children to replace the heavy plague losses. This was done only slowly and after the end of the plagues in the early Middle Ages, but in the fifteenth century parts of Italy and probably of France saw a steady increase in spite of the plague.

The distribution of population was largely determined by ter-ritoriality, a fundamental principle of the animal world as well as of the human. Each male normally defines an area or source of support which will care for him and his family or females depen-dent on him. He defends this area against his own kind and others who threaten the area. Until he has his territory he usually does not mate or arrange for the caring of a family. The necessity of support is a considerable factor in maintaining a stable and prosperous group. Since the opportunities for support were lim-ited, the principles of control and succession were developed to guard against subdivision of territories too small to support a family. In this respect ancient and medieval societies were more careful than our modern society which has overpopulation as one of its more terrible problems. While territoriality relates primarily to individuals, it also has relevance for villages and tribes. When German tribes moved into an area, they occasionally set off village sites at regular intervals in unoccupied territory, using their group experience in making village allotments which would care for their families.

In spite of this, there were the poor, their numbers relieved by drastic remedies, such as the plague. In Florence in 1400 their number declined with the epidemic of that year. Teruel in Spain had a drop in numbers with the plague of 1348 and later years. The examination of wealth at Albi before and after the plague of

1348 showed a redistribution of wealth among those who survived.[19]

In any case clerical influence tended to limit sexual relations to marriage and the family through the confessional and ecclesiastical legal system. Marriage is usually thought of as a means for furthering population. Its purposes were variously described in the Middle Ages but two were clear: to produce children and to save men from sin.[20] Actually it seems designed to restrict population growth almost as much as to foster it. Restrictions were many: persons were not allowed to marry within certain degrees of kinship, varying from about four to eight, settling finally on five degrees, (first cousin once removed); the godparent relationship was regarded as a first degree kinship relationship, thus cutting out another group; boys were normally not allowed to marry before fourteen and girls before twelve; Christians were permitted to marry each other and then only if they were not heretical. Divorce or annulment were not easy to come by. The clergy at the rank of subdeacon or of any regular persuasion might not marry. One might not marry a wife's sister.

Even the married were discouraged from conjugal relations in Lent and on certain holy days. Church laws regulated the positions of partners in sex and they were encouraged not to have them for personal enjoyment, else they might sin, if only venially. Treatises on marriages, mostly from a clerical point of view, are long on the negative side and have little to say even about the joys of parenthood and family life. Medieval society seems to have made certain that if one was born and allowed to live that there was a fair chance of employment and a steady place in society.

The attainment of a living allowed a couple to marry. Data for late medieval England shows that for the larger landholders an estimate may be made from the life tables for the size of a nuclear household, that is man, wife and children. Take the table for the generation born 1426-1450.[21] The problem is to follow such a family as long as they live in a house or cottage. We assume that the family may continue in that dwelling or another cottage until both parents died and that children live in it until they marry or leave on their own. The average expectation at age twenty (when we assume that they marry) was about twenty-eight years for men and probably a few years younger for women, say twenty-five. The surviving member had an expectation of about sixteen years of age for both. Thus the cottage would be occupied by one or the other

---

[19]Herlihy-Klopisch-Zuber, 1978, 453. Russell, 1962, 493-495. G. Prat, "Albi et le peste noire," *Annales du Midi* 64 (1952): 490-491. Cf. also Herlihy-Klapisch-Zuber, 1978, table 82 on p. 508.

[20]See ch. XIII.

[21]Russell, 1948, 185.

for about forty-four or forty-one years. Of normal average five children, one would die in the first year, another about age ten and the other three probably live out their adolescence at home. Thus the number of years lived by members would be:

father	44
mother	25
first	20
second	20
third	20
fourth	10
fifth	1
	140 years

The length of time the family lived in the dwelling would be the life of the longest, either father or mother, here estimated as forty-four. This would give an average number of persons to the year over the period as 3.2 for the household. Using the same method for the plague households of the generation born in 1348-1375 produces an average of 2.6. For both and particularly for the plague period there would be quite a number of orphans who would be accepted in other households, raising the average somewhat.

Much the same results come from another use of the life table. It is assumed that the T_x column represents the entire body of persons. The number of households would be represented by the number of women householders, perhaps 15 percent in the thirteenth century, as represented by extents, together with the number of men over the age when they seem to be holding land, about age twenty-two in preplague times and less than twenty during the plague. This gives an average of about 3.5 to the household for preplague and about 2.3 for plague.[22] Again the latter would almost certainly be increased by orphans from families where parents had died. If the men inherited or acquired land holdings where there was an average of five to the household they would have waited until about their thirtieth year before the plague and much later thereafter.

The actual evidence available for size of household before the changes in housing construction at the end of the Middle Ages seems to confirm this size, except for Italy and other places where more than one generation often lived in the same dwelling.

The poll tax returns for some 101 villages and a city or so for 1377 in England show about 3.5.[23] The number of persons in

[22]Russell, 1948, 31.
[23]Russell, 1948, 22-31.

households murdered in the thirteenth century was about the same.[24] The higher number suggested for the manor of Taunton is secured by not using medieval ratios for age and sex. The Spalding priory lists are highly unrepresentative, using only a fraction of one of three classes from unusually wealthy manors, leaving out the cotter class which pulls down the average on the normal manor.[25]

The question whether the English household was similar in size to the French and German is important since figures for great areas are based upon its size, notably the great French hearth assessments of 1328. The Polyptyque d'Irminon of the early ninth century near Paris is detailed enough so that one can safely estimate household size as about 3.6.[26] Tenth-century data from Burgundy would show about four.[27] The extent of Viry-Noueil of 1291 would seem to indicate a household even much lower.[28] Except in Italy the evidence would seem to show that medieval society preferred the nuclear family (man-wife-children) to a larger multi-generational set up. This is illustrated even in Italy, where the household in the large farm buildings was often larger. During the height of the plague, when there was plenty of space, the tendency was for the people to spread out in units of near 3.5.[29]

Unfortunately, skeletal evidence gives very little data about percentage of married persons in populations, as it also tells little about number to a household, except that obviously the very small cottages of the poor would tend to encourage the limitation of number of children. Most of the information about the number of the married comes from the second plague period and is considered there. There is some information about the eighth and ninth centuries and probably the data would be typical of centuries before the great expansion of feudal population. The places consist of five fairly large areas in Italy, France and Germany. The percentage seems to vary from 29 percent in the German areas to 44-45 in Italy and near Paris in France. The other two are 32-33 percent. The three lowest are quite consistent with a careful

---

[24]Russell, 1958, 15.

[25]J. C. Russell "Demographic Limitations of the Spalding Serf Lists," *Economic History Review* 2nd ser. 15 (1962), 144, note 2 for Taunton; 138-151 for serfs of Spalding Priory.

[26]Data summarized in Russell, 1958: 14.

[27]In the Maconnanois, A Delèage, *La vie en Burgundie* (4 vols.) (Macon, 1942): 4, 577.

[28]Robert Fossier, *La terre et les hommes en Picardie* (Paris, 1968, 2 vols.) 1: 276-277. The heads of households are given as 171 men and 65 women. If one assumes as many unmarried men as women, one has 130 single persons (men and women) and 106 married couples, for a total adult population of 342. Assuming an equal number of children gives a total of 684, of all ages and about 2.9 to the 236 households, a very low number.

[29]D. Herlihy, "Mapping Households in Medieval Italy," *Catholic Historical Review* 67 (1972): 5-6.

Table 38				
Sex Ratio by Time and Area				
Region	*1-542*	*542-750*	*750-1000*	*1000-1348*	*1348-1500*
1 Mediterranean	181		178	226	319
2 France	89	108	(180)		
3 Britain	124	121	(131)		143
4 Germany	121	110	135	147	(300)
5 Hungary-Balkans	85	82	108	118	143
6 Alps-Bohemia	212	86	109	112	206
7 Scandinavia	109	(106)	79	122	138
8 Poland	70	45	134	121	120
Total					
Number of Skeletons					
1 Mediterranean	419		1179	529	88	2215
2 France	151	755	38			944
3 Britain	711	483	131	142	536	2053
4 Germany	1555	2035	419	428	68	4505
5 Hungary-Balkans	986	1862	3883	2969	930	10603
6 Alps-Bohemia	496	1255	2852	294	220	6117
7 Scandinavia	307	64	504	762	1350	2987
Poland	253	115	290	2900	580	4138
Total	4878	6569	9296	8024	3722	

control of population (table 53). The fifteenth-century data will be discussed in the status of that period.[30]

WHY SO FEW WOMEN? THE SEX RATIO.

Sex ratio is one of the key factors in any culture so one must indeed turn to it. The data are cataloged in table 38. The shortage of women seems apparent: a total ratio of 132 for the entire period is very high and the subtotals for time and geographic phases are almost entirely high. Immediately the gap between potential fertility and actual births may be bridged by the mortality of women which would bring the birthrate down. Two possibilities before this rather obvious explanation need to be cleared.

Is it possible that the sex ratio at birth was higher than the present 102-105? We use 105 because it does seem that crisis or rough conditions sometimes raise the sex ratio at birth. The sex ratio at conception seems to have been as high as 200 at times and occasionally higher than normal sex ratios do occur.[31] Modern investigations have shown that people today often desire high sex ratios for their children, as high as 122. Attempts to determine the

---

[30]See table 53.
[31]See table 38.

sex of very young children are relatively infrequent since only recently acceptable criteria for such a determination are available. Thus far these attempts at identification of the very young have not turned up any remarkable cases of very high or low sex ratio. A second possibility is that the evidence itself is at fault. Some of the data point to a high sex ratio. Misuse or overuse of skeletal evidence in ossuaries and sometimes in museums have made it difficult to examine the smaller more fragile bones of women and children. This is especially true of the later English mortuary evidence which has been moved frequently.[32] Some attrition should normally have occurred over the centuries thus causing losses in the ground from unfavorable soil conditions or depredations from animals or men. There is, however, a bias in favor of determining females since their skeletons seem a little easier to recognize.

The sex ratio of the deceased varies considerably from one age division to another. Though the daughters nearly all seem to have suffered more from neglect and even organic problems, fewer of them died than did the sons.[33] Then there is the terrible loss within ages fourteen through thirty-nine when, despite the sex ratio of about 130 the sex ratio at death was only 105. It is not surprising then that the ratio from forty to sixty was a whopping 193. If one assumes a sex ratio at birth of 105 and that the number of female babies then should equal the male number divided by 1.05, an estimate may be made of the deficit of women in the population. The numbers for the four time periods are: A.D. 1-540, 16.4 percent; for 540-750 6.8 percent; for 750-1000 13.7 percent and for 1000-1340 24.8 percent. In other words the variation correlates with the needs for population. Similarly the low sex ratios of Hungary, Czechoslovakia, and Poland are in areas where less restraint was put upon women.

Earlier we found that data seemed to show that women on the average bore about 4.2 children each. Let us take the cemeteries where the total number of skeletons showed about 4.2 persons to those over age 20, since this tends to show what sex ratio seemed suitable to maintain the 4.2 average indefinitely. The data from 23 cemeteries and two Roman provinces show 432 males and 254 females for a sex ratio of 170.[34] The percentage of total mortality of infans I is 13.3 and of infans II 10.1. This is about right for infans II but much too low for infans I. The group must have borne more than 4.2 children apiece to have provided the babies lost to keep the 170 sex ratio. About 5.2 children each would have

---

[32]See II, Note 28.
[33]See table 39.
[34-37]In collections of the author.

Age Group	Total	Analyzed by sex			Sex Ratio	% not sexed	*Not analyzed by sex		
		Male	Fem.	?			Total	Sexed	%
Inf. I	1102	288	324	490	88.9	44.5	3691	402	10.8
Inf. II	801	155	219	427	70.8	53.3	2315	183	7.9
Juv	1664	472	746	446	63.2	26.8	1134	626	55.7
Adultus							5566	4292	77.1

Table 39

Age Specific Sex Number and Ratio (0-20 years).

*This section does not include all of those used in the other part of the table.

Adultus	2203	2089		105
Maturus	2977	1539		193
Senilis	810	540		150

produced the desired number. Possibly the very high sex ratio was caused by societal pressures for nearly all of the women to marry. The average of 4.2 to the female was probably in part due to lack of such pressure. The question naturally arises eventually about the percentage of those who did marry in the Middle Ages. Only about 75 of the nearly 500 cemeteries show an actual number exceeding the expected: cemeteries where there was evidence for more than five children on the average.[35]

The sex ratios of the other areas are as follows for the three periods:

	0-542	542-700	700-1000
German areas	121	110	135
Hungarian-Balkans	85	86	110
Bohemia-Austria	212	86	109
Poland	70	85	104
Scandinavia	109	106	79

With the exception of the very high ratio (because all the evidence came from one cemetery), the ratios are not high by medieval standards. The lowest are among the areas where herding and hunting were probably important. The very low ratio of Scandinavia came from loss of men outside of the villages, presumably those on the sea or in the forest.[36] The increase of the sex ratio is noticeable in all but the Scandinavian data. Only in the case of the German areas is the number beyond the possibility of chance.

The length of life of men in the period was nearly as low as in the preceding period, except for the Bohemian-Austrian region where

Table 40

Sex Ratio of Large Cemeteries

Place	Time	Century	Male	Female	Ratio	Source
Lauriacum-Austria	1	IV-V	92	29	312	Kloiber 1957
Mlodikaov Poland	1	II-IV	57	87	66	Zymaczlwski 1958
Reichenhall Germany	1	I-IV	184	203	91	Von Chlingenberg 1890
Tricciana Balkans	1	IV	90	104	87	Sz Burger 1966
Schretzhaim Germany	2	VI-VIII	72	72	100	Hitzeroth 1965
Szentes-Kajan	2	670-790	173	172	100	Korek 1943
Bedford, England	3		64	61	95	Brash 1935
Birka-Scandinavia	3		159	237	67	Arbman 1943
Bourogne France	3	VII-VIII	101	132	76	Scheuer-Lablatier 1914
Mikulcice Czechoslovakia	3	IX	324	246	132	Stloukal
Czechoslovakia	3	IX	555	464	136	Stloukal 1962a & b.

Table 40
Sex Ratio of Large Cemeteries (continued)

Place	Time	Century	Male	Female	Ratio	Source
Cezchoslovakia Burgwall						
Valy Czechoslovakia	3	IX	84	60	140	Stloukal 1964
Nové Zamky Czechoslovakia	3	VIII	162	157	104	Stloukal 1966
Ptuj-Jugosl.	3	X	92	87	106	Korosec 1950
Staré Město Czechoslovakia	3	X	233	279	84	Hruby 1955
Halimba Hungary	3-4	X-XI	309	291	106	Acsádi-Nemeskéri 1957: Torek 1962
Holiare Hungary	3-4	X-XI	114	203	56	Malá 1965
Kerpuszta Hungary	3-4	X-XI	104	103	101	Acsádi-Nemeskéri 1959
			121	119	102	Nemeskéri 1952
Nitry Hungary	3-4	X-XI	78	78	100	Malá 1960
Zalavár Hungary	3-4	X-XI	216	186	116	Acsádi 1962
Ptuj-Jugosl.	3-4	X-SI	104	94	111	Iranicek 1951
Üllo			104	72	144	László 1951

the expectation at age 20 was about 29 years in contrast to about 20-21 in Germany, Hungary, and Scandinavia. Women seem to have done rather well also in Bohemia-Austria (expectation of about 23-24) and in Hungary-Balkans (about 24). The data for Poland are too meager to use.[37]

The sex ratio seems also to be affected by the size of settlements. Table 40 gives the ratios of 23 cemeteries which are among the largest examined. The sex ratio is very low for most of them even though only a few are of the plague periods when the number of women was notably higher than in nonplague periods. The population was probably kept under control by refusing marriage to many of the women. The high ratio of Lauriacum is because it was largely an army camp with relatively small settlements of women about. As usual many single women must have migrated from the countryside into the cities even when these were relatively small.

WHAT HAPPENED TO THE CHILDREN OR INFANTICIDE.

Information about the sex ratio, especially when it is so high that it suggests infanticide, is unfortunate because the problem cannot be traced easily given the small amount of data about children. Skeletal evidence does not yield much yet about the percentage of living children since the information is primarily about the deceased. On the other hand it does suggest a wholesale loss of females in childhood, an inordinate number of girl babies were allowed to die at birth. If the sex ratio data is correct, the loss varies some. The sex ratios of the first four periods are given as roughly 129, 113, 122 and 132. These suggest a loss in each period of 18.7, 7.1, 13.8 and 25.9 percent respectively. It is quite possible that the 7.1 percent of girls born in the plague period might have died naturally amid plague conditions. It is very unlikely that the higher rates of the other three periods occurred without human interference with the lives of the children.[38]

In table 41 it is clear that the smaller the cemetery the less chance there was of finding remains of a high percentage of children under age twenty-one. Of the sample of 155 cemeteries where the data offered information about the number of children of infans I (0-6 years of age) and of infans II and juvenis, of the 44 which had no infans I, twenty-seven had twenty or less skeletons. It was, of course, easier to walk around and over the smaller cemeteries which, in many cases, were rather casual burying grounds.

---

[38]Salmon (I, Note 37) 70-76; Emily Coleman, *European Studies Newsletter* 3 (1973): 6-7; "Infanticide dans le Haut Moyen Age," *Annales, E. S. C.* 29 (1974): 315-335; Barbara A. Kellem, "Infanticide in England in the Late Middle Ages," *History of Childhood Quarterly* 1 (1974): 367-388; John Bongaarts, "Why High Birth Rates are so Low," *Population and Development Quarterly* 1 (1975): 389-396.

Table 41

Number of Cemeteries by Time Periods and Percentages
of Children (Aged 0-20) Compared to Adults

Percent Children	Total Number	Roman	1-540	540-750	750-1000	1000-1348	1348-1500
Over 100	30	1	4	4	10	8	3
90-99	10	1	1	2	4	2	
80-89	15	1	1	1	5	4	3
70-79	25	2	4	2	7	9	1
60-69	26	1	4	6	6	5	4
50-59	47	3	8	8	13	12	3
40-49	52	12	13	13	12	9	3
30-39	80	8	17	19	14	15	7
20-29	78	5	18	19	14	20	2
10-19	58	2	12	14	8	16	6
0-9	66		12	17	13	19	5
Total	487	36	94	105	106	119	37
Average*	36.5	33.4	31.1	36.8	47.2	39.5	41.2

*Each class calculated from its midpoint, i.e., 60-69 counted as 65.
Median average (if each counted a x5 would be 41.0)

The difficulty of accepting that a fifth of the female infants and probably a small number of males were allowed to die at birth is that the Church strongly opposed infanticide.[39] Yet when one examines the penitentials, the overlaying of infants, (probably the chief explanation of the deaths) was not punished as severely as murder and, if the excuse of poverty was given, the penance was not very heavy.

Brutal treatment of children, such as is envisioned by De Mause[40] in his horrifying explanation of the attitude toward medieval and ancient children, is not substantiated by broken bones or other evidence of maltreatment of the very young. The child had to be accepted by family and clan in Greece and by the family in Rome or it was exposed in the marketplace. Medieval folk, knowing their environment, also knew of their chances for a good life. Unlike today, the "right to life" was not as important as the right to a good life. As mentioned earlier, childrens' bones seem to show little of rickets or other cases of dietary deficiency and the spacing of births to three years or so for ordinary families presented very good conditions for growth.

---

[39]See chapter XIII.
[40]Lloyd de Mause, "The Evolution of Childhood," *History of Childhood Quarterly* 1 (1974): 503-575. It also appears as part of a book with the same title.

Table 42

Number of Cemeteries with Percentage of *Infans I*
in the Total Population, by Size of Cemetery.

Percent of Infans I in Cemetery	0	1-5	6-10	11-15	16-20	21-25	26 +	Total Average
Number of Persons in Cemetery								
0-20	27	3	7	3	6		46	2.5
21-40	7	4	5	4	3		23	6.8
41-100	4	7	10	6	2	3	4 36	11.1
101+	6	6	9	5	5	6	10 47	14.6
Total	44	20	31	18	16	9	14 152	

Read for first number in column: 27 cemeteries having 1-20 graves or persons had
no Infans I burials. Last number on lower right: 10 cemeteries having more than
100 graves or persons had 26 or more percent of Infans I burials.

The size of the communities, then, seem to have depended more
upon the opportunities for holdings which would support marriages than upon fertility of marriages. It is true that in time of
plague northern Europe took several centuries to recover from the
mortality, although Italy and several other areas recovered in one
hundred and fifty years.[41] The population changes then were
determined by the human estimate of the land and wages necessary to keep up a marriage. England in 1085 apparently thought
that thirty acres was enough to support a family. Yet by the middle
of the thirteenth century, population had tripled and was still in
reasonably good condition. For some reason, instead of rampant
overpopulation, the numbers seemed to have leveled off. The
additional people were accommodated by subdividing the holdings
down to ten or twelve acres to the homestead and in assarting
tracts of land around the edges or on unused territories. In many
cases the assarted lands were probably in addition to wages paid by
manor lords on their demesne lands and by the wealthier free-
holders or even serfs of wealth, particularly female landholders.
Climate was also a factor. The thirteenth century seems to have
enjoyed a singularly warm climate, conducive to large crops. Any
expansion based upon the warmer weather might easily be negated
by long spells of cold. However, changes based on weather were
bound to be slow and subject to considerable discussion on the part
of inhabitants of the villages. The primary decisions were voluntary choices of the people rather than involuntary dependence
upon weather or human fertility.

[41]Don E. Dumond, "The Limitation of Human Population, a Natural History," *Science*
187 (January-May 1975): 713-718.

X. *Population Stability, A.D. 0-1000*

The population of Europe and the western Mediterranean basin was about the same in A.D. 1000 as it had been a millenium earlier—about thirty-two million. In the interval (table 6) it had declined in the empire while the outside area increased slightly. After an apparently very stable period, A.D. 350-540, both suffered terribly from epidemics of the plague. At its conclusion population increased nearly everywhere. The history of the fall of the Roman Empire in the west, the barbarian kingdoms, the Islamic invasions and the rise of the Carolingian and Ottonian empires occurred in these thousand years. The problem is to relate demographic developments to the changes which took place then. In particular, were the demographic changes produced by nonhuman circumstances alone or did humanity share or even determine the course of population? This chapter is devoted primarily to define as far as possible the elements of population change, chiefly as they have been outlined in chapters four and nine. It is clear from earlier chapters that Europe did suffer terribly from new diseases, tuberculosis, the plague and probably malignant malaria in the period.[1]

The population was subdivided and distributed according to a general pattern of human distribution.[2] In the country villages their inhabitants usually occupied from one to several square kilometers with not very many isolated farms and homesteads. Every ten kilometers or so there was a small market town and often a larger one about every twenty kilometers. Small cities appeared at about a day's journey, forty kilometers or more. Great cities developed at greater distances, depending upon the geography of the area and its political organization. The rise of population in the early Roman Empire tended to increase the size of the metropolitan areas. Since the people had a higher birth rate and lower death rate in the countryside, there was a migration normally from the cities. Thus city folk were usually related to country folk, that is, village dwellers, within a considerable area about the city. Political ties often bound the areas about the cities into regions. Migration and marriage tended to produce regional physical similarities as the typical types married each other and exerted a pressure for the atypical to migrate into the city. Thus the typical increased while the atypical failed to marry and reproduce as rapidly as they. The political consequence of this

---

[1] Above, chapters V-VII.

[2] A map illustrating distribution of villages and cities appeared first in my "The Metropolitan City Region in the Middle Ages," *Journal of Regional Science* 2 (1960): 61.

Table 43

Life Table, Period 1 (A.D. 1-542)

	q_x		l_x	d_x	L_x	T_x	e_x^o
All (Males, Females, Uncertain)							
I	14.8	85.2	3332	494	20833	118717	35.6
II	9.5	90.5	2838	279	18750	91884	32.4
J	11.3	88.7	2559	290	14484	73134	28.6
A	49.9	50.1	2269	1132	34060	50650	22.3
M	77.0	23.0	1137	876	13980	16590	14.6
S	100.0	0.0	261	261	2610	2610	10.0
Males							
I			1324	81			
II			1243	30			
J	8.3	91.7	1213	101	6975	32335	26.7
A	44.4	55.6	1112	494	17300	25860	23.3
M	80.7	19.3	618	499	7370	8560	13.9
S	100.0	0.0	119	119	1190	1190	10.0
Females							
I			923	17			
II			906	20			
J	10.5	89.5	886	93	5035	22785	25.7
A	52.0	48.0	793	412	11740	17750	22.4
M	71.1	28.9	381	271	4910	6010	15.8
S	100.0	0.0	110	110	1100	1100	10.0

This table does not include an English cemetery, Trentholm (Wenham 1968) which, because it was near a Roman army camp had an excessively high rate for males, especially in the 20-40 age group.

regional movement was largely concealed by the universality of the Roman Empire and by the lesser amount of evidence remaining from that age as compared with the really striking manifestations of regionalism in the later Middle Ages.[3]

CONDITIONS A.D. 1-312

The movement was clearly, from east to west, as seen in chapters six, seven and eight. The Sahara Desert seems to have protected Europe from the reservoir of warm-climate diseases of central Africa so that the entrance would normally have been through the Nile Valley. This was allegedly the course of the plague in 541-542. The diseases of Indian and Central Asia also could have come in through the Nile gateway although there were more avenues to the

---

[3]Russell, 1972.

north.[4] The increase in the size of cities and of the warmth of the climate also offered more favorable conditions for the introduction of disease and the setting up of permanent reservoirs in the area. The early plague, however, did disappear although the later one (1348) continued for centuries. Geography made for a distinctly more deleterious state in the south as that for the north. The growth of the Roman Empire made for ideal conditions for the spread of the disease. Traffic moved along the great roads and in ships in the Mediterranean. The movement of large armies, with their series of army camps from the first century before Christ and for centuries after also aided in the spread. New diseases in an area are usually more harmful than those to which an area has acquired a certain amount of immunity. The Roman Empire then had the great handicap of absorbing and offsetting a series of human ailments—a burden to any society.

Population changes in the Mediterranean and southern European areas were quite different before A.D. 800 than later, apparently declining somewhat in the first three centuries in the south and remaining much the same in the north, perhaps increasing slightly. The expansion of the Slavs in the Balkans is largely responsible for the increase in the total population of the areas north of the Mediterranean following the plague period, A.D. 540-750.[5] In terms of percentage even the greatest increase, about 90 percent in two centuries, is not large compared with modern population change. This means that, if a test can be made of the change, it may be small and difficult to define accurately. The change was so slow that even boundary alterations must be considered carefully.

Some of the most remarkable declines in population in the first three centuries occurred in the rich grain lands of Campania in southern Italy and in the province of North Africa.[6] Since the weather was favorable for grain production in the entire period, except for a very rainy period in the fifth-sixth centuries, the population decline can hardly be blamed upon drought. For the eastern half of the Roman Empire, impoverishment of the soil has been alleged, but that was hardly the case with the west. After all, several countries, Italy, France and Britain, today support agriculture which sustains twice the population of the western half of the Roman Empire. Population fell and brought disuse of the land with it. In North Africa this happened despite the evident good health and long life of the inhabitants. The people must have

---

[4]M. W. Dols, *The Black Death in the Middle East*, (Princeton, 1977), especially 42-67; W. H. McNeill, *Plagues and Peoples* (Garden City, 1976).

[5]The Slavs had a lower sex ratio (more women than men) and thus presumably a higher birth rate, enabling them to fill the Balkans.

[6]Russell, 1958: 73, 76-77.

chosen to control their numbers. The worship of Moloch, indeed, at times involved the sacrifice of the first son, so great was the problem of too many children.

The quality of land cultivated and of pasture was important. Methods of cultivation were rather primitive: plows which were hardly more than a stick, poor harnesses and indifferent farm animals contributed to a low yield of grain. The English Tribal Hidage considers that the hide, an area of perhaps 120 acres, was the land of one family and must have included woods, pastures, and meadows as well as perhaps thirty tilled strips or acres. However, the farmers could see their allotments and knew how much land was necessary to maintain their families. As time went on, the area necessary for such a purpose declined. By Domesday Book (A.D. 1086) it was a virgate (about thirty acres), and it assumes more labor on the fields and less dependence upon animals as sources of food. The work was harder physically, with more effect upon the length of life of women than of men. The Mediterranean area suffered from overcultivation and overgrazing especially by goats. The forest area declined.

The population of the Roman cities fell along with the decline of the Empire itself. As seen earlier, the population of Rome was still at its height (about 175,000-200,000) well into the fifth century. Its population seems to have fallen rapidly, however, after that date as it lost its position as capital and sank to perhaps ten or twenty thousand well past the end of the millenium. In the west only Corduba had a considerable population of perhaps about ninety thousand at the height of the Omayyad Empire in the eighth and ninth centuries. Fez, probably the largest city of the Maghreb, had possibly about thirty thousand inhabitants while Constantinople was several times larger. For the period A.D. 500-1000 the cities of the west must have been very small with few over ten thousand in size. Aachen was as near a capital as Charlemagne held but it was probably not over ten thousand and may have been closer to five.[7] It illustrates the low state of government at that time. Nor did the minimal commerce of the period provide a suitable base for a large population.

The limits of habitation might be influenced by such a taboo as the Germanic hesitation to cut down a sacred forest so that great stretches of woodlands remained in Germany although both the Romans to the west and the Slavs to the east had no hesitation about deforestation. One result was apparently that rather than cut down trees to provide more cultivated lands, the tribes migrated from the forest areas. This animistic approach to the woods

---

[7]R. E. Sullivan, *Aix-la-Chapelle in the Age of Charlemagne* (Norman, 1963).

was probably carried by the tribes as they moved west,[8] where they have been welcomed by the Celts, since they also ascribed sacred qualities to trees individually or in groves.[9] It may help to explain the appearance and continuation of royal forests long into the Middle Ages. Since these ideas obviously tended to inhibit the cutting down of the forests for cultivation, they helped control population for a time. The new Germanic kingdoms of the Visigoths, Ostrogoths, Vandals, and Franks increased slowly in population before A.D. 1000 and this taboo may have been one of the reasons. As the tribes were christianized the taboo slowly disappeared, having been incorporated only sparingly by the converts. The taboo may also help explain why Christian monks of the west, except the Irish, seldom chose to settle as individuals or as monastic houses in the forests, as compared to eastern religious who settled in the deserts of the east.

Since the population was essentially stable during this period the problems accompanying increase of population were not seen. Obviously men had different numbers of heirs but, in general, they tended to be equal to their fathers. Even in areas of some increase, it was too small to make much difference. What happened then was a shuffling of lands among the heirs and heiresses. Thus if one man had three daughters, he supplied wives to heirs of estates. Moreover, the method of succession also mattered little. From the standpoint of inheritance, that of the youngest son was actually the most satisfactory. Many fathers lived until their eldest sons were thirty or older which meant, that unless the sons married heiresses, they must wait several years beyond the time when they might normally expect to receive land. If an elder son married an heiress, he might be expected to relinquish the heiress's holding to another relative or himself or his wife, preferably the latter. Even equal inheritance might result merely in reshuffling: of two sons one would receive the father's holding; the other would be expected to marry elsewhere. Mathematically, if a woman had four children, two male and two female, only one of each sex might be expected to succeed, each as holder or wife of a holder. The division of land among grandchildren or greatgrandchildren after several generations should have equaled only the original holders.[10]

---

[8]A. H. Price, "The Germanic Forest Taboo and Economic Growth,' *Vierteljahrschrift für Sozial- und Wirtschaftsgeschichte* 53 (1965): 368-378. On the forest in the period see Ch. Higounet, *Paysages et villages neufs du Moyen Age* (Bordeaux, 1975): 37-63.

[9]C. Plummer, *Vitae Sanctorum Hiberniae* (2v, London, 1920) 1: clii-clv.

[10]The idea that families constantly increased in size and made subdivision necessary appears in F. Seebohm, *The Tribal System in Wales* (New York, 1904), viii.

FERTILITY—CONDITIONS ON THE FRONTIER

In the study of effects of fertility the attitudes of various institutions are important. Roman emperors tried to encourage larger families but with little success. The population tended, at least in the first Christian centuries, to decline slightly; the Roman Church may have been partly responsible. Celibacy was encouraged as a means to sanctity. Great numbers took up the way of hermits and anchorites, even of the pillar dwellers, the Stylites. Nevertheless, the total number of celibates must have been small; the percentage of Christians themselves was not large, hardly more than 5 percent. Yet the celibates have received more attention, thus giving the impression that Christians as a whole opposed the increase of population. Some religious leaders, it is true, said that decline did not matter; many Christians thought they were living in the last days. Their attitude was that since the earth was full, the filling of heaven was more important. Yet the celibacy of the leaders was to have a profound effect upon the character of leadership. Catholic leadership has had to come from homes of the laity.[11]

On the other hand, ordinary Christians were urged to marry and to have children. The purposes of marriage according to the Roman Church are two: to have children and to prevent men from sinning.[12] Infanticide was discouraged in a society where it was widely practiced. The result must have been a differential fertility in favor of Christians. If the population was holding even with an average of four children to a marriage, the appearance of an additional child would increase the number of Christians fourteen times in three hundred years assuming a generation of twenty-five years. If there was such a differential fertility, mere births should have been one factor in the triumph of Christianity.

Earlier differential fertility has been mentioned as possibly a factor in the triumph of Christianity, although celibacy gradually became a way of life of the ecclesiastical leaders. As long as the Christian society was a persecuted or at least an under-privileged minority, the leaders and members shared a common experience and it probably made little difference about the source of leadership. However, as the Church attracted more and more members from the upper classes, (which they did fairly soon) the source of the leadership did become important. Frequently the leaders coming from the homes of wealth and power naturally carried over into their leadership roles practices to which they were accustomed from birth.[13] The worldly attitude of many of the

---

[11]Russell, 1958: 134-137.

[12]See above ch. IX.

[13]Even into the imperial family in the time of Domitian.

Catholic leaders was no accident. And as the discipline of the Church improved so fewer leaders came from clerical homes. Among Jews, and later among Protestants, a high percentage of the leaders came from the homes of religious men and their actions as leaders reflected this.

A second factor affecting population in the Roman Empire was the frontier between it and the barbarians, as the Romans and Greeks called them. One might anticipate that the frontier as a scene of danger and of constant fighting would be a poor place in which to live and that health and mortality conditions there would not be satisfactory. Fortunately the Roman inscriptions provide much information about the conditions on both sides of the frontier.

The data, presented by Szilagyi, are subject to another interpretation as set up in table 44. Four of the border provinces were on the edge of the Empire and four other areas within the Empire. Can their relationship to the frontier have had any effect upon the health of the persons or was the condition due largely to the spread and prevalence of disease? The change within the Empire is indeed striking: the data are particularly plentiful there. The average life expectancy of women and men at age 20 was not much different with the female average actually a little higher. Yet in centuries III-V the expectation of men is higher than for women. The same is true at age 40 but the difference is not so marked. Was it the excitement of war that raised the expectation of men and lowered that of the women or was it just a different mortality of disease? On the edge of the Empire the expectation declined a little at 20 and increased somewhat at 40. In both periods and for both sexes the expectation was better on the frontier than within the Empire. Here again the border provinces were largely mountainous and might have been expected to have better protection from malaria and tuberculosis than areas within the Empire on lower ground. The data for cemetery evidence, although not great, shows a male expectation at 20 of 24.1 and at 40 of 12. 6 in the preplague period, while the female expectations are 20. 8 and 12. 6. The expectations of Bohemia, Austria and Switzerland are slightly better than the German. The conditions of health then did not favor the Empire.[14]

What light does this throw upon the fall of Rome? Obviously, conditions were not good within the Empire. Perhaps the most serious change there was not in health conditions but in the decline in the number of men available for the defense of the Empire.[15]

---

[14]See chs. VI and VIII for these data.

[15]For instance: A. E. R. Boak, *Manpower Shortage and the Fall of the Roman Empire in the West* (Ann Arbor, 1955), 1-84.

Table 44

Expectation of life at 20 and 40; in areas on edge of and within later Roman Empire; from Roman inscriptions.

Area	At 20				At 40			
	Men		Women		Men		Women	
					Centuries			
	I-II	III-V	I-II	III-V	I-II	III-V	I-II	III-V
Within Empire Italy-small places	21.3	25.3	19.1	19.9	19.1	18.7	19.2	18.1
Gauls	17.7	25.2	18.1	17.5	15.0	20.2	21.4	14.5
Britain	22.3	24.0	23.3	18.4	14.2	17.6	16.7	16.7
Dalmatia	23.9	23.9	24.2	23.5	18.9	18.0	19.3	18.6
Average	21.3	24.6	21.2	19.8	16.8	18.6	19.2	17.0
On edge of Empire Moesia	32.7	28.5	24.2	24.5	20.6	20.2	16.2	17.8
Noricum	27.1		26.5		20.5		20.2	
Pannonia	28.9	25.3	25.3	21.2	19.7	19.0	19.6	22.2
Mainz-Koln	22.4	22.5	22.5	23.8	12.4	18.7	21.1	21.4
Average	28.0	25.4	24.6	23.2	18.3	19.3	19.0	20.5

Source: Szilágyi, 1961, 1962. His data are rearranged by anthropological age divisions. The data for Dacia are not included although they are of interest as showing some clues to the early history of modern Rumania. The data are rather few and haphazard in character.

The city armies had disappeared. The Empire was the victim of its own terrible fear of insurrection and thus allowed the cities to become virtually defenseless even after walls were built in the third century. The number of legions in the west was twelve or thirteen with two of these near the Mediterranean. There were only eight legions available on the Rhine and upper Danube frontier, four along the Rhine and four in Pannonia between Vienna and Budapest (to use the modern names). At full strength they had about 48,000 men together with perhaps an equal number of auxiliaries. The size of German tribes is in doubt: the Visigoths as they moved in North Africa are said with some degree of confidence to have had 80,000, which meant an army of 20,000 at the most. The Visigoths who overwhelmed an eastern Roman army at Adrianople of perhaps 20,000 was probably not much larger. In short the imperial forces in the continental west were not really prepared to fight off more than four large German tribes.

What had perhaps saved the Romans earlier was the German veneration of forests which prevented the cutting down and cultivating great areas of Germany. Had they done so, their military strength would certainly have had been more than Rome could have easily controlled. The defeat of the three legions under Varus in A.D. 9 was caused by an exceptional coalition drawn together by a remarkable leader. However, in 410 two great tribes, the Visigoths and Vandals were already within the Empire. The addition of Alemanni, Burgundians and Franks was too much. And one must remember that the Germans were bigger men as well as equal in numbers then.

The mortality of the Roman Empire from A.D. 100 to 542 barely held its own. A 70 percent decline from age 20 to 40 might be maintained by a population with a sex ratio of 100 and an equal mortality of the two sexes. However, since the people persisted in having a high sex ratio and women suffered generally a higher mortality rate, the Empire probably saw a population decline at least until A.D. 450. The eastern half of the Empire probably saw no decline at all but very little increase also. Proportionately, health conditions in the eastern half were better than in the west and that area continued a thousand years longer.[16]

PLAGUE CONDITIONS A.D. 542-750.

Before the plague struck Europe in 542 or the year before, conditions had stabilized by a strengthening of the Byzantine Empire and the consolidation of German tribal states in the west of Europe. The plague came in from the east. It is the first for which there is both a fair amount of written evidence and extensive skeletal information. The tribal movements, the Volkerwanderung, which preceded the outbreak of the plague, has been of tremendous interest to the nations that have come from it and it has led to extensive archaeological and anthropological research. This is particularly true of those states which have only a modest written record of the period, like Germany and the Balkans where there has not been as much interest in ancient history as in areas having outstanding Classical ages, like, Italy, France, Iberia and North Africa. Since cemeteries before the sixth century were pagan, there has been little inhibition about digging them up. Skeletal evidence is thus more abundant in the states in which Christianity developed early than for the period of the Black Death, 1348-1500. The data are especially valuable for understanding demographic conditions: sex, age, and potential fertility. In the countries beyond the Roman frontier which were deficient in written sources, skeletal data have been very useful. The splendid study of the Moravian Kingdom in the ninth century is based largely upon skeletal and artifact data from the graves of the period.

---

[16]For Egypt: J. C. Russell, "The Population of Medieval Egypt", *Journal of the American Research Center in Egypt* 5 (1966): 69-82.

Skeletal conditions tell much about the length of life during the first plague. The age of death of women (table 34) would have allowed them only about 71.6 percent of time between twenty and forty years of age for bearing children, that is, about 14.3 years, even if married throughout the twenty years. If the women were married only once and to men of their own age, they would have experienced only about 11.6 years of marriage, since many of the men died early also. Given three years between each child, these years should have seen the births of only about four children, not enough to replace those who died from the plague. Since after a century of the epidemics population remained constant or even increased, childbearing practices and customs must have been modified.[17] Perhaps like the later medieval English landholders, women married earlier, and probably there were more frequent second marriages.[18] Some apparently made use of wet nurses to speed up the births of children, especially in the wealthier families. The virulence of the first epidemic affected the people so greatly that they could not avoid the problems it produced.

The plague appeared abruptly at the end of 541 but disappeared sometime in the eighth century, more probably earlier in the west of Europe than in the east. The losses of population were probably heaviest in the first plague (541-544) and recurred at intervals of about four years of uneven mortality. If similar to the fourteenth-century epidemics, population must have dropped a quarter in the first plague and down to 60 percent in the first thirty years, leveling off at 50 percent after a century. The dry warm desert and semidesert regions probably suffered less, perhaps as little as a tenth.[19] As seen in earlier chapters, the plague covered the British Isles, France, Germany, Austria, Bohemia and the southeast of Europe. Demographic changes followed. The number of women in the population approached equality with men, as infanticide of females declined with the need for children. Overall life expectancy was shortened but the length after thirty was not.

The decline of total population meant also a decline in the average size of cities, since these are affected by the population changes of the countryside which supports them. This brought on a simplification of the commercial and intellectual life of the cities since large numbers enable persons to concentrate upon narrower bases of thought and sales. Of the great Church Fathers of the west only Gregory the Great appeared in the time of the plague, and, in

---

[17]Russell, 1948: 240-244.
[18]See p. 209.
[19]Dols (note 4 above) believes that Islamic areas suffered more.

general, the religious and intellectual life of the period seems less complicated and more superstitious. Another obvious effect was to reduce the human resources for military purposes. The tribes ceased largely to expand in this age. Into the vacuums of the Balkans the Slavs of the north drifted in this period.

Biraben and Le Goff suggested that Charlemagne's ascendancy may have resulted because the Germanic areas were not decimated by the plague. This conjecture relies entirely upon chronicle evidence for the period and assumes that no documentary evidence meant no disease. However, the dominance of Charlemagne may have accompanied the momentum of the population recovery beginning within the plague and continuing beyond A.D. 700.[20]

The most obvious effect of the plague was in its encouragement of the spread of Islam throughout the desert and semidesert areas from Arabia to Spain in the west and India in the east. There had usually been a kind of balance between the settled areas around the coasts of the seas and the nomadic and semi-nomadic peoples in the interior. The larger numbers within the settled areas were offset by the larger proportion of nomadic and semi-nomadic fighting men among the males of the desert peoples. The loss of population proportionately in the settled areas, together with the appearance of a religion which eminently suited and united the nomadic peoples, overturned the balance between settled and nomadic areas in the period. The plague also weakened the Byzantine and Persian Empires of the east as well as the Vandals and Visigoths of North Africa and Iberia. The Islamic religion was well suited to the simpler conditions produced by the plague.

One contrast to the usual social setup where the high sex ratio was an important factor in keeping down the population was the pattern offered by the Avars (table 45). The excess women probably included a large slave class, as did that of the Celts occasionally. The Avars came into Hungary just as the earlier plague struck there; it doubtless was a factor in the settlement. The Avars were essentially a ruling class in which the women occupied an important place. There is, of course, the question as to what extent the low sex ratio of the Avars was primarily a tribal pattern or whether it was influenced by the incidence of the plague.[21]

Unlike the society of the fifteenth century which was to develop social practices sufficiently prolific to offset the mortality of the plague, the earlier period saw only a slow increase even after the plague had disappeared.

---

[20]See table 45. (*Die archeologischen Denkmäler in Mittelalter*)

[21]For studies on Avars: G. Laszlo, "*Etudes archéologiques sur l'Histoire de la Société des Avars*," *Archaeologia Hungarica* N.S. 34 (1955).

Table 45

Sex Ratio in Avar Settlements

Place	Time	M	F	Sources
Adorjan I		27	13	Bartucz-Farkas 1957
Adorjan II		23	22	Bartucz-Farkas 1957
Alattyan-Tulat	VII-VIII	117	115	Wenger 1957; cf. also Wenger 1952
Aporkaiurböpuszta		8	8	Liptak 1951
Batida		6	6	Balint 1937, p. 99.
Csákberény		21	8	Tóth 1962, p. 530.
Csuny		37	55	László 1955, p. 127.
Donau-Theiss area		191	194	Liptak 1957, p. 202.
Jánoshida-Totkérpuszta		23	15	Wenger 1953, p. 232.
Kiskörös-Varosalatt		67	63	László 1955, p. 94.
Sidlisko		21	37	Tocik 1963, p. 177.
Szebeny		30	10	Toth 1961, p. 588.
Szentes-Kajan I		172	172	Korek 1943
Szentes-Kajan II		56	40	Wenger 1955, p. 403.
Üllo		72	104	László 1955, p. 110.
		871	862	

THE GREAT EMPIRES

Following the decline of the plague in the eighth century the population of Europe, especially in the west, was at a low point, perhaps forty or fifty percent or more below its level at the beginning of the plague in A.D. 541. One should expect then that the population would rise to meet the needs for persons to fill the countryside. This apparently can be seen in the data accumulated primarily to show the position of women in European society from A.D. 701 to 1200.[22] The number of children should be proportionate to the number of males as contiguous owners of property during those centuries; that is, the more children the more likely that males would inherit and own property. Thus it is an indirect result of more children. About A.D. 776-800 the number of owners who were male was about 82 percent. Then it arose to better than 90 percent in 876-900 and remained above 87 percent through 951-975 falling off slightly to the year A.D. 1000.

The period, 700-1000, saw rising population everywhere accompanied by increased aggression of states against neighbors. From the south and west Islamic forces took over Iberia and parts of Italy and threatened the Byzantine Empire. Hungarian and

---

[22]D. Herlihy, "Land, Family and Women in Continental Europe, 701-1200," *Traditio* 18 (1962); 89-120. See figure on p. 107.

Viking raids increased until they took over much of the Balkans, Russia and parts of France and Britain. The Lombards descended into Italy and a short lived but very interesting Moravian Kingdom appeared. Few areas have received more careful archaeological treatment than Moravia. In the west the rise and fall of the Carolingian Empire dominated political and military as well as cultural history. Anthropological evidence is greater for eastern than for western Europe and throws much light at a time when written sources are sparse. Communist states have tended to specialize in archaeology and anthropology, and as a result more is known about this phase of regional life in the east than in the west.

The density of individual villages, territories, was often as high as 30-40 persons to the k[m] although the lands about them were often forests until well past the year 1000.[23] Lords, often monasteries, encouraged landholders to remain in the village until the desired density had been reached. In Picardy. one of the most densely settled areas in western Europe, the estimates are of about the order above, although a case could be made for lowering the estimates. Usually, if one has an estimate for adult population, the total would be about twice that figure.[24] The density of the manors in the Polyptyque d'Irminon run to about the same figure.[24] In the villages, however, in Picardy and probably in many other places a stationary population was typical by the middle of the ninth century.

The tendency seems to be for local population of fair density to develop in largely forest areas, but the essential density might make for higher sex ratios. The evidence comes from both skeletal data and lists of inhabitants of villages in the period 700-1000. French villages of the lands of St. Germain des Pres, Paris, show a sex ratio of 125 for adults and 126 for children. This is based upon information about 4,773 persons, a large number.[25] A much smaller number of burials would show a very high sex ratio of 180 while a parallel series of documents from various German sites, shows a sex ratio of 156 for some 419 persons.[26] For cemetery data of the same period the ratio is 135.[27] In both countries the sex ratio has increased sharply from the preceding period, which was 108

[23]F. Lot, "Conjectures démographiques sur la France du ix siècle," *Le Moyen Age* 27 (1921): 1-27, 109-137. B. Guerard, ed, *Polyptyqye de l'Abbé Irminon* (Paris, 1844).

[24]R. Fossier, *La terre et les hommes en Picardie jusqu' à la fin du xiiˈ siécle* (Paris, 1968), 205. Fossier gets about the same figures (perhaps a little more) by adding two or three children to each menage. Van Werveke (*Miscellanea Mediaevalia*, Ghent, 1968, 290) gets about the same number, 34 to km[r].

[25]Russell, 1958: p. 14.

[26]Russell, 1958, p. 15.

[27]See pp. 153 above.

for France and 110 for Germany. It seems clear that the control by means of maintaining the high sex ratio, presumably by infanticide of females, had tightened after the disappearance of the plague, Christianity notwithstanding.[28]

The sex ratios of the other areas are as follows for the three periods:

	0-542	542-700	700-1000
German areas	121	110	135
Hungarian-Balkans	85	86	110
Bohemia-Austria	212	86	109
Poland	70	85	104
Scandinavia	109	106	79

With the exceptions of the very high ratio (evidence from one cemetery) others are not high by medieval standards. The lowest are among the areas where herding and hunting were probably important. The very low ratio of Scandinavia should have come from loss of men outside of the villages, presumably on the sea or forest. The increase of the sex ratio is noticeable in all but the Scandinavian data. Only in the case of the German areas is the number beyond the possibility of chance.

The length of life of men in the period was nearly as low as in the preceding period, except for the Bohemian-Austrian region where the expectation at age 20 was about 29 years in contrast to about 20-21 in Germany, Hungary, and Scandinavia. Women seem to have done rather well also in Bohemia-Austria (expectation of about 23-24) and in Hungary-Balkans (about 24). The data for Poland are too meagre to use.

The rise and fall of the Carolingians were due to a considerable extent to the chance survival of heirs to the throne. For several generations for more than a century (680-840) chance permitted only one candidate to the throne to survive for more than a few years and then the ruler lived on until his son was well grown: Pepin, Charles Martel, Pepin the Short, Charlemagne and Louis the Pious. Following the death of the last named, three sons succeeded and the Carolingians plunged from the heights as their lands were repeatedly divided. In fact the demographic history of the Merovingians was repeated. The family had never learned, at least permanently, how to provide for a succession by only one heir. In general in this period heirs were sons or near relatives: succession was determined by competence as well as relationship. If sons were not fully grown, or at least near enough to rule, brothers or others

---

[28]J. C. Russell, "Aspects démographiques des debuts de la Féodalité", *Annales: Economies, Sociétés, Civilisations* 20 (1965): 1120-1122.

Table 46							
Life Table, Period 3 (A.D. 750-1000)							

	q_x		l_x	d_x	L_x	T_x	e_x^o
All (Males, Females, Uncertain)							
I	19.2	80.8	10664	2045	66423	323872	30.4
II	12.0	88.0	8619	1031	56209	259409	30.1
J	9.8	90.2	7588	746	43280	203240	25.8
A	50.0	50.0	6842	2805	108670	1599	23.4
M	79.2	20.8	4037	3191	48230	57290	14.2
S	100.0	0.0	846	846	8460	8460	10.0
Males							
I	5.1	94.9	3333	171			
II	2.4	97.6	3162	75			
J	4.0	96.0	3079	122			
A	40.3	59.7	2960	952	49680	75420	25.8
M	80.9	9.1	2008	1625	23910	25740	17.8
S	100.0	0.0	383	383	3830	3830	10.0
Females							
I	7.0	93.0	3097	217			
II	6.8	93.2	2880	105			
J	8.9	91.1	2775	249			
A	46.7	53.3	2526	1179	38730	62610	24.8
M	75.7	24.3	1347	1020	0010	23280	17.3
S	100.0	0.0	327	327	3270	3270	10.0

might succeed. In the thirteenth century, the chance of any son succeeding was seventy percent: the chance of an adult son somewhat less, even if by adult is meant fifteen years of age.

Consolidation and strong development of other states besides the Carolingian in the period 700-1000 indicates that it was common. The Anglo-Saxon state in England reached its heights under Alfred and his descendants while in Iberia the Caliphate of Cordoba under Abd-er-Rahman III peaked as well. The Byzantine Empire and the Caliphate of Bagdad experienced some of their greater epochs in this period, not quite at the same time. All had suffered in the plague and presumably would be expected to share in its overall developments. Now the data of the English land-holders indicate that length of life began to increase markedly with the generation born about 1426-1450 over even the preplague times. This should have meant greater energy and vitality from that time on. The development of stronger governments may have been in part a result of the increase of vital elements. In this period the two areas which have received the most attention archae-ologically are Hungary and Bohemia. The latter concentrates the period of the Great Moravian Kingdom which flourished spec-tacularly in the ninth century; the end of the Avar period and coming of the Hungarians are of great interest to Hungarians. Both Rumania and the Scandinavian countries have an interest in this period also because of developments among Viking and Romance-speaking peoples. The movement of the Slavs was also a very significant phase of the history of this period. German, English and French interest in this period has hardly been demographic.

During the thousand years after the birth of Christ far-reaching demographic changes occurred in the Mediterranean-European world—not so much in terms of numbers which, as a total, changed little. Within the Empire new diseases, like tuberculosis and probably malignant malaria, spread and reduced the length of life of its people. Meanwhile health on the frontier and in pagan territories was much more satisfactory partly because the hilly or mountainous terrain was not accessible so easily to the contagion. Within the Empire also, only the army was well armed but this was expensive. Cities lost their power of resistance largely because the emperors were fearful of revolt. Among the barbarians the percentage of warriors was high, perhaps 20 percent, as compared to one percent of the Romans. The barbarians also were larger physically. The army whose leaders were emperors dominated the Empire. Gradually the barbarian element grew proportionately large within the army and came to provide even its generals. German tribes were usually restless and in the debacle of 400-410 tribal armies broke in and overran the western half of the Empire. The plague reduced both halves of the Roman Empire, by perhaps 40 percent in humid areas and by lesser degrees in the smaller dry areas. Thus semi-nomadic regions came to be as powerful as the settled areas at the time when Islam was making inroads. Thus North Africa, Iberia, Sicily and adjacent parts of the continent fell under Islamic rule. As population increased in the settled areas, Islam gradually lost its grip. Frankish power grew even when the Merovingian house died out. An almost unbelievable demographic accident, an uncontested succession of the Carolingian family, led to the development of a powerful empire culminating in the reign of Charlemagne. Eventually even the Carolingians succumbed to hereditary succession among sons and declined toward the end of the first thousand years.

XI. The Medieval Population Crisis, 1000-1348

Although population in Europe remained reasonably stable during the first Christian millennium, it rose rapidly during the first three and a half centuries of the second. Somewhere between 1280 and 1310 population increase either reached a peak or slowed down markedly. The question is whether people deliberately controlled their numbers or whether it was a Malthusian situation where reaching a limit in subsistence forced a limitation in population. As in the preceding chapter, effort will be made to determine, as far as the sources will permit, how the factors controlling population status operated, more particularly why the population increased so rapidly and why that increase slowed down. The increase is very obvious and well documented.[1] A controversy has occurred over the population course after the peak was reached, assuming that this happened in the second half of the thirteenth century. One theory is that population actually continued to increase until the outbreak of the plague in 1349, at least in most parts of Europe. The other is that a limit was reached about 1280 and then declined.[2]

Our estimate of population change in the period is given in table 6. Information about the eastern countries is much less reliable than for western and southern Europe. It is quite probable that further research will modify these conclusions considerably. However, the little data about Rumania and Czechoslovakia and others show that they also had a slow rate of growth in this period.

Not only did the area of settlement increase but the unit of cultivation necessary for keeping a family declined and thus allowed a denser population without much lowering standards of living, at least for a time. The introduction of a better plow, a more efficient harness and horseshoes encouraged the introduction of the three-field system of agriculture.[3] The quality of seed and animals may have improved some. Extensive agricultural leadership by clerical lords and laity should have led to some improvement. The food supply was supplemented by a more liberal use of fish from ocean fisheries and mill ponds. The typical family holding, villein class, may have been about thirty acres with a quota of animals and other lands. It was probably nearer fifteen or ten acres with appropriate animals in the thirteenth century.[4]

---

[1] L. Genicot, "On the Evidence of Growth of Population in the West from the Eleventh to the Thirteenth Century," in Sylvia Thrupp, *Change in Medieval Society* (New York, 1964): 1-29; Lynn White, Jr., "The Vitality of the Tenth Century," *Medievalia et Humanistica* 9 (1955): 26-29. Russell, 1980: 446-462.

[2] Russell, 1958: 99-113; also note 12 below.

[3] Lynn White, Jr. 1940: 151-153.

[4] Usually a few villages. There is a real need for a study of the size of knights' holdings.

The population increase of the period in the northern feudal areas, France, Britain and Germany, was about 300 percent in 350 years—by modern standards not a very rapid increase. It could be accomplished by relatively minor changes in marriage customs. The question, however, is whether population increased as a result of natural causes, for example an increase in fertility, or whether it was made possible by a change in attitudes of the ruling class. Since the possession of land was controlled by the lords of the day, was it to their advantages to subdivide the land and encourage movement onto other uncultivated areas? The political conditions upon the breakup of the Carolingian Empire favored such movements.

The division of the empire among the sons of Louis the Pious continued with more and more subdivisions with equal inheritance of noble holdings. Political power was more frequently in the hands of dukes, counts, and bishops with less and less restraint from above. Struggle for power encouraged lords to use every device to increase their resources in men and land at the expense of their rivals. Military action required expensive equipment, horse and armor with heavy expenditure for castles and their upkeep even of the manor houses of less important lords.

THE FEUDAL EXPANSION.

In all three areas where there was rapid expansion in population, territorial expansion also occurred. Britain's population moved north and west into areas where less settled people had lived before. Even in the more thickly settled areas waste lands belonging to the royal forest were assarted and appropriated while manors were subdivided into those distinguished by identifying words, such as North and South, large or small, or by owner's name or title. In France divisions appear in the names of the saints of the parishes added to their original names: Nogent-Saint-Pierre or other designation. In Germany the well known Drang nach Osten saw Germans with their denser settlements pushing into less densely settled Slavic lands, adding to urban populations as well. Extensive areas were redeemed from swamp and ocean in the northwest. One easily forgets that each settlement was authorized and usually encouraged by feudal lords and that they profited greatly by such colonizations. In short it was the driving force of noble ambition that upset the time honored reservations about expansion which had previously dominated the conditions of settlement.[5] The supreme driving force in the period was, of

[5]That is, permission to divide holdings or even to consolidate them, belonged to the lord who either by law directly or indirectly forced his vassals to conform. As examples: Bryce Lyon, "Medieval Real Estate Development and Freedom," *American Historical Review* 63 (1957): 47-61. Reprinted in *Variorum Reports, Studies of European Medieval Institutions* (London, 1978): 47-61; CH, Higounet, *Paysages et villages neufs du Moyen Age* (Bordeaux, 1975): 119-127, 236 ff.

course, the Norman expansion in many areas in northern Europe. With the decline of the Empire there was no longer a restraint upon the methods used by the feudal lords, except in England. The data used in the preceding chapter to secure some estimate of the fertility of the landholders continues into this period. It shows that after the height of fertility reached in the period 876-900 a long and important decline occurred, reaching a low point about A.D. 1126-1150. There was a sharp rise in the quarter century 1150-1175 and then a slower rise in the succeeding years.[6] Only Spain showed no decline in the eleventh century; indicating a low point in the tenth rather than the eleventh. By these data South France shows a little higher fertility than the Mediterranean countries. Data for northern France are less than for the others, but as far as it goes, it would indicate higher fertility than any except for Germany. German data, unfortunately, are missing after the ninth century. The data then are important for showing that the upward movement of fertility was not continuous following the first medieval plague but that there was a decline in the tenth century which continued into the eleventh and, indeed, from the quarter century total lasting to the middle of the twelfth century. The course of fertility is not so easy to follow thereafter.

Under ordinary circumstances (breast feeding by the mother) a lord might expect to have *one* son who lived to maturity. This was an average and many of course had two or more. However, the lords tended more and more to have their children nursed by others—a kind of nursing revolution in the twelfth century, and so had more children, as the data above show. Perhaps the change began even in the eleventh century, but its effects show only in the twelfth century as the initial expansion in holdings by subdivision began to produce too many small holdings. The extra sons might marry heiresses; or go into the Church. Often bishops or abbots ranked as high as dukes or counts and considerable numbers of them came from the nobility or gentry.[7]

The fractioning of fiefs could not continue indefinitely in a feudal setup. The support of an armed knight was very expensive. His upkeep would require perhaps ten manors of about five square kilometers[2] since it included his horses, his bachelors and other retainers. This group of manors should cover about 50 k[2] or about seven kilometers square. Thus an elder son or perhaps his father, who possessed a territory of about this size had to decide how the inheritance should be divided. If divided equally between two or more sons, none would have enough income to perform his duties as an armed knight. In general the older son, if the father had

[6]Herlihy 1962: 95.

[7]S. Painter, *William Marshall* (Baltimore, 1933); G. Duby, "Dans la France du Nord-Ouest au xii siecle: les Jeunes dans la société aristocratique," *Annales, E. S. C.* 19 (1964): 835-845.

made no prearrangements, was enough older than his brother (assuming that his father died at an average 45-50 yeras of age) to prevent his brother from inheriting.[8] Or their lord might decide that only one should inherit, since he needed one armed knight, not two halfknights. The sheer force of circumstances tended to pressure families to accept primogeniture to preserve the fighting strength of the knight's fee. The same type of problem, the proper support of a vassal's obligations, tended to suggest primogeniture for the feudality. Those who did not conform saw their families descend rapidly on the social scale: the Carolingians are the best example. Geographical realities seem to have forced primogeniture at both levels of feudalism.

The struggle to preserve family holdings intact led then to primogeniture and its corollary, wet nursing, which guaranteed a considerable number of children, males among them. Even with the hope of marrying heiresses holding perhaps an eighth of the lands available and the attractions of the Church, prospects were bleak for many sons. There were many young men to whom the Church, even at its most militant phase, did not appeal. Often their fathers could endow them with enough money for horse, armor, and modest subsistence, so that they could participate in the feudal tournaments and other activities of the knightly class. They tended to band together and in France were known as the *juvenes*, for a time. They formed the nuclei of the strongest armies of the time. They, at their most powerful age, could serve their lords all year instead of the usual forty days, and they had no bases from which they could revolt against them. Furthermore, although some dukes and counts could hire bands of their own, few could compete against the kings in terms of financial resources. The efforts to maintain families through primogeniture and wet nursing led in time to submission of families to the royal will.

The typical feudal solution of the problem of succession was primogeniture among sons and equal division among daughters, if there were no sons. This was an accumulative principle for families which had sons since the eldest son inherited not only his father's holdings but also those of his mother. The great problem of primogeniture has always been that the eldest son sometimes inherited mental and physical weaknesses as well as lands and power, leaving him with a real incapacity to rule. While exceptions might be made for children and advisers appointed to rule while the king was young, no such possibility existed for nobles. In England two kings were deposed because they seemed unable to meet the expectations of the nobility and people. The awful days of Caligula and Nero in the Roman Empire were good illustrations of the rule of primogeniture unmodified by any control.

---

[8]Russell, 1948: 202-207; Russell, 1965: 1122-1123.

While greater density of population does not of itself seem to limit life,[9] smaller farm holdings had to be tilled more intensely to derive greater subsistence from them. When tilling of lands began to replace pastoral activities, more work was done with the plow or hoe. The surprising decline in length of life among women in Bohemia and Hungary in A.D. 1000-1350 may have been a result of this. The great improvement in the life of Scandinavian women is harder to explain. There is little information about English and German women and none about the French. The increasing density of population in those areas probably means that their expectation declined from the previous period. Toward the end of the period some of the best information about length of life is available about landholders in England. Though limited to men it shows a decline of life expectancy as well as in the sex ratio in the period of Black Death. Data from farming areas seem to show that farmers' expectations were about as good as those for the landholders.

The highest natural growth occurred apparently in the middle ranks of feudal lords. A group of families of Picardy showed the following average of adult sons to households between A.D, 1075 and 1200, using quarter centuries:[10]

1075-1100	2.53
1100-1125	2.26
1125-1150	2.35
1150-1175	2.40
1175-1200	2.70

Average 2.44

Since about 1.8 sons were required at the most to continue with an even population, there was an excess of about .64 sons to a family.[11] In the Namuroise the Walcourt family from ca. 1130 to 1408 in eleven generations had 45 children attaining some age for an average of 4.1, but the later families were notably smaller. The Rumigny-Monalin family before about 1300 had 46 children in nine generations. A remarkable feature was the sex equality (24 male, 22 female). Of course, the total number of children was much higher, perhaps as much as 40 percent, with six to eight children to a family.[10] Farther south the larger number of heirs can be seen in the data of the religious house of La Fertesur-Grosse from 1113 to 1178.[11]

---

[9]A. Alland, *Adaptation in Cultural Environment* (New York, 1970): 84.

[10]Robert Fossier, *La terre et les hommes en Picardie jusqu' au fin du xiiie siecle* (Paris, 1968): 279-283.

[11]L. Genicot, *L'economie Naumurois au Moyen Age* (1190-1429): the Remigny-Florence family, 67; the Walcourts, 66. For Germany, J. W. Thompson, *Feudal Germany* (Chicago, 1928): 11.

The limit of fertility cannot be so well documented. In England no decline in the number of male heirs is clear from the data about the landholding class. It remains at about 75 percent until cut down by the Black Death. But 75 percent is low by continental standards so that England had achieved, at least in the ruling class, a control by the middle of the thirteenth century.[12] Similarly, the generation of English landholders born in the years A.D. 1276-1300 had a shorter life expectancy than the preceding generation. Since the landholders experienced no famine or shortage of food, this must have been caused by other health factors. Conditions were still better than England was to experience before the nineteenth century.

Just how overcrowded Europe was before the Black Death is uncertain. It was Postan's contention that population had reached a Malthusian condition of overpopulation by about 1280 and that it remained so until the Black Death relieved the situation. He has never presented any real evidence that this was so and neither have his students.[13] Nevertheless they have continued to make assertions to this effect despite good evidence that population was never too great and that it continued to rise until 1348. After all, Europe's population rose after the plague period and reached the preplague population by 1550, continuing to rise slightly in the succeeding centuries. Yet almost no one has suggested that the 1550-1750 population was overcrowded, although the economic situation was the same after the great plague period as it had been in the preplague era. Agricultural improvement began only in the eighteenth century and the commercial revolution , while increasing the size of the cities, did not help the countryside.

In general, cities did not provide enough children to keep up their population so that migration from the countryside was necessary. This is illustrated by Genoese documents of the twelfth century. In one series of 29 documents there were 25 male heirs and 15 females while a second series shows 18 documents with 24 male heirs and 11 female. There are great problems here, of course. Wills can be made at any time of life and thus cannot reflect the actual number alive at death, since these are notarial documents rather than probate series. Nevertheless they show the unusual preponderance of males over females and a low survival rate. The average for the first is 1.4 and for the second 1.7. Since it would take about 3.6 persons, if not more given a high civic

---

[12]Russell, 1966: 468-469.

[13]M. Postan, *The Famulus. The Estate Labourer in the Twelfth and the Thirteenth Century,* *Economic History Review,* supplement no. 2 (1954): p. 20; H. E. Hallam, "Further Observations on the Spalding Serf Lists," *Economic History Review,* second series, 16 (1963): 350; M. Postan and J. Titow, "Heriots and Prices on the Winchester Manors," *Economic History Review* 11 (1959): 409.

mortality—the city was supplying about half of the children needed to replace its population.[14]

As did other parts of population, the Church expanded. In it the sons of the higher classes had the usual advantage. A very good illustration can be seen in data from the members of the clergy in Hungary, which, through later than our data, are typical. The table below cites the ages at which members of the various social classes reached clerkship, the episcopate, and death in fifteenth-century Hungary.[15]

Class	Clerk	Bishop	Death	Years as bishop
Baronial	22	25	50	25
Noble	24	34	51	17
Commons	29	39	59	20
Peasant	39	47	66	19

The Church also had the problem of too few positions to be filled as the Middle Ages wore on. Education, and especially the universities, attracted an ever increasing number of young men, so many that only minor places were open, such as manor clerks and chantry priests. The bishops allowed only a limited number, even of the mendicant orders, to become priests.

NONFEUDAL EXPERIENCE

In this primitive societal setup, agriculture was the principal source of employment. On the social scale, above the peasants were clerical or military lords but the basis was still the fields and woods, grain and animals. Water mills and small shops constituted a modest industrial life. With increasing population, especially in the cities of the west, diversification took place and provided many more outlets for manual and mechanical expression. Of course, in the cities even earlier there was construction of churches and castles. New opportunities were apparently subjected to the same principles of control as the older agriculture; that is, possession of a means of support was assumed to be ownership of this means and newcomers who wished to participate in a trade or business had to get permission of those already in it. For this reason guilds were organized and maintained—simply an extension of the idea of territoriality from the fields into the city. It seemed as natural to the Middle Ages as our system of "free enterprise" seems to us. A

---

[14]M. Chiadano & R. Marusso della Rocca, *Notai liguri del secolo xii,* Oberto Scribo de Marcato (1190) (Torino, 1938): 4-240; M. Chiadano & M. Moresco, *Cartolare de Giovanni Scriba* (2 vols. Torino, 1935).

[15]E. Fugédi, "Hungarian Bishops in the Fifteenth Century," *Acta Historica, Journal of the Hungarian Academy of Sciences* 11 (1965): 375-391, esp. p. 376.

corollary to this was that something must be done to take care of
the surplus of those who were denied admission to the means of
support in that society: the problem of the control of population.
Thus means of control continued much as they had in the earlier
period.

Data for cities provide difficult problems, the most serious being
the amount of emigration, primarily to other cities. Lists of
admissions to citizen status suggest that there was a sizable immigration and that it replaced a high city loss by deaths. Just the
increase in the size of many cities in the period 1000-1348 required
quite a number of admissions. There was social mobility even in
the cities. A guildsman with several sons might wish to place some
of them in other guilds, preferably of greater social prestige.
However, his financial status, if poor, might necessitate gaining
admission for some in the lesser guilds. In theory he should have
been permitted to place them within his own guild, even if that
involved their marriage to daughters of other members of the
guild. The guilds set up apprenticeship which theoretically was a
synthetic sonship. The apprentices often married daughters of
guildsmen and, in times of rising population, were simply allowed
to set up shop as masters. However, the tendency in many guilds
was to reduce numbers of masters and keep the journeymen on as
hired workers—the masters becoming more and more merely
supervisors. The problem was whether the apprentices would be
allowed to marry. If the English example is typical the masters
were not replacing themselves with sons during the plague.[16]

Beginning in the late twelfth century and accelerating rapidly in
the thirteenth century was an increase in the members of the
clergy. Not only were parishes divided and the numbers of local
clergy increased but new orrders; the canons, Austin and Pre-
monstratensian, and the friars: Preachers, Friars Minor, and Car-
melite, set up hundreds of houses. Hospitals also increased.[17] The
improved educational and literacy conditions, with a more complicated society lead to wider need for educated men: in law,
medicine, clerkship and administrative assistants. The new orders
were mostly celibate and the more powerful papacy of the century
enforced the rules more effectively. From then on, the clergy
provided fewer of the clerical leaders of society.[18] Furthermore,
the new clerical professors and increased numbers of the older
clerical forces attracted more and more of the literate members of
the society. As mentioned earlier, the clergy had to draw recruits

---

[16]Sylvia Thrupp, *The Merchant Class of Medieval London* (Oxford, 1948).

[17]Listed in D. Knowles & R. N. Hadcock, *Medieval Religious Houses in England and Wales*
(London, 1953): 17-48; Russell, "The Clerical Population of Medieval England," *Traditio*
2 (1944): 177-212.

[18]Russell, "The Early Schools of Oxford and Cambridge," *The Historian* 5 (1943): 63-66.

from homes of ambitious and often wealthy families. The clergy could not provide for its members the underpinning of knowledge and inspiration given members of, say the legal profession, coming from homes of lawyers and jurists. The great leaders of the thirteenth century, and even more of later centuries of the Church, just were not born. No wonder the Church became ever more lay minded as it drew its recruits from lay families.

The clergy has associations with the freemen, especially with the laity of some wealth. Freemen had the same problems of subdivision of property and of smaller holdings as did the gentry and nobility. The decline in size of holdings meant also decline in social position in a society very sensitive to such. Even in villages the strong respect for position as indicated in charter witness lists is clearly indicated.[19]

An interesting case where the change from a static situation to an increasing population in an area of equal or partible inheritance are some data from the county of Cambridge in England in the tenth and eleventh centuries.[20] The tenth century average was two heirs to the father and the eleventh, 2.6 heirs which indicates (at a sex ratio of 100) families of 3.35 and 4.85. Assuming a generation of 25 years and using the life table for persons born before 1276, the number of persons at 20 is 692 and those at 45 is 389, giving division of the larger number by the smaller as 1.78. However, since the data deal with an entire family the number must be doubled to 3.56. Thus the families in the eleventh century were barely sustaining themselves. On the other hand twelfth-century data show an increase of about 38 percent a generation, a fairly rapid increase. Now Cambridgeshire, one of the faster growing counties of England was among those which increased from Domesday to the preplague years about 383 percent. However, even in the eleventh century, the subdivision of holdings among heirs must have led to severe reduction of size of holdings.

Of the English counties, only Kent generally used an equal inheritance among sons, a custom there called gavelkind. Fortunately the effect of this system can be tested against its neighboring counties between Domesday of 1086 and the mid-fourteenth century. We assume that the population of the counties was 60 percent in 1377 of what it had been just before the plague. Kent grew in population faster than any except Middlesex where the rapid growth of London produced a somewhat greater increase: about 310 percent whereas three of the neighboring counties were

---

[19]Russell, "The Significance of Charter Witness Lists in Thirteenth Century England," *New Mexico Normal University Bulletin* (August, 1930, supplement to no. 99). A summary of results is in *Speculum* 12 (1937): 319-329.

[20]Russell, 1948: 245.

Table 47

Effects of Equal Inheritance on Kent, in Comparison with Neighboring Counties, 1086-1346.

County	Increase in population, 1085-1346	Acres to inhabitant		Decrease percent
		1086	1377	
Essex	227	18.4	13.5	26.6
Kent	310	24.2	13.2	45.5
Middlesex	372	23.0	11.4	50.4
Suffolk	213	13.7	10.7	21.9
Surrey	283	31.3	18.4	41.2
Sussex	213	41.2	32.2	21.8

Sources: population at Domesday. Russell, 1948, p. 53; at 1346, multiply 1377 (p. 132) by .6 and divide by Domesday population. Acres Russell, 1948, p. 313.

Heirs, male, Kent gavelkind succession

0 sons	(21)	total	0
1 son	(26)		26
2 sons	14		28
3 sons	7		21
4 sons	4		16
5 sons	2		10
8 sons	1		8
	75		107 Average 1.5

Source: Russell, 1948, p. 245.

about 213-227 percent. This produced a lessened area of Kent for each inhabitant (table 47). One can test the rate of replacement in the early fourteenth century in a number of inquisitions post mortem when the number of sons inheriting is given. To get an estimate of succession one must add an appropriate number of deceased with one and no sons inheriting. Twenty-six sons are assumed as from deceased with one son because the numbers rise regularly to that number. Since the percentage of deceased with no sons or their heirs is 28 for this period, it is assumed that this would be true of the group and 21 is assumed. If the generation was about 30 years and the heirs inherited at about 20 years of age, there should have been about 2.1 sons to keep the population even.[21] If the sample of landholders is valid for the whole county, the county inhabitants must have already got their population under control. It does show that equal inheritance tended to increase population more than other forms of inheritance by individuals.

[21]Russell, 1948: 240-245.

THE PEASANTRY

Peasants formed the majority of population. When allowed opportunities to move to new manors, they would marry earlier and take their wives to the new holding. The process shortened the generation and allowed the population to increase more rapidly but stay within the limits of the new subsistence. In three areas of Europe people seemed to reach the limits of easy subsistence: northern Italy based on Venice, Florence and Milan; Paris in its larger sense, and an area of about twenty counties clearly related to London in England. Possibly other areas, perhaps the land about Bruges, might be added[22] In table 49: the total density is listed, but probably much more important, the density of the region without its ten largest cities. It is assumed that much of the supply to the largest cities comes from outside of the region by way of intercity commerce and trade. So defined, the regions tend to have a population of about thirty persons to the square kilometer. This would give about 3.3 hectares or 8.3 acres to each person. If the family in these areas was about 3.5 persons in these regions, its average holding would be about twelve hectares (29.05 acres) to the family. While the holdings of the families varied widely, many factors tended to spread the products of the land about.

Male landholders of England enjoyed an above average expectation of life in the later Middle Ages. It is not clear whether this expectation was typical of the mass of English landholders or just the result of a superior class expectation. Fortunately for the years 1259-60 and 1287 there remain two surveys of land belonging to Spalding Priory in eastern England giving names of the tenants. In the interval of 27 years, using the landholder table of the period for England (assuming them 20 years of age and older, about 22. 8 percent) 97 of 421 holders reappear at one manor, Pinchbek, while 94 of 426 reappear at Spalding itself, or 22. 1 percent. There are two minor factors: first, that some who did not reappear just moved away and that some in the 1287 list had the same names as some in the earlier manor thus offsetting each other.[23] Extensive evidence from the manors of the see of Winchester on the number of retirements or deaths for each show the number of years that the holders had held lands: normally the period from the acceptance of the holding of death (or retirement). This also shows about the same expectation as that of the landholders in the period.[24] The investigation may be pushed back into the early twelfth century with lists of 1114-5 and 1126, about 11.5 years

---

[22]Russell, 1972: 235 — 237.

[23]Hallam, 1957: 349.

[24]Russell, 1948: 70.

apart. Of 227 persons named in the first, 134 reappear in the
second, 93 dead in the period, a loss of 41 percent. Assuming that
the lists included those of 20 or more in the life table (born before
1276) the loss should have been 36.2 percent; if over 25, it should
have been 39.6 percent. Again the possibility of migration, increasing the loss, remains. It looks as if the expectation in the
twelfth century was about that of the thirteenth-century
landholders.

The process of reclaiming land from sea and swamp is well
illustrated by the lands of the Priory of Spalding on the east coast
of England. After the Norman Conquest several of the manors
were surveyed in Domesday and the prior surveyed them again in
1259-60. In that period the population of Spalding itself had
increased 6.45 times, that of Pinchbeck 11.3 and the manors of
Moulton and Weston 5.05 times.[25] The acreage to holding and
person were as follows:[26]

	Acreage	To Holding	To Person
Spalding	3334	7.83	1.15
Moulton	4160	18.45	4.72
Weston	2981	19.48	4.37
Sutton, 1304	847	5.13	
Pinchbeck	2847	8.92	

The number of persons to the holding is that given by Professor
Hallam which may be somewhat larger than actually stated. In any
case, since it is estimated that two normal acres and certainly two of
the richer Spalding acres could support one person, the holdings
at Moulton and Weston were more than ample to support the
population. Spalding was a large village which had its local business
and industry to add to the agricultural support. These villages are
not a good example of overpopulation.[27]

The reclamation had taken place in the long generation between
1160 and 1205 although the increase in population held for some
time. It was still increasing, if slowly in 1259-1285, because the
lands were still being partitioned.[28] However, the data come from
Spalding alone where village activity may have been responsible. If
we examine the ratio of survival, it seems very unlikely that there
was much increase. The number of surviving children seem to
have been: Spalding 2.81; Weston 3.4 and Moulton 3. 6. Hallam
thinks that the population was increasing, if more than one son

[25]Hallam, 1957: 340.
[26]Hallam, 1957: 343.
[27]Hallam, 1957: 340; Russell, 1962: 138-142.
[28]Hallam, 1957: 346.

succeeded his father.[29] If we assume that the fathers were on the average 45 years of age and their sons averaged fifteen years, it would have required 1. 83 sons or 3.66 children to merely keep the population even—using a very optimistic estimate of life table figures.[30] It might even be questioned if the areas *were* holding their own since the children on the Spalding manors probably included those who had migrated from the other manors. The sex ratios also show that the members of the manors were doing something about sex ratio: Moulton had a ratio of 125, Weston of 120 and Spalding of 115.[31] What all this seems to show is that the English population was able to expand quickly as a result of the reclamation of fen and sea and then to adjust to a stationary population again. The increase and adjustment had little to do with partibility of inheritance, despite Hallam's assertions that it was the decisive factor.[32]

Knowledge of the age and sex structure of Italian peasants before the Black Death is limited because few Christian cemeteries have been excavated. Indeed, the one thoroughly investigated was at Cannae where a Christian cemetery of this period was excavated because it was thought to have been the burying place for those slain at the famous battle of 215 B.C. The setup is as follows (Fedele, 1960):

	Male	Female	Uncertain	
I			32	
II		9		
J	1	5	7	
A	31	12	8	
M	25	18	4	
S	2	2	2	
?	8	5	7	
	67	42	69	178

If we assume that the number of adult women was the number identified as females older than the *juvenis* class (37) plus about 40 percent of those in the same classes not identified (8), the total was 45 women who should have produced 189 children at 4.2 percent. This is not much above 178 and makes the setup reasonably satisfactory. The surplus of males is large and has been discussed in the last chapter. If this cemetery presents a typical Italian village, it indicates a controlled population. Cannae is in southern Italy, the area in which overpopulation seems to have appeared in the following century.

---

[29]Hallam, 1957: 355-361; Russell, 1962: 142.
[30]Russell, 1948: 186.
[31]Hallam, 1957: 354-355. The division is mine.
[32]Hallam, 1957: 352-354.

SEX RATIO AND MARRIAGE

In the question of control of population sex ratio is a vital factor. A high sex ratio raises the probability of infanticide, a very definite indication of population control. For four of the areas, Hungary, Bohemia-Switzerland, Scandinavia, and Poland there is sufficient cemetery evidence for an opinion in the matter. The sex ratios of these areas are all about the same, from 112 to 122. Since the average should be about 105, these figures indicate some infanticide. Their health was apparently a little worse than in the preceding age but not bad. Their slow population growth also indicates some control. Altogether, it seems that most of the control was through prevention of marriage to a sizable proportion of the population. Girls and women presumably would serve as servants or field workers and the men farm workers. Cities were not important in the population field then, although they probably had a surplus of women already. Since the demographic conditions were much the same as for the preceding period, the methods of control were also.

For western Europe cemetery evidence is very limited. Some data from Germany give a ratio of 147. English data are even

Table 48

Life Table, Period 4 (A.D. 1000-1348)

	q_x		l_x	d_x	L_x	T_x	e_x^0
	All (Males, Females, Uncertain)						
I	13.5	86.5	9701	1309	61362	316573	32.6
II	7.8	92.2	8392	653	56132	255211	30.4
J	7.6	92.4	7739	592	44658	209079	27.0
A	44.9	55.1	7147	3210	110840	164410	23.0
M	95.7	4.3	3937	3227	45470	53570	13.6
S	100.0	0.0	710	710	7100	7100	10.0
	Males						
I			3828	4			
II			3824	18			
J			3806	107			
A	39.3	61.7	3699	1417	59810	90270	24.4
M	83.3	16.7	2282	1900	26640	30460	13.3
S	100.0	0.0	382	382	3820	3820	10.0
	Females						
I			2870	7			
II			2863	14			
J			2849	210			
A	52.1	47.9	2639	1376	39020	56510	21.4
M	82.8	19.2	1263	1020	15030	17490	13.8
S	100.0	0.0	243	243	2430	2430	10.0

higher but come from deposits of skeletons showing much wear severely on the frailer female and infant bones. French evidence is lacking. For England, however, there are two other sources. The data for the gentry show a normal ratio about 1250-86 but one which rises considerably as one moves toward the plague. The sex ratio of serf children in the Fens in the later thirteenth century was about 120. Furthermore, the high sex ratios of France and Germany for the preceding period suggest that they continued into the period 1000-1340. And in England they continued even after the outbreak of the plague.

In Picardy which had one of the densest populations of the medieval period the number of males and females seems to have been about even in the landholding classes. Along with this was an increasing participation of women in the documents of the period from 10 percent just before 1150 gradually until 68 percent in the first quarter of the fourteenth century.[33] Was this a decline in the masculinity of feudalism? Female participation had been as high as 50 percent before 1150. The percentage of sterile marriages seems to have been as high as a fifth to a third: 52 childless marriages to 109 with children, some 375. The 109 fertile marriages produced 375 children or a ratio of succession of 1.72; just about enough to continue the population. If all are included the 322 adults had 375 children or a ratio of 1.16, not enough given the loss of the length of the generation. These figures give the number of children alive at a specific time and thus do not give the total born.

The crisis produced by the population growth of 1000-1348 seems to have ended by control of population by 1280. After that, it increased only slowly, not at all, or even declined. It seems to have been caused by the desire of the feudal lords, scattered over Europe, to increase their wealth and military power. After the military power was limited by feudal kings, the wealth of increased population still attracted their attention. Many cities were built by lords for the same reason. The control was attained probably a little easier than expected, because of deterioration in climate. The main method was probably based on territoriality—no marriage until there were means of support. More went into the clergy as expansion of monks and friars in the thirteenth century shows. And the high sex ratio suggests a certain amount of infanticide. This will not satisfy those who believe in Malthusianism for they see famine and plague as the chief causes of the population restraint, even before the Black Death. The problems of over-population were ended by the Black Death and its recurring epidemics. Only in Italy did factors develop which led to continued overpopulation even in the face of the plague, smallpox, sweating

---

[33]Herlihy, 1962: 95.

sickness and syphilis in the second half of the fifteenth century and
even more in the seventeenth.[34]

THE AGE OF REGIONALISM

The collapse of the Carolingian family because of their failure
to practice primogeniture led to the dissolution of political power
among lesser political units—the counties and duchies of the ninth
and tenth centuries. Although these centuries were part of the age
of feudalism, this system cannot be blamed entirely for the
changed in societal structure. With rapid increase in population,
by medieval standards the power structure changed and developed
along regional lines, especially with the rise of much larger cities.
During the period the great powers: Russia the Byzantine Empire,
Germany and other states also declined and saw themselves replaced by city-centered tribes or states. The central powers did not
adjust to new conditions.

When Iaroslav died in 1054 Russia was divided among five sons
and a grandson. Theoretically, the family was supposed to act
together and follow a system, the Rota, of succession, but actually
it redivided constantly into more independent states. Russia isolated
herself from Western Europe with which she was developing closer
relations and even separated more from Byzantium. In 1054 also
the schism of Greek Orthodox and Roman Catholic branches of
the Christian Church drew Russia farther away from the west.
Sharper changes in customs followed over the centuries.[35]

Islamic countries seem to have recovered more slowly from the
first plague than did the West. Egypt had only a fraction of the
population in 1000 that she had before the plague and the others
were apparently also in short supply of men. It was an ideal time
for the Crusades from the West in 1095. However, bad planning
and feudal habits and state of mind led to eventual loss of even
what was captured in the First Crusade. The crusaders took the
hard road by land instead of the commercial sea routes, requiring
months instead of weeks. They also insisted on crossing Asia Minor
where their most powerful enemy did terrible damage to the
crusading armies: one after the other. Moreover, the feudal knight
had to fight every twenty miles or so thus getting into trouble even
with inhabitants of friendly countries through which they passed.
Even the most famous had trouble. Richard I fought twice before
he reached Palestine even though he went by sea, and Louis IX got
neither of his two crusading armies to Palestine.

Perhaps the most effective armies were those from England and
the Low Countries in the Second Crusade—but they represented a

[34]J. Hajnal, "European Marriage Patterns in Perspective," in D. V. Glass and D. E. C.
Eversley, *Population in History* 101-143.
[35]Russell, 1972: ch. 12.

Table 49

Comparative Data on Area and Population of Regions, ca. A.D. 1250-1348.

Region	Area 1000 km²	Population 1000s	Density to km^m	Top 10 Cities 1000s	Urban Index
Toledo	184.0	2,800	15.2	128	4.6
Prague	158.6	2,000	12.6	112	5.6
Paris	156.0	5,226	33.5	257	4.9
Cordoba	115.8	1,320	8.6	224	17.0
Toulouse	135.4	3,372	25.0	111	3.3
London	131.8	3,700	28.1	163	4.4
Augsburg	130.9	1,667	12.7	117	7.0*
Barcelona	125.2	1,221	9.8	170	14.0
Cologne	107.3	2,670	25.0	152	5.6*
Palermo	102.2	2,500	24.5	190	7.6
Magdeburg	100.0	1,330	13.3	100	7.5*
Montpellier	95.4	1,296	13.6	146	11.3
Lisbon	89.4	1,252	14.0	93	7.4
Dijon	84.8	1,130	13.3	70	6.2*
Dublin	84.3	675	8.0	41	6.1
Ghent	76.6	1,500	19.5	211	14.1
Lübeck	75.0	1,500	12.7	124	8.3*
Milan	51.0	1,745	34.5	337	19.1
Venice	38.8	1,473	38.0	356	23.4
Florence	28.0	1,140	40.0	296	26.0

*This has little significance since the total population is based upon the size of the largest city at 1.5% of the total. Source: Russell, 1972, 235.

more disciplined society. As the great states declined, regional groups of city states became more prominent. These were based upon an extensive commercial life in the West. The great cities were mostly trading centers: Venice, Florence of about a hundred thousand by the end of the thirteenth century. Not much smaller were Milan and Genoa; the demographic dominance of northern Italy was striking. In the north the cities of Belgium had about the same population with their great cloth trade. Paris had perhaps eighty thousand by 1300 and London twenty thousand less. And there were large cities in Spain remaining from the Islamic era of Mediterranean trade. Novgorod in Russia showed that the Slavic east could participate effectively when free of Asiatic domination.

The population development of the period, 1000-138, had a double thrust. First, the feudal lords, released from central control by the decline of the Carolingians, pressured their inferiors to increase in size and taxation, doubling or tripling their population of the countryside. To some extent the cities increased also. As royal or noble power increased inferiors were forced to control their population through infanticide, later marriage, migration to cities. In the second half of the period the countryside control was exercised in the ancient ways, even among the upper classes. However, the cities continued to grow as new techniques and inventions broadened the economic base of civic life and drew more workers to them. The mutual association of countryside and cities tended to form great regions with their peculiar dialects, social customs, architecture and political institutions. They often created parliaments in which clergy, feudal lords, and representatives of the cities participated, usually as separate estates or houses. Only in England was the division by dignity rather than by order thus producing a two-house Parliament. This very interesting and promising development was damaged by the plague which encouraged the lords to move into the political arena more effectively as the economic base of the regional groups was eroded.

The expansion within the European area tended to hold off the groups of tribes beyond its borders. The Turks moved west across Asia Minor and consolidated their position as the Byzantine Empire lost ground. The Slavic groups strengthened their position in the Balkans, forming the basis for their later nations. The Tartar tribes consolidated and ruled across Eurasia, leaving permanent traces of their customs and ideas. Even earlier, the might of the Normans or Northmen was dissipated as it was divided among many peoples speaking different languages, so that in a few centuries they were only parts of ruling classes speaking the language of the formerly defeated and dominated peoples.

In general the population of Europe seems to have risen only slowly from 1250-1280 to 1348. This was apparently true of the British Isles and of Scandinavia. It is hard to say what happened in eastern Europe, although probably the same increase occurred. In Provence some areas had definitely begun to decline by the plague. The same was apparently true of some of the Italian cities, particularly those which enjoyed a very rapid expansion in the thirteenth century. On the whole there seems to have been little overpopulation and similarly the people seem to have had its numbers under control. The fourteenth century suffered rather unusual climatic conditions, including very cold years in 1303 and 1307. The only severe crisis was the very wet era of 1313-16 which brought on very poor crops with some famine following it with a heavy mortality from dysentery. The mortality seems to have sent many prematurely to their deaths as the death rate after the epidemic was less than before. Conditions for the first four decades of the fourteenth century seem to have been satisfactory, although they worsened in 1340-1348. One can hardly present the picture as one of Malthusian solution of overpopulation.

XII. Divergent Trends in Population Control, 1348-1500.

The appearance of the bubonic plague in Europe in 1347-1348 was a terrible blow. Except for the famine and pestilence of 1315-1316 the area had enjoyed remarkably good health in the preceding half millennium, better than it was to enjoy again until well into the eighteenth or early nineteenth century. Conditions were somewhat different from those of the preceding plague, A.D. 542-750: the climate was much colder and therefore, presumably, less receptive to it; the density of population was much greater then, making it easier to spread the disease; medical attention was greater but not much more enlightened. Our knowledge about the plague is considerably greater but problems still remain.[1] Perhaps the most serious is, why, if the disease kills about 80 per cent of those who are stricken, only 25 to 40 percent of the population died, generally in the first epidemic which lasted two or three years. The second epidemic came ten to twelve years later and a large but lesser number died. Following these attacks, at intervals or multiples of about 3.9 years (a rat cycle) other epidemics occurred, killing off perhaps 8 to 10 percent, mostly of the age group seven to twenty. During the plague period the expectation of life of those over thirty years of age did not change much from nonplague periods. The number of fleas to a person and their dislike to certain animals and plants were factors in the spread of the plague. The subject then is a relatively complicated one, as was seen earlier. It was further complicated by occasional periods of little plague followed by very serious epidemics.

An important question is what happened to land holdings during epidemics; how did it happen that lands were so quickly occupied if so many holders died? A look at data about landholding in England in 1279 helps us conjecture what would happen if a plague took 40 percent of the holders in an epidemic.[2] The holdings were as follows:

---

[1] J-N Biraben, *Les hommes et la peste en France et dans les pays européens et méditerranéens des origines à 1950* (2 vols., The Hague, 1974); M.W.Dols, *The Black Death in the Middle East* (Princeton, 1977), especially good on origins and movement of plague. For bibliography, W.M.Bowsky, *The Black Death* (New York, 1971): 126-128. For the demographic problems of the period: Roger Mols, S.J. *Introduction à la démographie historique des villes d'Europe de xiv⁰ au xviii⁰ siecle* (3 vols. Louvain, 1954-1956). Russell, 1980: 255-266.

[2] E.A.Kosminsky, *Studies in the Agrarian History of England in the Thirteenth Century* (Oxford, 1936): 228.

Major holdings. Over a virgate	520
Virgate holdings	3143
One-half virgate holdings	3448
	7001
90% males	6391
Minor holdings ¼ virgaters	1474
Petty landholders	4929
	6303
80% males	5122
Total males holding lands	11513
60% men surviving plague	6908

If the number of men with major holdings on the manor lands had been about 6,391, that would have barely sufficed to give them proper care. This assumes, that all men even with petty holdings would have been able and willing to take up the larger ones. Some would have been cotters, men too old or too feeble to work the thirty acres or so of the virgates. Others with minor holdings used their few acres to supplement their duties as millers, carpenters, bakers, and so forth. Some, indeed, might consolidate half-virgate holdings in virgates. Nevertheless, there was a considerable shortage of land workers caused by a heavy mortality. Similarly, for many, a plague provided openings for larger and more profitable careers as landholders thus decreasing indigency for the time.

THE COURSE OF THE PLAGUE, 1348-1440.

After the initial epidemic (1348-1350) the decline in population continued, reaching perhaps about 60 percent of the preplague population by 1380. From there it seems to have declined slowly until it reached bottom at about 1440. Perhaps its low point can be defined as after the epidemic—about 1440 when it must have been at about 50 percent of the preplague figures, although it varied from place to place. The course of the plague was somewhat erratic. Parts of the Netherlands escaped the first attack as did the plain of Castillon in Catalonia.[3]

The aridity of Iberia probably kept the loss below average. This is well illustrated by the city and countryside of Teruel in east central Spain for which data come from 1342 and 1385 about number of households.[4] The registers give the numbers of both

---

[3] For the Netherlands, Hans Van Werveke, "De zwarte Dood in de Zuidelijke Nederlanden," *Verhandelingen van de Koninklijke Vlaamse Akademie voor Wettenschappen,* Klasse der Letteren jg. 12 (1950): 1-28. (The author has seen an English copy.) For the plain of Castillon, J. San Martin Bayo, "La mas antigua estadistica de la diocesis de Palencia," *Publicaciones de la Institucione Tello Tellez Menasis,* 1896: 100.

[4] Russell, 1962: 493-495.

the paying and indigent persons. The decline was about 37 percent for the city and 36 for the countryside. Since Teruel seems to have about average temperature and humidity for the Iberian peninsula, the loss of the plague was probably about 36-37 percent. Except for Estelta[5] and the plain of Castillon there seems little evidence about the decline of the first epidemic. Egypt, also an arid country, seems to have had a 20 to 25 percent loss, although the data for the province of Sharkieh (probably the most accurate) shows only 15 to 19 percent. There are problems because during the period the Nile did considerable damage and some famine occurred because of low water in the river.[6]

By medieval standards Italy had reasonably abundant statistics with respect to demography as can be seen in Beloch's volumes. Florence, which had about 95,000 before the plague dropped to 54,700 in 1380, less in 1400 and about the same in 1404. The magnificent catasto of 1427 shows a city population of 19,953 men and 16,119 women in the city and 137,993 men with 125,645 women in the countryside and lesser cities. The decline continued until 1441.[7] Orvieto by 1402 had less than half of its preplague numbers. Bologna had fallen from about 70,000 to 40,000 in 1371. Padua, Pavia, and Pistoia fell to less than half like the others.[8] The loss of life was a little less than half by 1380 and clearly a half by the middle of the fifteenth century.

Southern France also suffered heavily. Provence had an average mortality of more than one-half even in the first epidemic of the plague.[9] Millau, in the mountains, declined even before the plague but fell another 30 percent in the first attack. Albi lost half of her population in the initial epidemic.[10] In the north of France the losses were apparently not much less. An area of Normandy lost about 49 percent. Toulouse seems to have done rather well for France with a loss of about 40 percent.[11]

English population fell from about 3.6 millions before the plague to 2.2 millions in the poll tax of 1377, a 40 percent decline. Sweden lost about 42 percent in the period. Not much has been

[5]For Estelta, San Martin Bayo, 88, 91, 101.

[6]J. C. Russell, "The Population of Medieval Egypt," *Journal of the American Research Center in Egypt* 5 (1966): p. 80.

[7]Beloch, 1940: p. 124. Herlihy & Klapisch-Zuber, 1978: 99, 165-181 and 656-663.

[8]For Orvieto, Beloch, 1961: 67-69, 74; for Padua, Beloch, 1940: 213, 217; for Pistoia, D. Herlihy, *Medieval and Renaissance Pistoia* (New Haven, 1967): 76.

[9]For Provence: Baratier, 1961: 147, 152, 161, 172-173, 174-175, 179, 184, 186-187 188. For Millau, A. Guery; "La population de Rouerge de la fin du Moyen Age," *Annales* 28 (1973); Rodez, 1558.

[10]G. Prat, "Albi et la peste noire," *Annales du Midi* 64 (1952): 18-25. For Normandy, Russell, 1958: 45.

[11]J-H. Biraben, "La population de Toulouse du xiv^{c}e et au xv^{c}e siècles", *Journal des Savants* 1964: 284-300.

estimated for the other countries in the north and east of
Europe.[12]

Some other effects of the plague can be ascertained. In the very
interesting data of Albi, the worth of the holdings just before and
after the plague are given. Since Albi had a numerical loss of about
fifty percent, the survivors on the average had about twice as
much property.[13] The rise in prices reduced some of this advantage, however. The number of landholders in England in the
records declined about as did the population.[14] The percentage of
pobres at Teruel had been 33.7 for the city and 13.6 for the
countryside; in 1385 the numbers were 10.4 for the city and 20.7
for the countryside. In Morella, a city not too far from Teruel, the
number of pobres was at 25.4% in 1397 in the city and only 12.1 in
the country.[15] Thus whatever the advantage achieved by the gains
in the first epidemic, they were apparently lost in the next
generation.

This plague, like the earlier one, showed certain effects upon the
population. Faced by need for more inhabitants, the number of
girls increased relative to boys: the sex ratio tended to become
near 100. The English poll tax of 1377 showed about as many men
as women, particularly in the larger places.[16] Similarly the great
Italian cities in the fifteenth century showed low sex ratios. This
was true of the German cities as well in that century. Of course in
every medieval century the sex ratio was lower in the larger places.
Another characteristic was the great mortality of clergy and other
small households. The older persons suffered more since they
often lived alone and the segregated group of lepers largely died
out.[17]

LOSS OF POPULATION CONTROL IN SOUTHERN ITALY

Tracing the loss of population control is difficult. Clearly the
population of Naples at 212,103 in 1547 indicated a loss of control:
that figure is at least a tenth of the total number for southern
Italy.[18] In the thirteenth century Florence at the height of her
banking and industrial strength only numbered about 9 percent of
the region of which she was the metropolitan city.[19] The normal
share for the top city of a region as widespread and as agricultural

---

[12]Russell, 1948: 263; for others, Russell, 1958; 45.
[13]Prat (note 10).
[14]Russell, 1948: 202-207. The total dead run about the same as the level of population.
[15]Russell, 1962: 489-492, for both Teruel and Morella.
[16]Russell, 1948: 150-154.
[17]Russell, 1958: 13-17.
[18]Beloch, 1937: 171.
[19]Russell, 1972: 235.

and pastoral as southern Italy should have been about 1.5 percent. When such control is lost, the surplus people tend to flock to the large cities. This also happened with Palermo in Sicily during the plague. With available evidence, some suggestions can be made about the peculiar political and economic conditions of the thirteenth century which led to the demographic breakdown beginning at that time. The evidence about the cities is worth examining more closely.

At the time of the Angevin Conquest, Naples had a population of perhaps 25,000.[20] Charles I made that city his capital and it grew rapidly. Even in 1270 he added an additional wall to the enclosed area so that the city covered about 200 hectares.[21] Charles II spoke of the city as abounding with people (*abundens multitudine populorum*) so that we may assume 150-200 to the hectare or about 30,000-40,000 before the Black Death.[22] Perhaps it was higher. A Neapolitan chronicler stated that the plague carried off 27,000 persons in 1382 and 16,000 in 1400, but, of course, this may well be exaggerated. One would have expected the post-plague population to have been about 20,000-25,000. In 1484 an enlargement of the walled area began—to include about four hundred hectares which should have provided for a population of 60 to 80,000 persons.[23] Even at the larger figure the population must have grown very rapidly to reach 212,000 in 1547.[24] This figure is based on actual numbers of persons as well as the hearth total of 35,325 hearths. This was nearly six persons to the hearth which meant crowded housing as well.

The Sicilian Vespers of 1282 had separated Sicily from Italy and thus reduced the base for its capital, Palermo. The population of Palermo was about twenty thousand in 1374.[25] If the decline had been about 40 percent, as occurred elsewhere, the population of preplague Palermo should have been about 33,000. Even then it had declined by several thousands from its mid-thirteenth century size of perhaps 40,000-50,000 which it had enjoyed as capital of the Hohenstaufen kingdom of Sicily and southern Italy.[26] In the century before 1479 Palermo had increased to about 25,000 but jumped to 40,000 by 1548. Thus the population of the city had doubled from 1378 to 1548. In the same period the population of

---

[20]Beloch, 1937: 170, 198, 214.

[21]Beloch, 1937: 203-212.

[22]Beloch, 1937: 169-170.

[23]*Diaria Napolitano anonymo,* in Muratori, 21:1043 for A. D. 1382; 16,000 in 1400, 1067.

[24]Beloch, 1937: 171.

[25]Beloch, 1937: 119. Traselli suggests only 10,000-15,000 but that is much too low for 4,088 hearths.

[26]Russell, 1972: 54-56.

all of Sicily had increased from 70,000 to 152,989 hearths, about the same rate of increase as for Palermo.[27] The city then had about 5.7 percent of the population of Sicily, about three times what a metropolitan city should have had. This was not as overpopulated as Naples was, but bad enough to show that control was probably lost. It probably had lost control in the decades after the capital was moved to Naples and the Sicilian Vespers since the population relationship between Palermo and Sicily had not changed during the fifteenth century. Sicily became part of the Kingdom of Aragon for the rest of the Middle Ages and enjoyed a relatively prosperous existence. It had a remarkable parliamentary history in addition to a satisfactory economic life, as a part of an almost constitutional monarchy.

Over the centuries the Norman kings of Sicily and Italy had adjusted to the life of the area. By the thirteenth century a common language had developed, shared by the rulers of the country.[28] Both Frederick II and his son, Manfred, had grown up there and had patronized Italian poetry as well as Latin literature. It was a period of Apulian magnificence.[29] Frederick II loved the area and had built in its cities a series of outstanding churches. The kings had not only organized a strong absolute government, but they possessed monopolies over many of the most important economic activities, such as transhumance, mining, and fairs. Their one weakness, and it was a fatal one, was their attempt to rule northern Italy against the wishes of both the vigorous re-publics there and of the Popes. King Manfred had proved an excellent king and ruler of southern Italy and Sicily for sixteen years before he was defeated and killed in 1266. By founding Manfredia he joined the successful city founders of his day. Though he did not endanger the papacy or northern cities and preserved good relations with other Mediterranean states, the popes decided that he had to go.

By contrast the man whom the popes invited into Italy was an ambitious, able administrator with a peculiar genius for irritating neighboring states: the Byzantine Empire, north Africa, and even the popes. He came in with the great population of France at his back. The triumph of Charles in the battles of Benevento in 1266 and of Tagliacozzo in 1268 brought a prolific family to the throne.[30] Charles was one of eleven children, his brother Saint Louis IX of France had twelve and his son, Charles I, had

---

[27]Beloch, 1937: 119-120

[28]Saverio la Sorsa, *Storia di Puglia* (2v., Bari, 1953) 2: 268-269.

[29]La Sorsa, *Storia di Puglia* 2: 298.

[30]J.C.Russell, "Aspects démographiques des débuts de la feodalité," *Annales: Economies, Sociétés, Civilsations* 20 (1965): 1123-1125.

fourteen. In a sense population control broke down with the royal family.

The kingdom over which Frederick II and Manfred reigned was divided economically into three commercial zones.[31] One was Sicily and a second, Italy west of the mountains. Through these zones in which Palermo, Naples, and Messina were the great ports, went the commerce of Genoa and Barcelona to Tunis and the Levant. West of the Appenines lay a series of sizable cities along the coast of the Adriatic which participated in the Venetian trade with the Byzantine Empire and the east. The factors in the cities were apparently local men who sold mostly agricultural products destined for the cities along the trade routes: wheat, oil from the olive orchards, and wine from the vineyards. For this trade the southern Italian cities supplied ships in small numbers. The prosperity of the farmers was thought to have been one of the best in Europe then. Nevertheless, much of the farming was done on annual leases of a temporary nature, which did not bode well for the future.

Commerce in animals was also extensive; for example, more than six thousand hogs were moved through Foggia in one year.[32] The same city was the center of the great movement of sheep to the mountains in early summer from the plains of Apulia and back again in the autumn.[33] There is no account of this transhumance in Italy to compare with that of Spain.[34] It was the basis for a very considerable trade in wool in Apulia's extensive foreign trade.[35] The summer herders of the sheep were an important part of the winter population of the cities of Apulia. The economic life centered in the long series of fairs which lasted ten months of the year in the Apulian cities.[36] To these fairs merchants came from the northern Italian cities to participate in an extensive commerce, mostly in agricultural produce, but also in some mining products.[37]

Charles II's conquest of southern Italy had been given the status of a crusade and his victories brought a horde of French adventurers into Italy.[38] Great numbers of supporters of Manfred were

---

[31]Russell, 1972: 52-61 for a discussion of the region of Palermo and its relation to mainland cities.

[32]V. Spola, "I precedenti storici della legislazione della dogana di Foggia nel regno di Napoli," *Archivio Storico Pugliese* 25 (1972): 477.

[33]G. de Gennaro, "Produzione e commerci delle lane di Puglia dalla epoca federiciana al periodo spagnuolo," *Archivio Storico Pugliese* 24 (1972): 49-80.

[34]J. Klein, *The Mesta* (Cambridge, Mass., 1926).

[35]La Sorsa, *Storia di Puglia* 2: 253.

[36]E. Kantorowicz, *Frederick the Second*, 1194-1250, tr. E.O. Loran (New York, 1936), 283-286. La Sorsa, *Storia di Puglia* 3: 93-95.

[37]A. Gradilone, "Logobocco e le sue miniere," *Archivio Storico per la Calabria e Lucania* 32 (1963): 53-66.

[38]E: Jordan, *Les origenes de la domination angevin en Italie* (Paris, 1909.).

driven out and their lands and offices given to Charles I's men.[39] They included at least four different groups: the royal family and their retainers, the merchants and other businessmen, the clerical and governmental employees, and the army, both officers and ordinary soldiers.

Charles entered Italy deeply in debt to the bankers of Tuscany.[40] Thus he had to collect as much money as possible from the people of southern Italy and Sicily in order to repay his debts. With great sums of money leaving the south, the balance of payments in its favor of that area was lost. Charles also permitted many Italian merchants of Siena and other Italian cities to do business throughout the south, displacing the rebellious native Italian merchants in the area.[41] He also led attacks on "heretics" in a number of places.[42] These were often industrial workers or merchants. Thus the introduction of merchants and other north Italians from the most sophisticated business communities did not promote business in the south, but led to a flight of money there.[43] A part of the trouble was the loss of markets for Sicilian grain, sugar, sweet wine, fruits, and nuts.

The turnover in officials was serious, the new officials affecting the inhabitants of the cities and countryside. Their coming meant the substitution of French for the vernacular as the official language and the introduction of Frenchmen who neither spoke the vernacular nor understood it. These included French soldiers in the various garrisons who were there to keep order, thus arousing intense hostility. It was the action of a French soldier at Palermo which set off the Sicilian Vespers in 1282 and ended the Angevin occupation there. The relations of the French to the Italians on the mainland could hardly have been unhappier, and were certainly disturbing to economic relations there.

Charles, of course, turned over extensive estates to his followers, as was usually done by thirteenth-century victors. These French (and other followers) found life on the estates which the king had expropriated from the "rebels" intolerable. Growing numbers of the French nobles tended to live in the cities, especially Naples, where they were relatively safe.[44] The French left control of their estates to local characters whose sole interest was collecting money for their lords rather than in farming. The tendency was to allow

---

[39]G. del Giudice, *Codice diplomatico di Carlo I e II* (see note 41)

[40]Jordan, *Les origenes*, 536 ff.

[41]Del Giudice, *Codice diplomatico di Carlo I e Carlo II d'Angio dal 1265 al 1309* (2v, Napoli, 1963) 2: 32-33. G.Iver, *Le commerce et les marchands dans l'Italie meridianale du xiii au xiv siècles* (Paris, 1903).

[42]Del Giudice, *Codice* 2: 42-46.

[43]H.A.Miskimin, *The Economy of Early Renaissance Europe* (Englewood, 1969), 66 ff.

[44]La Sorsa 3: 140.

the estates to run down and to erode the agricultural base of the south. As the estates declined, malaria advanced and became the scourge of southern Italy, as it has remained until the present century. Employment lessened and became more precarious. The very widespread prevalence of seasonal or yearly holdings eroded the permanence and responsibility of the southern Italians. It just did not seem worthwhile to observe the age-old restrictions of marriage to permanent sources of income. So the check on population became less and less effective.

Before the plague southern Italy had a population of about two million, including Naples.[45] Even in 1448 it had 230,000 hearths for a population of perhaps 1,150,000 which was above the expected number (of a million). That number further reflects a failure of the preplague population to decline after the arrival of the Angevins.[46] By 1545 the population had risen above two million and was rapidly increasing. Control was lost.

This loss of control in southern Italy came from a sense of defeat. There were pressures to have more children—the Church condemned any forms of birth control and infanticide, and there was the feeling that children were insurance against extreme poverty in old age. The wonder, perhaps, is that the population of southern Italy did not rise more rapidly than it did.

LOSS OF POPULATION CONTROL IN NORTHERN ITALY

In the northern half of Italy city states struggled against each other, much as the feudal lords had done in the period 1000-1250. The effect upon population attitudes was much the same, there was an effort to increase manpower. Cities encouraged immigration by letting new settlers postpone paying their debts. Sometimes cities tried to stimulate the birthrate by giving dowries to girls or by forbidding women to dress expensively, assuming that women preferred expensive dresses to children. Even before the plague Siena had tried to limit the cloth in women's dresses but ran into the objection that the law discriminated against large women.[47]

The pressure for more population in the cities was paralleled by the urge to have more sons in the great families which dominated the life of north Italy. Unlike southern Italy the literature on the subject is large and persuasive. The humanist, Leon Battista Alberti, wrote about the families at some length.[48] In addition

---

[45]Beloch, 1937: 203. Estimated from the general subvention. Beloch, 1937: 191-203.

[46]Beloch, 1937: 203-212.

[47]M. Pierro, "Le legge suntuarie e la problema demografica nel Medioevo," *Politica sociale* 2 (1930): 20-22. D.Herlihy, "Family Solidarity in Medieval Italian History," *Explorations in Economic History* 7 (1969-1970) 173-184, esp. 181-184.

[48]G.Mancini, ed. Leon Battista Alberti, *Libri della familia* (Florence, 1908).

several Italian men of affairs kept diaries which often give clues to their thoughts and even to the number and appearance of their children.[49] There are also more demographic data for the north of Italy in the fourteenth and fifteenth centuries than for the south.

Alberti in his book of advice on the family suggests that the proper age for a man to marry is twenty-five years but does not urge, as in earlier population control, that the man have a job to support himself. The duty of the father in a family was tribal; he should increase the fame of the family, of the city, and its citizens. This meant raising children—particularly sons. He should choose a wife and a daughter-in-law with a number of brothers on the theory that their families tended to run to sons. He should marry "a well stacked person likely to bear a supply of most beautiful sons. Let us have a house, as we have said, full of youth."[50] The only real check on marriage was the matter of dowries for the girls.[51] Alberti did advise that mothers nurse their own children but that naturally would have limited the number of children: there were grave dangers in trusting children to wet nurses. In the great palazzos of the north Italian cities there was plenty of room for married sons and their families.[52]

Records show they did have children. One Coluccio Salutati had ten sons from two marriages and Poggio Bracciolini had twelve sons and two daughters.[53] Few could equal the paternal record of Gregory Dati, as recorded in his diary. One of seventeen children, he had a child before marriage, then married Isabetta who died quickly. A second marriage brought eight children in eight years. His third wife was the most prolific: eleven children in sixteen years. His fourth marriage produced six children in six years, at this point he quit—writing his diary.[54] It is obvious, even if other evidence did not show it, that the babies were given wet nurses. Dati was very fond of his wives. Never more grieved than when they were dying in childbirth, he usually honored his deceased wife by naming the first girl of the succeeding marriage for her.

[49]G. Brucker, *Two Memoirs of Renaissance Florence* (New York, 1967). D.Herlihy, "Family Solidarity in Medieval Italian History," *Exploration in Economic History* 7 (1969-1970): 173-184. V. Branca, ed. Ricordi di G. de Pagola Morelli (1377-1444) (Florence, 1969). J. K. Hyde, "Italian Social Chroniclers in the Middle Ages," *Bull of the John Rylands Library* 49 (1966): 107-132. P.J. Jones, "Florentine Families and Florentine Diaries in the Fourteenth Century," *Papers of the British School at Rome* 24 (1956): 183-205.

[50]Mancini, ed. Alberti: 15, 30-31, 102, 164, 103 and 121 respectively. "Formosa e apta a portare e produci una copia di bellisimi figluoli." N. Tamassia, *La famiglia italiana nel secolo decimoquinto decimosesto* (Milan, 1910).

[51]Tamassia, chapter on dowries, 166-167.

[52]Branca, ed. Morelli, 102; Tamassia, 170.

[53]V. Cronin, *The Florentine Renaissance* (New York, 1967), 37, 48.

[54]Brucker, *Two Memoirs*, 107-144.

The ideal seems to have been to keep wives perpetually pregnant.[55] It was a system hard on the mother and even harder on the child, but it produced the desired progeny. Something may even be said for the system, despite its hardship on the mothers. In time of plague with its recurring harvesting of children, the great number of infants was a hedge against total loss of successors. One must always remember the shadow of the Black Death in the background—a constant pressure to forget the need for population control. The system did center attention upon children and gave them more status in the family. Parents, or at least the men, seem to have enjoyed children and paid more attention to them. There is the story of Cosimo di Medici who interrupted his conference with Luccan ambassadors to play with his grandchild and asked his guests if they did not love their children. He not only had made the child's whistle, but would even play it.[56]

These examples have all been of the literary and business classes of Florence. What about the other classes? A recent article has suggested infanticide among the poor.[57] Clearly there was infanticide in Florence as evidence from hospitals and ecclesiastical documents show; the number was considerable. Before the plague Florentine evidence shows that the sex ratio for babies was about 115 which is certainly higher than the normal 104 or 105.[58] Such a disparity comes either from infanticide or failure of parents to have female babies baptized in the cathedral at Florence. However, each of the five decades beginning with 1451 shows a sex ratio of baptized in the cathedral in the range of 103.5 to 105.[59] The same results come from the Tuscan city of Siena.[60] And this is generally true, with some exceptions, in the following century. Only among the illegitimate children in the fifteenth century was a high sex ratio apparent.[61]

Usually a low sex ratio means that population was increasing rapidly. This would be especially true if girls married at from fourteen to twenty years of age, as is alleged.[62] The problem is whether the population would increase even during the severe epidemics of the Black Death.

---

[55] Jones, "Florentine Families," 189.

[56] Cronin, *The Florentine Renaissance,* 99. Diametrically opposed in thought to L. DeMause, "The Evolution of Childhood," *History of Childhood Quarterly* 1 (1973): 503-575.

[57] R. C. Trexler, "Infanticide in Florence: New Sources and First Results," *History of Childhood Quarterly* 1 (1973): 98-116.

[58] Beloch, 1937: 10. Evidence from Giovanni Villani.

[59] Beloch, 1937; 10.

[60] Beloch, 1937: 11.

[61] Beloch, 1937: 13.

[62] Laura Martines, *The Social World of the Florentine Humanists, 1390-1460* (Princeton, 1963), 200.

Florence, together with much of central Italy, did increase rapidly from the middle of the fifteenth century until the middle of the next. Umbria was the exception. In the north of Italy Bologna, Milan, and Venice followed the same pattern as Florence. Genoa probably did also, but the evidence is poor. On the other hand the smaller cities of the Po Valley increased only slowly if at all: Mantua, Reggio Emilia, Parma, Piacenza and Padua.[63] Since all of these smaller places, except Mantua, had been absorbed by larger neighbors, the incentive to increase population to achieve greater manpower no longer existed. And Mantua was too small to compete effectively in the struggle in the north. Outside of Italy only Portugal shows definite, rapid increase while the emigration of Jews and Muslims into Spain complicated matters there.[64]

Everywhere, it seems, about the middle of the fifteenth century the level of population stabilized or barely increased. The problem then is why there were no further declines and why in some places population began to increase rapidly and persisted until the areas were thoroughly overpopulated, as they have remained until the present. After a century of plague, a number of possibilities existed which should be studied further. The microbes may have weakened to produce a less severe mortality, although the occasional severe epidemics do not seem to bear this out. People or rats may have developed at least a partial immunity to it but research has not shown this to be true. Perhaps even the more frequent deaths of persons who attracted fleas may have created a kind of immunity. Or the reservoirs of plague may have declined. The answer to the second is clearer. When the will to restrain population weakened, population could increase even in the face of plague.

The lack of population control in Italy led to very definite overpopulation by 1550; the problem continuing to the present time. Two very different factors created this. In the south too many workers owed their living to temporary or short-term employment in agriculture, viticulture, transhumance and other pursuits. The relatively large population then found itself either jobless or displaced in the continuing Angevin depression in the country, increasing perhaps about 1320.[65] Unsure of permanent employment, men found it difficult to plan for marriage or children. For some time the plague solved the problem with its shortage of manpower and increased holdings for those who

[63]Beloch, 1940: 5 for Rome, 136-142 for Florence; 60 for Umbria; 90-94 for Bologna; 297 for Mantua; 270 for Reggio Emilia; 243 for Parma; 249-250; for Piacenza; Beloch, 1961 6-8 for Venice; 69-70 for Padua and 172-182 for Milan.

[63]Russell, 1958: 113-118.

[65]George Iver, *Le commerce et les merchants dans l'Italie meridionale au xiii et au xiv siècle* (Paris, 1903), 119. Trouble at Naples because of *pluralitatum incolarum*.

survived. However, when somehow or other the pressure of the plague declined, the way was open for overpopulation and its accompanying depression and misery.

In the north the reverse situation led to loss of population control, the competing cities needed more manpower and families wanted more members, especially sons. With Church and civic approval, the people of Florence and the north happily threw aside their previous mastery of population control—a strange phenomenon in the wealthiest and most sophisticated people of Europe. It is sometimes debated whether modern Europe began with the Italian Renaissance.[66] In the matter of overpopulation and loss of control, it certainly did.

POPULATION CONDITIONS IN ENGLAND

From the data about the landholders of late medieval England it is possible to see how the distribution of heirs occurred from about the middle of the thirteenth century into the sixteenth. At the beginning the population of that country was rapidly increasing by medieval standards. As might be expected the sex ratio was low. About two thirds of the deceased had either sons or grandsons as heirs, while the number of heiresses was about 10 percent. Other inheritors (17.7%) were not direct descendents.[67] Beginning about 1300 the sex ratio of heirs jumps very high, to about 193. This presupposes a change in the handling of children some twenty-five years earlier since the highest number of heirs were about that age in 1300. Evidently the declining condition of the country by that year produced enough worry for the beginning of population control then. With probably better conditions of the generation before the plague, the sex ratio arose somewhat but was still not as drastic as earlier. The plague surprisingly enough did not lead in England to a rising sex ratio at once; even in spite of the severe mortality it remained high. With the beginning of the fifteenth century it declined to a still very high 160. Suddenly about 1460 or thereabout a radical change occurred; the sex ratio dropped to a modest 98. During that period the age of marriage seems also to have been lowered. The number of the landholder class must have grown very markedly in this period: it coincided with the reign of Edward IV who brought England peace after years of civil war. The rate of succession in families was so low during the preceding century that some should have died out. It illustrates the problem of succession during times of high mortality.

---

[66]G. Brucker, *The Renaissance. Was it the Birthplace of the Modern World?* (New York, 1965).
[67]Russell, 1948; 240-245.

The use of the T column of the life table is helpful in establishing population trends of those represented by it if a series can be secured of that population. Three samples of T appear in life tables of landholders in England in 1280-1282,[68] 1310-1312 and 1340-1342. Comparative percentages, using the first as unity are for age 0: 1.00, 0.99 and 1.21 and for age 20: 1.00, 1.01 and 1.43. If this is a fair sample of the landholding age pattern, the population of landholders was hardly growing at all between 1280-1282 and quite rapidly between 1300-1302 and 1340-1342. It seems clear that it is not representative of the country at large which apparently grew only slowly during the whole period. This growth of what was also the military class may account for the enthusiasm which led to the outbreak of the Hundred Years War. If so it is easier to understand the decline of enthusiasm after the outbreak of the plague, particularly after it continued.

Somewhat the same development is characteristic of the period from 1348 to 1425. The country at large hardly experienced any growth before the opening of the sixteenth century. Yet see what was happening according to the T column in the life tables of the period. If we take the experience of the generation 1348-75 as a base, the figures are:[69]

	T_0	% increase	T_{20}	% increase
1348-75	17331		7659	
1376-1400	20533	18.5	9011	17.7
1401-1425	23780	37.2	11871	55.0

Table 50

Status of Heirs, England landholders, to 1505.

Period	Total	No direct heirs		Sons or their heirs		Daughters or their heirs		Sex ratio
		Number	%	Number	%	Number	%	
To 1300	1317	233	17.7	952	72.2	133	10.1	113
1301-48	2015	364	18.1	1452	72.1	199	9.9	193
1348-1400	2115	606	28.7	1198	56.6	311	14.6	150
1401-1430	919	256	27.9	535	58.2	128	13.9	192
1431-1450	508	104	20.5	324	63.8	80	15.7	166
1451-1475	688	109	15.8	496	72.1	83	12.1	166
1476-1505	1252	188	15.0	900	71.9	164	13.1	98

Source: Russell, 1948, 240-242.

[68]S.Thrupp, *The Merchant Class of Medieval London* (Chicago, 1948), 200.
[69]R. S. Gottfried, *Epidemic Disease in Fifteenth Century England* (Rutgers, 1978), 204.

This rise in the number of the military class may account for the enthusiasm for a renewal of the Hundred Years War in the second decade of the fifteenth century. It does not account for the failure of the increasing population of this class to continue enthusiasm for the war after about 1430, but it may have added impetus to the Wars of the Roses.

Landed men in England inherited at ages nineteen to twenty-one rather then twenty-four to twenty-eight. This includes brothers and other heirs as well as sons. This shortened the generation and tended to overcome loss by the plague. Furthermore, girls married earlier—in England at about eighteen instead of twenty to twenty-four and this was even more effective in increasing numbers of children. However, the childbearing period was also shortened by the plague. Under the circumstances it would not have been surprising if wet nurses had been employed, as in Italy, so that women could have more children faster.

	Males			Females	
	Age at inheritance, median	Age at death, median	Primo-geniture generation	Age at marriage, median	Generation
Born before 1276	28	54	26	24-	30
Born 1276-1300	24	51	27	24	30
Born 1301-1325	22	46	24	20	26
Born 1326-1348	20	43	23	18*	24
Born 1348-1375	21	43	22	18*	24
Born 1376-1400	21	48	27	18*	24
Born 1401-1425	19	48	29	18*	24
Born 1426-1450	24	55	31	18 plus	24

Table 51

Age at Inheritance, Marriage and Death, English Inquisitions post mortem.

Sources: data for inheritance and death, medians: Russell, 1947: 202-207; for marriage: 156-158.

*Probably many married earlier but since few women had children before 18, this is assumed as the age of effective marriage. The generation is assumed to be the years between a mother's birth and birth of her middle child, roughly six years after marriage.

The same table (no. 51), of the age of inheritance of English medieval landholders shows that the generation born A.D. 1426-1450 had a markedly longer life than earlier plague generations. It was even longer than the preplague generations of the same type of English landholder. If this was true of people elsewhere in Europe, it should have meant more healthy and long-lived generations during the Renaissance in Europe and may have been partially responsible for the outburst of energy and production in that period.

In general one may assume that the age of marriage for males in the upper landowning class would be about the same as the age of inheritance or coming of age (21) whichever was the higher. The age of marriage for girls comes from the inquisitions post mortem,[70] where the ages given are for inheritance of status often listed. The estimate of age of marriage then is a quantitative matter based on the age when most women seem to be married when they inherit. It is assumed that the generation based on females is the woman's age at marriage plus six years, assuming that she will have had then half of the 4.2 children which women had, on the average. This is based on the assumption that the number of child marriages was too small to be important. The male generation is based on primogeniture, from one eldest son to his eldest son. It should then include only enough time for the eldest son, other sons if eldest has died and daughters if no sons survive, and is estimated at three or four years after marriage or inheritance. This also assumes that in England, in this class, wet nurses were not normally employed in this period. If this was so, the generation would be reduced perhaps a year or so since more children would be born in the marriage.

OTHER PLAGUE AREAS

How the plague affected people at the end of the fifteenth century can best be seen by studying England and Italy which show extremes of population increase and stability. In between came most of the other areas of Europe and the Mediterranean. Even though Mols's work sheds some light on that period, there is still much to be done. Just why population began to increase in some areas after 1440 is not clear—especially since the plague recurs at intervals in epidemic form and was constantly endemic; its toll often devastating.[71] New diseases cropped up, for example the sweating sickness which seems to have been a form of influenza, as well as syphilis which may have come from America. Later, more virulent forms of smallpox appeared. Malthus would have been

---

[70]Russell, 1948; 189-191.
[71]Russell, 1948: 180-191.

bewildered by the failure of these diseases to keep population under control.

Cities seem to have recovered and pushed on faster than the countryside, probably as a result of the new technology and ensuing commerce. Paris having about eighty thousand before the plague, experienced the customary reduction during the plague, but pulled up rapidly by 1500 although its actual population cannot be estimated from the overenthusiastic description of observers. Smaller places like Cambresis and Carpentras which also increased rapidly may well illustrate a general increase in France. The recovery of Normandy from the Hundred Years War led to rapid increase there.[72]

The southern Iberian ports of Seville and Lisbon grew rapidly with increased oceanic trade. Indeed, all of Portugal and parts of Spain also increased, possibly with the help of the fleas' aversion to olives. Valencia also grew rapidly in this period, but it seems to have been largely at the expense of Barcelona. At this time deep ports improved their position while the smaller and shallower ports which could not accommodate the larger vessels then coming into use decreased. Better equipment made it possible for ships to strike boldly across wider stretches of water and tended to concentrate shipping in fewer ports as well. Iberia came out of the Middle Ages as the most powerful nation in Europe though it had a smaller population than France.

Not much is known of Scandinavian population. Norway seems to have increased rapidly and possibly the others did as well.[73] Similarly Russia may have increased as better trading conditions developed under the Tartars.

Population seems to have increased slowly in Germany: where conditions during the later Middle Ages were not too good. Some of the best information comes from the German cities of Nurnberg, 1449; Nordlingen 1459 and Strasbourg, 1473-1477. These compiled censuses of all the citizens: their totals of 20,185, 5,295 and 20,612-20,722, give some idea of the size of German cities in that century. Danzig, however, seems to have increased rapidly with the help of the Hanseatic trade. Brabant, Switzerland and Luxemburg also stayed about the same in numbers of inhabitants.[74]

Aragon expanded as mountain people emigrated there. The sources of its high male sex ratio in the eleventh century raises a question. The answer may be found if we assume that the pattern of life in the fifteenth century is a continuation of earlier times.

---

[72]Russell, 1948: 156-158.

[73]Russell, "Recent Advances in Mediaeval Demography," *Speculum* 40 (1965): 100.

[74]Russell, 1956: 121.

Professor Riú has edited two lists of persons and their children from Sant Lorenc in the Pyrenees of the years 1429 and 1470. (Table 52). There are remarkable similarities in the two lists. The number of families with children are 55 and 53; the number of male children 77 and 76 and of female children 20 in both. A problem, of course, is why such remarkable similarities as well, as the more obvious disparity of sexes of the children. The difference is not caused by out migration of girls since it is nearly as great among families with one child as of those with many. One must then consider seriously the probability of female infanticide. The expansion of Aragon then may have been an increase in the infanticide, permitting the male babies to survive in considerable numbers.

Infanticide was probably the result of the environment. Instead of allowing an indefinitely large number of babies to survive in poverty and squalor, the mountain society reacted by limiting the number of surviving children. It was probably a healthy society (tuberculosis and malaria were not a serious threat). The killing of baby girls enabled families to avoid costs of rearing them and to profit by exacting dowries from mountain girls who married there.

Table 52

Distribution of Children by Family and Sex in Sant Lorenc in 1429 and 1470.

Combination if each family		Number of each combinations		Total Number of Children 1429		1470	
Son	Daughter	1429	1470	Male	Female	Male	Female
0	0	76	54	0	0	0	0
1	0	23	29	23		29	
0	1	8	5		8		5
1	1	5	4	5	5	4	4
2	0	5	3	10		6	
2	1	6	1	12	6	2	1
3	0	4	4	12		12	
3	1	1	1	3	1	3	1
3	2		3			9	6
3	3		1			3	3
4	0	3	1	12		4	
4	1		1			4	1
Total		131	107	77	20	76	21

Source: Manuel Riú, "Una posible fuente para la estadistica demográfica medieval: los'cartells' de cofradias de laicos," *Homenaje á Jaime Vicens Vives* (2 v, Barcelona, 1965), 1:597.

The marriage percentage at Sant Lorenc was obviously rather high with the number of daughters so low,—close to fifty percent. There are data also for some other places, but, of course, no skeletal evidence on marriage. (Table 53). Ninth-century data seem to average from 29 to 44, but the other two are 32-33 percent. The data from the earlier plague, in Italy, show a high (45) percentage—and this seems to be typical of the mass of the data which also come from a plague period. Fourteenth-century (1377) figures from three English cities show a lower percentage than those from the villages. One would expect that, as usual, population in the cities would not reproduce themselves and would draw from the countryside. The Tirol villages show also a higher percentage of married persons than the German cities. One has

Table 53

Percent of Population Married

Time, Century	Country, Place	Percentage	Plague or Nonplague
7,	Italy, S. Lorenzo d'Oulx	45	Plague
9,	France, S. Germain des Pres	44	Nonplague
9,	France, S. Remi, Reims	33	Nonplague
9,	France, St. Victor, Marseilles	32	Nonplague
9,	Germany, several sites	29	Nonplague
14,	Carlisle, England, 1377	38	Plague
14,	Dartmouth, England,	45	Plague
14,	Colchester, England,	40	Plague
14,	Kingston-on-Hull, 1377 England	39	Plague
14,	Towns, 200-200 inhabitants, England	44	Plague
14,	Towns 100-200 England	47	Plague
14,	Towns, 50-100 England	49	Plague
14,	Towns, 25-50 England	47	Plague
14,	Towns, 1-25 England	56	Plague
15,	France, Reims, 1422 (part)	47	Plague
15,	Germany, Basel, 1454	33	Plague
15,	Germany, Dresden (part), 1430	49	Plague
15,	Freiburg i. Uchtland	39	Plague
15,	Germany, Tirol villages, 1427	43	Plague
16,	Low Countries, Ypres (part) 1421	35	Plague
15,	Italy, Florence, 1427		
	City 34.4, County 42.2	35	Plague

Sources: English Sites: Russell, 1948: 156; for Reims: Desportes, 1422; for others Russell 1958:18. Florence, Herlihy & Klapisch-Zuber 1978:663,659.

to be careful about using data from only parts of cities since it probably varied from one part to another: the central, wealthier parts would probably have a higher percentage of the married than the outer less wealthy areas.

Some records of births remain for Barcelona from the second half of the fifteenth-century[75]

1457	1121	1494	1380
1483	998	1497	1256
1489-1490	1580	1501	1619

The range thus is roughly from about a thousand a year to about 1600. The attacks of the plague were probably a complicating factor. A second factor is that cathedral baptismal records may have included children from the countryside. If we assume, however, that there were few of these and that most of the children were baptized there, the birthrate may be estimated. The number of hearths in the city was about 7,000 and, assuming 4.5 to the hearth, the total population would be about 31,500 persons. The birthrate then would have been about 3.2 to 5.1 percent a year, with an average of about 4.2, quite reasonable for plague periods.

The plague's effects upon the Middle East are less certain than in the West, largely because sources are unsatisfactory. Some records remain, but their value is uncertain, as M.W. Dols's work shows. Many numbers, even in allegedly official data, are obviously exaggerated most of them probably are—since public opinion tended to make plague mortality too high. Dols stresses the importance of pneumonic plague, but little is known of its prevalence.[76] His tendency is to accept large figures, for example, he lists 451,008 for Cairo and its suburbs before the Black Death of 1348. This flaws an otherwise very welcome account of the plague's bibliography, geographic spread, and effects upon the Middle East. He closes with this statement:

The pandemic initiated a series of plague epidemics that contributed to a marked decline in Middle East population from the middle of the fourteenth century. What must be emphasized is that this decline was continual in large part because of the recurrence of severe epidemics that included pneumonic plague. This decrease in population was the essential phenomenon of the social and economic life of Egypt and Syria in the later Middle Ages.[77]

---

[75]Russell 1956: 123-126.

[76]M.W. Dols, *The Black Death in the Middle East,* 72-83. and elsewhere. The pneumonic form is characterized by the spitting of blood and appearance in winter, both typical of pneumonia itself. Years when it apparently occurred were: 1348-1349, 1374-1375, 1379-1381. 1403-1404, 1410-1411, 1429-1430, 1437, 1448-1449 and 1459-1460. 230. Wu Lien-Teh, *A Treatise on Pneumonic Plague* (Geneva, 1926) which I have not seen. The chief problem is why, if the disease is about 100 percent fatal, more did not die in each epidemic?

[77]Dols, 202. The effect of dry climate in reducing plague mortality is not considered.

Devastating plague brought equally devastating consequences and much has been written about them. However, the effect upon population control was probably not very great. Except for Italy, European countries seemed to have maintained control for generations after 1500. In Italy the economic situation in the south and the civic pressure for greater population may well have reduced control despite the plague. Obviously the plague did affect the custom of infanticide and other methods of control.

The plague of 542-750 seems to have aided in the advance and triumph of Islam in the desert and semidesert areas of the world, probably because it apparently did not bring the mortality in dry areas that it did in damp ones. In the fourteenth century the Ottoman Empire, based in Asia Minor and the Balkans, did advance and take over great territories in Europe and in Asia. Doubtless, population did increase in those areas faster than in most of Europe except Italy. However, if the pneumonic form of the plague was prevalent in Islamic lands, as has recently been suggested, even this hypothesis might be doubted. And in western Europe, the greatness of Spain in the sixteenth century might rest in part upon the lesser mortality of the plague there. Perhaps this may have been true of Portugal as well.

During the plague period many of the stronger governments of Europe: the Papacy, France, Germany, England, and even the Hispanic nations were shaken by serious civil wars and other problems. Central authority was rather tenuous in any case and doubtless plague-related disturbances undermined their strength and validity. During the change from feudal anarchy, much strength had been left in the hands of feudal lords and their organizations. The plague tended to upset financial arrangements for taxation and raised question about the validity of ancient customs which had kept the poorer classes in subjection.

The loss of manpower meant that many men and probably some women inherited lands and civic positions which they had not expected and which raised them to much more comfortable places in society. If in a generation nearly half the population died, those remaining should have inherited extensive sources of income and prestige. The fifteenth century probably saw a closer approach to democracy than Europe would see until the end of the nineteenth century. Of course the initial series of distributions of money and property was followed by a reshuffling of money and positions, so that the old structure of power and wealth tended to return. The generation of the less endowed must have had their finest days in the period after the first epidemic of 1348-1350.

XIII. Of Interest to History

Population varied from country to country and from time to time in the late ancient and medieval world. The reason for the catastrophic decline in the two plague periods is obvious and might tend to ascribe most changes to the effects of disease. Yet the decline varied from place to place even in the plague periods. Drier areas suffered less, some areas even escaped a time: Scotland and northmost parts of England in the first and the Netherlands for a time in the second. One might have expected recovery of similar proportions to fill the vacancies created by the plague, but recoveries also were uneven. Italy increased rapidly after 1450 even though the plague was still rampant there, indicating that the human race, if it wished, could overcome terrible population losses, almost at will. The experience of the Roman Empire showed that people could decrease their numbers at will also. The question is why the people willed an increase or decrease, given the choices of population control available.

First, the tests will be examined which might indicate that people actually wished a control of population rather than a supine acceptance of demographic fate. This assumes that attitudes of peoples may be indicated by types of actions showing approval or disapproval of policies. Then the influence of climate and disease will be briefly discussed. Some attempt will be made to estimate the importance of population size and change in the late ancient and medieval Europe. Finally some suggestions will be made about needed research in the field.

As we have seen, several factors control the course of population:

1 Territoriality. If marriage is associated with possession of land, population would be stable unless the territories are divided.

2 The age of marriage of the bride determines what part of her potential childbearing period may be utilized. Generally this period is from about eighteen to death of herself or of her husband or to menopause, usually about ten to seventeen years or less.

3 The number of children is reduced by breast feeding or increased by the use of wet nurses.

4 The parent, family or midwife may decide whether the newborn, especially the girls, may be allowed to live, normally in the first days of life.

5 Abortion and contraception, although well known, do not seem to have been important in the period.

---

[1]A very good introduction to Malthus by an outstanding demographer is J.J. Spengler, "Malthus's Total Population Theory," *Canadian Journal of Economics and Political Science* 7 (1945): 83-110, 234-264.

The first four alternatives offer a considerable range of population controls. Given the ordinary circumstances of the period territorial stability, late marriage, breast feeding and normal death rate control was automatic. In times of high mortality, plague or otherwise, the substitution of wet nurses, earlier marriage, and, the marriage of more women was geared to increase population. As we have seen, this did occur in places in Italy and elsewhere in the fifteenth century.

Thus if disease caused a heavier than usual death rate, people would marry earlier or more often and thus make up the difference. This assumes that some factors would remain stable for instance, territoriality. This would also assume that the ideas of territoriality would persist and not change. Obviously, if the concept of the proper size of a territory altered, the population would adjust to it.

In the long run the important question is what did people think about population and the environment. In a people's total concept of its life, what importance did it place on it? If one did not regard population as important, over-population would ensue, as is the case in much of the world today. The problem then becomes one of understanding the main motives of each age and determining what effect they have upon the problem of population. But how does one discover the important driving motives of an age?

Expression of these ideas varied widely in the ancient and medieval world. Greeks were a very articulate people who tended to discuss nearly every phase of life; Romans somewhat less so.[2] The Church inheriting their traditions constantly discussed and wrote about their ideas. Moreover, some traditions of the Church, such as celibacy, were somewhat unusual and thus required defense. The opinions of the common man, though widely held, were seldom written down. To understand how the majority felt, one has to look at their practices and their treatment of persons either agreeing with or hostile to their common opinions.

TEST OF DEMOGRAPHIC INTERESTS

Marriage and family, a central demographic factor, illustrates the first test, that of *institutionalization* of the relationship of the sexes and parental customs. Institutions are protected by customs and eventually by legal agencies and processes. The extent and power of institutions are then illustrative of the strength of the ideas held by people at the time. The second test is that of *rationalization*, the ways in which a society explains and defends the reasons for its ideas and institutions. Why Jewish men should

---

[2]Paul Veyne, "La famille et l'amour sous le Haut-Empire Romain," *Annales, Economies, Sociétés, Civilisations* 33 (1978); 35-63, esp. 46-48.

marry their brother's widow and Christian men should not are good illustrations. The third test is *canonization*, the tendency to raise beyond criticism the chief exponents of general beliefs. The fourth test is that of *intolerance*. Those hostile to the commonly held opinion are subjected to various forms of persecution or dislike since people do not like to have their fondest beliefs questioned. Finally there is *taxation*, used in its broadest sense of any burden or requirement imposed upon persons in the name of the general idea.[3]

Leadership is not included although it frequently does indicate widespread interests. However, it is often a highly personal attraction often produced by dislike for particular conditions or persons rather than by the leader's manifestation of a generally held opinion.

In general there were two bases for demographic types of the late ancient and medieval world: the more ancient family-territorial system whose chief aim was to control population and the Catholic system which was directed primarily toward a Christian heaven and hell.

In terms of the tests, the older system had as its aim the material well-being of the entire society. Among the Romans and Greeks the extended family sometimes had to accept children into the clan and could decide whether to keep or expose the clan's offspring. With the German and Celtic groups the responsibility for acceptance or rejection is not clear. Possibly it was a joint midwife-parent decision at birth. As mentioned earlier many provisions with respect to marriage affected the birthrate. It is hard to determine the customs or their operation since peasants seldom wrote or apparently talked much about them. The ancient system apparently did not need to rationalize: the ideal of enough for everyone was clear. Even infanticide fell within the need to protect all against famine. Societal intolerance was expressed in infanticide and against women who had children outside of wedlock. Taxation put restraints on human conduct, primarily that of the women who might have to wait for marriage until men with holdings, sufficient to maintain a family appeared; breast feeding was the norm, being preferable to pregnancy at shorter intervals.

Generally speaking the ancient system was good: fewer children at longer intervals were better for both women and children, a child was assured of a living when he came of age. Marriages were respected since illegitimate children were outcasts. Despite the talk

---

[3]These ideas were used by Archie Bahm, *The Specialist: His Philosophy, His Disease, His Cure*, (New Delhi and Albuquerque, 1953): 132-134.

of famines, skeletal evidence shows generally good conditions of
bones and teeth, almost no rickets, and relatively few instances of
violence.[4]

Christian sex and marriage patterns differed little from customary practices but they were modified by the long and bitter
struggle with unorthodox and heretical beliefs—manichees and
Gnostics among others.[5] Their main contentions involved
Christology and other theological beliefs; for them followers died
and killed. Sexual practices also differed and aroused very strong
feelings with lesser penalties for deviation from custom. The
unorthodox seem to have questioned marriage and countenanced
sexual relations which were not primarily for reproduction. The
Church developed strong views on marriage and family. Yet
neither the early nor the medieval Church seemed interested in
increasing population. The most influential thinker, St. Augustine,
"achieved a balance which saved Christian marriage, explained
original sin and rejected Manicheanism." Population however, was
not given much consideration.[6]

Out of the controversies arose the Church's theory of marriage.
The purposes of marriage were defined as children, faith (fides),
and sacrament (sacramentum).[7] Children were to be produced and
trained as Christians. Fides restricted sexual relations to one's wife
and precluded other relations. Sacramentum emphasized mutual
companionship of the sexes, but married love was seldom mentioned. St. Thomas Aquinas and other thirteenth-century theologians were rather ahead of their time in discussing these.[8]
Marriage became a sacrament of the Church, although some had
doubts that it actually led the way to salvation.[9]

As one of the sacraments, marriage took on the religious
practices and thinking of other sacraments becoming regulated
with respect to persons, times and conditions of sexual relations.
These sanctions took on a significance often not easily understood
by the uninitiated. One may consider the sanctions through the
several approaches mentioned above: institutionalization, rationalization, canonization, intolerance, and taxation.

As an institution, marriage was clearly defined: age limits were
set at fourteen for males and twelve for females. There were blood

---

[4]Russell, 1958: 132-134. For superior interests in love as a factor: John M. Ferrante,
"Cortes 'Amor' in Medieval Texts." *Speculum* 55 (1980): 686-695.

[5]For many of the data and information about attitudes to vital questions and the Church:
J.T. Noonan, *Contraception. A Historical Treatment by the Catholic Theologians and Canonists*
(Cambridge, Mass., 1965). Manicheanism, p. 120.

[6]Noonan, 1965: 138.

[7]Noonan, 1965: 127.

[8]Noonan, 1965: 255-256.

[9]Russell, 1958: 135-137.

barriers: one might not marry within certain blood relationships, usually above first cousin once removed. These degrees included god parenthood as a first degree, and one could not marry his wife's sister. In general this was probably good since it tended to force marriage with those outside of the immediate community. For a long time the ceremony was not well defined: a chance remark in the presence of witnesses that one intended to marry a certain woman might have serious consequences in an ecclesiastical court. Generally the romantic element of marriage was not very obvious. Lack of a dowry was often an impediment. In short, medieval marriage seems to have been directed as much to preventing children as to producing them.[10]

Ecclesiastical rationalization assumed that marriage relations should be "natural" with the almost sole function sexually of producing children. "A norm is postulated, consisting of hetero-sexual marital coitus, a man above the woman and insemination resulting."[11] The position was defined because it was uncertain whether insemination would occur in other ways. How seriously regarded it was is illustrated by two remarks by theologians. "It is bad for a man to have intercourse with his mother but it is much worse for him to have intercourse with his wife against nature," (St. Bernadine). "If the penitent has confessed to unlawful coition, the priest should inquire further: whether it was fornication, adultery, incest or against nature. The inquiry is important. for the sin against nature is the gravest of the sins." (Alan de Lisle).[12] Marriage partners should acknowledge their marital debt to each other and pay it but it would be better to remain celibate.[13] Yet it should be noticed that the penances required were not too severe.

Christian saints seldom had children or were married, although there was no rule against canonization of the married. Higher values were assigned to celibacy. When a person with children was canonized, his or her parental status was secondary, as with Louis IX with his dozen children, certainly enough to secure the succession to his family.

There was not a marked intolerance for sexual matters even for the illegitimate although they had handicaps in succession and in attainment of ecclesiastical positions. Lack of intolerance indeed illustrates a lack of interest in demographic matters, as is true also of other phases of marriage relationships.[14]

In taxation, death and sexual relationships were important. The Church exacted ten years penance usually for infanticide, unless,

---

[10]See *Catholic Encyclopaedia* on marriage.
[11]Noonan, 1965: 246
[12]Noonan, 1965: 261,271.
[13]Noonan, 1965: 121-126.
[14]Noonan, 1965: 228-230.

occasionally, the parents were very poor.[15] For the dead, mortuaries had to be paid as well as the parish or priest—often the second best animal or its equivalent. This was the price of entrance into heaven through the agency of the Church. Over sexual relations a price was exacted: members were penalized for coition during certain more sacred times, notably Lent. Perhaps the heaviest tax was exacted on the unhappily married since there was technically no divorce. Failure of a marriage resulted in loss of sexual relations for the rest of one's life, if a member of the Church. And the Church required celibacy of its clergy throughout life.

The ecclesiastical pattern was more different in theory than it was in practice,[16] since neither secular nor sacred authority sought an increase in population as an ideal, although the former approach was based upon control of population. Both practiced some restraint upon growth of population, favoring nursing of one's own children and discouraging coition and childbirth outside of the family. The ecclesiastical restriction of divorce probably discouraged population growth also. The divergence of approach came because, under the Church's rules, population did tend to increase in many families. The problem was a family matter. The family found itself faced with another birth while the next older child was still very young, or the possibility of another girl when they felt they already had too many, or the prospect of another child when they had enough children already. No remedy was available for the family which followed the Church's direction,[17] but the skeletal evidence apparently shows that many families followed the age old traditions of tribal custom. The number of people had to be kept in line with available resources.

THE STRENGTH OF THE WILL TO CONTROL

The tests of interest can be used to show strength of other concerns than of population control. A series of comparisons of such interests with the urge for population control can give indications of the power of such an urge. These will be given for five periods: the Roman Empire, the later Roman Empire, from the earlier medieval plague and subsequent recovery, the period of population increase, A.D. 1000-1348, and the later plague. The amount of infanticide is one indication of the will to restrain population growth and a second, of course, is the actual trend of population. What will be shown is that the control remained strong in spite of indications that it sometimes ran counter to other strong forces.

---

[15]Noonan, 1965: 157-160, 165.

[16]Noonan, 1965: 167,170.

[17]Noonan, 1965: 6.

The Roman Empire had until A.D. 312 a notable unity. The most highly regarded persons were the more esteemed emperors. Augustus, Claudius and the Good Emperors; these were deified. Theories of absolute monarchy were provided by the rationalizers of the time. The institutionalization occurred in the development of the empire, a professional army, an extensive bureaucracy and a widespread ruling class. Treason or even hostility toward the government was heavily punished. The empire demanded very heavy taxes and other services from its people. People acquiesced, apparently preferring a rather colorless peace to the inter-city warfare and civic independence of an earlier day.

In the western half of Europe population was apparently falling gradually within the empire and not increasing outside. The conditions of health were declining with the spread of tuberculosis and the two periods of epidemics of the second and third centuries. Persons noticed the decline, commented upon it and felt that the world was getting old. The emperors adopted policies to stimulate the growth of population, encouraging marriage and discouraging abortion and infanticide. The emperors failed in spite of their prestige and power. The ancient control of population remained stronger than the imperial government, even reinforced by the pronatal policy of the rising Catholic Church, which may have been the only group with increasing numbers at the time. The sex ratio, as usual, provides the chief information about population control.

After A.D. 312 conditions changed. As a student once wrote, "The Edict of Milan made Christianity tolerable." Thousands now joined whom earlier intolerance and persecution kept in a state of approval but not of membership. They were not the stuff of which martyrs are made. Many of them were members of the Roman ruling class and found their way easily to positions of leadership, once they joined. Thus it happened that the possible enthusiasm for Christianity, expansion of the family and rapid population increase did not occur. The Roman middle and upper class, except for the imperial circle, had never been particularly enthusiastic for larger families. Thus in spite of the apparent strength of the Christians and their antagonism to birth control, the sex ratio declined little and infanticide must have continued to keep the population from increasing. The eagerness of Christians for celibacy found a vicarious satisfaction by gradually forcing the clergy to be celibate, perhaps against their original wishes. The Christian[18] influence was probably enough to produce a mild increase before the plague of A.D. 542.

---

[18]Helen R. Bitterman, "The Beginning of the Struggle of the Regular and Secular Clergy," *James Westfall Thompson Essays* (Chicago, 1938): 19-27.

The low point of European population was probably about A.D. 600 at the bottom of the decline caused by the plague. It took two hundred years before the population returned to preplague numbers, and then moved modestly above it in the succeeding two centuries. Christianity spread over the continent and the Church had an ever firmer grip upon the people. German reverence for the forest continued keeping population down as they moved into the forest only slowly. The Slavs in eastern Europe were Christianized in these centuries also and moved over much of eastern Europe. In the semi-arid and arid areas Islam tended to expand rapidly with the plague and then to retreat gradually as the plague-stricken areas recovered their population. Yet despite the pronatalist tendencies of the Christians, the forces restricting population growth continued to hold it down and kept up a relatively high sex ratio. Indeed Ireland alone seems to have recovered rapidly from the earlier of the sixth-century plagues.

The strongly religious Weltanschauung which dominated the period before the end of the first millennium shifted considerably in the succeeding centuries. It was a great age for the Church with such saints as Bernard, Francis, and Thomas Aquinas influencing not only theology but the world as a whole. Institutionally, the Papacy, backed by canon law, increased its power throughout Europe, dominating the educational institutions. Rationalization of the ecclesiastical position developed in the Investiture Struggle and in the scholastic debates following it. Interference in the lives of the faithful increased as did the tendency for a celibate clergy, especially in the monastic orders. The Inquisition in the thirteenth century epitomized the strength of Church control.

There was, however, a great lay revival as well. Feudal heroes were celebrated in the romance epics of the period. The Roman Empire of the Germans struggled with the Papacy and local legal systems developed as well as feudal custom. Feudal forces were not as good at rationalizing their positions of power as the more literate institutions such as the Church. They did set up the body of duties which vassals owed lords and peasants owed the manor, all causing considerable interference in the lives of the people. Kingdoms developed even in eastern Europe. At the beginning of the period the characteristic political unit of power was the local feudal lord. He spent his life, often struggling fiercely against his neighbors, and this shaped his thinking about increasing his power by founding cities, villages, and even monasteries which produced villages alongside them. Feudalism was not really very intolerant, usually merely contemptuous of others. So the period had a kind of schizophrenic appearance, with strong motivation along both ecclesiastical and lay lines.

Ecclesiastical forces increased both among local clergy and in the orders. The percentage of secular then among the total population increased from a half percent of the total population to more than one percent, mostly of men.[19] While professions recruited heavily from their own families, the celibate Church lost the potential for a religiously minded and literate family group, particularly after the reforms of the Fourth Lateran Council of 1215. Part of the decline of the Church after 1250 owes something to this. The popes, for instance, were increasingly lay minded in their politics in the second half of the thirteenth century. Moreover, the directives of the Church against infanticide, abortion, and contraception must have been a factor in the population increase so marked then.

The chief cause of the rapid increase was the founding of villages, cities, and monasteries by the feudal lords as a part of their struggle for military and financial strength against each other. In the thirteenth century consolidation of royal power reduced the local urge for greater strength and, in any case, the evidences of pressure against subsistence became clearer. Nevertheless, there was a real danger that a runaway population might occur. Territoriality as a principle tended to give way before the pressure. The average holding in the west declined from about thirty acres to about fifteen or even less. After the middle of the thirteenth century a reaction seems to have taken place.

Population also had an effect upon the Papacy itself. Located in the largest city in the West before the decline in the fifth-eighth centuries, the Papacy as an institution had become firmly fixed there by tradition. The wide interests of the Papacy contributed to the population and prestige of Rome, so that even in the time of its smallest population, eighth-tenth centuries, no effort was made to force its removal. Even the overpowering strength of the German (Roman) Empire brought only German popes, but not a German residence. In the thirteenth century, it proved to be different. The Papacy, fearing too much power for the Hohenstauffens, delivered their fate to the French, under Charles of Anjou, and inevitably to the power of the French, who were in that century both very numerous and very powerful.[20] The awesome decline of French royal power in the second half of the fourteenth century allowed the Papacy to return only temporarily, long enough to form the basis for the Great Schism which rent the Church a half century later.[21] Fortunately for the Papacy, the French power was at its lowest ebb when a temporary accession of German, English, and

---

[19]Estimate from numbers of regular clergy (and secular): Russell, "The Clerical Population of Medieval England," *Traditio* 2 (1944): 212.

[20]G. Barraclough, *The Medieval Papacy* (New York, 1968): 142-144, 164-181. Also A. C. Leighton, *Transport and Communication in Early Medieval Europe, A.D. 500-1150* (Newton Abbot, 1972).

[21]Russell, 1972; esp. 15-38.

Iberian strength led to the reunification of the Church with its head again in Rome. The influence of population was indirect but nevertheless of considerable strength. The rise of modern nations together with the decline of political importance of the Church has removed population as an important if indirect influence upon the Papacy.

While population in general reached a plateau about 1250, the cities tended to increase for another generation. Thus it is hard to define the last period: perhaps 1348-1500 will do as well as any other. In the economic sense it was the age of reason but economics had a low place in Christian and even feudal thinking. There were few Christian saints and fewer rulers who were seen as noble figures. Several women saints achieved distinction for their efforts toward peace. Some men led mass movements which again were too early to arouse eternal renown. Parlements were widespread and tried novel and somewhat democratic ideas. Perhaps Europe was at that time nearer democracy than she was to be again before the nineteenth century. If anything, there was an atmosphere of anti-interference. The chief intolerance was directed toward the Jews who stood out from the mass of persons who seem to have moved toward more uniform political customs and habits. The circulation of commerce produced leading cities which were centers of their regions. Secularization advanced rapidly in this period.

The plague, or course, dominated the thinking of the period. Its awful mortality sent the fear of death through all; the dance of death was a favorite theme of the time. Yet the reaction varied: from those who became terribly religious to those who simply said, "Let us eat, drink and be merry, for tomorrow we die." The elderly, prone to die more alone were forced to live with the rest of the family. Subjected to such pressures, many became mentally tormented, Often women were considered witches. The Flagellants appeared. Jews were suspected of being the cause of the plague and were persecuted.

Everywhere, especially in Italy, underpopulation was fought by multiple wives and births, one after the other, thus overcoming the heavy mortality. The Renaissance writers popularized infants and children, leading to less control of population.

It is difficult to get an objective picture since most of the writing was done by clerics. The laity produced little written evidence. There is information, of course, of the imperial Roman attitude and from the highly literate Renaissance. The ordinary people went their way, carefully controlling population by later marriage, nursing their babies, and letting unwanted children die at birth. They made their peace with the Church with modest penances and questionable explanations, but they kept their eye on the availability of subsistence and held their numbers within it. The attitudes toward population details and problems conform fairly well with the attitudes of the people. It is a good illustration of the difficulty of following public opinion of groups which do not write down their thoughts and feelings.

In earlier times continuity of family was not too pressing a problem. The leading families of Rome were the exception, as shown by family tombs and dovecotes. Others seemed curiously careless about preserving memories in cemeteries. Christians, of course, had the Church as a reference point for burials. The more important were often buried within the church: others could arrange burials nearby and provide for family groupings. But they did not encourage limitless births in order to preserve the continuity of the family.

With the Renaissance all this changed. The importance can be seen by applying the tests. The "saint" was the pater familias, the male head. The institution was the arranged marriage, usually to very young women to make the most of their fertile years, and all lived in a great house with numerous relatives and servants. It was an impressive institution. The rationalization for this arrangement was not only for the continuation of the family but for the strengthening of cities as well, often with close ties to particular churches. The system forced relatives, often quite hostile families, to live under the same roof and defend the whole family as well as to keep the women as perpetually pregnant as possible. Hostilities developed constantly among the great families as well as among those who disliked the system. That the family feeling was superior even to civic feeling is indicated by the frequent struggles among the families which erupted into desperate, internecine fights in the cities, especially those where the family feeling was the strongest.

CLIMATE AS A FACTOR

The effects of climate upon the human race has been a subject of interest for some time. The people of Europe obviously enjoyed a superior climate. Although lying relatively far to the north, the winds from the Atlantic Ocean, modified by the Gulf Stream, warm western Europe far more than might be expected. The mountainous areas lie east and west and thus do not create the deserts which are typical of the Americas. The continental areas to the east can be very cold in the winter and hot in the summer. For western Europe cold winters which killed insects and warm or hot summers which ripened grain well were most satisfactory. Spring rains were important while summer rains often injured the grain crops. Warm winters were also not very helpful.

The diagram (fig. 1) shows the general course of temperature over the centuries as recorded on the Greenland ice sheet.[22] If the influences which affected the ice pack were about the some as those which influenced western Europe, it should give some idea of the situation there. The plan is continued to the present so that comparisons may be made. The recent high of about A.D. 1940-60 was about the same as that reached in the highs of the Middle Ages. However, from A.D. 600 to 1150 there was a warm period of continued length. Actually length of life was greatest in this period. It was a period of relatively low population and a time devoted to pastoral life in the areas from which much of the data come. It is hard to separate the influences of the climate and agricultural operations. Certainly plow culture was harder on farmers than pastoral. It was not a very stimulating period intellectually, a condition which some would attribute to the weather.[23]

Within general climatic areas there were, of course, miniclimates created by land height and distance from the sea.These were important for access to fish as well as sources of warmth and chill.

Before the long warm period, there was a long continued dip from A.D. 1-200 down to 450 and then a rise to 650. Length of life does not seem to have declined with the climate. There was a long wet spell in the fourth century, indicated by darker soil from the deposits used in soil analysis. For example, kilns were used in Britain to dry grain. This period was the beginning of the great migrations into the Roman Empire from Scandinavia and central Europe. Here the worsening climate was almost certainly an important factor. The climatic change also pushed the area of grain culture south.

A second period of damp weather occurred in the twelfth century and was accompanied for at least part of the time by apparently much colder weather. It continued off and on through the succeeding centuries as the Little Ice Age.The coincidence of this frigid period with the second plague makes it difficult to determine its effects on the health of the people. However, the length of life of the English landowners certainly was declining even before the plague appeared, so the increasing chill probably did affect it. In Provence, population descended on the hillsides into lower altitudes which seem to have been affected by the decline in temperature.[24] Since it was harder to grow and ripen

[22]See also Herlihy 1974: 12-16. The periods of cold weather do not quite coincide with the Greenland evidence.

[23]Clarence A, Mills, *Climate Makes the Man* (New York, 1942).

[24]Russell, 1948 182-186: E. Baratier, *La dèmographie provencale du xiii⁴ au xvi⁴ siècle* (Paris, 1961), 119-124.

crops every year, sections of Scandinavia became depopulated. Even the fish moved farther south.

Climate also was a factor in disease. The second and third-century pestilences and epidemics came at a time of relatively high temperature which would spawn the more lethal type of malaria. And its recurrence at Rome and Latium in the middle period (A.D. 600-1100) was appropriate in those centuries. The warmth of the first two centuries would have been helpful in the spread of tuberculosis, as was the warmer middle period. On the other hand, the plague occurred in the sixth and seventh centuries, starting when the temperatures were not excessive, while the plague recurred in the Little Ice Age and remained in Europe for centuries. The disease was hindered by very hot and very cold times. The second half of the fourteenth century, for example, saw a warm spell coincident with a temporary lapse in the course of the plague. The relationship between plague and climate needs further study.

Another factor to be studied is climate and housing as they affect population. Many Roman buildings had good heating systems, useful even in the northern part of Europe. The more pretentious buildings in the north were also heated by fireplaces and chimneys. In the north also peasant cottages were often built above dugouts of a foot or so below the ground level. Above were walls of earth and sticks (adobe like) topped by a thatched roof. These were rude and elementary but also rather efficient. The fire in the center kept the room warm and even the earth beneath helped. Later houses (usually thirteenth century and after) had wooden floors and walls and sometimes fireplaces with chimneys. Not well insulated, it is doubtful if these houses were as warm as the earlier cottages. They cost more and so families tended to keep their elderly in with them, thus enlarging the household from about 3.5 upwards.[25]

The difference between the cooler surroundings of the later period and of the earlier was equalized by the use of more and warmer clothing. In the earlier times the Mediterranean people protected themselves with flowing garments; togas and the like, although the ordinary persons wore shirt-like garments. Often made of wool, they were quite effective. The barbarians to the north wore trousers, particularly in the winter time. They became more like a second skin for both men and women. The closer fitting garments also offered more havens to fleas and other insects of the time. It must have been easier to shake them out of togas than the trousers of a later day.

---

[25]See pp. 150-152.

The building of larger houses to withstand the weather also tended to increase the size and density of city population, but this had a negative effect on disease. Tuberculosis spread more easily in densely populated areas. With the plague the question is more difficult. The rat is a territorial animal so that crowding might actually reduce the chance for association with the rat and indirectly with the infection by the fleas. Certainly the increase in size of cities produced problems of sanitation, especially in the later Middle Ages. In the cities reservoirs of disease were created. Perhaps it was the smaller populations of the sixth-seventh centuries which caused the plague to die out then.

The control of population, to judge from methods used to enforce it, was one of the strongest drives in the ancient and medieval world. It was apparently closely associated with what is known in animal behavior as territoriality, the preservation of an area in which an animal or groups of animals feed. In villages sources of subsistence were easily determined as was also their quantity. When acres would not yield enough grain or the meadows enough pasture or the woods enough nuts for men and animals, perceptive people knew how to cope to maintain a satisfactory living to be handed on to successors. The desire to pass a comfortable living to the next generation was so strong that one might even suggest sociobiologically that it was handed on as part of inheritance of the genes. From this point of view one had the duty to make certain that too many children did not live to face a dwindling subsistence: that one had not the right not only to life but to a good life even if it meant infanticide to decrease the surplus. Such thinking somewhat mimicked wolves, where only one pair of a pack would breed each year. A sex ratio of 140 means that two of each five female infants somehow did not live. The cemeteries show that women died at birth rather than of hard work at a later date.

The problem of meeting the need for more children during the plague periods was not difficult. Society simply permitted and encouraged earlier marriage and permitted larger numbers of female children to live. As the 1427 catasto data for Florence and Tuscany show, even in the midst of the plague, the sex ratio was still high.

MIGRATION

Migration is only indirectly involved as a factor in the control of population, mostly by relieving pressure in overpopulated areas. Our concern here is primarily with population information and factors which are illustrated by cemetery and similar evidence.[26]

---

[26]Peter McClure, "Patterns of Migration in Late Middle Ages," *Economic Historical Review* 32 (1979): 167-182.

Obviously if population was not increasing there should be no serious need for migration except for such normal demands as were made for pilgrimages, fairs and overland trade, clerical and secular official visits, and other forms of travel. The subject is far too complicated to be treated in these few pages. The evidence presented by the cemeteries will be suggested and also the problems for migration caused by the high sex ratio (the surplus of unmarried in the population.)

Cemetery data illustrating migration are of two types; the first, artifacts and burial customs and the second, information about bone structure and blood types. The first have, of course, been studied for infomation about migration of nations and tribes as a part of racial study since the nineteenth century. More recently blood types, a much more difficult study, have been examined to trace migration and settlement, particularly in eastern Europe, notably in Hungary.

As noted earlier the sex ratio was often very high in the late ancient and medieval period, often over 120 men to 100 women. Except in time of plague and occasionally in the larger cities, the ratio was always too large to have been natural, that is more than 102-105 men to 100 women. The most impressive evidence, other than the persistently high sex ratio in the cemetery evidence came, as has been seen, from Florence and Tuscany in the great catasto of 1427. For the city the ratio of children from 0 to 3 runs from 112 to 118 while in the rest of the country it is from 116 to 128. This condition can hardly have had natural causes and must therefore have been a result of consistent infanticide of girl babies, even though the plague should have been favorable for conservation of all human resources. Now such a disparity of the sexes should have had some results for the people of the time.

One obvious indication is that society then was much more favorable to men and male babies than to females. This meant the setting up of a large, privileged class of men who were probably frustrated by their inability to marry and participate in landholding activities. The condition of one group, the juvenes of eleventh-twelfth century France has been discussed brilliantly. However, the military group as a whole could hardly have been more than two or three percent of the total male population over age fourteen and thus even military ventures could hardly care for a large part of the unmarried men. However, they were the armed and fighting group, readily available for exploitation by the political leaders of the time. Indeed they were a vital factor in the final triumph of the kings over feudalism in most countries of Europe.

Earlier, unmarried men had been an important source of manpower for the Roman Army which included perhaps one percent of the population, or about three percent of the total number of men. Whatever lack of manpower occurred, it should not have been the result of the lack of single men who must have numbered several times that percent. The drawing together of single men in the army camps should have reduced the disparity of sexes, at least on the farms.

In the German tribes military groups constituted much of the ordinary fighting folk and even in the tribal migrations may have constituted the larger part, although this again needs study.

The greatest sublimation of the fighting instinct was in the Crusades, of course, where the act of fighting was believed to be of religious significance. The failure of the Crusades was apparently not the result of either lack of sufficient manpower nor of motivation, but rather in lack of proper planning for their execution. The leaders repeatedly chose to try to force the campaigns through Asia Minor where the Turks provided the most effective opposition. It would have been so much easier to go, as many pilgrims and some crusaders, directly by sea. A further handicap was the urge of the feudal hosts to fight at short distances.

The great majority of the unmarried males would have been of the farming population. Some wandered about as the anlepimen of medieval England. Most of them waited until opportunities opened as landholders died or they found heiresses to marry. Some place was usually found for the retired and the mentally disturbed among the cotter population. In the period from about 1,000 to 1,260 many lords opened up forest lands or pushed into eastern territories held by the Slavs and thus offered opportunities to many waiting for places. (The Pied Piper was probably followed by many more young adults than children.) The difficulty was that sooner or later the limits of opportunity were reached and the final problem of population control had to be faced.

Many of the unmarried men found places in the clergy as the councils tightened the requirements of celibacy, particularly after the Fourth Lateran Council of 1215. In the thirteenth century not only were many new parishes set up to fill the needs of the increasing population but the larger parishes added to the number of clerks. The spread of literacy added to the need for clerks even on the manors. Even many of the ordinary village clerks seem to have held off from marrying to be available if better ecclesiastic positions became available. The plagues reduced the number of men rather than of positions so that about three percent of adult males in the population were ecclesiastics. The number of monks seems to have declined in the plague period since they were more directly supported by the agricultural population.

NEEDED INFORMATION

One runs the risk, of course, of exaggerating the influence of demographic factors in enthusiasm for new material and different approaches to history. However, an offsetting influence is the emphasis which has been placed upon quantitative methods and data. It is encouraging that so many of the ideas worked out on the basis of limited evidence or evidence from areas and times prove to be true for wider areas and longer times, that is if they have proved to be reasonable samples of the whole. Much remains to be done, as can be seen from the information presented thus far. There are great time gaps in the evidence. Much of the evidence can also be put to more and better use; much can be restudied in the light of much more exact methods today. And approaches used in other fields can be tried for their application to medieval data.

Perhaps the most obvious opportunity is in the vast amount of information about skeletal evidence available at Pompeii. Information is available there about a considerable fraction of the inhabitants, perhaps from one third to a half of the total. In addition to the skeletal remains, archaeologists and anthropologists can see more of the total environment than is possible elsewhere.

There are great areas of the world and large periods of time which are not well illustrated by the data now available. Table 7 in an earlier chapter gives the number of skeletons for study by country and time. France, for instance, shows barely more than a hundred graves for the last three time periods. The Mediterranean shows more but a considerable proportion of them come from the very interesting remains from the Canary Islands. In both of these areas the primary interest has been archaeological and limited to the Classical and prehistoric periods of time, understandably so. When they became Christian lands, there was strong feeling that graves should not be disturbed except for important reasons. Excavation for anthropological purposes are not considered of that great importance. The cemetery at Cannae was excavated because it was thought to contain the dead from the great battle in the war against Carthage. The French have been much interested in the great migrations of the first five Christian centuries but not of later times. It is obvious then that one great need is the systematic study of at least a few cemeteries in each of the great time periods.

The others are also weak in periods of little interest. Britain in the first two periods, Germany very strong in the second and moderately so in the others, Scandinavia better in the last two periods and Poland in the third. Bohemia's great Moravian Empire has concentrated interest in the third period. Far and away the most has been done in Hungary with a considerable emphasis on the Avar and Hungarian (Arpadian) time. Thus great areas remain where much needs to be done.

The methods of physical anthropology have improved very rapidly in the last fifty years in detection of sex and age. Many of the collections could be done again, especially to add information about the younger age skeletons. This would give better clues as to the relative mortality of male and female in the two infant classifications. And, of course, there is need of standardization of results so that one knows if adultus includes those 20-30 or 20-40 and even more bizarre series of years. Classification is a vital part of scientific advance but the classifications need to be well known and carefully observed.

Some of the advances in physical anthropology need to be more carefully checked. The Harris lines in bones show serious illness or trauma—very valuable information—but more needs to be known about them, perhaps from study of modern corpses. The problem of the ridges in pubic bones which were thought to indicate childbirths also remains. Modern study of women today show a much more blurred effect which is not closely related to number of childbirths. Could the habits of childbirth in former ages have been more decisive in producing distinct ridges? A study of female diet would seem to show women could not have lived as well or so long as they seem to have done. Could the diet of the women have been more sustaining and satisfactory than has been assumed? And Lanyel's study of blood types is fascinating for its possibilities of following lines of migration.

Diseases came from the greater centers of all animal and insect life of the world, the warmer and damper areas which fostered a tremendous variety of life. Disease was a microbian form of life which enveloped not only animals but men as part of the animal world. The great proliferation of forms of life produced more dangers for all as the new varieties of life fed upon other and earlier forms of life. These naturally spread into adjacent areas, limited only by opportunities for dissemination and the restraints placed by such limiting factors as temperature, moisture, and quality of air and water. Population increase was a factor. Considerable concentrations of men, particularly in cities, provided a reservoir for retention of diseases. Even if the size of areas like India has been overestimated these areas were large enough to preserve and transmit diseases to new ones, like the west. And the vast tropical areas of Africa might also have been expected to send out new diseases to the Mediterranean and Asia. The Roman Empire with its great roads and water communication was ideal for transmitting diseases over its roads and by ships. On the other hand the Empire was a greater danger to its northern neighbors from a disease standpoint than those neighbors were to it. This can be seen in the expectation of life along the northern border.

Of the diseases which increased in intensity during the period 1-1500 tuberculosis can be followed—with some reservations. In north Africa it moved in along the roads into the more desert country through Carthage and other coast cities. Into the north it followed roads and probably moved with merchants and especially

Roman soldiers into northern cities. Soldiers traveled in some numbers from one end of the empire to the other, even in times of peace. Thus it was only natural that along with their religious interests which are indicated by shrines, they would bring their diseases with them. It was a kind of *unification microbiene* previous to the later world movement but upon a lesser scale: European instead of world.[27] It was a part of the price that the empire had to pay for its unity. After all twenty-year-old soldiers were much more apt to carry tuberculosis with them than forty or fifty-year-old merchants. The disease was probably responsible for the increase of mortality of men in their twenties and thirties. However, as had been seen, there seems a much greater mortality in certain areas: Rome, Gaul, the Rhineland, where contemporary sources say the plague of the second (and probably the third) centuries were carried from Seleucia by the Roman army under Varus. This may possibly have a more malignant form of malaria, the *P. falciparum*.

Very little has been done in regard to mental conditions which would affect health or employability in the Middle Ages. It would seem that mental retardation did not prevent children and adults from care of animals. Indeed it might even have been an advantage to those who herded animals in the montains during the summers. For mental illness there is an interesting article on mental states in the Middle Ages and a hypothesis that the impostor who claimed that he was Edward II of England was a schizophrenic.[28]

Then there is the problem of the fundamental influence in the question of population control: free will or determinism.[29] Malthus held for a kind of determinism which might be modified by moral attitudes. The medieval church did the same although the restraints which it suggested (chastity, celibacy) were probably not going to keep population from increasing beyond limits of subsistence in the course of a few generations. Apparently the differences of number of men and women (except in times of plague and occasionally other times) derived from death at or near birth in much of ancient and medieval Europe. Infant mortality occurred in defiance of the clear ecclesiastical prohibitions of infanticide and abortion. Clerical oversight might have been responsible. Or it may have been that the determination of a people to control its population caused a majority of clergy to look

---

[27]E. Le Roy Ladurie, "Un concept: l'unification microbienne du Monde (xive-xviie siècles)," *Revue suisse d'histoire* 23 (1973): 627-696.

[28]S.W. Jackson, "Unusual Mental States in Medieval Europe," *Journal of the History of Medicine and Allied Sciences* 27 (1972): 262-297. J.C. Russell and E.W. Russell, "He Said He was the King's Father," *Res Publica Litterarum* 5 (1982) 197-201. S.Rubin, *Medieval English Medicine* (Newton Abbot, 1974): 198-200.

[29]An excellent description of medieval determinism appears in Howard R. Patch, "Troilus on Determinism," *Speculum* 6 (1931): 226-230 where the author discusses the subject as an introduction to his particular application of the problem. See also Patch, "Necessity in Boethius and the Neoplatonists," *Speculum* 10 (1935): 393-404.

the other way—as is the case today in the United States as growing numbers of Roman Catholic laity practice birth control.

The study of population has been a victim of the mutual dislike of history and sociology. While history has expanded by incorporating some social and intellectual fields and has even developed social history, it has been very slow to accept sociology. It is too professional and perhaps too statistical. Sociology, unlike economics, has never cared for the history of its subject, although many phases of the subject are clearly factors in history. This study of the control of population tries to show how important the history of population is, largely through the use of anthropological evidence, which is, in a sense, an extension of sociology backwards into ancient and medieval history. It shows that the human race has controlled its numbers and can do better than it is now doing with overpopulation. It also reveals that control of population was one of the really great achievements of the late ancient and medieval world.

Appendix 1

BURIALS OF HERETICS IN THE MIDDLE AGES

Walter L. Wakefield, Professor Emeritus of History
State University of New York, Potsdam

Knowledge of burial practices among heretics in the Middle Ages is far from abundant. The use of consecrated ground, of course, was forbidden to them, a ban that was often avoided with the tacit compliance of priests or despite their objections. Most of the information we have of these and other acts comes from the records of the Inquisition.[1]

The attitude of the Waldenses toward death and resurrection was entirely orthodox and virtually nothing is recorded of them in this respect. One witness before the inquisitor Friar Peter Seila in Montauban in 1241 did say that at an undisclosed date his wife "gave herself to the Waldenses at death and was buried in their cemetery."[2] It is commonly supposed that because the Cathars of Languedoc denied the resurrection of bodies and scorned the services of the Church they were indifferent to the fate of human remains. However, disregard for the dead does not seem to have been entirely true of the Albigensian heretics in the years before the Albigensian Crusade (1209-1229), for the deceased among them were interred with at least some formalities. The chronicler, William of Puylaurens, attested the practice, writing that heretics were held in such reverence that they had their own cemeteries in which they were publicly buried.[3]

There was one such cemetery at Montesquieu and inquisitors in 1245 questioned at least ten witnesses about it. They were told of fourteen burials before 1209, including those of seigneurs of the place and other knights.[4] At Lordat, when the priest forbade putting the body of Raymond of Rabat in the village cemetery, it was taken to a nearby height called "Bec en Barra"; the knight,

---

[1] The subject has been discussed by, among others, Jean Guiraud, *Histoire de l'Inquisition au moyen âge* (2.v.. Paris, 1935-1938), 1: 165-167; Christine Thouzellier, *Cathares et valdenses en Languedoc à la fin du xii°et au début du xiii° siècle* (2nd ed., Paris) 1869) 248; and Ives Dossat, "Les Cathares d'après les documents de l'Inquisition," *Cahiers de Fanjeaux* 3 (1968): 80-81.

[2] Paris, Bibliothèque nationale, Collection Doat, XXI, f.232r. Another witness reported that she had attended the funeral of a Waldensian but did not state the place: ibid., f.281r-v.

[3] *Cronica*, ed. Beyssier, "Troisième mélanges d'histoire du moyen âge," *Bibliothèque de la Faculté des lettres de Paris* 18 (1904): 120.

[4] Toulouse Bibliothèque municipale, MS 609,ff.99r-102v *passim*. William of Puylaurens attested that heretics "were held in such respect that they had cemeteries in which they publically buried those whom they had hereticated, from whom they had received their beds and clothing." Chronica, ed. by Jean Duvernoy, *Guillaume de Puylaurens, Chronique* (Paris, 1876), 24.

William Cat, was buried in the same place.[5] Before the coming of the crusaders Peitavin of Sorèze was buried in a cemetery of the heretics at Puylaurens in the presence of many knights and ladies.[6] At Saint-Paul-Cap-de-Joux the body of Raymond was escorted to the cemetery of heretics by numerous persons, some carrying candles; Guilabert of Saint-Paul who died in a house of the heretics was taken to the same spot.[7] It is most probable that there was also a Cathar cemetery at Saint-Martin-la-Lande, for two members of the Arrufat family of nearby Castelnaudary, having received the heretical baptism (*consolamentum*) about 1206, were taken there to die in the hands of the heretics.[8]

Despite their disrespect for clerical services, Cathars and their sympathizers sometimes made use of them. When Roger of Latour died at Laurac about 1234 after receiving the *consolamentum* knights of the Hospital of Saint John at Pexiora gave him prompt burial.[9] They did this also for William of Niort, father of a thoroughly heretical family, and promised to allow burial in their precincts also to Bernard Oth, most notorious of his sons for allegiance to the Cathars.[10] Some eighty years later, the rector of Montaillou caused gossip because he buried his mother, well-known as a believer in the last of the Cathars, at the altar of the village church.[11]

After the crusade, attempts were made to cast out of holy ground those who had been wrongfully buried. In Toulouse about 1231, the Dominican friar, Roland of Cremona, led parties of friars and clerics to disinter and take to the fire the remains of two men: one was Galvan, thought to be an important figure among the Waldenses; the other was A. Peter, a donat of the monastery of Saint-Sernin, who was buried in the cemetery of Villeneuve although before his death, without the knowledge of the canons, he had become a perfected heretic. Among acts of the first inquisitors in 1234 were those of Friar Arnald Catalan who provoked a riot at Albi by personally taking charge of an exhumation; of Friars Peter Seila and William Arnald who had bodies dug up and dragged to the fire at Cahors; one loyal son succeeded in removing his father's bones from the cemetery before they were discovered. Similar actions in Toulouse preceded riotous protests

---

[5]Collection Doat, XXIV, f. 277r-v.

[6]Ibid., ff. 127v-141r-v.

[7]Collection Doat, XXIII, ff.76v-r; XXIV, ff.112v, 134v; respectively.

[8]Toulouse, Bibliothèque municipale, MS 609, f. 250. Cf. Elie Griffe, *Le Languedoc cathare de 1190 à 1210* (Paris, 1971), 123, 125.

[9]Toulouse, Bibl. mun. MS 609, f. 141r.

[10]Collection Doat, XXI, f. 38r-v.

[11]*Les Registres d'Inquisition de Jacques Fournier (1318-1325)*, ed. Jean Duvernoy. (3v., Toulouse, 1965) 3: 182; Emmanuel Le Roy Ladurie, *Montaillou, village occitan de 1294 à 1324* (Paris, 1975), 98, 335; trans. by Barbara Bray as *Montaillou, Promised Land of Error* (New York, 1978), 61, 224-225.

in 1235, although exhumation and burning of more than a score of bodies was peacefully accomplished two years later.[12] In evidence also is the sentence of Friar Ferrier at Castres in 1244, ordering that the bones of a condemned man be recovered and burned if they could be distinguished from others.[13]

In dangerous times and places, if burial in an orthodox cemetery could not be arranged, treatment of the dead became more casual. According to Bernard Oth of Niort, when his brother, Raymond of Roquefeuil, died of wounds after he was given the *consolamentum* at some time between 1223 and 1227, the body was placed in a crypt because of an interdict that lay on the region.[14] Bernard Oth also spoke of another interment at Roquefeuil, giving the name of a man who knew where a female heretic was buried.[15] Ada, a lady of Montgaillard, about 1226 was buried in a nearby wood with no other heretics present.[16]

As prosecution continued in peacetime, the need for secrecy was paramount. At Villemur several men consulted on disposal of the body of an unnamed heretic, deciding to give it to a fisherman to be thrown in the Tarn, which was done. It was also at Villemur that the brother of the deceased heretic, P. Gralh, provided cloth to wrap the body before it was placed in an old pit.[17] About 1231 at Avignonet the corpse of Aymengarda was taken outside the town at night to an orchard owned by her brother-in-law.[18] When P. Barta died at Mirepoix about 1233 men placed him in a gravel pit outside the village.[19] Arnalda of Lamothe spoke laconically to inquisitors about an incident in her career over three decades as a perfected heretic. About 1233 she and her sister, Peirona, were living in a wood near Lanta, "in a little house below ground," and there Peirona died. She was buried by Arnalda with the help of two male heretics and three other men.[20] At Montferrand about 1235,

---

[12]All described in the chronicle of William Pelhisson, trans. in Walter L. Wakefield, *Heresy, Crusade and Inquisition in Southern France, 1100-1250* (Berkeley and Los Angeles, 1974), 210, 214, 217-223, 224-225.

[13]Collection Doat, XXI, ff.313r-315r. Even participation in a burial was punishable. Among the crimes for which Arnalda Maurin and Maria, wife of Hugo, were sentenced to prison for life in 1246 and 1247 respectively, were that Arnalda had been present when a heretic was buried, Maria had collected money to buy a winding-sheet for another: Célestin Douais, *Documents pour servir à l'histoire de l'Inquisition en Languedoc* (2v., Paris, 1900), 2: 9,45.

[14]Collection Doat, XXIV, ff. 99v-100v.

[15]Ibid., f. 91r-v.

[16]Celestin Fouais, *Les Sources de l'histoire de l'Inquisition dans le midi de la France en xiiie et xive siècles* (Paris, 1881), 128.

[17]Collection Doat, XXII, ff.47v-48r, 49v respectively.

[18]Ms 609, f. 133v.

[19]Collection Doat, XXIV, f. 189r-v.

[20]Collection Doat, XXIII, ff. 22v-23r.

En Peirota, who had been "received by the heretics at death," was immediately buried by them in an undisclosed place.[21] There were two burials of like kind at Villefloure: at dates not stated Alazaicia d'En Arneil was interred near a stream[22] and a male heretic was also buried with little or no ceremony.[23] Finally, much later, when heretics and their devotees were seeking refuge in Italy, Pons Boyer died at Pavia about 1272-1274. His companion heretic with some helpers buried him in the basement of a house.[24]

Archaeological investigation has done little to illuminate burials of heretics in special cemeteries or elsewhere. It has been speculated that various discoidal and other crosses which have been found were connected with Cathar practices.[25] No burial site for defenders killed in the fighting at the heretical refuge of Montségur in 1243-1244 has been discovered, although two skeletons of persons probably killed by arrows were found in 1964 in a grotto into which the bodies apparently had been thrown.[26] There is a remote possibility that an older discovery is a memento of the days of heresy and prosecution. In 1836 in a grotto between Carcassonne and Cabaret were found three groups of carefully arrayed skeletons. Cros-Mayreville in 1896 concluded without any supporting evidence that these had been exhumed from private properties to prevent their being come upon by agents of the inquisitors with subsequent action against the owners of the original burial sites.[27]

---

[21]Ms 609, f. 144r-v.

[22]"In recco de Rippis," Douais, *Documents* 2: 289.

[23]"Sepultus in aperio": ibid. Douais conjectures (n. 4). that aperio = opertorio, i.e. tomb. *Opertorium* can also mean workshop.

[24]Collection Doat, XXIV, ff. 304v-305r, 305r, 305v; XXVI.f. 16r.

[25]Cf. René Nelli, *Le Musée du Catharisme* (Toulouse, 1966); Jean Duvernay, "Des discoidales du Lauragais au auges funéraires du Comminges," *Actes du XVIII ͤ congrès de la Fédération des societés académiques et savantes Pyrenées-Languedoc-Gascogne* (Tarbes, 1963).

[26]Fernand Niel, *Les Cathares de Monségur* (1973), 62, 246-247.

[27]Jean-Pierre Cros-Mayreville, *Histoire du comté et de la vicinité de Carcassonne* (Paris, 1896) 1: 190-196.

Bibliography of Sources of Demographic Data

The bibliography is designed to furnish data as economically as possible. The information is listed as follows:

Author or authors and date of publication.

Title of publication.

Number of area and time (i.e. 4-2 for fourth area Germany) and the second period A. D.540-750).

Direction of graves in cemetery (i.e. ENE for east northeast).

Table of age and sex data (T. p.000).

Plan or map of cemetery (P.p000 or M. p.000).

Age groups, singly or by groups. One number indicates all or undifferentiated. Two numbers indicate male and female numbers of skeletons. Three indicate male,female and uncertain. i.e.

II: 14, fourteen skeletons of infans II.

AMS 2,4,6. two male, four female and 6 uncertain which includes *adultus, maturus* and *senilis* ages undifferentiated by age.

M:7,10 for seven male and ten females of the *maturus* group.

If the articles are written in Hungarian or Slavic, the titles of the western language summaries are used. The use of the original languages would add an immensely greater burden upon printers and editors with relatively little value as information. The data are frequently given in tables or catalogs which can be handled with relative ease by those who know only the terms of the relevant data. I am indebted to Professor Charles C. Bajza of the Department of Geography of Texas A & I University for assistance with these language terms.

Abramowicz, A. 1962. "Results of Investigations of an Eleventh Century Cemetery at Lutomiersk near Lodź," *Archaeologia Polona* 5: 123-132. 8-4. M.p. 124. AMS: 48, 54.

Acsádi, G. & J. Nemeskéri. 1957a. "Contributions à la reconstruction de la population de Vesprém, x^e et xie siècles," *Annales Historico-Naturales Musei Nationalis Hungarici* 49: 435-467. 5-3. T. 437. II:1. J:0.2. A: 6, 9. M: 16, 8.

———. 1957b. "Paläodemographische Probleme am Beispiel des frühmittelalterlichen Gräberfeldes von Halimba-Cseres, Kom.Veszprém, Ungarn," *Homo* 8: 133-148. 5-4. T.p. 138. I:254. II:78. J: 18, 38. AA: 81, 106. M: 126, 95. S: 84-92. Actually given in five year intervals.

———. 1958. "La Population de la Transdanubie Nord-Est, x^e et xi siècles", *Annales Historico — Naturales Musei Nationalis Hungarici* 50: 359-415. 5-3. I:4. II:10. J:1, 9. A: 25, 20. M: 17, 9. S: 4.0. Consolidated from several lists.

———. 1959, 1960. "La Population de Székesfehérvár, x^e et xie siècles", *Annales Historico-Naturales Musei Nationalis* 51: 493-564 and 52: 481-495. 5-4. A: 6, 7. M: 8, 0. S: 1, 1.

———. 1970. *History of Human Life Span and Mortality.* Budapest.

Acsádi, G. & J. Nemeskéri & L. Harsányi. 1959. "Analyse des Trouvailles anthropologiques du cimetière de Kerpuszta, xie siecle, etc.," *Acta Archaeologica Academiae Scientiarum Hungaricae* 11: 419-455. 5-4. I:123. II:40. J: 20. A: 33, 41. M: 55, 50. S: 16, 22. Converted from lists by ten, after estimates for ages: 0, 1, 2, 3, 4, 5, 10 and 15 are given.

Acsádi, G., L. Harsanyi, & J. Nemeskéri. 1962. "The Population of Zalavár in the Middle Ages", *Acta Archaeologica Academiae Scientiarum Hungaricae* 14: 113-141. Not used: data set in percentages.

Akerman, J.Y. 1853. "An Account of Excavations in an Anglo-Saxon Burial Ground at Harnham Hill, near Salisbury." *Archaeologia* 35: 259-278. 3-1,NE. I:20. II: 16. J: 2, 5. A: 34, 20, 27. M: 17, 7, 10. S: 6, 4, 2. Rough guesses probably.

Alenus, J. 1961. "Fouille mérovingienne à Folx-les-Caves," *Bulletin de la Société royale belge d'anthropologie et de pré-histoire* 72: 5-80. 2-2. SE. M.p.7. AMS: 13, 3, 12. Not used.

Antoniu, S. & M. Unofrei. 1975. "Étude anthropologique des schelettes de la nécropole du ive siècle de n.e. de Lefcani, dep. Jassy," *Arheologia Moldouei* 8: 281-287. 5-1. I:7. II:3. A:4, 12, 14. M:0, 6, 8. S:1, 1, 2. Rumanian with French summary.

Apel, G. 1963. "Die Slawenpopulation vom Alt-Spandau", *Bericht der deutschen Gesellschaft für Anthropologie* 8: 242-244. *Homo*, Supplement. 4-4. T.p. 243.I: 6. II: 4. J: 2, 0, 2. A: 12, 4. M: 6, 4. S: 2, 0.

Arbman, H. 1943. *Birka*. I *die Gräber* (Stockholm, K. Vitterhets Historie och Antikvitets Akademien). 7-3. AMS: 165, 249, 749.

Aries, P. 1977. *L'homme avant la mort* (Paris), especially 21-67.

Arnal, J. & M. Riquet, 1959. "Le cimetière Wisigothique des Piñedes à Saint-Mathieu de Tréviers (Hérault)," *Gallia* 17: 161-177. 2-2. ESE. P.p. 162. I:4. II:3. J:1. A:3, 3. M:1.1. S: 1, 0.

Arne, T.J. 1934. "Das Bootgräberfeld von Tuna in Alsike, Uppland," (Stockholm, *K. Vitterhets Historie och Antikvitets Akademien*). 7-3. I-II-J: 2. AMS: 12, 4.

Asmus, Gisela. 1939. "Frühkaiserliche Schädelfunde aus Mecklenburg und Pommern," *Offa* 4 (2): 136-153. 4-1. I:1. A:7, 2. M:1.1.

————. & K. Schwarz. 1959. "Beobachtungen zur Tracht und zur Bevölkerungenstruktur der karolingisch-ottonischen Zeit in Oberfranken," *Bayerische Vorgeschichts-Blätter* 24: 172-183. 4-3, NE, T.p. 173. I:10. II:1. A:8, 4. M:9, 0. AMS: 9, 9. Holzendorf.

Avenariova, I. 1970. "Anthropologische Analyse der Gräberfeldes von der Bratislaver Burg," *Acta Facultatis Rerum Naturalium Universitatis Comenianae Anthropologica* 15: 181-190. 6-4. T.p. 183. J: 4, 6. A: 9, 17. M: 28, 13. S: 6, 2.

Bach, Herbert. 1960. "Slawisches Gräberfeld bei Espenfeld bei Arnstadt," *Ausgrabungen und Funde* 5: 244-246. 4-4. E. I:19. II:6. J:2. AMS 13, 16.

————. & W. Timpel. 1962. "Frühmittelalterliches Gräberfeld mit Schläfeuringen von Possendorf, kr. Weimar," *Ausgrabungen und Funde* 7: 242-248. 4-4. ENE. P.p. 243. I:3. II:3. J:1, 0, 1. A: 6, 0, 3. AMS: 6, 1.

Bacic, B. 1958. "The Medieval Acropolis at Zminj," *Starohrtska Prosvjeta*, 3rd ser. 6: 77-92. Serbian with English summary. 5-3.I-II:44. AMS: 18, 6.

Backoczi, A. 1968. "A Sixth Century Cemetery from Keszthely-Fenékpuszta," *Acta Archaeologica Academiae Scientiarum Hungaricae* 20:275-311. 5-1, EW. P.p. 227. Data not used.

Bakay, K. 1963-1964. "Gräberfelder aus dem 10-11 Jahrhunderten in dem Umgegend von Székesfehérvar und die Frage der fürstlichen Residenz," *Alba Regia* 6-7: 43-88. 5-3. Ist cemetery. II:1. J: 1,0. A: 5, 1. M: 5, 2. 2nd cemetery. II: 0, 1, 6. J: 1, 7. M: 7, 3. S: 2, 0.

Bálint, Alajos. 1936. "Gräberfeld aus der Arpadenzeit in Szakálhát," *Dolgozatok* 12: 205-222. 5-4. NE Hungarian with German summary.

————. 1937. "Gräber aus der Awarenzeit in Batida," *Dolgozatok* 13: 98-104. 5-2. ENE. I-II: 4. AMS 6,6. Hungarian with German summary.

————. 1938. "Das Gräberfeld und die Kirche von Kaszper aus dem Mittelalter," *Dolgozatok* 14: 184-190. 5-4. E. I-II-J: 125. AMS: 82,87. Hungarian with German summary.

————. 1939a. "Ausgrabungen in Mëzokovácsházá," *Dolgozatok* 15: 161-164. 5-5. EW. I-II-J: 19. AMS: 36, 15.

————. 1939b. "Die Ausgrabungen in Csanádapáca," *Dolgozatok* 15:182. 5-5. EW. I-II-J:6. AMS:4, 3.

————. 1956. "Le cimetière de Kiskunfélegyháza-Templomhalom," *A Móra Ferenc Museum Evkönyve* 1:55-84. 5-5, EW. M.p. 57.I-II-J: 23. AMS:17, 17.

Banner, J. 1927. "Gräber aus der Völkerwanderungzeit bei Nagykamóras," *Dolgozatok* 3:141-159. 5-3. ESE. AMS 11, 2. Hungarian with German summary.

Bartucz, L. 1936. "Die Gepiden-Schädel des Gräberfeldes von Kiszomber," *Dolgozatok* 11:178-204, 4-5. EW, I-II-J:6. AMS:38-18. S:1 Hungarian with German summary.

Bartucz, L. & G. Farkas. 1956, "Anthropologische Untersuchung der in Csongrád-Felgyó gefundenen Skelette aus der Arpadzeit," *Acta Biologica* (Szeged) 2:235-261. 5-3. T.p. 236. II:2. J:0, 1, 3. A:6, 7. M:5, 7. S:1, 1.

_____. 1957. "Zwei Adorjaner Gräberfelder der Awarenzeit," *Acta Biologica* 3:315-348. 5-3. NS. T.p. 321. M.p. 318. I:8. II : 5. J:3, 5. A:9, 15. M:29, 10. S:9, 5.

_____. 1958. "Die Bevölkerung von 'Csĕsztó' in der Arpadzeit aus anthropologischen Gesichtspunkte betrachtet," *Acta Biologica* 4:246-284. 5-3. T.p. 247. II:1, 0, 4. J:1, 2. A: 2, 2. M: 4, 0. S: 2, 1. Second cemetery. Zeuta 5-3. T.p. 247. II:1, 0, 4. J: 1, 2. A: 2, 2. M: 4, 0. S: 2, 1.

Bata, B. 1949. "La cimetière avar de Vachartyan," *Annales Historic-Naturales Musei Nationalis Hungarici* 57: 213-233. 5-2. T.p. 213. I-II:3. J: 0, 2. A: 3, 8. M: 10,8. S: 0, 1.

Bay, R. 1968. "Die menschliche Skelettreste aus dem spatrömischen Gräberfeld vom Kaiseraugst," *Provincialia. Festschrift für Rudolf Laur-Belart* (Basel), 6-14. 6-1. I:7. II:10. J:4. A: 9, 8, 2. M: 18, 8, 1. S: 2, 0.

Belniak, T. 1951. "Cemetery of Gródek on the Bug River, xiii-xvii c.," *Materialy i Prace Antropologiczne*, no. 50 (Wrocaw). 8-4. J: 3, 5. A: 97, 66. M: 55, 30. S: 4, 3. Polish with English summary, revised from Martin to scale.

Beloch, K.J. 1937, 1940, 1961. *Bevölkerungsgeschichte Italiens* (Berlin).

Bengmark, S., N.G. Gejvall & E. Hjortsjö. 1952. "Das mittelalterliche Schädelgut aus der Klosterkirche in Gudhem," *Anthropologische Untersuchungen. Acta Universitatis Lundensis* 49: no. 14 (Lunds Universitets Arsskrift). 7-4 (13c). II:1. J: 0, 1. A:4, 2. M: 2, 1.

Betzler, P.S. & H. Köthe. 1964. "Merowingerzeitliche Gräber bei Niederweisel, kr. Friedberg," *Funderichte aus Hessen* 4: 117-124. 4-2. ENE. II: 0,1. J: 0, 1. A: 2, 2. M: 1, 0. (A.D. 550-600).

Bidder, M.F. 1906. "Excavations in an Anglo-Saxon Burial Ground at Mitcham, Surrey," *Archaeologia* 60: 49-68. 3-2. ENE. P.p. 57. I-III-J:5. AMS: 11, 3.

Biraben, J.N. & J. Le Goff. 1969. "Le Peste dans le Haut Moyen Age," *Annales, E.S.C.* 24: 1494-1510.

Blajerova, M. 1961. "Die Körpereigenschaften der mittelalterlichen Einwohner von Teplice (Friedhof bei der Römanische "Basilika")," *Památky Archeologické* 52: 652-660. 6-5. EW. A: 1, 3. M: 7, 7. S: 2, 3. Czech with German summary.

_____. 1973. "Die anthropologische Characteristik des Skelettmaterials von mittelalterliche Friedhof Oškobrh," *Památky Archeologické* 65: 185-217. Ist cemetery, probably preplague. 6-4. T.p. 186. I: 10. II: 9. J: 13. A: 22, 14, 7. M: 16,, 8, 10. S: 3, 1, 33. 2nd cemetery, in time of plague. 6-5. I: 42. II: 24. J: 12. A: 15, 12, 6. M: 11, 6, 7. S: 1, 3, 1. Czech with German summary.

_____. 1978. "Frühmittelalterliche Skelettreste aus Hradsko-kanina (kr. Mělnïk)," *Památky Archeologické* 69: 396-422. 6-2. T.p. 397. I: 12. II: 3. J: 3. A: 7, 8. M: 10, 5. S: 1, 2. Czech with German summary.

Böhner, K. 1949. "Die frankischen Gräber von Orsoy, Kr. Mors," *Bonner Jahrbücher* 1949: 146-196. 4-2. EW. ?. 5, 4, 1.

Botezatu, D. & G. Stefanescu. 1969. "Contributii la studiul antropologie al populatiei feudale timpurii din Moldava din sec. xiii en.," *Studii si cercetari de Antropologie* 7: 13-18. 5-4. I: 0, 1, 1. II: 1. A: 1, 1. M: 2, 1. S: 1, 0. Coconi.

_____. 1970. "Contributii la studiul antropologie al populatiei timpurii din Moldava din sec. xiii e.n.," *Studii si cercetari de Antropologie* 7: 13-18. Two villages of Bitca Doamne and Trifesti. 5-4. I:5. II: 10. J: 2, 1, 2. A: 0, 4. M: 3, 3.

Bottyán, Olga. 1966. "Data to the Anthropology of the Avar Period Population of Budapest." *Anthropologia Hungarica* 7: 3-34. Two cemeteries, early Avar. 5-2. J: 1. M: 2, 1. S: 1, 0. Late Avar. 5-3. J: 0, 2. A: 3, 4. M: 3, 4. T.p. 12.

_____. 1968. "The Outlines of an Anthropological Reconstruction of the Cemetery (xi-xv c) at Sopronbánfalva, West Hungary," *Anthropologia Hungarica* 8: 97-120. 5-5. T.p. 102. I: 1. II:1. J:2. A: 14, 3. M: 10, 5. S: 2.

_____. 1971. "A Short Anthropological Analysis of an Eleventh Century Cemetery at Csorna-Hosszŭdomb," *Anthropologia Hungarica* 10: 31-48. 5-3.EW. T.p. 33. I: 6. II: 2. J: 0. 3. A: 4, 4. M: 5, 5. S: 3, 4. Revised, assuming a Martin scale.

_____. 1972. "An Anthropological Examination of the x-xi Century Population at Oroszavár," *Anthropologia Hungarica* 11: 83-136. 5-4. T.p. 85. I: 4. II: 3. J: 6. A: 12, 16. M. 8, 8. S: 1, 0. ?: 1, 0. English summary.

_____. 1973. "The Anthropological Assessment of a x-xiii Century Cemetery at Mosonmagyaróvár," *Anthropologia Hungarica* 12: 13-40. 5-4. T.p. 28. II: 2. II: 8. J: 6. A: 4, 7. M: 25, 3. S: 0, 1. ?: 1, 0. English summary.

_____. 1975. "Anthropologische Auswertung des Pokaszepetker Friedhof aus der Früh-Awaren Periode," *Anthropologia Hungarica* 14: 5-56. 5-3. T.p. 34. I: 83. II: 9. J: 15. A: 25, 23. M: 24, 12. S: 1, 1.?: 3, 5.

Bradford, J.S.P. & R.G. Goodchild. 1939. "Excavations at Frelford, Berks., 1937," *Oxoniensia* 4: 1-70. 3-1. (4c). EW. P.p. 55. II: 1, 1. A: 4.
Brash J.C. & M. Young, 1935. "The Anglo-Saxon Skulls from Bidford-on-Avon; Worcs., and Burwell, Cambs.," *Biometrika* 27: 373-387. 3-1. SE. I: 25. II: 21. J: 6, 3, 2. A: 32, 20, 20. M: 15, 9, 16. S: 3, 5, 2. Not exact standard classification.
Breuer, J. & H. Roosens. 1957. "Le cimetière de Haillot," *Annales de la Société Archéologique de Namur* 48: 340-341. 3-1. II: 0, 1. J: 1, 0. A: 4, 1. M: 4, 0.
Brothwell, D.R. 1962. In John Morris, "The Marina Drive Settlement," *Bedfordshire Archaeological Journal* 1: 45-47. 3-2. NE. P.p. 42. I:6. II: 8. J: 6, 1, 3. A:11, 3. M: 1, 2.
_____. 1967. *Diseases in Antiquity* (Springfield).
_____. & Patricia. 1969. *Food in Antiquity* (New York)
Bruce-Mitford, R.L.S. 1956. *Recent Archaeological Excavations in Britain* (London): 187-189. Mawgan Porth. 3-3. I-II-J:9. AMS: 12.
Büchi, E.C. 1949-1950. "Mittelalterliche Skelette vom Lindenhof Zürich," *Bulletin der schweitzerischen Gesellschaft für Anthropologie und Ethnologie* 26: 77-97. 6-4. I: 6. II:3. J:3. A: 1, 1. M: 1, 7. S: 3, 1.
Budinský-Krička, V. 1959. "Slawische Hügelgräber in Skalica," *Archaeologica Slovaca, Fontes* 2: 7-162. 6-3. I-II-J: 17. AMS: 23, 24. Czech with German summary.
Bullough V. & C. Campbell. 1980. "Female Longevity and Diet in the Middle Ages," *Speculum* 55: 317-325.
Burger, A.S. 1966. "The Late Roman Cemetery at Ságvár," *Acta Archaeologica Academiae Scientiarum Hungaricae* 18: 99-234. 5-1. SE. I: 54. II: 25. J: 11. AMS:90, 104. Age estimated from length of skeleton.
_____. 1966-1977. "Das awarenzeitlichen Gräberfeld von Dunaszekcsö", *Folia Archaeologica* 18: 91-122. 5-3 (8c). SE. I:6. II:4. J:4. A: 5, 4. M:10, 7. S: 8, 7.
Busse, Herta. 1934. "Altskelettreste in Potsdamer Havelland," *Zeitschrift für Ethnologie* 66: 111-128. 4-3. II: 1. J:1. A:2. M: 15. S:3.
Capitano, Mariantonia. 1974. "La necroppoli di Potenzia (Maceratu) de época romana," *Notizie antropologiche* 104: 179-209. 5-1. I: 2, 0, 10. II: 1, 0, 3. A: 13, 11, 3. M: 2, 1. S: 1, 3.
Caplovic, P. 1953. "Nécropole slave de xme siècle à Nitra au pied du Zobor," *Archeologické Rozhledy* 5: 173-283. 8-3. I-II-J: 52. AMS: 39, 52. Czech with French summary.
_____. 1965. "Gräberfeld und Siedlung aus dem Frühmittelalter in Hurbanovo," *Slovanská Archeológia* 13: 237-247. 5-4. ENE. P.p. 239. Czech with German summary. No age data.
Carettone, G. et al. 1960. *La Pianta Marmorea di Roma Antica* (Rome).
Cebak-Holubowiczowa, Helena. 1955. "Sixth and Seventh Century Barrows at Karmazyny near Troki (LSSR)" *Wiadomosci Archeologiczne* 22: 312-331. 8-2. I-II-J: 2. AMS: 5, 13. Polish with English summary.
Chadwick, Sonia E. 1958. "The Anglo-Saxon Cemetery at Finglesham, Kent, a Reconsideration," *Medieval Archaeology* 2:1-71. 3-2. NE. P.p.2. I-II:4. AMS 15.
Chadwick-Hawkes, S. & A.C. Hogarth. 1974. "The Anglo-Saxon Cemetery at Monkton Thanet," *Archaeologia Cantiana* 89:85-89. 3-2 (6c). ENE. J:1. A:8,3. M:2,0. Skeletal data by C.B. Denston.
Charzewska, Jadwiga. 1963. "Opis szczatków kostnych z cmentarzyska wczesnośredniowiecznego w Gorys Lawicach, pow. Busko," *Raspravy Badania Archeologické* 2:199-212. 8-5. T.p.207. I:0,1. II:1,0. J:5,3. A:3,8. M:6,3. S:0,1. (Martin pattern?)
Chastagnol, A. 1960. *La Préfecture urbain á Rome sous la Bas-Empire* (Paris).
Chlingensperg-Berg. Max von. 1890. *Das Gräberfeld von Reichenhall in Oberbayern* (Reichenhall). I-II-J:136. AMS:184,203. Map separate.
Chochol, J. 1963. "Anthropologische Untersuchung der Leichenbrandes auf der Begräbnisstätte aus der Römerzeit in Tišice," *Památky Archeologické* 54:438-466. 6-1. I:5. II:4. J:2. A:1,3. M:5,29. S:1, Czech with German summary.
_____. 1970. "Menschliche Überreste aus dem römerzeitlichen Brandgräberfeld in Lušec," *Památky Archeologické* 61:378-394. 6-1. I:3. J:1. A:2,4,6. M:8,3,4. S:2,0 Czech with German summary.
_____. 1973. "Anthropologie der altslawischen Gruppe von Lahovice bei Prag," *Památky Archeologické* 64:393-462. 6-3. T.p.428. I:112. II:24. J:12. A:22,37,12. M:79,55,30. S:12,16,6. Czech with German summary.
_____. M. Blajerová & H. Paléčková. 1960. "Überreste von Skeletten der slawischen Einwohnerschaft von Alt-Koufim," *Památky Archeologické* 51:294-331. 6-3. I:38. II:16. J:1,3,7. A:16,11,11. M:19,18,5. S:8,5,2. ?:8. Czech with German summary. Altered from Martin Classification.

_____. & H. Hana. 1961. "Anthropologischer Beitrag zur Erforschung der slawischen Population in Böman," *Památky Archeologické* 52:631-651. Brandysek bei Slany. 6-3. I:3. II:2. J:0,1,4. A:4,8. M:11,7,1. S:2,2. Sulejuvice bei Luvosice. 6-4. I:16. II:1. J:5. A:4,7. M:3,2. S:1,0. Czech with German summary. Figures converted from Martin system.

Christlein, R. 1966. "Das alemannische Reihengräberfeld von Marktoberdorf im Altgau," *Materialhefte zur bayerische Vorgeschichte* 21:1-169. 4-3. NE. I:5,4. II:2,4. J:7,5. A:29,23. M:69,47. S:9,10. ?:2,1.

_____. 1971. "Das alemannische Gräberfeld vom Dirlewang bei Mindelheim," *Materialhefte zur bayerische Vorgeschichte* 25:1-102. 4-2. ENE. Tafel 23. J:1,0. A:3,1. M:2,7. S:2,0. ?:2,1. Martin classification?

Chropovsky, B. 1962. "Das slawische Gräberfeld auf Lukpa," *Slovenská Archeológia* 10:175-240. 5-3. ESE. 184. I-II-J:43. AMS:56. Czech with German summary.

Cilinska, Zlata. 1963. "Slawisch-awarisches Gräberfeld in Žitavská Tony," *Slovenská Archeológia* 11:87-120. 6-3. EW. I-II-J:15. AM:33. Czech with German summary.

_____. 1966. "Slawisch-awarisches Gräberfeld in Nové Zamsky," *Archeologia Slovaka, Fontes* 9:325-327. P.p.326. SE. Few data.

Clarke, Giles, 1981. *The Roman Cemetery at Lankhills* 3-1. Oxford E-ENE, I-II, 72. J: 1,2. A: 24,21.7 m 25 71,61.

Cochet, L'Abbé. 1851. *Sépultures gauloises, romanes, franques et normandes* (Paris).

_____. 1857. *La Normandie souterraine* (Rouen).

Cook, Jean. 1958. "An Anglo-Saxon Cemetery at Broadway Hill, Broadway, Worcs.," *The Antiquaries Journal* 38:58-84. 3-2. EW. Pl.p.60. A:3,2. M:1,1.

Cordier, G., R. Riquet & H. Brabant. 1974. "Le site archéologique du dolmen de Villaine á Sublaines (Indre et Loire)," *Gallia* 32:163-221. 2-2, ENE. M.p.163. P.p.209. 1:25 II:8. J:1,11. A:13,14,3. M:23,14,2. S:1,0.

Creel, N. 1966. "Die Skelettreste aus dem Reihengräberfriedhof, Sontheim an der Brenz," in art. by C. Neuffer-Muller, *Veröffentlichen des Staatlichen Amtes für Denkmalpflege Stuttgart* 1966: heft 11, 73-102. 4-2. NNE. 1:12. II:6. J:1,4,7. A:21,21,1. M:11,5. S:1,1. Also data on children aged 1-12.

_____. 1967. "Die Skelettreste von Wendlingen-Unterboihingen, kr. Nürtingen," *Fundberichte aus Schwaben* 18:297-306. 4-3. J:0.1. A:4,1, M:2,2.

Csallany, D. 1961. "Archäologische Denkmäler der Gepiden in mitteldonaubecker (454-568)," *Archaeologia Hungarica* 38.

Dambski. J. 1950. "Report on Human Remains from the Cemetery at Kónskie," *Materialy Wczesnósredniowieczne* 2:177-200. 8-4. T.p.24-25. 1:2. A:6,4. M:24,10. S:5,3. Polish with English Summary.

_____. 1955. "Crania et alia Ossa Polonica: Early medieval Cemetery at Kónskie," *Materialy i Prace Antropologiczne*, new series 3. 8-4. 11:12. A:6,4. M:24,10. S:5,3. Polish with English summary.

Dannheimer, H. 1960. *Die Alemannen in Südbaden* (Berlin, Germannische Denkamäler der Völkerwanderugenzeit.) *A.* 10.

_____. 1968. "Lauterhofen in früheren Mittelalter," *Materialhefte zur bayerische Vorgeschichte* 22: 1-150. 4-3. ESE. II:3, J:2,2,2. A:16,15,12. M:19,9,4. S: 1,0,1.

Dastugue, J. 1959. "Le cimetière du Mont-Joly," *Annales de Normandie* 9: 245-256. 2.2. A:1,1. M:0,2.

_____. 1964. "Le nouveau cimetière du moyen-age à Fleury-sur-Orne (Calvados)," *Annales de Normandie* 14: 111-172. 2-2. NE. 11:1. A:1,5. M:2,0. S:1,0.

_____. & R.S. Torre. 1961, "Sèpultures du haut moyen age à Saint-Aubin-sur-Mer, étude anthropologique," *Annales de Normandie* 11:96-99. 2-1. II-1. A:1,1. M:20,1. S:1,0.

_____. & R.S. Torre. 1965. "Etude anthropologique des Ossement du cimetière de Saint-Martin de Caen," *Annales de Normandie* 15: 329-352. 2-3. SE. J:1. A:5,3. M:8,3. S:3,3.

Della Corte, M. 1954. *Case ed abitanti di Pompei* (Rome, 2nd edition).

Denston, C.G. see S. Chadwick-Hawkes 1963 and W.I. Evison 1956.

Desportes, P. 1966. "La population de Reims au xv siècle d'àpres un dénombrement de 1422," *Le Moyen Age* 72: 97.

Diacanu, G. 1965. "Ein Gräberfeld aus dem 3.u.4. Jahrhundert u.Zeit," *Biblioteca de Arheologie* (Bucarest) 8: pp.53-72. 5-1. I-II:45. J:8. AMS:15,3,72. Rumanian with German summary.

Dienes, I. 1956. "Le cimetière de Hongrois conquérante à Bashalom (Fouilles exécutées a L. Kiss)." *Acta Archaeologica Academiae Scientiarum Hungaricae* 7: 245-273. 5-3. EW. P.p. 246. I-II:1,5. AMS: 12,5.

Diez, Christiana & May Volker. 1975. "Stomatologisch-anthropologische Untersuchung der Skelette des frümittelalteriche Gräberfelder Zöllnitz, kr. Jena." *Ausgrabungen und Funde* 20: 243-248. 4-3. Pl.p.244. I:29. II:13. J:2. A:23,20. M:9:6. S:2,2. Good study for dental conditions.

Dolinar-Osoletova, Z. 1954. "Altslawische Skelette aus Dubrača. bez. Kragujevac," *Arheoloski Vestnik* 25: 63-83. 5-4. T.p.65. I-II: 14. J:1,2,1. A:6,3,5. M:4,2,1. S:2,1. ?:2. Slovak with German summary.

Dymaczewski, A. 1958. "Un cimetière de la période romaine à Miodzikowo, dist. de Sroda," *Fontes Archaeologici Posnanienses* 8-9: 179-442. 8-1. AMS: 57,87. Polish with French summary.

Dzierzykray-Rogalski, T. 1956. "Skulls from a Prussian Cemetery at Rówina Dolna, the Ketrzyn dist.," *Wiadomosci Archeologicke* 23: 197-202. 8-4. J:0,2. M:0,3. S:0,1. Polish with English summary.

_____. 1962a "Analysis of Bone Remains in the 5th-6th Century Cemetery Cremation Graves at Osowa in the Years 1958-9," *Rocznik Bialostocki* 3: 299-336. 8-1. I:1 A:3,2. Polish with English summary.

_____. 1962b. "Research of Bone Remains of the III-IV Century A.D. from Jadwing at Szwajcaria, Dist. Suwalki," *Przeglad Antropologiczny* (Posnan) 4: 309-320.8-1. J:2,8. A:4,10. M:3,2. Polish with English summary.

_____. 1963. "Examination of Bone Remains from Inhumation Graves in Barrows at Osowa, Suwalki District," *Rocznik Bialostocki* 4: 309-320, I-II:2. J:1,1. A:2,3. M: 1,0. Polish with English summary.

_____. 1966. "Bone Remains from the 5th-6th Century in Cremation Graves at Wolownia, pow. Suwalki," *Rocznik Bialostocki* 6: 209-227. 8-1. J:0,6. A:7,16. M:7,7. S:2,2. Corrected from Martin scale.

Dzierzykray-Rogalski, T. & E. Prominska. 1961. "Bone Remains found in the 5th and 6th Century Cremation Graves at Osowa, Suwalki Dist. in 1957." *Rocznik Bialostocki* 2: 281-308. 8-2. 1:1,2. II:1. J:1,1. A:8,5. M:2. Polish with English summary.

Eblé, E. 1948. "Découverte á Saint-Aubin-sur-Mer (Calvados)," *Gallia* 6: 365-383. 2-1. P.p. 368. I-II—JJ: 12 AMS: 21.

Eck. T. 1888. "Découverte d'un cimetière Gallo-Romain á Saint-Quentin (Aisne)," *Mémoires de la Sociètè Academique — de St. Quentin*, 4th ser. no. 9, 25. 2-1. I-II-J: 14. AMS:8, 12.

Ehgartner, W. 1947. "Der spätrömische Friedhof von Oggau, Burgenland," *Mitteilungen der österreichischen Gesellschaft für Anthropologie*, E. & P. 73-77: 2-33. 4-1. NE. II:0,6. J:1,1,2. A:3,1,6. M: 3,0,4. S:0,1,1. ?2.

Ery, K. K. 1966. "The Osteological Data of the Ninth Century Population of Artánd," *Anthropologia Hungarica* 5: 85-114. 5-3. I:23. II:20. J:0,3. A:35,40 M:27,27. S:0,2.

_____. 1967. "An Anthropological Study of the late Avar Period Population of Artánd," *Annales Historic-Naturales Musei Nationalis Hungarici* 59: 464-484. 5-3. T. 466. I:42. II:25. J:9,12. A:21,27. M:47,27. S:10,15. ? 8,9.

_____. 1967-1968. "Reconstruction of the Tenth Century Population of Sárbogárd on the Basis of Archaeological and Anthropological Data," *Alba Regia* 8-9: 9-148. 5-3. SE. T. p.96. I:23. II: 11. J:7,3. A:14,5. M:13,13. S:2,9.

_____. 1968. "Anthropological Studies on a late Roman Population at Majs, Hungary," *Anthropologia Hungarica* 8: 31-57. 5-1. T.p. 40 1:6. II.4. J:2,2. A:2,4. M:12,7. S:0,2. ?: 3,0. Of about A.D. 250-400.

_____. 1969. "Anthropological Studies on a Tenth Century Population at Kál, Hungary," *Anthropologia Hungarica* 9: 9-62. 5-3. T.p. 33. I:14. II:4. J:1,2. A:8,4. M:12,14. S:2,4.

_____. 1970. "The Skeletal Remains of a Tenth Century Population at Dunaalmás, Hungary," *Annales Historico-Naturales Musei Nationalis Hungarici* 52: 405-412 5-4. EW. I:2.J:0.1. A:1,4.1. M:2,0. S:0,2. Com Komaron.

_____. 1971. "The Anthropological Examination of a Tenth Century Population at Tengelic, Hungary," *Anthropologia Hungarica* 10: 49-90. 5-3. T.2. I:5. II:6. A:3,4. M:5,8, S:1,1.

_____. 1973. "Anthropological Data to the Late-Roman Population at Pécs, Hungary," *Anthropologia Hungarica* 12: 63-114. 5-1.T.p.82. I:53. II:10. J:3,2. A:8,10. M:19,26. ?:4,8.

Ery, Kunga K. & A. Kralovanszky. 1960. "Analyse paléosociographique des cimetières de Székesfehérvár, et xi siècles," *Annales Historico-Naturales Musei Nationalis Hungarici* 52: 497-522. 5-4. T. 507. I:21. II:4. J:4. A:20. M:10. S:9. 7:3.

Evison, V.I. 1956. "An Anglo-Saxon Cemetery at Holborough, Kent," *Archaeologia Cantiana* 70: 84-141. 3-2 (7c). ENE. Pl.p.86 I:6. II:2. J:0,1,1. A:10,10. M:6,0. S:0,1. ?:4.

Faider-Feytmans, G. 1970. *Les nécropoles mérovingiennes. Les collections arch.régional du Musée de Mariement,* 207. (Tertre). 2-2. I:2. II:2. J:3,1. A:2,3.1. M:9,1,1. S:5,1. ?:4,5,4. Museum data.

Farkas, G., I. Lenguel & A. Marksik. 1971. "Supposition of Greater Connections between the Finds of the Cemetery at Mélykút-Sancdúló (Southern Hungary) on the Basis of Blood Grouping ABO," *Acta Biologica* (Szeged) 17: 199-207. 5-2. NS. T.p. 200. M:p. 201.1:3. II:4. J:1,3. A;8,13. M:7,9.

Fedeli, M. 1960. "Ricerche antropologiche sulla necropoli di Canne," *Rivista di antropologia* 47: 174-206. 1-4. T.p. 193. I:32. II:19. J:1,5. A:31,12,8. M:25,18,4. S:2,2.2. ?:8,5,7.

Fettich, N. 1965. "Das awarzeitliche Gräberfeld von Pilismarót-Basahare," *Studia Archaeologica* III, Akadémiai Kiadó. 5-3. I:0, 3,15. II:10,4,5. J:3,8,0. A:20,19,1. M: 40,22,1. S:10,9. Ages defined individually: consolidated here.

Fingerlin, G. 1971. *Die alemannische Gräberfelder von Güttingen und Merdingen in Südbaden* (Berlin). Merdingen. 4-2. NE. P.p. 308. I:1,4,18. II:2,5,6. J:6,14,5. A:29,50,5. M:54,44,1. S:5,7. ?:1,1. If this a Martin arrangement, it should be revised to: A:56,72,5. M:30,26,1. S:2,3,7. Date is 6-7c. *Germanische Denkmälere der Volkerwanderungszeit.* ser. A, 12.

Fischer-Møller, K. 1942. "The Mediaeval Norse Settlements in Greenland," *Meddelelser om Grønland* 89: 72. 7-4 & 5. I.1. II:7. J:5. A:4,23. M:8,8.

Flinn, M.W. 1981. *The European Demographic System* (Baltimore).

Florkowski, A. 1970. "Human Remains from a Cemetery of the Roman Period at Gostkowo, Torun district," *Wiadomosci Archeologiczno* 35: 552-556. 8-1, T.p.552. I:1,2. II:2,2. J:4,3. M:9,6. Polish with English summary.

Fremersdorf, F. 1955. *Das fränkische Reihengräberfeld Köln-Müngersdorf* (Köln). 4-1. EW, I-II:4,5. J:2,2. A:5,13,1. M:19, 15,1. S:2,0.

Fricke, W. 1960. "Untersuchungen an Leichenbränden der Gräber felder von Prositz und Niederkaina," *Arbeits-und Forschungsberichte zur sächsische Bodendenkmalpflege* 7: 320-356. 4-1. T.p.348. I:1, II:6. J:2. A:7, M:5, 5:2. ?:2.

Friesinger, M. 1971. "Frühmittelalterliche Körpergräber in Tullu, NÖ," *Archaeologia Austriaca* 50:197-249. 6-3, EW. I:13. II:2. J:1,0,4. A:7,4. M:2,2. S:2,3.

Fusté, A.M. 1954. "La duración de la vida en la población española desde la prehistoria hasta nuestros días," *Trabajos del Instituto Bernadino de Sahagún* 14:81-104. Duraton. p.90 1-2. NE, A:46,23. M:51,21. S:28,11. From Prevosti 1951.

_____. 1961-1962. "Estudio antropologico de los esqueletos inhumados en túmulos de la región de Gáldar, (Gran Canaria)," *El Museo Canario* 22-23: 1-122. 4-1. Same skeletons as in Schwidetsky 1958.

Garan, Eva. 1972. "Avar Cemeteries at Andoca," *Folia Archaeologia* 23: 129-182. 5-2. ENE. Pl.p. 179. I:1 II:1. AMS: 28,57,32. Hungarian with English summary.

Garsha, F. 1970. *Die Alemannen in Südbaden* (Berlin).

Gejvall, N-G. 1951. "Untersukning av de brända fran Mellby grävfelt," *Västergotlands Fornminnesförenings Tidskift* 5(2):53,77. 7-1? I:5. II:II. J:2,0. A:5,9,5. M:7,10,4. S:3,4.

_____. 1955. "The Cremations at Vallhagar," (pp.700-723) and "The Skeletons" (pp. 724-765). in M. Stenberger, *Vallhager: a Migration Period Settlement in Gotland, Sweden* (Copenhagen). P.p.1.6. 7-1. I:4. A:10,7,2. M:7,8,1. S:3,6. ?:3,2. For skeletons. 7-1. I:2. II:1. A:11,16,20. M:8,11,2. S:5,8,4. For cremations.

_____. 1960. *Westerhus. Medieval Population and Church in the Light of Skeletal Remains* (Lund). 7-4. I:183. II: 27. J:12,3. A:31,38. M:27,36. S:2,3. Very detailed data about age.

_____. 1968. *The Archaeology of Skedemosse* (Stockholm) 3: 223-236. 7-1. I:5. II:1. J:2,0,3. A:II,3,2. M:3,1, S:4,4.

Gierlach, B. 1965. "An Early Medieval Cemetery in Warsaw Wilanow in the Light of the 1961 Excavation," *Wiadomosci Archeologiczne* 31: 68-74. 8-4. I-II-J:8. AMS:6,21. Polish with English summary.

Gladykowska Rzeczycka, Judyta. 1968. "Knochenmaterial aus dem frühmittelalterliche Gräberfeld in Mlodzikowo, bez. Sroda," *Fontes archaeologici Posnanienses* 19: 160-173. 8-4. I:0,2,1. II:1,7. J:1,2,2. A:5,26,3. M:14,12,3. S:5,3. ?:1,0. Polish with English Summary.

Gläser, R. 1935. "Die spätgermanische Kultur Schlesiens in Gräberfeld von Gross-Sürding," *Quellenschriften für ostdeutschen Vorund Frühgeschichte* 2: 88-115. 4-1. T.p. 88. J:0,1. A:12,3. M:5,2.

Gralla, Gertruda. 1964a. "Report of Bone Remains from Cremation Graves at Zakrzow, Krapkowice dist," *Materialy Starozytne* 10: 225-228. 8-1. I:2. II:1. J:0,1,1. A:2,2. M:0. ?4.3,3. Polish with English summary.

———. 1964b. "On Estimating Total Body Height in Cremated Skeletal Materials," *Materialy i Prace Antropologiczne*, Polska Akademia Nauk, Wroclaw, no. 70, 95-98. 8-4. AMS:91,71. Milicz, Lower Silesia.

———. 1967. "Cimetière à squelettes du haut moyen age, de Ciëlmice, près de Tychy," *Studia Archeologiczne* 2: 283-288. 8-5. I:5. II:3. J:1,0. A:6,8 M:4,1. Polish with French summary.

Grimm, H. 1953. "Anthropologische Bemerkungen an der Gräber von Leuna," in W. Schulz, "Leuna, ein germanischer Bestattungsplatz der spätrömischen Kaiserzeit," *Schriften der Sektion für Vor- und Fruhgeschichte*, Deutsche Akademie der Wissenschiften zu Berlin, 1:74-84. 4-1, T.p. 83. J:1,2. A:2,9,1. M:4,7. S:2,2,1.

———. 1959. "Anthropologische Beschreibungen zu einigen kaiserzeitlichen Skelett-gräbern von Rügen und dem benachbarten Festland," *Bodendenkmalpflege in Mecklen-burg*, Jhb. 1959: 88-100. 4-1. I:2. J:1. A:1,2.5. M:2,,1. S:1. ?:2.

———. 1969. "Anthropologische Untersuchung der Leichenbrandreste und einer Kör-perbestattung aus dem kaiserzeitlicher Gräberfeld von Zauschwitz, kz. Bonn," *Arbeit-sund Forschungsberichte zur sächsischen Bodendenkpflege*, beiheft 6. Anhang — Elmar Meyer (Berlin). 195-221. 4-1. NNE. I:12. II:2. J:1,0,2. A:7,12,2. M:12,5,5. S:4,1.?:1,0,2.

Guyan, W.U. 1958. "Das alamannische Gräberfeld von Beggingen-Löbern," *Schriften des Institute für Ur- und Frühgeschichte der Schweiz* 12. 4-2. ESE. I:1. J:0,5,1. A:0,2,5. M:1,2. AMS: 24,29,24.

Hajnis, K. 1965. "Römerzeitliche Schädel des 4-5 Jahrhunderts aus Warna in Bulgarien," *Anthropologie* (Brne) 2: 63-70 (7c). 5-1. J:2,1. A:6,8,1. M:3,1,1. Extra: AMS: 24,29,24.

Hallam, H.E. 1957-1958. "Some thirteenth Century Censuses," *Economic History Review*, 2nd ser. 10: 343-356.

Hampe, H. 1959. "Die Reihengräberfriedhof in der Schlafkammer in Grone," *Göttinger Jahrbuch* 1959: 27. 27-36. 4-1. I:6. II:3. J:2,0. A:3,3. M:5,2.

Hampl, F. 1961. "Ein frühgeschichtliches Gräberfeld in Wartmannstetten p.B. Neu-nkirchen, NÖ," *Archaeologia Austriaca* 29: 18-37 6-4. NE. I:10. II:2. J:1,1,2. A:3,0,3. M:0,1.1.

———. 1965. "Die langobardischen Gräberfelder von Rohrendorf und Erpersdorf, N.O.," *Archaeologia Austriaca* 37: 40-78. 6-2. EW. 1:1. II:9. J:0,2,3. A:1,1,1. M:3,0,3. S:2.1. ?:4,2.

Hanáková, H. 1963. "Anthropologische Analyse der slawischen Skelettüberreste aus Žalany, bez. Teplice," *Památky Archeologické* 54: 308-314. 6-4. SE. II:2. A:1. M:3,1. S:1.1 ?:5,2.2. Czech with German summary.

———. 1969. "Eine anthropologische Analyse der slawischen Skelette aus dem Burgwall von Libice nad Cidlinon," *Anthropologie* (Brno) 7: 3-40. 6-3. EW. T.p. 4-5. I:220. II:30. J:12. A:28,27,17. M:49,25,10. S:6,11,14. ?:9,11.14. In the first year: 66, included above in Inf.1.

———. 1971. "Die slawische Begräbnisstätte aus Bílina: anthropologische Analyse," *Anthropologie* (Brno)) 9:111-128. 6-4. T.p. 114. I:48. II:15. J:18. A:2,25,2. M:46,19,1. S:1,4. ?:19,12,21. Also information about first year of life.

Harman, Mary. 1979. In Giles Clarke, *The Roman Cemetery at Lankhills* (Oxford): 24-95. 3-1. E-NE. M.p.377. I:88. II:19. J: 1, 11,5. A:86,52,44. M:3,0.

Harster, T. 1913. "Das bajuwarische Reihengräberfeld bei Kelheim," *Praehistorische Zeitschrift* 5: 227-261. 4-2. EW. M.p. 229. I-II-J: 13. AMS:20,22.

Hauschild, M.W. 1925. "Die menschlichen Skelettfunds des Gräberfelds von Anderten bei Hannover," *Zeitschrift für Morphologie und Anthropologie* 25: 221-242. 4-2. NE. ?:41,38.

Hauser, U. 1940. *Anthropologische Untersuchung des alammanischen Gräberfeldes Oerlingen*, kr. Zurich. (Zurich). 4-2 (7c). I:7. II:3. J:13-4. A:18.4. M:18,8. S:1,1. ?:1,0. Perhaps: A:22,8. A:11,5.

Helmuth, H. 1966. "Die menschlichen Skelettfunde des mittelalterlichen Gertrudenhof in Kiel," *Zeitschrift für Morphologie und Anthropologie* 57: 272-298. 4-5. EW. I:30. II:51. J:21. A:78. M. 36. S:31.

———. 1970. "Zur Paläodemographie der völkerwanderszeitlichen Skelettserie von Altenerding bei Müchen," *Homo* 21: 85-88. 4-2. EW. I:99. II:86. J.82. A:127,155,25. M:81,62,5. S: 67,83,5.

Hencken, H.O. 1950. "Lagore Crannog: an Irish Royal Residence of the 7th to 10th Centuries, A.D.", *Proceedings of the Royal Irish Academy* 53 C: 199-203. 3-3. I:2. II:6. J:1,2,3.A:1,4. ?:6,2.2. (A massacre).

Henshall, A.S. 1958. "A long Cist Cemetery at Parkburn Sand Pit, Lasswade, Midlothian," *Proceedings of the Society of Antiquaries of Scotland* 89: 252-283. 3-2. ENE. M.p. 252. I-II-J:4. AMS:10,14.

Herlihy, David. 1958. *Pisa in the Early Renaissance* (New Haven).

———. 1962. "Land, Family and Women in Continental Europe," 701-1200, *Traditio* 18: 89-120.

———.1965. "Population, Plague and Social Conditions in Rural Pistoia," *Economic History Review* 18: 225-244.

———. 1967. *Medieval and Renaissance Pistoia* (New Haven). especially appendix 11.

———. 1974. "Ecological Conditions and Demographic Change," in *1000 Years,* ed. Richard L. de Molen (Boston), 3-44.

———. 1974. "The Generation in Medieval History." *Viator* 5: 347-364.

——— & C. Klapisch-Zuber. 1978. *Les Toscans et leurs familles: un étude de catasto florentin de 1427* (Paris).

Hermansen, G. 1978. "The Population of Imperial Rome: the Regionares," *Historia* 27: 129-169.

Heuertz, M. 1957. "Études des squelettes du cimetière franc d'Ennery (Moselle)," *Bulletins et Mémoires de la Société d'Anthropologie de Paris* 8: 81-141. 2-1.P.p. 132. 1:15. II:10. J:5,5,12.A:27,8,5. M:36,8,5. S:20,8,8.

Hitzeroth, H.W. 1965. "Morphogenetische Untersuchung der Schretzheimer Reihengräber," *Anthropologische Anzeiger* 29: 96-107. 4-2. EW. 1:18. II:27. J:0,11,10. A:42,37,12. M:21,21,16. S:3,1. ?:3,2 ??:25. Changed from A:21,17: M:42,41.

Hjortsjö, C-H. & T. Kraskau. 1944. "Antropologiska data beträffande befolkingen i Lund unter 1000, 1100, och 1200 talen," *Lunds Universitets Arsskrift,* n.f. 1-44. 7-4. J:1,4. A:3,0. M:1,0.

Hollnagel, A. 1965. "Das slawische Körpergräberfeld von Behren-Lübchin," in E. Schuldt, *Behren-Lubchin* (Berlin). Deutsche Akademie der Wissenschaften, *Schriften der Sektion für Vorund Frühgeschichte* 19: 133-143. 4-4. P.p. 134. I:1. J:0,1,2. A:5,5,2. M:9,2.2. S:2,0. ?:3,0,6.

Holter, K.R. 1925. "Das Gräberfeld bei Obermölern aus der Zeit des alten Thüringen," *Jahresschrift für die Vorgeschichte des sächsisch-thuringischen Länder* 12: 1-114. 4-2. I-II-J:5. AMS:5,9.

Hopkins, K. 1967. "On the Probable Age Structure of the Roman Population," *Population Studies* 20: 245-263.

Horne, D.E. 1928. "Saxon Cemetery at Camerton, Somerset," *Proceedings of the Somersetshire Archaeological and Natural History Society* 74: 61-90. 3-2. ENE. Definition uncertain.

Howells, W.W. 1941. "The Early Christian Irish: the Skeletons at Gallen Priory" *Proceedings of the Royal Irish Academy* 46 C: 103-202. 3-4. EW. Corrected for age. A:36. M:65. S:26.

Hruby, V. 1965. *Staré Město. Die grossmärische Begräbnisstätte 'Na Valach'* (Prague, Monumenta Archaeologica 14). 6-3. I:5,27,130. II:9,34,92. J:3,27,56. A:40,68,29. M:79,59,10. S:69,48,7. The figures for M and S seem much too high. Calculated by substituting for five and ten-year periods.

Hruby, V., H. Hochmanová & J. Pavelcik. 1955. "Die grossmärische Kirche und begräbnisstätte in Modrá bei Velehrad (Mähren)," *Casopis Moraského Musea v Brně* 40: 42-126. 5-3. ESE. I:8. II:4. A:6,2. M:10,8,1. S:1,2. Czech with German summary.

Hug, E. 1940. "Die Schädel der frühmittelalterlichen Gräber aus dem solothurnischen Aargebiest in ihrer Stellung zur Reihengräberbevölkerung Mitteleuropas,," *Zeitschrift für Morphologie und Anthropologie* 38: 359-528. 6-2. J:1. A:0,2. M:2,0. S:0,1.

Hyslop see p. 263.

Isager, Kr. & E. Sjovall. 1936. *Skeleton Finds at Cara Insula Monastery MCXXII-MDLX* (Copenhagen). 7-5. I:29. II:20. J:22,5,11. A:109,33,14. M:35,10,9. S:3,0,17. Presumably many monks.

Ivanicek, F. 1951. "Ancient Slav Necropolis at Ptuj," *Dela* 5. Slovenska Academija Znanosti in Umetnosti, Ljubljana, 5-4. T.p.9. I:12. II:54. J:0,7,9. A:30,44,8. M:58,-28,9. S:14,15,2. ?:2,0,7. Slovak with English summary.

Jakab, J. 1977. "Anthropologische Analysevon Skelettrestenaus dem frühmittelalterlichen Gräberfeld von Nové Zámky," *Slovenská Archeológiaa* 25: 161-218, 6-4. T.p. 161. I:2. II:12. J:1,2,1. A:3,8. M:8,8,1. S:4,1. Slovak with German summary.

———. 1978. "Anthropologische Analyse des Gräberfeldes aus dem 9. -10. Jahrhundert in Nitra am Fuss des Zobor," *Slovenská Archeológia* 26: 127-148. 6-3. I:8 II:5. J:1,2. A:2,7. M:11,12. S:2,0.

Janocha, H. 1966. "Ergebnisse der Untersuchungsarbeiten durchgeführt in den Jahren 1959-1960 auf Góra Chelmska (Krzyzanka). bei Koszalin," *Materialy Zachodniopomorska* 12: 383-472, NE. 8-4. P.p. 388. J:0,5. A:2,3,2. M:1. Polish with German summary.

Jungwirth, J. 1968. "Die Skelette aus dem Longobardenfriedhof von Poysdorf, N.Ö." *Mitteilungen der anthropologischen Gesellschaft in Wien* 98: 15-33. 4-1. I:1. A:1,1. M:3.1.

Kastelic, J. & B. Škerlj. 1950. "The Slav Necropolis at Bled," *Dela* 2, S.A.Z.U. 5-3. EW. I-II-J: 90. AMS: 99:86. Serb with English summary.

Kaszewski, E. 1960. "An Early Medieval Cemetery at Kaldus, district of Chelmo (1957 Excavations)," *Prace i Materialy*, Museum Archeologicznego i Etnograficznego w Lodzi, ser. arch. 5: 145-191. 8-4. ESE. I-II-J:13. AMS: 17,30. Polish with English summary.

Kazmierczyk, J. 1957. "Das frühmittelalterliche Korpergräberfeld bei dorf Kranowice, kr. Opole," *Archeologia Slaska* 1: 112-134. 8-4. EW.M. p. 128. I:2. II:3. J:1,0.A:9,8. M:3,1 ?:2. Polish with German summary.

Keil, B. 1970. "Demographische Beobachtungen an einer frühneuzeitliches Population aus Langd in Oberhessen," *Homo:* 21: 89-93. 4-4 (12c), I:2,0,22. II:17. J:0.1.8. A:43,47,24. M:36,24,13. S:12,13,7.

Keith, A. 1936 in R.E.M. Wheeler, *Verulamium. A Belgic and Two Roman Cities* (1936, Reports of the Research Committee of the Society of Antiquaries no. 11) 3-1. T.p. 136. I-11: 10. J:1,1. A:4,5. Infant burials in houses.

Keller, E. 1971. *Die spätrömischen Grabfunde in Südbayern* (Munich, Deutsche Akademie der Wissenschaften). Weissling (Starnburg), 259. 4-1. ENE. I:0,2. II:2. J:0,2. A:2,2. M:5,2. S:2,0,1.

Kietlinska, S. & Teresa Dabrowska. 1963. "A Cemetery from the Period of Roman Influences at Spicymierz, dist. Turek," *Materialy Starozytne* 9: 143-254, 8-1. ?:60,46. Polish with English summary.

Kiszely, I. 1966. "Anthropological Examination of a Longobard Graveyard in Szentendre," *Antropoligiai Közlemények* 10: 57-90. 5-1 (mid.6c). ESE. M.p. 79. I:1,2. II:2,6 J:2,4. A:12,8. M:16,16. S:4,3.

Kloiber, A. 1957. *Die Gräberfelder von Lauriacum. Das Ziegelfeld.* (Linz, Oberösterreichischer Landesverlag: in Kommision der Institut für Landeskunde Osterreich). 6-1. I:13. II:8. J:6,1.4. A:27,12,5. M:29,6,12. S:12,3,7. ?:18,7,28.

———. 1962. *Die Gräberfelder von Lauriacum. Das Espelmayrfeld.* (Linz, as above). 6-1. I:9. II:9. J:2.3. A:13,9. M:37,15. S:5,1 ?:5,6.

———. 1966. "Ein Bestattungsplatz des 9/10 Jht. in Gusen. polit. bez. Perg, Ö.Ö." *Jahrbuch des oberösterreichischen Musealvereines* 111: 261-277. And: Kloiber, A. & M. Pertlwieser, 1967. "Die Ausgrabungen" 1966 auf der 'Berglitzl'" in Gusen und auf bem "Hausberg" in Anhof bei Perg, pol. bez. Perg, 00," same journal: 112: 75-90. 6-3. I:6. II:2. J::2,1.1. A:7,3,1. M:6,3,2. S:1,1.

Kmiecinskiego, J. 1968. "A Cemetery of the Roman Period at Odry," *Acta Archaelogica Lodziensia*, no. 15. 8-1. I:1,0,3. II:4.J:4,7,1. A:7,8. M:2,4 ?:3,16. Polish with English summary.

Koch, Ursula. 1968. *Die Grabfunde des Merowinger zeit aus dem Donautal um Regensburg* (Berlin, Germanische Denkmäler der Volkerwanderungszeit.) ser. A, 10.

Korosec, J. 1950. "The Old Slav Burial Place in the Castle Hill of Ptuj," Slovenska Akademija Znanosti in Umetnosti, *Dela* 1. I:II-J:92. AMS:99,86. Slovak with English summary.

Kovrig, I. & J. Korek. 1960 "Le cimetière de l'époque avare de Csóka (Čoka)," *Acta Archaeologica Hungarica* 12: 257-297. 5-2. SE.I-II-J: 3. AMS; 13,9,5.

———. 1963. "Die avarenzeitliche Gräberfelde von Alattyan," *Archaeologia Hungarica* 40:5-267. Cemetery I, p. 114. 5-2. I-II-J: 10. AMS:8,23,6. 7c. Cemetery II, p. 114. 5-2.I-II-J:55. AMS: 90,83,25. Cemetery III, p. 124. 5-2. A:5.4. M:2.2. ?:1.1. Cemetery IV, p. 141. 5-2. I:58. II:25. J:33. A:60,87. M:45.17.

Kozikowska, Janina. 1960. "Les débris des ossements de la nécropole à squelettes de Góra, dep. de Turek," *Fontes Archaeologici Posnanenses* 11: 194-199. 8-4. J:2. A:1,1. M:4,1,1. S:1,0. ?:0,1. Polish with French summary.

Kral, L. 1959. "Das slawische Hügelgräberfeld in Vyzočany an der Thaya," *Památky Archeologické* 50: 197-226. I-II:12. AMS:9,9. Czech with German summary.

Kraskovská, L. 1955. "Cimetière slave de Bratislava-Kárlova Ves," *Archeologické rozhledy* 7: 487-566. 6-3. I-II-J:6. AMS:9.

———. 1958. EW. "Ausgrabung in Bešeňov im Jahr 1950," *Slovenská archaeológia* 6: 419-447. 6-4. EW. P.p. 423. I-II:17. J:18. AMS:46. Czech with German summary.

———. 1960. "Awarisch-slawisches Gräberfeld in Bernolákovo in der Slovakei," *Archeologické rozledy* 12: 366-369. 6-3. NE. I-II-J: 28. AMS: 54. Czech with German summary.

———. 1963. "Slawisches Gräberfeld in Devin auf der Flur," *Slovenská Archeológia* 11: 391-406. 6-3. EW. I-II-J: 11. AMS: 4,3,4. Czech with German summary.

———. 1965. "Slawisches Gräberfeld in Kopčany," *Sborník Slovenského Národneho Musea, ročník* 59: 19-48. 6-3. ENE I-II-J:18. AMS: 33. Czech with German summary.

———. 1966. "Un lieu de sépulture à Blatné," *Sborník Slovenského Národneho Musea, ročník* 60: 95-116. 6-3. SE. I:1. AMS:5,2. Czech with German summary.

Krüger, B. 1967. "Ein frühslawischer Siedlungsplatz im mittleren Elbegegiet," *Deutsche Akad. der Wissenschaften im Berlin, Schriften der Sektin für Vor-und Fruhgeschichte* 22. 4-2. P. 102. I:6. II:5. J:1,1.1. A:6,9,3. M:4,0,5. Infant ages given.

Kunter, M. 1974. "Frühkarolingische Skelettreste von Zullestein. gem. Nordheim, kr. Bergstrasser," *Zeitschrift für Morphologie und Anthropologie* 65: 305-323. 4-3. A:3,3. M:8,3. S:2,1.

Kytlikova au Czav, Olga. 1968. "Das slawische Gräberfeld in Brandysek," *Památky Archeologické* 59: 193-248. 6-3. Children only.

La Baume, P. 1967. "Das fränkische Gräberfeld von Junkersdorf bei Köln," *Römisch-Germanische Kommission des Deutschen Archäologischen Instituts, Germanische Denkmäler der Volkwanderungszeit,* ser. B. 2: 7-271. 4-2. T.p. 262. 1:0,3,7. II: 2,4,6. J:4,2. A:15, 14,3. M:5,5.2.

Lantier, R. 1948. "Un cimetière du ive siecle au 'Mont Augé' (Vert-le-Gravelle, Marne)," *L'Antiquité Classique* 17:373-401. 2-1. ESE. 1:2. II:4. J:2. A:0,3. M:4,3. S:3,0. ?:5,4.

———. 1949. "Le cimetière Wisigothique d'Estagel," *Gallia* 7: 55-80. 2-2. ENE. T.p. 57. I-II-J: 63. AMS; 20,28,20.

Laser, R. 1963. "Ein Brandgräberfeld der spätrömischen Kaiserzeit bei Schönebeck (Elbe)," *Jahresschrift für mitteldeutsche Vorgeschichte* 47: 325-341. 4-1. I:17, II:16. J-A: 36. M-S: 30. ?.1.

Laszlo, Gyula. 1955. "Études archéologiques sur l'histoire de société des Avars," *Archaeologia Hungarica,* new ser. 34: 1-301. 5-2. I-II-J:46. AMS: 37,55,138.

Laur-Belart, R. 1948. "Betrachtungen über das alamannische Gräberfeld am Bernerring in Basel," *Festschrift für Otto Tschumi* (Fravenfeld): 112-125. 6-2. P. 14. I-II:1 J:3,3. AMS:14,16,3.

Leciejewicz, L. 1960 "Le cimetière du haut moyen-age de Mlodzikowie, dist. de Šroda," *Fontes Archaeologici Posnanienses* II: 105-165. 8-4. EW. I-II-J: 25. AMS: 46, 18,89. Polish with French summary.

Leeds, E.T. 1909. "Anglo-Saxon Cemetery at Holdenby, Northants," *Northamptonshire Natural History and Field Club* 15: 91-99. 3-2 7c, 1st half. NE. ?: 4,3.

———. 1940. "Two Saxon Cemeteries in North Oxfordshire," *Oxoniensia* 5: 21-30. Chadlington, p. 23. 3-2. ENE. J:0,1. A:2,2. M:3,2. S:0,1. North Leigh, p. 21 3-2. ?: 2,3.

———. & D.B. Darden. 1936. *The Anglo-Saxon Cemetery* at *Abingdon.* Berks (Oxford). 3-2. ENE, I:6,6,9. II:5,7,6. J:2,2. A:33,26. M:2,2,. S:3,1.

———. & H. de Shortt. 1953. *An Anglo-Saxon Cemetery at Petersfinger near Salsbury, Wilts* (Salisbury). 3-2. EW. I:6. II:1,0,5. J: 2,1,3. A: 2,0. S:1,1. ?:15,16,6.

Lethridge, T.C. 1936. "A Cemetery at Shudy Camps, Cambridgeshire," *Cambridge Antiquarian Society, Quarto Publications* N.S.5: 30. 3-3. I-II J:33. AMS:148,115.

Lindegard, B. & F. Löfgren. 1949. "Anthropologische Untersuchung mittelalterlicher Skelettfund aus den Aussetzigenspital Jørgen in Åhus," *Lunds Universitets Arsskift,* N.F. 245.

Lippert, A. 1967. "Die zeitgeschichtliche Stellung des frühgeschichtlichen Gräberfeldes in Zwölfoxing, pol. u. Gev. Bez. Schwachat, N.Ö., *Mitteilungen der Anthrpologischen Gesellschaft in Wien* 96-97: 298-309. 6-2. P.p. 309. I:0,13,63. II:1,3,1. J:3,6. A:26,32,3. M:35,17. S:0,6. ?:8,6,8.

———. 1969. "Das awarenzeitliche Gräberfeld von Zwölfoxing in Nieder-Österreich," *Praehistorische Forschungen* 7: 1-159. T.p. 106. As in preceding study. Estimates also of children aged 0-8.

Lipták, P. 1949. "Étude anthropologique du cimetière avare d'Aporkaiurbopuszta (commune de Bugyi)," *Annales Historico-Nationalis,* pars anthropologica, 42: 232-259 5-2. J:2,1. A:1,2. M:5,3. S:0,2. ?:8,8.

———. 1955. "Récherches anthropologiques sur les ossements avares des environs d'Üllo." *Acta Archaeologica Academiae Scientiarum Hungaricae* 6: 231-316. 5-2. T.p. 232. I:2. II:7. J:4,4,2. A:13,28,2. M:23,27,2. S:0,2,2.

———. 1956. "Contributions à anthropologie des temps avars de la région de Kiskoros," *Crania Hungarica* 1: 47-52. 5-2. J:2. A:5,2. M:2,1.

————. 1957a. "Awaren und Magyaren in Donau-Theiss Zwischenstromgebiet (zur Anthropologie des VII-XIII Jahrhunderts)," *Acta Archaeologica Academiae Scientiarum Hungaricae* 8: 199-268. Three parts 1: Avarenzeit vii-ix c.p. 202. I:3,4 II:7,8. J:5. I-II:45. AMS: 191, 194, 5. 2: Landnahmzeit x c. I-II: 11. AMS: 36,26, 3. 3: Arpadenzeit. I-II:27. AMS: 82,59.

————. 1957. b. Same. p. 206. for Csatalja. 1951-1953. 5-2. I:2. II:8. J:3. A:10,27.1. M:8,10,1. S:1,1.

————. 1961. "Germanische Skelettreste von Hács-Béndekpuszta aus dem 5 Jht. u,z." *Acta Archaeologica Academiae Scientiarum Hungaricae* 13: 231-246. 5-1. I-II-J:3. AMS: 2,10,1.

————. 1963. "Anthropologie der awarenzeitlichen Bevölkerung von Budapest, I," *Budapest Régiségei* 20: 327-334. J:4. A:2,3. M:4. Hungarian with German summary.

————. & Antonia Marcsik. 1965. "Das anthropologisches Material sus Gräberfeldes Téglás-Angolkert vom Mittelalter aus dem XI-XIV Jahrhundert," *A Debreceni déri Múzeum Évkönyve* 48: 69-96. 5-4. I:6. II:6. J:5. A:6,5. M:8,6,1. S:1.0.

————. 1966-67. "Recherches anthropologiques sur le ossement de la cimetière Nádud-var-Töröklaponyag des x-xi siècles," *A. Debreceni déri Múzeum Évkönyve* 49: 179-195. 5-4. I:3, II:4. J:2. A:6,9. M:8,6. Hungarian with French summary.

————. & G. Farkas. 1962. "Anthropological Analysis of the Arpadian Age Population of Orozháza-Rákóczitelep," *Acta Biologica* N. S. 8: 221-232. 5-4. T.p. 222. I:1. II:15. J:11. A:34,48,4. M:46,26. S:13,4.

————. 1974. "Anthropological Analysis of the Avar-period Population of Szakszärd-Palánkpuszta," *Acta Biologica* 20: 200-205. 5-2. T.p. 200. I:5. II:10. J:1,1,10. A:14,32,2. M:31,19,4. S:3,4.

————. & A. Marcsik. 1966. "Die anthropologische Untersuchung des Gräberfeldes Szeged-Kindomb aus der Awarenperiode," *Anthropológiai Kozlemények* 10: 13-55. 5-2. T.p. 14. I:1. II:22. J:10. A:15,45. M:27,23. S: 20,9. ?:5,8.

————. & G. Farkas. 1967a. "Anthropological Examination of the Arpadian Population of Szatymax (10th and 12th centuries)," *Acta Biologica* 13: 71-119. 5-4. I:15. II:38. J:7. A:28,31. M:45,24,1. S:20,7,1. ?:21,25,21.

————. & G. Farkas. 1967b. "Anthropologische Untersuchung an den aus der Urzeit und aus den 10-12 Jahrhundert stammenden Skelettmaterial des Gräberfeldes Békés-Povádzug," *Anthropológiai Közlemenyek* 11: 127-163. 5-4. T.p. 128. I:44. II:21. J:7. A:8,23,. M:14,11. S:8,6. ?:1,,1.

————. & K. Vamus. 1969. "Anthropologische Untersuchung des Skelettmaterials des Awarenzeitliche Gräberfeldes von Fehertó A," *Anthropologiai Kozlemenyek* 13: 3-30. 5-2. T.p.5. II:18. J:7. A:6,25. M:67,38. S:16,24. ? 7:0,1. Perhaps correct classification. A:40,44. M:41,31. S:2,12. Hungarian with German summary.

————. & A. Marcsik. 1970. "Skelettreste von Szarvas-Kákapuszta-Kettöshalom," *A Móra Ferenc Múzeum Évkönyve* 1970: 45-57. 5-4. T.46. I:4. II:3. J:8,4. A:84. M:8,3. S:0,2.

————. & V. Imre. 1971-1972. "Characterizierung des anthropologischen Materials des Awarischen Gräberfeldes von Kunszállas," *A Móra Ferenc Múzeum Évkönyve* 1971-2: 71-84. 5-3 (late Avar). SE. T.p. 72. I:8. II:9 J:0, 4,1. A:5,10. M:6,3. S:0,3.

————. & A. Marcsik. 1971. "Anthropological Investigation of the Cemeteries excavated at Szarvas," *Acta Biologica*, Szeged 17: 209-221. 5-4. EW. II:2 A:1,1,1. M:5,1. ?:2. T.p. 210.

————. & A. Marcsik. 1975. "Skeletal Remains of the Avar Period in a 10th Century Cemetery, excavated at Rakóczifalva-Kastélydomb near Szelnook," *Acta Biologica* 21: 165-179. 5-3. I:1. II:6. J:0,1, A:3,9. M:14,8. S:1,0.

————. & A. Marcsik. 1976. "Anthropologische Characteristik der Skelettreste aus dem Awarischen Gräberfeld bei Madaras-Téglavetö," *Cumania* 4: 115-140. 5-2.T.p. 116. I:11. II:11. J:0,2,6. A:13,27. M:11,6. S:0,1.

Liptakowá, Zora. 1963. "Slawisches Gräberfeld aus dem x.-xi. Jahrhundert in Úlany nad Žitavou," *Slovenská Archeológia* 11: 223-236. 6-4. 6-4. EW. P.p. 223. I-II-J. 7. AMS: 26. Slovak with German summary.

Lorencova, Anna. 1960. "Die Brandgräber von Staré Břeclav," *Sborník prací filisofické fakulty brněnské university* 10: 83-95. 6-3. I:5. II:4. J:0,1. AA:a,4,2. M:4,1.1. S:1,2. Czech with German summary.

Losinski, W. 1958. "Ein frühmittelalterliches Gräberfeld in Cewlino, kr. Koszalin," *Materialy Zachodnio-Pomorske* 4: 251-284. 8-4. ?:8,5,2. Polish with German summary.

Lotterhof, Edith. 1968. "Anthropological Investigation of the Skeletal Material of a Cemetery at Baja-Pétö from the xi-xvi Centuries," *Acta Biologica* (Szeged) 14: 81-89. 5-5.T.p. 81. I;15. II:29. J:18. A:34,21. M:7,2. S:1,3.

———. 1971. "Anthropological Investigation of the Skeletal Material from the Cemetery of Roszke-Koszo," *Acta Biologica* 7: 221-229. 5-1. T.p. 223. I:13. II:6. J:5. A:10,14. M:16,9. S:1,0.

———. 1973. "The Anthropological Investigation of the Tenth Century Population of Nagytarcsa," *Anthropologia Hungarica* 12: 41-62. T.p. 55. I:3. II:1. J:1. A:5,10. M:2,5.

———. 1974. "Some Data to the Anthropology of the Population of North Plains in the Arpadian Age," *Anthropologia Hungarica* 13: 87-127. 5-3. T.2. I:1. II:4. J:0,2,1. A:30,24. M:25,19. S:1,0.

Macalister, R.A.S. 1935. "The excavation of Kiltera, co. Waterford," *Proceedings of the Royal Irish Academy* 43 C: 15-16. 4-3. II:1. J:1. A:2.1. M:3,0,4, S:2,1 ?:3,3. Data by C.P. Martin.

Malá, Helena. 1960. "Beitrag zur Anthropologie der Slawen aus den X-Xl Jht. von Zobor un Mlynarka bei Nitra." *Slovenska Archeologia* 8: 231-262. 5-4. I:13. II:12. J:5. A:4,14,1. M:16,8,3. S:8,2. ?:1,0,2.

———. 1961. "Der morphologische Character des Volkes aus dem 10. und 11. Jht. aus den Gräberfelden von Zobor und Mlynarce bei nitra," *Studijne Zvesti.* AUSAV 4: pp. 207-290. 5-4. I:16. II:5. J:2,4. A:12,5. M:11,9. S:5,1,1. ?:2,0,4. Czech with German summary.

———. 1965. "Anthropologische Analyse von Skelettresten aus dem slawisch-awarischen Gräberfeld in Holiare," *Slovenská Archeólogia* 13: 432-451. 5-3. T.p. 424. I:54. II:40. J:3,28,24. A:38,88,17. M:39,36,7. S:13,21,4. Revised to standard classification.

———. & H. Karlové. 1972. "Age Differentiation in some Slavonic Burial-Places in southern Slovakia," *Anthropologie*, Brno. 1: 13-18. P. 16 for Stefanikovce. 5-3. P.p. 15. I:2. II:2. J:0,2. A:1,2. M:1,1,1. Data for Holiare given in Mala 1965, Hungarian with English summary.

Malan, M. 1952. "Zur Anthropologie des langobardischen Gräberfeldes in Várpolata," *Annales Historico-Naturales Musei Nationalis Hungarici* 44: 257-275. J:0,1. A:5,3. M:0,2.

Malinowska, H. 1969. "Archäologische Froschungen auf dem Gräberfeld in Cedynia in den Jahren 1967-1969," *Materialy Zachodniopomorskie* 15: 111-159. 8-1. I:75,7. II:24,4. J:28,13. A:54,21. M:71,4. S:2,?:38,0. Odd distribution. Data also in *Zeitschrift für Archäologie* 7 (1973): pp. 13-23.

———. 1973. "Einige Probleme anthropologischen Untersuching von Leichenbrand-Gestätten in West Pommern in Hinblick auf allgemein-polonischen Unterlagen," *Zeitschrift für Archäologie* 7: 13-23. 8-3? I:75,7. II:24,4. J:28,13. A:54,21. M:71,4. S:2,0. ?:38.

Malinówska-Lazarczyk, H. & J. Budzynska. 1975. "Mittelalterliches und neuzeitliches Gräberfeld in Cedynia. kr. Clujna, in lichte archäologischen Forschungen," *Materialy Zachodniopomorske* 21: 1-39. 8-5. II:3,0. A:5,6. M:5,6. S:0,1 Hungarian with German summary.

Marciniak, J. 1960a. "An Early Medieval Settlement Center at Bazar Novy in Maków Mazowiecki district," *Materialy Wczesnosredniowieczne* 5: 99-140. 8-4. I-II-J:16 AMS:31,28. Polish with English summary.

———. 1960b. "Early Mediaeval Inhumation Burials at Strzemierzyce Wielke, the Bedzin District," *Materialy Wczesnosredniowieczny* 5: 141-185. 8-4. EW and ESE. AMS:44,20. Polish with English summary.

Marcsik, Antonia 1967. "Analysis of the Anthropological Material of the 10-11 Century Cemetery in Alderö-Macsáros," *Acta Biologica. Acta U. Szegediensis* 13: 163-177. 5-3. EW. I:4. II:4. J:3. A:2,6. M:7,1. S:1,1. Hungarian with English summary.

———. 1970. "Anthropological Investigation of the Cemetery at Kardoskút-Fehértó from the 11-12 Centuries," *Acta Biologica* 16: 155-162. 5-4. I:4. II:16. J:21. A:44,66. M:90,52. S:2,1. ?:1,0. Hungarian with English summary.

———. 1971. "Anthropological Investigation of a Cemetery at Mélykut from the Avar Period," *Anthropologiai Kozlemnyek* 15: 87-95. 5-2. T.p.88. I:2. II:4. J:2,3. A:8,11. M:8,8.

———. 1972. "Data to the Paleoanthropology of the Environs of Nagybaracska," *Acta Biologica* 18: 269-277. 5-4. I:1. II:1. J:0,4. A:4,0. M:1,2. ?:1.

Martin, Rudolf. 1914. *Lehrbuch der Anthropologie in systematischer Darstellung* (Jena). Third edition under names of Martin and K. Saller published in Munich 1959-1964.

McLoughlin, E.P. 1950. *Report on the Anatomical Investigation of the Skeletal Remains — at Castelknoch* (Dublin). 3-3. T.p. vi.I:46. II:18. J:20. A:153. M:68. S:5. Revised.

Meaney, A.L. 1964. *A Gazetteer of Early English Burial Sites* (London). One specific site: Stratford-Alveston, p. 263. 3-2. I-II-J: 7. AMS:29,28.

_____. & S.C. Hawkins. 1970. "Two Anglo-Saxon Cemeteries at Winnall, Winchester, Hampshire," *Society for Medieval Archaeology, Monograph Series*, no. 4. Winnall I. 3-2. I-II: 0,2,7. J:2,2. A:5,7. M:8,5. S:1,3. ?:1,1. Winnall II. 3-2.EW. P.p.8. T.p. 20. I:5. II:0,2,3. J:1,2.1. A:6,10. M:7,4. S:1,2. ?:1,0. 7c.

Megay, G. 1963. "Das landnahmezeitliche ungarische Gräberfeld von Mozözombor-Bálványdomb," *A. Herman Ottó Múzeum Evkönyve* 3: 37-53. 5-3. EW AMS:6,5,1. Hungarian with German summary.

Méroc, L. & G. Fouet. 1961. "Le cimetière mérovingien de Saint-Peyre à Félines-Minervois (Hérault)," *Gallia* 19: 191-200. 2-1. ESE. I:4. II:3. J:1. AMS:13.

Méry, A. 1968. "Le cimetière mérovingien de Blossangeaux (Doubs)," *Annales litteraires de l'Université de Besançon* 94. 2-2. SE. Pl.p.14. I:20. II:16. J:1,8,1. A:15,11. M:17,12. S:1,1. ?:13,18,1.

Meyers, A. 1969. "Frühgeschichtliche Gräber aus Tullü, NÖ," *Archaeologia Austriaca* 45: 59-76. 6-2. EW. I:2. II:1. A:1. ?:4.

Miskiewicz, B. 1957. "Crania Lithuanian, Polish and Ruthenian. Graves from the Bronze and Early Middle Ages," *Materialy i Prace Antropologiczne* no. 25. (Wroclaw). Two sets of small cemeteries. Zwirble and Poszuswie. 8-3. J:1,1. A:0,3. M:7,2. Turow, Bazar Novy and Salabiacizki. 8-4. J:2. A:2,1. M:11,12. Perhaps should be revised to A:77. M:66. Polish with English summary.

_____. 1967. "Die mittelalterliche Bevölkerung auf Opole (xiii-xiv Jht) im lichte anthropologischer Untersuchungen," *Materialy i Prace Antrologiczne* no. 74. 199-216. 8-4. I:9. II:6. J:1,0. A:13,8. M:8,1. Polish with German summary.

_____. 1968. "Anthropologische Analyse der mittelalterlichen Bevölkerung aus Pawlow, kr. Trzebnicá (xv-xvi Jht.)," *Materialy i Prace Antropologiczne* 76: 197-218. 8-5. I:13. II:3. J:0,3. A:20,14. M:13,10. Polish with German summary.

_____. 1969. "Die anthropologische Struktur der mittelalterlichen Bevölkerung der Stadt Genf (xv Jht)," *Materialy i Prace Antropologiczne* 78: 355-374. 6-5. J:0,1,1. A:58,39. M:73,19. S:7.

_____. 1973. "Die anthropolgische Struktur der mittelalterliche Bevölkerung der Stadt Gubin, kr. Krosno Rodrzanskie (xiii-x v Jht)," *Materialy i Prace Antropologiczne* no. 86, 157-168. 8-5. II:1 J:2. A:31,19. M:32, 19. S:3,1. Original: A:21,15, AM:10,4. M:32,19. MS:3,1.

Mitscha-Märaheim, H. 1955. "Völkerwanderungszeitliche Gräber aus Mannersdorf aus Leithagebirge, N.O.," *Archaeologia Austriaca* 22: 45-53. 6-3. SE. Kleinkind:18 Kind:15. Jugend:2. Erwachsen 26.

Modrzewska, K. 1958. "Life Expectancy of Early Medieval Inhabitants of Podlachia," *Czlowick w Czasie i Przestrzeni* 1:65-72. 8-3. I:23. II:1,1,8. J:3,12. A:9,12. M:16,4. S:7,7,2. Revised from five year age groups. Polish with English summary.

Møller-Christensen, V. 1958. *Bøgen om Aebelholt Kloster* (Copenhagen). Three cemeteries. Kirke. 7-4. I-II:21. J:0,2,3. A:34,13,10. M:45,13,14. S:8,2,4. Fratergard. 7-4. I-II:40. J:5,20,4. A:56,53,33. M:90,69,31. S:17,19,8. Kirkegard. 7-5. I-II:74. J:3,0. A:18,7,1. M:26,10,5. S:1,1.

Morawski, W & E. Zaitz. 1977. "Nécropole à inhumation du Moyen-Age à Cracovie-Zekrzówek," *Materialy Archeologiczne* 17: 53-170. 8-4. ENE. T.pp. 64-68. M.p. 58. I:4. II:9. J:1. A:5,14,3. M:16,6. S:5,4,1. ?:0,1,5. Polish with French summary.

Moss-Eccardt, J. 1971. "The Anglo-Saxon Cemetery at Blackhorse Road, Letchworth," *Hertfordshire and Bedfordshire Arch. Jour.* 6: 27. 3-2. ENE.I:1: II:1. A:4,0. M:2.2.

Mossler, Gertrud. 1975. "Das awarenzeitliche Gräberfeld von Wien-Lessing," *Mitteilungen der anthropologischen Gesellschaft von Wien* 105: 79-95. 6-2. ESE T.n.iv. I:3. II:2. J:1,0,2. A:3,2. M:1,0. S:1. ?:1,1.

Müller, C. 1961. "Das anthropologische Material zur Bevölkerungsgeschichte Obermöllerns," *Praehistorische Zeitschrift* 39: 115-142. 4-2. I:7. II:2,0,1. J:1,2. A:7,3,2. M:2,3,1. S:1. ?:1,1.

_____. 1963. in E. Reinbacher, "Die alteste Baugeschichte der Nikolaikirche in Alt-Berlin," Berlin, Deutsche Akademie der Wissenschaften zu Berlin, *Schriften der Sektion für Vorund Frühgeschichte*, 15: 93-109. 4-4. I:3. II:1. J:0,1. A:5,2. M:4,0. ?:0,1.

Mols, Roger, S. J. 1954, 1955, 1956. *Introduction à la démographie historique des villes d'Europe du xiv au xviii° siècle* (Louvain).

Musty, J. & J.F.D. Stratton. 1954. "A Saxon Cemetery at Winterbourne Gunner, near Salisbury," *The Wiltshire Archaeological and Natural History Magazine* 59: 86-109. 3-2. EW. I:1. II:1. A:4,4.

Necrasov see p. 263.

Nemeskéri, J. 1949. "Anthropological Examination of the Finds Discovered in the Precincts of Csepel, dating from the Early Period of the Arpad Dynasty," *Archaeolgiai Ertesito* 76: 91-99. 5-3. NE. T.p. 95. II:1. J:0,2. M:6,1. S:1,0. Hungarian with English summary.

————. 1950. "Examination of the Anthropological Finds found in the Graves of the Eleventh Century in the Municipal Gallery Garden (Budapest)," *Budapest Régisegei* 15: 403-415. 5-4. J:0,1. A:2,0. M:5,2. Hungarian with English summary.

————. 1952a. "Anthropologische Untersuchung der Skelettfunde von Alsónémedi," *Acta Archaeologica Academiae Scientiarum Hungaricae* 1: 55-72. 5-4 (9-10c). I:13. II:2. J:0,1, A:8,2,2. M:5,2. S:2,0. ?:6. Hungarian with German summary.

————. 1955. "Étude anthropologique des squelettes du clan princier avare découvertes en cimetière de Kiskorös-Vágóhid," *Archaeologia Hungarica* 34: 189-210. 5-2. P.p. 190. II;1.A:1,1. M:2,8.

————. 1956a. "La population de Csakvar dans l'epoch romaine tardive," *Crania Hungarica* 1: 3-12. 5-1 J:0,1. A:2,4. M:4,2 S:3,0.

————. 1963. "Die spätmittelalterliche Bevölkerung von Fonyód," *Anthropologia Hungarica* 6: 131-137. 5-4. T. 133. I;36. II:16. J:5,2.1. A:26,18. M:33,24. S:4,2.

————. & D. Botezatu. 1964. "Étude anthropologique des squelettes de Doina datant au xiiie-xive siècles," *Annuaire Roumain d'Anthropologie* 1: 29-37. 5-4. I:11. II:4. J:1. A:10. M:7. ?:12,7.

————. D. Botezatu, & C. Teodorescu. 1967. "Contributie la studial Antropologic al populariei feudale timpurii din Romania: seria de la Izvoral (R. Giurgin) datiud diu secolol al vii-lea E-N," *Studii si cercetari de antropologie* 4: 3-24. 5-3. T.p.8. I:26. II:5. J:5,3. A:8,18,1. M:25,32. S:1,1.

————. V. Ursache, D. Botezatu & G. Stefanescu. 1969. "Sur les restes osseux trouvés dans les cimetièrelov birituel de Gabara-Moldoveni et Sabaoan I (dept. de Neaml)" *Studii si cercetari de antropologie* 6: 7-15. 5-1. Gabora: 1:22. II:10. Sabaoani: I:45. II:6. A:12. M:9. ?:1. Ages for children are given to the year.

————. & G. Acsádi. 11952b. "Les materiaux de cimetière de Kerpuszti (xi siècle) vue à la lumière de le démographie historique," *Archaeologiai Ertesito* 79: 134-147. 5-4. Table by five year periods p. 145: and by years of childhood. I:125. II:0,1.28. J:5,9,3. A:71,74,4. M:45,34,1. S:1. ?:121,119. Hungarian with French summary.

————. P. Lipták, and B. Szöke. 1953. "Le cimetière du xie siècle de Kérpuszta," *Acta Archeologica Academiae Scientiarum Hungaricae* 3: 305-370. 5-4. M. 280. I:19. II:9. J:11. A:62. M:129. S:1.

————. & G. Gaspardy. 1954. "Remarques concernant les rapports anthropologiques — de Üllö et de Eger," *Annales Historico-Naturales Musei Nationalis Hungarici* 46: 485-527. T.p. 53. for both. I-II:3. J:2,1. A:10,7. M:6,3. S:1,0. Hungarian with French summary.

————. M. Deak, & A. Mohacs. 1956b. (No western summary-Cselei). *Archaeologiai Ertesito* 83: 52-65. 5-5. T.p. 53. I:13. II:0,19. J:4,4. A:16,12,2. M:17,8,8. S:1,0. ?:11,7.

————. K. Éry, A. Kralavansary, & L. Harsányi. 1961. "Data to the Reconstruction of the Population of an 11c Cemetery, Gava Market, a Methodological Study." *Crania Hungarica* 4: 2-63. 5-4. T.p.46. I:4,5. II:0,1 J:2,1 A:3,2. M:6,4. S:2,1. ?:2,0. See second list on p. 46.

————. & L. Harsányi. 1966. "Prospettive d'una antropologia storica condotta con metodi biologici," *Archivio per antropologia e l'etymologia* 96: 97-104.

Nenquin, J.A.E. 1953. "La nécropolle de Furfooz" (Bruges, *Dissertationes Acheologicae Gandenses* vol.1). 2-1 (4c). P.p. 22. I-II:1. J:1,5,1. A: 3,2,2. M:4,1 S:0,1,4.

Neuffer, E. M. 1972. "Die Reihengräberfriedhof von Donzdorf, kr. Göppingen," *Forschungen und Berichte zur Vor- und Frühgeschichte in Baden-Würtemburg*, Landesdenkmalamt Baden-Würtemberg. 4-3. EW. I:1,1,6. II:2,1. J:0,1,2. A:7,21,4. M:12,8,2. S:1,0.?:5,5,2.

Neuffer-Müller, Christine & H. Ament. 1973. "Das fränkische Gräberfeld um Rübenach," *Germanische Denkmaler der Volkerwander ungszeit* ser. B. 7.

Nicolescu-Plopsor, D. 1972a. "La nécropole Feodale d'Ipotesti (de. d'Olt)," *Apulum* 10: 235-257. 5-5. NE. T.p. 252. M.p. 238. I:2.J:0,5. A:2,3,2. M:1,0.

————. & Wanda Wolski, 1971. "Les tombes à incineration de la nécropole du ivme siècle à Mogosani," *Studii si cercetari de antropologie* 8: 157-163. 5-1. I:1,0. II:2,0. J:0,1. A:1,1. M:1,0.

————. & D. Wolski. 1972b. "Nécropole de secol iv e.n.din Muntonia," *Studii si cercetari de Antropologie* 9: 109-118. 5-1. (4c). I:66. II:34. J:23. A:167. S:2.

256   ANCIENT & MEDIEVAL POPULATION CONTROL

Noonan J. T. 1965. *Contraception. A History of the Treatment by the Catholic Theologians and Canonists* (Cambridge, Mass.)

Nowak, M. & B. Schmidt. 1966. "Ein thüringesches Gräberfeld des 6. Jahrhunderts bei Altweddington, kr. Wanzleben," *Jahreschrift für mitteldeutsche Vorgeschichte* 50: 287-292. 4-1. ENE. J:0,1. A:2,1. M:1,1.

Olmerova, H. 1959. "Das slawische Gräberfeld in Radětice bei Příbram," *Památky archeologické* 50: 227-245. 6-3. EW. I-II-J: 7. AMS: 24. Czech with German summary.

Palol, P. de. 1963. "Excavaciones en la nécropolis de San Juan de Bañes (Palencia)," *Excavaciones Arqueologicas en España*, no. 32: 1-24. 1-3. I-II:7. J:4. AMS:22.

Paret, O. 1935-1938. "Das alamannische Gräberfeld von Sernäre, gem. Ellington." *Fundberichte aus Schwaben* 9: 136-139. 4-2. ESE. I-II-J: 5. AMS:82,62,81.

Parsons, F.G. 1908. "Report on the Hythe Crania," *Journal of the Royal Anthropological Institute* 38: 419-450. 3-5. Museum data. I-II-J:34. AMS:320,220.

Passarello, P. & G. Alciati. 1968."Su una collezione dei cranii antichi della Sicilia orientale," *Rivista de antropologia* 56: 81-96. (Michelica). I:1. II:0,1 J:0,2. A:4,1. M:1,0. S:1,2.

Pástor, J. 1955. (Somatore — no western summary-Slovak). *Slovenská Archeológia* 3: 276-285. 6-4. I-II-J: 11. AMS: 11.8,11.

Paul, K-P. 1979. "Somatlogische Untersuchungen des Slawischen Körpergräberfelds vom Spandauer Burgwall, Berlin," *Anthropologisches Anzeiger* 37: 68-79. 4-4. J:2,2. A:4,9. M:13,3. S:2,0. Good on teeth.

Paulsen, P. 1967. "Alamannische Adelsgräber von Niederstützingen (kr. Hildenheim)," *Veröffentlichen des Statischen Amtes für Denkmalpflege*, Stuttgart 12, pt. 2. by N. Creel, 27-32. 4-2. I:1,1. II:1. J:1,0. A:4,0,2. M:1,0,2.

Pavelcik, J. 1949. "Material des os trouvé dans les fouilles à Staré Město in 1948," *Zprávy Anthropologické Spolecnosti* 3-4: 24-31. 6-3. I:3,14,24. II:2,4,6. J:0,1,1. A:4,2. M:5,2. S:8,5. ?:4,3,1. Czech with German summary.

———. 1959. "Das Knockenmaterial aus dem altmahrischen Gräberfelde in Veletiny bei Uberský Brod," *Anthropologie. Acta Facultatis Rerum Naturialium Universitatis Comenianae* 3: 237-246. 6-3. I-II-J:3. AMS: 6,7,3.

Peake, H., & E. A. Hooten. 1915. "Saxon Graveyard at East Shelford, Berks.," *Bulletin of the Royal Anthropological Society* 45: 92-130. 5-1 (5c). ENE. 1:1,0,4. II:1,0. J:2,1. A:4,5. M:2,5. S:1,1.

Perez de Barradas. J. 1933. "Excavaciones en la necropolis Visigoda de Vega del Mar (San Pedro Alcantara, Malaga)," *Junta Superior el Tesoro Artistico, Memoria* no. 128. I-1. I-II:10. J:1. AMS: 14,13.

Picard, C. 1963. (Cortrat, Loiret) *Gallia* 21: 397-403. 2-11 NS. I-11:6. J:0,1. A:0,4. M:2,0. ?:4.

Pieczynski. Z. 1959. "Le cimetière du haut moyen-age de Strzekno, dist de Mogilno," *Przeglad Archeologiczny* 11: 80-87. 8-4. I-II:3. J:1. A:1,3. M:1,4. ?:5. Polish with French summary.

Piepers, W. 1963. "Ein fränkisches Gräberfeld bei Lamersdorf, kr. Düren," *Bonner Jahrbücher* 1963: 424-468. 4-3. EW. I-II-J: 17. AMS: 11,13.

Pilaric, Georgina. 1968. "Phenotypical Characteristics of the Skulls of Bijelo Brdo from Early Middle Ages," *Arheoloski Radovi i Rásprave* 6: 263-291. 5-2? I:1,1. II:2,1. J:1,1. A:1,0. M:2,1. S:1. Serbian with English summary.

Pointek, J. 1974. "Early Medieval Cemetery in Brzeg Glogowski, district Glogow," *Przeglad Anthropologiczny* 40: 281-289. 8-3. ENE. P.p. 282. I:10. II:3. A:17,10. M:6,5. S:1,0. Revised from Martin scale. Polish with English summary.

Popovici, Ioana. 1966. "Récherches anthropologiques sur la population valague a l'époque féodale," *Annuaire Roumain d'Anthropologie* 3: 9-22. Several cemeteries. Dinogetia: 5-4. J:3. A:10. S:5. Verbicio. 5-4. I:1.II:2. J:4. A:25. M:17. S:4. Strautesi-Bucurest (1).5-4. I:6.II:5. J:1. A:12. II:14. J:2. A:36. M:21. S:5.Turnu-Severin. 5-4. A:42. M:23. S:8. Doina. I:11. II:4. J:1. A:10. M:7.

———. 1967. Same as Strautesi-Bucuresti (2), Popvici 1966 except: ages 18-30:6,11; 30-40:12,7; 40-50:10,4; 50-60;5,2;60:2,2.

———. 1968. "Consideratii antropologice asupra unor schelete din cimitirul din secolulual xiv-lea de Cunhea-Maramures," *Studii si cercetari de antropologie* 5: 33-37. 5-4. I:1. II:2. J:1,2. A:3,0. M:3,1.

———. 1970. "Données anthropologiques concernant la population d'une petite communauté villageoise (cimetière I-Straulesti-Maicanesti, xiv-xv siecles)," *Annuaire Roumain d'Anthropologie* 7: 15-20. 5-5. I:17. II:10. J:0,2,1. A:8,8,2. M:11,3. ?:2. In ten years age periods.

———. 1972. "Nouvelles données anthropologiques concernant le population di Dinogetia (x-xi siècles)," *Annuaire Roumain d'Anthropologie* 9: 51-60. 5-4. I:3. II:3. A:8,10. M:20,6,1. S:7,3,1.

Poulik, J. 1959. "The Latest Archaeological Discoveries from the Period of the Great Moravian Empire," *Historica* 1: 7-70.

———. 1963. *Zwei Grossmärische Rotunden in Mikulčice* (Prague, Monumenta Archaeologica XII), 6-3. I:69. II:15. J:13. A.8,14,1. M:26,18,3. Czech with German summary.

Preuschoff, H. & H. Schneider. 1969. "Die Skelettreste aus der evangelische Pfarrkirche St. Veit zu Unterregenbach," *Anthropologie*, Brno 7: 55-71. T.p. 57. 1st cemetery. 9-11c. T.p. 57 1:4. II:2. J:0,1 A:1,2. M:8,3. 2nd cemetery. 12-15 c. I:2. II:1. A:0,1. M:2,1. S:2,0.

Prevosti, Maria & Antonio. 1951. "Restos humanos procedentes de una necropolis judaica de Montjuich (Barcelona)," *Trabajos del Instituto Bernadino de Sahagun* 12: 65-148. 1-5. EW. I-II:15. J:4,1,7. A:21,10. M:21,5,2. S:21,5,1. S:4,1.

Prominska, E. 1963. "Bone remains of Early Medieval Cremation Graves at Zaswirtz, Swir Region in the BSSR," *Rocznik Bialosticki* 4: 397-404. 5-1. I-II-J:1. A:0,2. M:1,0. ?:2,1. Polish with English summary.

Raddatz, K. 1962. "Kaiserliche Korpergräbe von Heiligenhafen, kr. Oldenburg," *Offa* 19: 91-128. 4-1. II:1. J:1.A:2. M:1.

Rahtz, P. A. 1960. (Excavations at Sewerby, Suffolk). *Medieval Archaeology* 4: 137. 3-2. I-II-J:9. AMS: 20,20.

Ranke, J. 1897. "Frühmittelalterliche Schädel und Gebeine aus Lindau," *Sitzungsberichte der K. bayerischen Akademie der Wissenschaften*, math-phys. 27: 1-192. 4-4. I-II:1. A:1,4. M:5,2. S:2,0.

Rauhut,L. & L. Dlugopolska. 1972. " An Early Mediaeval Cemetery with Stone Setting at Laczyno Stare, Przasnysz District," *Wiadomosci Archeologiczne* 37: 320-393. 8-4. ENE. I:2. II:1. J:1,4. A:7.7 M:12,2. ?:9,13. Revised from Martin scale: A:13,8. M:8,1. Polish with English summary.

———. 1973. "Early Mediaeval Graves in Stone Setting at Tańsk-Przedbory, Przasnysz District," *Wiadomosci Archeologiczne* 38: 383-441. 8-4. SE. I-5. II:0,1,3. J:1,0. A:2,6.. M:6,1. S:1,1,1. Polish with English summary.

Razi, Zvi. 1980. *Life, Marriage and Death in a Medieval Parish: Economy, Society and Demography in Halesowen. 1270-1400* (Cambridge, Cambridge University Press).

Redfield, A. 1970. "A New Aid to Aging Immature Skeletons: the Development of the Occipital Bone," *American Journal of Physical Anthropology* 33: 207-220. Mistihalj. 5-5. I:75. II:19. J:13. A:41,38. M:44,21. S:20,25. Very detailed data for ages.

Rempel, H. 1966. "Reihengräberfriedhöfe des 8. bis 11. Jahrhunderts aus Sachsen-Anhalt, Sachsen und Thüringen," (Cambury-Jena). Deutsche Akademie der Wissenschaften, Berlin *Schriften der Sektion für Vor- und Frühgeschichte* 20: 1-194. 4-3. I:4. J:1,2. A:3,3. M:2,3. S:2.2. ?:0,1,3.

Reymond, M. 1911. "Le cimetière barbare de Saint-Sulpice (Vaud)," *Revue Charlemagne* 1: 81-86, 146-155,171-179. ENE. P.p. 179. I-II-J: 13. AMS:155.

Ried, H. A. 1909. "Skelette aus dem Reihengräberfelde zu Tettlham, bez. Laufen" *Beiträge zur Anthropologie und Urgeschichte Bayerns* 17:63-95. 4-2 or 3. I:3. J:0,1. A:3,3. M:4,1. S:2,0.

Rieth, A. 1939. Alemmannische Grabfunde von Bingen bei Sigmarinen (Hohenzollern)," *Mannus* 31: 126-140. 4-2. EW. Pl. 127. I:2. J:2,0. A:0,3.

Riquet, R. 1959. "Note anthropologique sur les crânes wisigothiques des Piñedes," *Gallia* 17: 171-177. 2-1. ESE. I:0,4,3. II:2. J:0,2. A:3,4. M:2,1. S:1,0. ?:6,7.

Rosinski, B. 1950-1951. "Anthropological Description of Human Bone Remains — in Radom," *Wiadomosci Archeologiczne* 17: 327-340. 8-4. I-II-J:2. AMS: 11,6,1. Polish with English summary.

Russell, J.C. 1948. *British Medieval Population* (Albuquerque).

———. 1958. "Late Ancient and Medieval Population," *Transactions of the American Philosophical Society* 48, 3, 152 pp.

———. 1969. "Population in Europe, 500-1500," *Fontana Economic History of Europe* 1: 25-70.

———. 1972. *Medieval Regions and their Cities* (Newton abbot and Bloomington, Indiana.)

———. 1973. "Medieval Cemetery Patterns: Plague and Nonplague," *Économies et Sociétés au Moyen Age. Mélanges offerts à Edouard Perroy* (Paris), 525-530.

———. 1980. "La expansion demográfica," *Historia Universal, Salvat* 4: 7-20; "La crisis demográfica, 4." 257-266.

Sagi, K. 1960. "Die spätromische Bevölkerung der Umgebung von Keszthely," *Acta Archaeologica Academiae Scientiarum Hungaricae* 12: 187-256. 5-1. ENE. I-II-J: 11. AMS:17,15.

―――. 1964. "Das Langobardische Gräberfeld von Vörs," *Acta Archaeologica Academiae Scientiarum Hungaricae* 16: 359-408. 5-2. EW. I-II-J:5. AMS: 8,28,4.

Sählstrom, K.E. & N-G. Gejvall. 1954. "Westgothische Urnenfriedhöfe aus Bänkalla und Stora Ro." *K. Vitterhets Historie oc Antikvitets Akademiens Handlingar* (Stockholm) *del* 89. 7-1. I:35. II:3. J:1. A:6,5,1. M:4,3 S:1,1. ?:7,2. Swedish with English summary.

Salamon, A. 1969. "Über die ethnischen und historischen Beziehungen des Gräberfeldes von Kornye (VI Jhr)," *Acta Archaeologica Academiae Scientiarum Hungaricae* 21: 273-297. 5-2. NE. I:0,1. II:1,2. J:1,1. A:10,4. M:3,1.

Salin, E. 1922. *Le cimetière de Lezéville* (Nancy). 2-2. NE. P.p. 1. I,II,J. 9. AMS:78,60,123. Sex determined by grave goods.

―――. 1949-1959. *Le civilization mérovingiens d'après les sépulture, les textes et le laboratoire* (Paris, 4 vols.).

Salin, E. & A. France-Lanord. 1946. "Traditions et art mérovingiens. Le cimetière di Varangeville (Meurth-et-Moselle)," *Gallia* 4: 199-245. 2-2. ESE. P.p. 202. AMS:11,11,12.

Salman, P. 1974. *Population et depopulation dans l'Empire romain* (Brussels).

Sarama, L. 1956. "The Early Mediaeval Graveyard at Samborzec," *Materialy i Prace Antropologicne*, Wroclaw, no. 7: 1-49. 8-4. J:0,1,1. A:0,5. M:18,19. S:4,1, Polish and English summary.

Sauter, M-R. 1950. "Crañes burgondes de Château de Curtilles (Vaud)," *Mélanges — Louis Bosset* (Lausanne), 47-56. 2-3. I:1. A:2,1.

Schaefer, U. 1955. "Demographiche Beobachtungen an der wikingerzeitlichen Bevölkerung von Haithabu," *Zeitschrift für Morphologie und Anthropologie* 47: 221-228. 7-3. T.p.222. I:7. II:11.J:2,1. A:20,18. M:15,7. S:2,1. ?:6,2.

Schaefer, U. 1961. "Anthropologische Untersuchung der Skelettreste aus den Voerden-Ork und den Grabhügein von Voerde-Emmelsum, Kr. Dinslaike," *Bonner Jahrbücher* 1961: 308-318. 4-1. T.p. 314. I·3. II:3. J:4 A:1,0,3. ?:3.

―――. 1963. "Anthropologische Untersuchung der Skelette von Haithabu," in *Das Ausgrabung in Haithabu*, 4 (Kiel, Institut für Ur- und Frühgeschichte in Kiel). 7-3. T.p. 213. I:7. II:11. J:2,1. A:20,18. M:15,7. S:2,1.

Schahl, A. 1938-1951. "Das alamannische Gräberfeld von Nusplingen, kr. Ballingen," *Fundberichte aus Schwaben* 12: 120-136. 4-2. I-II-J: 38. AMS: 54,56.

Scheuer, F. & Lablotier, 1914. *Feuilles de cimetière barbare de Bourgne* (Paris). 2-2- SE. I-II-J:16. AMS: 101.132,33.

Schmidt, Berthold, 1953. "Ein Reihengräberfeld des 6. Jahrhunderts bei Schönbeck (Elbe)," *Jahreschrift für mitteldeutsche Vorgeschichte* 37: pp. 281-311. 4-2. J:0,1.A:1,2. M:0,1. ?:7,4. Also 3 horses. The site is Rudelsdorf bei Schönebeck.

―――. 1964. "Das frühvölkerwanderungszeitliche Gräberfeld von Niemburg, Saalkreis," *Jahreschrift für mitteldeutsche Vorgeschichte* 48: 315-332. 4-1. (4-4c). I:3. I:3. J:5. A:0,1. S:1,0. ?:1,4,1.

―――. 1970. *Die späte Volkerwanderungszeit in Mitteldeutschland* (Berlin), south and east parts, Stösse, kr. Hohnemölsen, P. 20. 4-1. SE. II:1. A:2,3. M:2,3. Oberwersden, kr. Hohemölsen, p.1. 4-2. ENE. A:0,1. M:1,1. S:0,1.

―――. 1975. *Die späte Volkerwanderungszeit in Mitteldeutschland* (Berlin) south part. P. 101. Obermüllern, kr. Naumberg. 4-1. ESE. I:4. II:2. J:1,1,1. A:4,5. M:3,4. S:2,1. P. 109. Rathewitz, kr. Naumberg. 4-1. ENE. II:0,1,1. A:4,5. M:4,1. S:1,1. P. 144. Muhlhausen. 4-2 (6c). II:6.II:2. J:1,2. A:15,10. M5,3. ?:1,0,1.

―――. 1976. *Die späte Volkerwanderungszeit im Mitteldeutschland* (Berlin), north and east parts.

Schneiter, C. 1939. *Die Skelette aus den Alamannengräbern des Zurichsee- Limmat- und Glattales —* (Zurich), 14-16. 6-1. I:1,0. II:1. J:1,3. A:15,26. M:14,1. S:3,2. ?:2,0.

Schoppa, H. 1952. "Spätfrankische Gräber im Limburger Becker," *Nassauische Heimatblätter* 42: 16-42. 4-3, I-II-J:2. AMS:2,9,1.

―――. 1959. "Die fränkischen Friedhöfe von Weilbach, Maintaunuskreis," *Veröffentlichungen des Landesamts für kulturgeschichtliche Bodenaltertümer*, Wiesbaden: 1: 1-81. 4-2. P.P. 82. ENE. I-II-J:20. AMS:21,11. Cemetery. 1,NE. Cemetery II, EW.

Schott, L. 1960. "Zur Anthropologie des slawischen Gräberfeldes von Güstavel, kr. Sternburg," *Bodenkmalplege in Mecklinibur 1960:* 169-200. 4-5. I:1. II:1. J:1,2. A:7,3. M:3,3.

_____. 1961. "Zur Kräniologie von Leipziger Mönchen des ausgehended Mittelalters," *Arbeits- und Forschungensberichte zur sächsische Bodendenkmalplege* 9: 59-206. 4-5. I-II:1,0,2. J:1,1. A:24,5,19. M:13,4,1. S:1.

Schreiner, K.E. 1939, 1946. *Crania Norvegica* (Oslo) 7-1. AMS: 56,33.

_____. 1962. *Crania Norvegica* (Oslo). 7-1. AMS: 1049, 1009.

Schroter, E. 1965. "Neue slawische Reihengräberfelder im Kreise Barnburg," *Jahresschrift für mitteldeutsche Vorgeschichte* 49: 51-86. Two cemeteries. Sixdorf, pp. 52-67. 4-2. ENE. P.p. 57. I:10. II:6. J:5. AMS:31,16,2. Latforf. pp. 67-77. 4-3. ESE. P.p. 73. I-II-J: 38. AMS:31,16,2.

Schulz, Walter. 1933. "Das Fürstengrab und das Grabfeld von Hassleben," *Römisch-Germanische Forschungen* 1933, 4-1. I:1. II:4. J:0,1. A:1,1. M:3,1. ?:0,1.

Schwarz, K. 1958. "Neue archeologischen zeugnisse frühmittelalterlichen Landesaufbaues," *Bayerische Vorgeschichtsblätter* 23: 101-126. Pulling. 4-1. ESE. M.p. 103. I-II:13. J:3. A:4,1. M:5,0. S:1,0. ?:5,18,16.

Schwidetsky, Ilse. 1958. "In welchem Alter starben die Altkanier?" *Homo* 8: 98-102: 9: 31-33. I:3. A: 199,148. M:438, 195. S:118,81. Same title. *Homo* 8: 98-102.

_____. 1960. "Die Sterbalter bei den Alt-Kanariern," *El Museo Canario* 2: 377-383.

_____. 1963. "Die vorspanische Bevölkerung der Kanarischen Inseln,": *Homo*, beiheft 1. Teneriffa. I-4. A:118,44. M:132,50. S:50,26. Gran Canaria, 1-3. A:199,148. M:438, 195. S:118,81.

Sellman, H. 1905. "Die Frühgeschichliche Gräber von Ammarn, Landkreis Mühlhausen i, Th.," *Jahresschrift für die Vorgeschichte der sächsisch-Thuringen Länder* 4: 43-63. 4-1. A:0,1. M:1,1. S:1,1.

Seracsin, A. 1936. "Das langobardische Reiherngräberfeld von Schwechat bei Wien," *Mannus* 28: 521-533. 6-1. ESE. M.p. 523. II:0,1,1. A:0,2. M:1,3. S:2,1. ?:3,2.

Skerlj, B. 1952. "The Orientation of Graves in Some Mediaeval Necropoles of Slovenia," *Slovenska Akademija Znosti in Umetnost, Arholoski Vestnik* 3: 108-136. 5-3. P.p. 117. Bled, p. 116. 5-3. I:11. II:16. J:18. A:23. M:16. S:5. Slovenia, p. 117. 5-2 (7c). ESE. I:99. II:14. J:18. A:22. M:15. S:5.P.124. Bled, 5-3 (8-10c). I:14. II:13. J:2. A:11. M:39. S:6. P. 127, Pruj, 5-3 (10-11c). I:12. II:53. J:13. A:80. M:86. S:25. ?:5.

Sós, Agnes Cs. 1954. "Rapport préliminaire des fouilles exécutés autour de la chapelle de chateau de Zalavar," *Acta Archaeologica Academiae Scientiarum Hungarica* 4: 267-274. 5-?.I:13, II:22. ?:5. AMS: 57,54. ?:8.

_____. 1955. "Le deuxième cimetière avare d'Üllö," *Acta Archaeologica Academiae Scientiarum Hungarica* 6: 192,230. 5-3. SE. M: p.224. I-II:27. J:7. AMS: 43,67.

_____. 1961b. "Das frühmittelalterliche Gräberfeld von Keszthely-Fenékpuczta," *Acta Archaeologica Academiae Scientiarum Hungarica* 13: 247-305. 5-3. ENE P.p. 251. I:14. II:11. A:3,2. M:5,0. S:2,1. ?:8,4.

_____. 1961a. "Neue awarenzeitliche Funde auf der Csepel-Insel." *Archaeologiai Értesítö* 88: 32-51. 5-2. I:1. II:1. A:1,1. M:1,0. ?:2,6,8. Hungarian with German summary.

_____. 1963. "Die Ausgrabungen Géza Fehérs in Zalavár," *Archaeologia Hungarica* n.s. 41: 1-310. Three cemeteries. 9c. Army camp: pp. 42-48. 5-3. I:13. II:3. J:1,1. A:7,5,1. M:12,1. S:7,1.?:1. 10c civilian: pp. 68-85 5-3. I:43. II:23. J:6,2,4. A:30,20,21. M:49,28. S:20,10. 11c civilian: pp. 85-100. 5-4. I:9. II:4. J:1. A:14,7,17. M:15,9. S:6,4,1.

_____. 1966. "Das awarenzitliche Gräberfeld von Dunaszekcšo," *Folia Archaelogica* 18: 91-122. 5-3. E or ESE. I:0,1,10. II:3 J:4. A:16,8. M:13,7. S:5,4. Revised from Martin. Hungarian with German summary.

_____. 1971. "Arpadian Period Cemetery and Settlement at Csátalja," *Folia Archaeologica* 222: 105-140. 5-4. NE. I:11. II:8. J:0,1,2. A:21,9. M:8,7. S:1. ?:5,1,11. Hungarian with English summary.

Steffensen, J. 1943. "Skelettmaterial," in M. Stenberger. *Forntida Gardar i Island* (Copenhagen). Two cemeteries. Hedensk, 9c. 7-3. J:3. A:24. M:21. S:3. Seljastir. A.D. 1000-1050. 7-4. A:24. M:23. S:3. Danish.

Stenburger, M. 1961. "Das Gräberfeld bei Ihre im Kirchspiel Hellvi auf Gotland: der wikingerzeitliche Abschnitt," *Acta Archaeologica* (Copenhagen) 32: 1-134. 7-2.AMS: 34,32.

Stloukal, Milan. 1961. "Skelette aus dem slawisches Burgwall 'Hrudy' bei Sudoměřice," *Sbornik ceskoslovenskě spolecností archeologické* 1: 81-84. 6-4. I:2. II:3. A:1,4,1. M:7,2,1. S:1,0. Czech with German summary.

_____. 1962. "Mikulciče," *Fontes Archaeologicae Moravicae* 3: 1-100. 6-3 (9c). T.p. 83. I:152,138. II:47,46. J:32,34. A:71, 114. M:236, 125. S:17,7. Total 555, 464. Same data in *Homo* 1: 145-152, esp. p. 146.

———. 1963. 1963a. "Die erste Begräbnisstätte aus dem Burgwall 'Valy" bei Mikulcice-Anthropologische Analyse," *Památky Archaeologické* 54: 114-140. 6-3. I:0,7,45. II:2,2,-17. J:0,3,11. A:10,25. M:59,18. S:13,5. Czech with German summary. Also in *Archeologie Ertesito* 80: p. 115, as 1963b.

———. 1963c. "Velaticer Brandgräber aus Oblekovice," *Přehled Výskum'* Brno, 1964. 32-33. I-II-J: 17. A:35. M:17. Czech with German summary.

———. 1964a. "Die vierte Begräbnistätte aus dem Burgwall 'Valy' bei Mikulcice," *Památky Archeologické* 55: 479-505. 6-3. T.p. 479. I:5,3,61. II:2,1,12. J:3,1,9. A:7,16. M:38.21.3. S:2,6. Czech with German summary.

———. 1964b. "Untersuchung der skelette von den mittelalterlichen Gräberfelder in Moravicanech," *Preheled Výzkum*, Brno, 1964: 63-65. 6-3. I:5. II:2. J:2.A:3.5. M:4,3. S:2,0. Czech with German summary.

———. & H. Hanakova 1966. "Anthropologie der Slawen aus dem Gräberfeld in Nové Zámky," *Slovenská archeológia* 14: 167-204. 6-3. T.p. 180. I:69. II:28. J:2,9,14. A:28,47. M:70,36,6. S:2,4.

———. 1967. "Die zweite Begräbnisstätte aus dem burgwall 'Valy' bei Mikulcice," *Památky Archeologické* 58: 272-1399. 6-3. I:5,21,122. II:1,2,41. J:9,4,16. A:48,58,2. M:119,78,3. S:4,3. ?:14,8,2. Czech with German summary.

———. 1969. "Die dritte Begräbnissätte auf dem Burgwall 'Valy' bei Mikulcice," *Památky Archeologické* 60: 498-532. 6-3. I:0,2,25. II:0,1,11. J:0,6. A:5,16. M:17,12. ?:3. Czech with German summary.

———. 1973. "Anthropologische Material von der Grabung in Konurky, gem. Herspice, vyz. Výskum," *Přehled Výskum* 32: 1971. 94-98. 6-3. I-II-J:24. AMS: 59.

———. & H. Hanakova. 1974. "Anthropologische Erforschung des Gräberfeldes aus dem 7-8 Jahrhunderts in Zelovich," *Slovenská Archeológia* 20: 129-188. 6-2. (600-800). I:162. II:58. J:1,2,40. A:41,144,8. M:106,100,7 S:6,14. ?:13,27,65. Czech with German summary.

Stoll, H. 1939. *Die Alamannen Gräber von Hailfingen* (Berlin,Römisch-Germanische Kommission des Archäologische Institute des deutsches Reiches. 4-2 (late 7c). NE. P.p.8. I-II-J:19. AMS:23,24. G.D.V.4.

Szilagyi, J. 1961. "Beiträge zur Statistik der Sterblichkeit in den Westeuropäischen Provinzen des Römischen Imperiums," *Acta Archaeologica Academiae Scientificarum Hungarica* 13: 125-155.

———. 1962. "Beiträge zur Statistik der Sterblichkeit in der illyrischen Provinzgruppe und in Norditalien (Gallia Padana)," ibid 14: 297-396.

———. 1963. "Die Sterblichkeit in den Städten Mittel und Süd-Italiens sowie in Hispanien (in der römischen Kaiserzeit)," ibid 15: 129-224.

———. 1965, 1966. "Die Sterblichkeit in den Nordafrikanischen Provinzen, I, II", ibid 17: 309-321: 18:235-262.

Szöke, B. & J. Nemeskéri. 1954. (Běsenoře pri Šuranoch). *Slovenská Archeológia* 2: 105-135. 6-4. T.p. 119. I:15, II:8. J:1,3. A:16,12.M:6,2. Hungarian with Russian summary.

Tajti, T. & T. Tóth. 1976-1977. "Data to the Anthropology of the Avar Period Population of the South-East Transdanubia," *Anthropologia Hungarica* 15: 5-124. Two cemeteries. Bóly. 5-2 (7-8c). T.p. 32.A:7,9. M:4,7. ?:2,1. Nagyharsany. 5-2 (6-7c). T.p. 52. A:11,12. M:7,6. S:0,2. ?:1,1. Hungarian with English summary.

Tengroth, B. & T. Lewin. 1961. "Injuries and Pathological Changes in the Skeletal Remains from the Excavations at the City of Kongahälla," *Fornvännen* 56: 177-190. 7-5. II:2. J:3,2,1. A:24,5,1. M:10,1,1. S:2,0. ?:6,0,12. Swedish with English summary.

Tester, P.J. 1968. "An Anglo-Saxon Cemetery at Orpington," *Archaeologia Cantiana* 83: 125-150. 3-1 (450-550). ESE. P.p. 129.I:3. II:0,1,2. A:9,5. M:2,1. S:0,1 ?:0,1.

Tetramanti, S. 1971. "Das Gräberfeld num. 1. von Zalavár-Kózég (11 Jh.)," *Archeologiai Ertesito* 98: 216-244. 5-4. ENE. I:45. II:0,1,9. J:1,1,2. A:14,9. M:9,18. S:7,6. Good data for infant years.

Thomas, C. 1967. "An Early Christian Cemetery and Chapel on Ardwall Isle, Kirkcudbright," *Medieval Archeology* 11: 127-188. 3-2. ENE. M.p. 132. II:2. A:6,3,1. M:8,0,8. S:1,0.

Tocik, A. 1968. "Slawisch-awarisches Gräberfeld in Holiare," *Archaeologia Slovaca* 1: 1-208. 5-3. SE. I:54. II:40. J:3,33,26. A:38,83,13. M:39,36,7. S:32,48,7. ?:2,3,19. Unrevised. See also Mala 1965.

Todd, T.W. 1927. "The Skeletal Remains of Mortality," *The Scientific Monthly* 24: 490-492. Scarborough. 3-4. I:17. II:12. J:8. A:35. M:63. S:8.

Torgersen, J., B. Getz & E. Berle. 1964. "Die mittelalteriche Bevölkerrung von Oslo," *Zeitschrift für Morphologie und Anthropologie* 56: 53-59. Total: 521,493.

Török, Gyula. 1962. "Die Bewöhner von Halimba im 10. und 11. Jahrhundert," *Archaeologia Hungarica* 39: 1-275. 5-3. P.p. 11. ENE. 5-4. (Halimba-Cseres).

Tóth, T. 1961. "The Cemetery of Szebény (viiie) from the Avar Epoch," *Annales Historico-Naturales Musei Nationalis Hungarici* 53: 571-613. 5-3. T.p. 588. II-1. J:1,,1. A:8,8. M:9,1. S:2,0. Russian with English summary.

———. 1962. "Le cimetière di Csákberény provenant des débuts de l'époque avare (vi[e]-viiie siècles). Esquisse paléoanthropologique," *Annales Historico-Naturales Musei Nationalis Hungarici* 54: 521-549. 5-2. T.p. 530. J:1. A:14,4. M:7,3.

———. 1964. "The German Cemetery of Hegykö (vi.c.). A paleoanthropological Sketch," *Annales Historico-Naturales Musei Nationalis Hungarici* 56: 529-557. 5-2. T. 532. I:3. II:12. J:5. A:9,16. M:7,6. S:2,1.

———. 1977. "Die völkerwanderungszeitische Gräberfeld von Környe," *Studia Archaeologica* 5: 292-296. 5-2 (6-7c). ENE. T. 156. I:7. II:6. J:6. A:27,19. M:16,7. S:3,7.

Trebaczkiewicz, Teresa. 1963. "The Early Medieval Cemetery at the Village of Psary Piotrków, Trybunalski district," *Prace i Materialy*, Museum Lodz, ser, arc. no. 9: 131-151. 8-4 (11c). M. p. 134. I-II-J: 9. AMS:18,11. Polish with English summary.

Trudel, W. 1938. *Die Alamanni von Elgg* (Zurich, Inaug.Diss.,) 6-2 (7c). EW. I-II-J:8. AMS:32,38.

Ulcek, K. 1956. "Das anthropologische Material von Žitavski Tön," *Slovenská Archeologia* 4: 132-135. 6-3. ESE. T.p. 133. I:15. II:3. A:6,3,1. M:4,2. Czech with German summary.

Urbánska, Halina. 1959. "Ein frühpolnisches Reihengräberfeld bei Groszowice, kr. Opole." *Archeologia Slaska* 2: 165-189. I:II-J:12.A:6,3. M:63. Polish with German summary.

Valic, A. 1969. "Altslawisches Gräberfeld 'Na Sedlu' unterhalb der Burg von Bled," *Arheoloski Vestnik*, S.A.Z.U. 20: 218-238. 5-3. NE. II:6. J:0,1,1. A:7,5. M:4,1 S:1,0. ?:1. Serb with German summary. Revised from Martin scale.

Vamos, K. 1973. "Die anthropologische Untersuchung avarenzeitliche Bevölkerung von Szeged-Makkoserdö," *Anthropologia Közlemények* 17: 29-39. 5-2 (late Avar). II:16,2. J:1,7,15. A:36,28,5. M:17,15,37. S:4,2. Hungarian with German summary.

Veeck, W. 1926. "Der Reihengräberfriedhof von Holzgerlungen," *Fundberichte aus Schwaben* 3: 154-201. 4-1. ESE.T.p. xxxiv. 1-LL-J: 25. AMS:88,78.

———. 1931. *Die Alamannen in Würtemburg* (Berlin, Germanische Denkmäler in Völkerwanderungszeit). 4-1. I-II: 7. J:9. A:31. M:11. S:5.

Viollier, D. 1908. "Fouilles executées sur les soins du Musée National," *Anzeiger für schweiziger Altertumskunde* 10: 276-286. Premploz. 6-1. ENE. I-II-J: 8. AMS: 23.

———. 1910-1912. "Fouilles — de la cimetière barbare de Kaiser-Augst (Ct. de Schaffhouse)," *Anzeiger für schweiziger Altertumskunde* 11: 130-140; 12: 22-39, 286-292; 13: 146-164, 222-233; 14: pp. 269-286. 6-2. ENE. I-II-J:79. AMS: 81,46.

———. 1911. "Le cimetière barbare de Beringen," *Anzeiger für schweizerische Altertumskunde* 13: 20-37. 6-2. EW. I-II:3.J:1. AMS: 4,6.

Voinot, J. 1904. "Les fouilles de Chaouilley, Cimetièrre mérovingien," *Mémoires de la Société d'archéologie lorraine et de musée historique lorraine* 54: 5-80. 2-2. I:3. II:4. J:1,2. A:5,4. M:5,2,1. S:1,0. ?:7,3.

Vollmayer, T. & G. Glowatzki. 1971. "Statistische Methodik zur Bearbeitung eines frühmittelalterlicher Gräberfelds von Goldberg bei Turkheim in bayerische-Schwaben," *Homo* 22: 165-181. 4-4. T.p. 167. I:4. II:1. J:4,0,1. A:5,1. M:7,7. S:6,1. ?:4,3,5.

Wachowski, K. 1970. "Frühmittelalterliches Skelettgräberfeld in Milicz," *Silesia Antiqua* 11: 199-222. 8-4. P. 200. I:53. II:52. J:8,12,12. A:122,142,26. M:85,72,24. S:3,5.1. Polish with German summary.

Warhurst, A. 1955. "The Jutish Cemetery at Lymynge," *Archaeologia Cantiana* 69: 1-40. 3-2. EW. P.p. 2. I:0,1,2. II:0,1,2. J:2,0. A:4,6. M:11,6. S:1,4.

R. Warwick, in Wenham, L.P. 1968. *The Romano-British Cemetery at Trentholm Drive, York* (London, Ministry of Public Building and Works, *Archaeological Reports* no.5.), 129-245. 3-1. NE. I:9. II:6,1,11. J:20,10,3. A:167,40,1. M:65,9.

Wein, G. 1959. "Das alamannische Gräberfeld in Weingarten, kr. Ravensburg," *Fundberichts aus Schwaben* 14: 142-144; 15: 194. 4-2. (6c-early 7c) EW; mid-end 7c-ENE. I-II:34. J:16,24. AMS:280,163.

Wells, Calvin. 1966 in Patricia Hutchinson, "The Anglo-Saxon Cemetery at Little Eriswell, Suffolk," *Proceedings of the Cambridge Antiquarian Society* 59: 21-28. 3-2 (6c). ESE. I:4. II:1. J:2,1.1. A:7,9. M:1,2.

Wenger, Sandor. 1952. "Contributions à anthropologie des Avars en Hongrie (le cimeti ère d'Alattyán-Tulát)," *Annales Historico-Naturales Musei Nationalis Hungaricae* 44: 205-212. 5-2. EW. T.p. 206. I:1. II:10. J:0,7,1. A:67,91. M:50,17. Much like Wenger 1957.

———. 1953. "L'anthropologie du cimetière de Jánoshida-Tótkérpuszta," *Annales Historico-Naturales Musei Nationalis Hungarici*, 45: 231-244. 5-2 (7-8c). T.p. 232. I:2. II:6. J:0,1. A:12,6.M:9,6. S:2,2.

———. 1955. "Types anthropologiques de la population de Szentes-Kajan provenant du viie siècles," *Annales Historico-Naturales Musei Nationalis Hungarici* 47: 391-410. 5-2. II:1.J:1,13. A:30,16. M:21,9. S:4,2. Hungarian with French summary.

———. 1957. "Données osteométriques sur la matérial anthropologiques du cimetière d'Alattyán-Tulát," *Crania Hungarica* 2: 1-55. See also Wenger 1952, same data.

———. 1966. "Anthropologie de la population d'Elöszállás-Bajceihegy provenant de temp avar," *Anthropologia Hungarica* 7: 115-200. 5-2. T.p. 152-153. I:29.II:21. J:0,3,8. A:35,40. M:27,27. S:0,2. ?:7,2,1.

———. 1967a. "Data to the Anthropology of the Avar Period Cemetery of the Transdanubia (Kékesd)," *Anthropologia Hungarica* 8: 59-119. 5-2. T.p. 76. II:1. J:0,1. A:16,61. M:4,4. S:1,0.

———. 1976b. "Data to the Anthropology in the Avar Age," *Anthropologiai Kozlemenyek* 11: 199-215. 5-2. I:4. II:9. J:4. AMS:49,49.

———. 1968. "Data to the Anthropology of a Late Roman Period Population of the S-E Transdanubia," *Annales Historico-Naturales Musei Nationalis Hungarici* 60: 313-342. 5-1. T.p. 314. I:4.II:1. J:1,2. A:10,8. M:5,1.

———. 1970. "Data to the Anthropology of the Early Arpadian Age of the Balaton Area," *Anthropologia Hungarica* 9: 63-145. Zalavar-Kapölna. 5-3. T.p. 95. I:2. II:18. J:5. A:19,18. M:19,21. S:2,4. ?:9,5.

———. 1971a. "Contributions à l'anthropologie de la population hongroise du Moyen Age," *Anthropologia Hungarica* 10: 91-161. Helemba. 5-1. T.p. I:33. I:32. II:9. J:6. AMS:93.

———. 1971b. "Anthropological Data of the Arpadian Epoch Population at the Great Bend of the Danube in Hungary," *Annales Historico-Naturales Musei Nationalis Hungarici* 68: 421-432. 5-5. I:16. II:6. J:14,13. A:14,10. M:1,1.

———. 1972a. "Anthropological Examination of the Osteological Material deriving from the Avar Period Cemetery at Tiszavasvár," *Anthropolgia Hungarica* 11: 5-82. 5-2. T.p. 40. I:12. II:7. J:0,5,4. A: 26,43. M:14,18. S:0,1.

———. 1972b. "Data to the Anthropology of the Avar Period Population in the Northern Plains, Hungary," *Annales Historico-Naturales Musei Hungarici* 64: 401-413. 5-2 (7c). I:13. II:9. J:0,5,4. A:26,43. M:14,8.

———. 1974. "On the Anthropological Problems of the Avar Age Populations in the Southern Transdanubia," *Anthropologia Hungarica* 13: 5-85. 5-2. T.2. I:40. II:12. J:0,2,1. A:20,24. M:18,16. S:0,4. Hungarian with English summary.

———. 1975. "Paleoanthropology of the Population deriving from the Avar Period at Fészerlakepuszta (Transdanubia)," *Anthropologia Hungarica* 14: 57-110. 5-3 (8c). T.p. 75. I:17. II:5. A:7,21. M:4,7.

———. 1976. "Analyses anthropologiques de nouvelles découvertes de Keszthely (Transdanubia) provenant de l'époque avar," *Anthropologia Hungarica* 15: 125-190. 5-2. T.p. 146. Both skulls and skeletons. I:11. II:4. A:11,26. M:6,4. S:0,1,1. Skulls or skeletons, I:3. II:1. J:0,1,1. A:3,6. M:7,6. S:3,5,1. Kestheley-Belvaros.

Wenham, L.P. see R. Warwick.

Werner, J. 1953. "Das alamannische Gräberfeld von Büloch Basel," *Monographien zur Ur und Frühgeschichte der Schweiz*, Schweizerische Gesellschaft für Urgeschichte, no. 9. 6-2 (6c). NE. Pl.1. I-II-J:29 AMS:108,71,92.

———. 1955. "Das alamannische Gräberfeld von Mindelheim," *Veröffentlichungen der Schwäbischen Forschungsgemeinschaft bei dem Kommission für bayerische Landesgeschichte* 1: 3-40. 4-?. ENE. I-II-J:14. AMS: 43-27.

Wheeler, R.E.M. 1943. Maiden Castle. Dorset, (Oxford, Society of Antiquaries of London), 3-1. J:1. A:14,9. M:1,0. S:1,0.

Wierchinska, Aline. 1968. "Anthropological Analysis of the Bone Material from Cremation Graves of the Roman Period at Korzén, Gostynin dist," *Materialy Starozytne* 11: 417-421. 8-1. T.p. 419. I:33. II:9. J:1,4,6. A:9,14,30. M:3,2,5.S:0,1,1. Revised from A (20-30):2,11,18. M:(30-45): 10,5,17. Polish with English summary.

————. 1969. "Examination of Anthropological Structure of Skulls from early Medieval Cemetery in Warsaw-Wilanow," *Wiadomosci Archeologiczne* 24: 270-279. 88-5? I:1. II:6. J:3. A:2,3. M:26,30,1. Revised to A:11,13. M:7,20. Polish with English summary.

————. 1970. "Anthropological Investigations of Human Bone Remains of the Cremation Cemeteries at Korkliny, Sawalki District," *Rocznik Bialostocki* 9: 177-196. 8-1. I;4,7. II:2.2. J:1,1.A:7,3. M:7,8. Not corrected. Polish with English summary. Probably should be A:10,4. M:4,4.

Wilson, D.M. 1956. "The Initial Examination of an Anglo-Saxon Cemetery at Melburn, Cambs.," *Proceedings of the Cambridge Antiquarian Society* 49: 29-41. 3-3. I:1. II:0,1,3. J:0,1. M:0,1. S:3,2. ?:2,4,1.

Wokroj, F. 1955. "Early Medieval Polish Skulls of Ostrow Lednicki," *Crania Plonica*. *Materialy i prace antropoliczne* 1. 8-4. I:7. II:7. J:2,25,12. A:114,149. M:212,98. S:30,15. Polish with English summary. Scale may be same as Wokroj 1967.

————. 1967. "Frühmittelalterliches Gräberfeld 'Mlynowka'. in Wolin in lichte des Anthropologie," *Materialy Zachodniopomorske* 13: 295-336. 8-3. EW. I:21. II:13. A:2,7,1. M:21,13,2. S:3,2. ?:7,1,0. Scale: J: years 15-18. A: 18-35. M:36-55. S:56-.

————. 1972. "Anthropologische Analysis von menschlichen Knockenreste aus dem Mittelalterlichen Gräberfeld von Chelmska Gora,": *Materialy Zachodnie-pomorske* 17: 273-203. 8-5. Converted from percentages. II-II-J:20. A:36,35.M:67,47. S:1,1. Corrected to A:70,59. M:33,23. Polish with German summary.

Wolanski, N. 1954. "Human Remains of an Early Cemetery (xi-xiic)) in Novy Bazar, dist. Makow Mazowiecki," *Przeglad Antropologiczny* 20: 180-217. T.p. 183. 8-4. I;1. II:1. J:3. A:17. M:1. Probably should be revised to A:11. M:9.

Woszczyk, J. 1966. "Early Medieval Inhabitants of the Village Lad, d. Slupea, in the Light of Craniometrical Data," *Przeglad Antropologiczny* 32: 239-247. 8-4. T.p. 240. J:1,0. A:6,5. M:7,3. Revised to A:9,6. M:4,2. Polish with English summary.

————. 1967. "Craniological Materials from Old Burial Grounds in Kruszwica," *Przeglad Antropologiczny* 33: 65-81. First Cemetery. 8-5. J:0,1. A:6,6,1. M:4,2. S:1. Revised to A:8,7. M:2,1. Polish with English summary. Second Cemetery. 8-4. II:1. A:16,13. M:8,5,1. S:1,1. Revised to: A:20,15. M:4,3. S:1,1.

Wuilleumier, P., A Audin, & A. Leroi-Gourhan. 1949. *L'Église de la Nécropole Saint-Laurent dans le quartier Lyonnais de Choulans* (Lyons), 33-49. 2-1 (A,D, 259-660). SE. I:9. II:0,1,2. J:0,1. A:8,7. M:14,3. S:5,0. ?:2,5,6.

Xavier de Cunha, A. & M.A.M. Neto. 1955. "Characteristics of the Visigothic Population of Silveirona (Estremoz)," Instituto de Antropologia, Universidade de Coimbra, *Contribuiçoñes para o Estudo da Antropologia Portuguesa*. 5: 239-309. 1-2/ II:1.II:1. JAMS: 20,6,1. Portuguese with English summary.

Zarzycka, Barbara. 1953. "Report on Human Bones found at Zlota," *Wiadomosci Archeologiczne* 19: 93-104. 8-4. (11-12c). II:1. A:1,1. M:4,3. S:0,1. Revised to: A:3,2. M:2,2. Polish with English summary.

Zawadzka, B. & B. Antosik. 1973. "Early Medieval Cemetery with Graves in Stone Setting at Grzebsk, Mlawa District," *Wiadomosci Archeologiczne* 38: 461-492. 8-4. NE. I:2. A:4,1,1. M:1,1. S:1. ?:2. Polish with English summary.

Zeman, J. 1958. "Das völkerwanderungszeitliche Gräberfeld in Mochov," *Památky Archeologické* 49: 423-451. 5-1. ESE. I:2. II:1. M:6,2. S:0,2. ?:1,0. Czech with German summary.

Žlvanovic, S. 1964. "The Anthropological Characteristics of the Avarian Skeletons from Vojka (Srem)," *Glasnik*, Anthropologsko G.A. Drustva Jugoslavije. 1: 105-113. 5-3. All: 39,33.

Zoll-Adamikowa, Helena. 1966a. "Nécropoles à squelettes du haut moyen age en Petite Poland," *Prace Komisji Archeologiecznej* 6: 1-203. 8-4. I:3. II:2,4. J:4,1,1. A:24,33,5. M:23,17,5. S:4,2. ?:20,6. Polish with English summary.

————. 1966b. "An Early Medieval Inhumation Cemetery on Site 4 at Stradow, dist. Kazimierza Wielka," *Sprawozdenia Archeologiczne* 18: 258-270. 8-4.T. 268. I:3. M:2,1. Polish with English summary.

Hyslop, Miranda. 1963. "Two Anglo-Saxon Cemeteries at Chamberlain Barn, Leighton Buzzard, Bedfordshire," *The Archaeological Journal* 102: 161-200. 2-3. ENE No data.

Necrasov, Olga & D. Botezatu. 1964. "Etude anthropologique squelettes de Doina datant du xiii[e]-xiv siecles," *Annuaire Roumain d'Anthropologie* 1: 29-37. 5-4. I: 11. II: 4. J: 1. A:10. M:7.

Necrasov, O., D. Botezatu & C. Teodorescu. 1967. "Contributie la studial Anthropolic al populatiei feudale timpurii din Romania; seria de la Izvoral (R. Giurgin) datiud diu secolo al vii- lea E-N," *Studii si cercetari de antropologie* 4: 3-24. 5-3. T.p. 8. I:26. II:5. A:8, 18, 1. M: 25,32. S: 1,1.

Necrasov, O., V. Ursache, D. Botezatu & G. Stefanescu, 1969. "Stuisal restoritor osoase diu Mormintele cimitirelov pirituale de la Gabara-Moldoveni si Sabaoani I (Jud. Neamt) (Sec. ii-iii E-N)," *Studii si cercetari de antropologie* 6: 7-15. 5-1. Gabara I:22. II:10. J-S ? Sabaoani I:45, II:6. A:12. M:9. ?:1. Ages are given to the year for children.

Index